ANTHONY BURGESS

Collected Poems

T0307481

ANTHONY BURGESS

Collected Poems

Edited with an introduction by Jonathan Mann

CARCANET
CLASSICS

First published in Great Britain in 2020 by
Carcanet
Alliance House, 30 Cross Street
Manchester M2 7AQ
www.carcanet.co.uk

A CIP catalogue record for this book is
available from the British Library.
ISBN 978 1 80017 012 4

Typesetting by Thomas Bohm, User Design, Illustration and Typesetting
Printed in Great Britain by SRP Ltd, Exeter, Devon

The publisher acknowledges financial
assistance from Arts Council England.

THE COLLECTED POEMS
OF ANTHONY BURGESS

John Anthony Burgess Wilson (1917–93) was an industrious writer. Through over fifty published books, thousands of essays, and countless other drafts and fragments, he articulated the struggles, freedoms and changes that he saw around him, and predicted many more to come. Perhaps his most famous example is *A Clockwork Orange* (1962), originally an indifferently-received novella which was later adapted into a controversial film by Stanley Kubrick, and provided Burgess with plentiful opportunities to explain his particular artistic vision. The linguistic innovations of that novel, the strict formal devices used to contain them, and its remarkable range of themes are all firmly present in Burgess's poetry.

Now he no longer appears on our screens, it is easy to forget that Burgess was an irrepressible international literary figure whose work was disseminated through the mass media of the 1970s and 1980s. He was many things at once, some of them seemingly irreconcilable. There are in fact many Burgesses to choose from: novelist, composer, teacher, drinker, linguist, husband, rebel, journalist, diarist, extrovert, family man, cook, smoker, art critic, literary critic, television critic, television personality, collector of matchbooks, and – last but not least – poet. His flair for words, formal discipline, experimentalism, and fondness for *variousness* echoes equally through his music, his novels, his journalism and his literary criticism. These aesthetic competences are abundantly represented in this book.

THE COLLECTED POEMS
OF ANTHONY BURGESS

Anthony Burgess

Edited with an introduction by Jonathan Mann

Per Liana e Antonio

CONTENTS

INTRODUCTION

Anthony Burgess was a versatile and productive poet whose career began in 1935 when a few adolescent poems were published in Manchester Xaverian College's magazine *The Electron*. Over the course of his career, Burgess wrote many hundreds of poems, lyrics, fragments, and occasional verses – everything from epic poetry to linguistically innovative experiments. Most of his novels include original poetry, frequently as a central plot device. This is especially evident in the *Enderby* novels, which feature poems written by Burgess but published under the fictional *nom de plume* F.X. Enderby. Notably, his words for music were heard on and off Broadway, and almost featured in a Warner Brothers film (*Will!*, 1968). The 1973 musical *Cyrano* (starring Christopher Plummer) was a commercial success thanks in no small part to Burgess's verse. Burgess's 1976 epic verse novel *Moses* was the literary product of an equally epic Italian television series. Likewise, the verses and songs from Burgess's *Man of Nazareth* (1979) arose out of a collaboration with the award-winning film and television director Franco Zeffirelli. His poetry career ended with a remarkable novel in verse (*Byrne*, posthumously published 1995), whose form was borrowed from Byron.

In his autobiography *You've Had Your Time*, Burgess says he sent his poems to T. S. Eliot, who sent back a mildly approving letter of rejection. Whilst that letter remains unfound, another letter in a private collection shows that, in 1954, Burgess's poetry *was* subject to the formal scrutiny of another literary critic. Gareth Lloyd-Evans, a noted Shakespearean scholar, judged Burgess's poetry as a part of a competition held by his local newspaper. Burgess won the competition, and saw his work published on the front page of the *Banbury Guardian* on 27 May 1954. In his note to the winner, the judge praised Burgess's imagery and linguistic innovation, but found his rhythm a little shaky. The short note is (so far) the only available review of Burgess's earlier poetry by an informed contemporary critic, who found:

> These are very accomplished poems indeed, and I suspect you are an old hand at the game. Have you published? If you haven't, then you ought to, immediately. I find your imagery particularly exacting – e.g. in Sonnet 1. The image of the cock is brilliant. The 'idea' in Sonnet 1 is simple enough, but your language has given it a depth (almost a mystery) which is most satisfying. You might look over your rhythm again – it is occasionally jerky – noticeably so in Sonnet 2 where the transition from line 8 to 9 is rhythmically awkward. Congratulations on two first rate poems which easily take the prize.

The critical note is signed 'G.L.E.'. The two sonnets in question were 'A dream yes, but for everyone the same' and 'They lit the sun, and their day began', part of the *Revolutionary Sonnets* sequence. Writing about this competition, Burgess notes that the newspaper regretted having to publish his poems. 'What the readers of the *Banbury Guardian* made of this sonnet', he says, 'was never recorded'.[1]

Another analysis of a Burgess poem came from the poet himself in the 1970s. Perhaps as a literary joke, Burgess reviewed a poem by F.X. Enderby in *They Wrote in English*, an anthology of major Western writers.[2] That poem is 'Garrison Town, Evening' (see p. 00). As the only available example of Burgess explicating his own poetry at length, it is worth reproducing here:

> The opening line is a reminiscence of the opening line of a song by Henry Purcell – 'Nymphs and shepherds, come away.' The scene is a

---

1   *Little Wilson and Big God* (London: Heinemann, 1987), p. 356.
2   *They Wrote in English* (Milan: Tramontana, 1979), vol. 2, p. 553.

town in which a great number of soldiers are stationed in wartime. In the evening they emerge from their barracks and look for girls, who are willing to be looked for. Thus, Faunus, the god of fertility or certainly physical love, uncovers what was hidden during the day – the libido, or human will. This reminds the poet of the philosopher Schopenhauer, who taught that the only real thing in nature was a huge impersonal Will, or '*Wille*,' that created illusions or phenomena or representations ('*Vorstellungen*') which we take for reality. The '*Wille*' is a cinema projector, and it projects these '*Vorstellungen*' (German for cinema shows) on to a screen. The projector is also a penis, and also a pig's snout, thoroughly bestial. Pigs thrust their snouts into the earth, looking for truffles. Low girls, or doxies (an Elizabethan term), instead of being ill-favoured and pimply, become matt, smooth, silver screens. The projectors or penises of the soldiers, expressive of the great natural Will, shine light [on] them which makes them appear attractive. Their 'trappings of the sport' are those physical appurtenances which are engaged in the act of sex. An ejaculation is achieved, and it is likened to a fiery rocket shooting high into the air. At the moment of ejaculation the girls seemed at their most beautiful. But there is an immediate re-vulsion of '*tristia post coitum*', and this is likened to the theory of another German philosopher, Spengler, who in his 'Decline of the West' says that all civilisations decay, tracing a falling curve or parabola.[3]

The decision to include and review the poetry of his fictional alter ego may have been a literary joke, or a convenient way to explain a favourite own poem. Either way, it demonstrates that Burgess wished to explain the poem. It was not the first time he reviewed his own work. In 1968, Burgess lost his job at the *Yorkshire Post* when he supplied an unflattering review of *Inside Mr Enderby*. Later, in *This Man and Music* (1982), Burgess discussed his own poetry again in his analysis of a novel with verse interludes, *Napoleon Symphony* (1974). This time, though, there was no trickery; readers knew it was

---

3   *Ibid.*

Burgess reviewing Burgess. His short analysis does not explain how the language of the poems *functions*, but it does name T.S. Eliot, Tennyson and Gerard Manley Hopkins as key influences for the work.

The fictional poet F.X. Enderby remains a core connection between Burgess's novels and poetry. All the way through the four *Enderby* novels (published in 1963, 1968, 1974 and 1984), Burgess's poetry is described as written by the eponymous poet. This raises a question about authorship that has only been tackled in passing by a few critics of Burgess's poetry, and remains unresolved. In a 2003 article, the French writer and critic Sylvère Monod – who edited a short selection of poems for the journal *TREMA* in 1980 – points out that Burgess was a poet in his own right, and one with an already long poetic career by 1980. While he admits to initially overlooking the Enderby/Burgess authorship issue, Monod focuses his attention on exploring the Enderby poems simply as plot devices in the novels. However, the discipline and linguistic inventiveness of the poetry suggests it is more than just functional plot-matter. As Kevin Jackson puts it in his foreword to *Revolutionary Sonnets* (2002), 'a man who set scant if any store by verses he had composed more than thirty years earlier would hardly have troubled to embed them so prominently'. In a foreword to the essay collection *Anthony Burgess and Modernism* (2008), David Lodge tackles the identity problem by simply focusing on Enderby as the author. Viewing Enderby as a modernist poet, Lodge compares Enderby to William Empson or Edward Thomas. Lodge and Monod, then, provide some brief commentary on Burgess's *Enderby* poems, but do not fully define the relationship between Enderby and Burgess.

Laurette Véza – also writing in *TREMA* in 1980 – explores how Burgess's influences are frequently echoed in the *Enderby* poems. Unlike Monod, Véza seems to separate Burgess from Enderby. She describes Burgess as a *formalist* poet who loves words, not emotion, praising the word play and clarity of the Enderby poems. In exploring this relationship between allusion and lucidity, she highlights how the *Enderby* poems seem to verge on parody, deciding that such parody is related to cultural heritage. Véza's critical appraisal passes comment on the poems *in their own right*, and not just as plot devices. Usefully, Véza emphasises the difference between the *fictional* poet *Enderby* and the *actual* poet Burgess.

Although they are substantial, the *Enderby* poems are only part of Burgess's career as a poet. In the 1970s especially, Burgess's long-form poetry found large audiences away from the *Enderby* books. He was at his most productive in this form between 1974 and 1976, although long poems had featured in his novels *The Worm and the Ring* (1961) and *One Hand Clapping* (1961). In just two years, Burgess published *Moses* and *Napoleon Symphony*, as well as including the long poem 'Augustine and Pelagius' in *The Clockwork Testament*. Then, in 1975, Burgess published another long poem ('In Memoriam Wystan Hugh Auden KMT') in the *Mark Twain Journal*.

To be sure, writing much is no qualification for greatness in itself. And yet, Burgess's poetry manages to combine sheer volume with linguistic ambition, frequently achieving equal levels of success. Indeed, the current corpus would be an impressive collection for one who had simply focused on being a professional poet. Given that – by the 1970s – Burgess had achieved fame and fortune as a journalist, translator, prolific novelist, visiting lecturer and vociferous literary critic, it is tempting to ask how he managed to produce such varied and voluminous poetry in between everything else. Moreover, longer poetry within *Napoleon Symphony*, *ABBA ABBA*, *Moses*, and – later – *Byrne* reveals Burgess as a fastidious formalist with a sharp eye for literary tradition and a keenness to exploit the quirks of the English language to the full. His poetry of the 1970s is enormous and enormously ambitious. In his poetry as much as his novels, he is unafraid to play with the words of his literary predecessors. Moreover, following T.S. Eliot especially, Burgess was keen to unite old traditions with modern sensibilities. In this way, the poetry records or extends the multiplicity of styles and traditions he devoured with such delight. No wonder Malcolm

Bradbury's obituary of Burgess described him as a 'postmodern storehouse'. His poetry – like the rest of his literary and musical endeavours – moves the borders of western traditions. Especially in these more expansive works, Burgess's regard for poetic tradition is so strong that it is sometimes hard to hear his own voice in among the celebratory echoes of other poets. Yet, the scale of the enterprise, alongside the regard for literary history, offers his readers a unique opportunity to explore nothing less than this.

Revolutionary Sonnets (2002), edited by Kevin Jackson, introduces Burgess's poetry to the general public via a small selection of previously-published verse, following a brief but extremely helpful introductory essay. This compact edition contains miscellaneous poems and poem fragments as well as extracts from *Moses* (1976). These are presented alongside translated verse and libretti, including *Cyrano de Bergerac* (1971 and 1985), *Oberon* (1985), *Carmen* (1986), and *Oedipus the King* (1972). Jackson's edition does not include any unpublished works from the archives, such as 'The End of Things' or 'An Essay on Censorship'. Nor is there any reference to *St. Winefred's Well*. A notable editorial decision in Jackson's selection is to 'hand the daunting task of editing *The Complete Poems of Anthony Burgess* on, with all good wishes to someone who finally has the nerve to tackle it'. He does, though, identify some poets who he believes are influential to Burgess. Eliot, William Empson, and Ezra Pound are found to be likely influences, along with 'perhaps a jigger or two of Robert Graves'. Jackson's edition is brisk, entertaining, and shines a light on some notable representative samples while avoiding archival adventures.

The present collection is the first to bring Burgess's significant poetic works into one volume. However, readers may be surprised to learn that the present edition is technically the *fourth* attempted collection of Burgess's poetry. In February 1978, a J.J.W. Wilson contacted Burgess to propose an anthology based on the poems published in *The Serpent*, Manchester University's student magazine. This would have included eight poems by Burgess, alongside other poets' work[4], and would have been called *Juvenilia*. Wilson proposed that he and Burgess share 40% of the fees, with 60% going to the other contributors. The other poets would have been Peter Cadle, Ashley Merlin Cox, and John Allan Wilson (the John A. Wilson who appears in *Little Wilson and Big God*), all former Manchester University students. In a later letter to Burgess from April 1978, Wilson notes that he has asked Glenda Jackson to write a short introduction, no doubt hoping to boost sales. Signalling Burgess's evident ambitions to have a reputable publisher commit his work to print, Wilson says he 'sent a copy of the typescript to Frank Pike of Faber & Faber as you suggested', who – in a later phone call – said the anthology would probably not see publication. Pike was, of course, correct.

Two years after Wilson's proposed anthology, a short collection by the French literary journal *TREMA* (1980) gave a handful of poems exposure to a limited specialist readership. The third, twenty-two years after that, *Revolutionary Sonnets* (Carcanet, 2002), made good ground in representing the range while acknowledging its incompleteness. The present *fourth* published collection, then, adds to at least thirty-seven years of Burgess scholarship, including around eighteen years of my own. Despite its long genesis, the present collection remains a work in progress, given that new material is frequently being discovered around the world. It is likely that even more Burgess poems will have been uncovered after *Collected Poems* is published. Perhaps they will be previously unknown poems, or 'new' versions of poems included in the present edition that further help us understand Burgess's compositional processes. Perhaps another verse novel will appear, or yet another verse play. Editors of Burgess have to be resilient and organised in the face of his sometimes overwhelming posthumous productivity.

---

4   'When It is All Over', 'Wir Danken Unsrem Führer', 'Girl', 'To Amaryllis after the Dance', 'Orpheus and Eurydice', 'All the ore' (retitled 'Jeweller' by J.J.W. Wilson), 'A History', and 'The Lowdown on Art'.

In an obituary published in the *Independent on Sunday*, Malcolm Bradbury called Burgess a 'postmodern storehouse'. However, Burgess was also a key component of the literary marketplace. His archival papers reveal a professional writer whose poetic ambition was mirrored by his large (and mostly extant) library. His literary criticism was erudite and relevant. That is to say, Burgess's poetry articulates the multiplicity of traditions, forms, and styles of his time, some of which were arguably pushed forward by his plentiful contributions. Projects such as 'Belli's Blasphemous Bible', Moses, and 'An Essay on Censorship' crucially combine respect for traditional forms, epic intention, and linguistic experimentation. More modestly-sized works such as *Revolutionary Sonnets* and many other individual pieces share this combination, but in an artfully compressed way. Both the shorter and the longer poems speak to his modernist influences. Burgess's linguistic gifts are equally balanced in a hundred or a hundred thousand words.

The present new and representative collection brings together more than four hundred pieces. One fifth of this work is published here for the first time, including the major poem 'An Essay on Censorship' (1989). In addition to that large 'new' work is a number of hitherto unpublished sonnets and occasional verses.

Where possible, *Collected Poems* (including 'Belli's Blasphemous Bible') draws on material that is either archived, or in first edition out-of-print novels. Manuscripts have been sourced from two archives. Roughly sixty percent comes from the Harry Ransom Center at the University of Texas at Austin. The rest comes from the International Anthony Burgess Foundation (IABF) in Manchester; this remarkably useful collection has received substantial investment recently, and its catalogue has been made available online. The IABF also has most of Burgess's own books. These were also inspected, and a few poems were found in inserted notes or on flyleaves. The present book is the first time Burgess manuscript material from the Austin and Manchester archives have been combined into a single substantive poetry collection.

Collected Poems has been an assuredly difficult work to compile. The multitude of manuscripts and published variants – mainly resulting from Burgess's sometimes revisionist approach to writing poetry – has presented significant editorial challenges. Where possible, the edition has drawn directly on material from the archive collections, and/or from first editions of novels, generally favouring earlier drafts. Sometimes, this has purely been for sanity's sake. Frequently, the level of difference is only slight, and perhaps results from Burgess typing later versions from memory. For example, the first line of the short poem spoken by Sir Benjamin in *The Eve of St Venus* (written c. 1951, published 1964) begins 'Heroes are dead to them'. In Burgess's Banbury diary (1954), the poem begins 'Heroes are dead to us'. In this case, the earlier version not only works better as a self-contained stanza, but also seems more generalizable. Complexities concerning which version to use are especially present in the poems that were eventually reused in *Byrne* (such as 'The Music of the Spheres'), but which have differing words and punctuation. Here, earlier forms have been used. A multiplicity of these sorts of decisions have been made, and the endnotes provide brief accounts where appropriate.

Collected Poems features a long sequence of bawdy and mainly biblical sonnets from a manuscript titled 'Belli's Blasphemous Bible'. Burgess also called this 'Belli's Bible for Blasphemers'; there are two main manuscripts of these translations, and both titles are used. (I have opted for the former title, preferring its brevity.) Most of these are translations of the nineteenth-century Roman poet G. G. Belli: five of the sonnets were published in *Times Literary Supplement* on 23 January 1976 and the complete sequence in *ABBA ABBA* (1977), a novel about a theoretical meeting between John Keats and Belli. Drafts of these sonnets were handwritten in a 1974 diary, and then worked up into intermediate typewritten drafts. Although the diary shows that Burgess may have translated them in the order that is used in *ABBA ABBA*, the present edition follows the order of the heavily corrected typescript. This order does not greatly deviate from the sequence as it appeared in *ABBA ABBA*, but the endnotes provide guidance where there are variations. As Paul Howard notes[5], the translation methods Burgess adopted meant that they each existed in numerous versions before their appearance in the *Times Literary Supplement* and the subsequent novel *ABBA ABBA* (1977). Given that these translations of Belli's Romanesco sonnets were built up through layers of redrafts, it follows that the versions used in *Collected Poems* should be based on the far more developed sonnets that appeared in *TLS* and *ABBA ABBA*. The present sequence draws on these original manuscripts.

As well as some slight lexical variations, these intermediate drafts have different titles to those that appeared in *ABBA ABBA*. A full account of these differences is provided in the endnotes. The manuscript can in many respects be read as proof of Burgess's growing confidence in his translations, since there seem to be – on the whole – fewer handwritten corrections added as the manuscript sequence develops. Moreover, Burgess seemingly worked out his line indentation system only around halfway through the 'Bible'. Accordingly, readers will note that the shape of the sonnets visibly changes; it was decided to maintain these non-standard indentations as they help us learn more about Burgess's poetics of space. Another striking feature of the manuscript transcriptions is that the word-choices show no particular regard for editorial conservatism. Sometimes, the rude language was amplified for the 'final' *ABBA ABBA* version. Conversely, in other places, the lexis is more conservative in the published book. The pen-corrected sequence of drafts also demonstrates that Burgess's intentions were chiefly auditory. A peculiar example can be seen in the last sonnet in the *ABBA ABBA* sequence ('The Last Judgment'). On the last line of this sonnet, 'Er-phwoo' – the sound of a candle being blown out – was originally written

---

5   Paul Howard, 'All Right, That's Not a Literal Translation': Cribs, Licence and Embellishment in the Burgess Versions of Belli's Sonetti Romaneschi', *Modern Language Review* 108:3, July 2013, pp. 700–20.

as 'Phwoo', and then corrected by hand. Even wind effects were subject to careful sonic reassessment; as well as a poet, Burgess was a musician.

In addition to the source manuscripts used in this edition, a large number of early handwritten translations of the Belli sonnets are held at the Harry Ransom Center archive in Austin, Texas. Additionally, early drafts can be inspected in the Burgess Foundation archive in Manchester. While many of these fragments seem quite different from the versions that were eventually published in *ABBA ABBA*, none of them offer a particularly elegant array of words upon the page; there are gaps in the lines and rhymes are often still to be worked out. Many sonnets have indeterminately re-worked words and phrases, and to display them here would not make for smooth reading. Hence, the later drafts were used. The sequence, then, draws on a single set of manuscripts, which presumably formed the basis for *ABBA ABBA*. Four other completed sonnets that are Burgess originals are included in the sequence, just as they are in *ABBA ABBA* ('The Bet', 'Two Uses for Ashes', 'Privy Matters' and 'The orchidaceous catalogue begins'). The previously published versions of these sonnets are substantially the same as the later drafts that are held at the archive in Texas, with one exception. The poem beginning 'The orchidaceous catalogue begins' does not go as far as spelling out that the name in question is that of the critic Geoffrey Grigson, whereas the archive version does. The full name is restored in the present version.

There are notable exceptions to the overall sequential logic of the Belli translations. Three previously unpublished sonnets ('Spaniards', 'Work' and 'Local Industry') have simply been added at the end of the 'Bible', just before Burgess's own sonnets from the novel. 'Local Industry' was originally included as part of the sequence, and appears at the end of the draft sequence, but wasn't used in *ABBA ABBA*. Another two were found elsewhere, but – being bawdy sonnets that reference the trappings of Catholicism – fit in quite naturally. Unlike the other sonnets that Burgess chose to translate, they have a markedly personal tone ('Work? Me?'), and do not directly tell biblical tales. These fruity sonnets were seemingly not produced as part of the main sequence of translations. Accordingly, it is unclear where they were meant to be placed.

Within the manuscripts used for 'Belli's Blasphemous Bible' is a shorter sequence of works that were seemingly intended to be published for a larger audience, in *Playboy* magazine. The choice of this magazine is not as surprising as it seems. A year before Burgess started his translations[6], an interview with Burgess by C. Robert Jennings appeared in the September 1974 edition of *Playboy*. Through this, and no doubt through his voracious general reading, Burgess would have been aware that the magazine published contemporaries such as Ian Fleming, Ray Bradbury, Roald Dahl, Norman Mailer and – much later – Vladimir Nabokov. The obscene sonnets intended for *Playboy* may, accordingly, have been intended as a sampler of the current work in progress. In this respect, it would have been comparable with the sequence that was published in *Times Literary Supplement*, although the poems selected for inclusion in *Playboy* were completely different. The intended selection was: 'Joseph the Jew (II)' 'All About Eve'; 'A Reply'; 'The First Clothes'; 'The State of Innocence' and; 'Joseph the Jew (I)'. Ultimately, it is unclear as to why the sequence never saw publication in *Playboy*, but that Burgess selected works for inclusion demonstrates that he was seeking wider audiences for his translations beyond specialist literary journals.

Burgess's verse manuscripts were either typewritten or handwritten. Many of his poems and translations (especially the Belli sonnets) are playfully illustrated, which frequently brings fun to otherwise mechanical transcription and inspection work. He seemingly wrote on any available material, including envelopes, matchboxes, scraps of card, foolscap paper, diaries and large, small, or very small notebooks. Later evidence of digital manuscripts exists in the

---

6   See Howard (2013), p. 702.

form of printouts (including sections from *Byrne* and an unfinished opera about Freud); Burgess possessed an IBM personal computer, bought in 1985. The sonnet addressed 'To Chas' was sent to the IABF by email, and the sonnet about Agincourt derived from an image of a typescript posted online by a manuscript dealer. Sometimes, drafts appear in multiple places. Much of the work is neatly typed, especially on note-o-gram business communication forms, such as the manuscript of 'The trouble is, you see, getting there'. The original copies of the note-o-gram sonnets are available at the IABF, and photocopies are held in the Harry Ransom Center. Burgess's use of paper suggests a predilection for tactility, playfulness, and a creative use of space, which – regrettably – is not always easy to convey in print. Generally speaking, it seems Burgess preferred pen and paper, even though his later works were written in the era of the PC.

Deciding which poems to exclude has followed a general logic which is open to debate and may be found to be faulty. As a guiding principle, texts have been selected which have been unavailable for a long time, either because they were out of print, or because they were previously unpublished. Generally speaking, verses that appear to be deliberately bad (usually in the service of a novel's plot) have been excluded. However, some texts in this general category are so entertaining, so *rounded*, or so creative that they *are* included here. A notable example of this is the long poem 'Not, of course, that either of us thought' from *One Hand Clapping* (1961), which – while reflecting its fictional writer's sense of camp drama – shows a remarkable understanding of the excesses of the emerging styles of the time. Some texts, while determinedly possessing a *poetic* quality, are too undeveloped for inclusion and would make for uneven reading. A number of fragments, most especially from the Enderby novels, appear in an unfinished state, with words like 'plonk' or 'something' used to describe a poet's mind at work; many of these are not included. It will be noted that *Byrne* is not included here, and – arguably – it should be. However, as a major work that is still in print, and one that has recently seen new editions, it is excluded.

Readers are strongly recommended to read *Byrne* immediately after *Collected Poems*. The same goes for *Napoleon Symphony*. Likewise, with a handful of notable exceptions (mainly from *The Complete Enderby*), other works currently in print (usually meaning embedded within novels) are not included. A collection of the plays is expected to be published as a separate edition. Accordingly, extracts from dramatic works are not included here. Whether these omissions detract from the book, and whether the general logic of the edition stands up to scrutiny is, of course, for the reader to decide.

It is difficult to provide a neat summary of the many styles, the linguistic inventiveness, the endless formal experimentation and the bewildering expansiveness of Burgess's poetic subjects. For all that, some readers may accuse Burgess of burning his poetic candle at both ends. Of course, his detractors were already saying that in the 1970s when he was yet to write long works like *Napoleon Symphony*, *Byrne*, 'Augustine and Pelagius' and the 'Essay on Censorship'. And yet, Burgess wrote a lot of very good poetry in between other massive literary, film, and journalistic endeavours. In all of his chosen forms – poetry, music and prose – Burgess's intention remained (mainly) serious, and the scale impressive.

Either way, Burgess's poetry was a central part of his career as a best-selling novelist, and his verse was performed on screens and stages the world over. His poetry was seen, heard, read and watched – in cinemas and on television – by millions of people. It may be the ultimate irony that the widespread availability of the work may have obscured the fact that Anthony Burgess was, first and last, a poet. He also *remains* a productive writer. There is still much to surprise and delight new and existing readers. Hopefully, that includes the present work for all its faults.

ACKNOWLEDGEMENTS

While collecting the poetry of Anthony Burgess has taken much longer than first anticipated, the experience has provided me with the exceptional opportunities to work with some truly extraordinary people. The sense of responsibility has been enormous, but the sense of collegiality has been much bigger. I am indebted to many people. The first person to support me in this particular pursuit was Liana Burgess, the poet's widow in the meadow. Through Liana, I met Professor Andrew Biswell, whose exceptional tutelage, knowledge, and incredible patience has been of central importance to the production of this work and its editor. The following staff at the International Anthony Burgess Foundation (past and present) provided unequalled motivation and practical assistance both directly and indirectly: Dr Alan Roughley, Will Carr, Anna Edwards, Paula Price, Tina Green, Ian Carrington, and Dr Graham Foster. I have been lucky to benefit from the camaraderie and wisdom of the following Burgessians: Dr Rob Spence, the sadly-missed Dr Alan Shockley, Dr Nuria Belastgui, Yves Buelens, and Dr Jim Clarke. Particular thanks go to Michael Schmidt from Carcanet Press for his quiet and enduring patience. Peter Philpott was an especially careful examiner of both prose and punctuation. Georgina Gibbs helped me begin the end. Dr Katy Beavers provided more help than can be adequately recorded here.

LONGER POEMS, SEQUENCES,
AND NARRATIVE WORKS

AN ESSAY ON CENSORSHIP

A book is perilous, a book can slay:
This is the text we ponder on today,
Hence sing the Censor, though our preference is
To swing the censer at his obsequies,
The Censor, whose twin tasks, when Rome held sway,
Were to count citizens, then make them pay,
But now whose proper function is defined
As preying not on money but on mind.
Suppression is the word: it operates
When free intelligence communicates
With free intelligence to clarify
The nature of this life beneath the sky,
Even beyond it. Image, verse or prose,
The actor's rhetoric or nudist's pose,
The painter's brush-strokes or the camera's clicks,
Whether the field be faith or politics,
The social ambit or the amorous life,
The Censor's poised, with napalm or with knife,
Communicate with structure and in stone,
As does the architect; or else intone
A complex symphony or artless tune,
And then your skill's theoretically immune,
Unless you were a son of Israel
In the bad German time or, sad to tell,
Your name was Wagner in the Jewish state,
Though briefly. Humanly communicate
Then fear inhuman seekers to suppress.
To freedom's partisans this breeds distress,
Though the degree of it depends upon

The status of the functionaries who don
The censor's robes. When small, they underline
The squirm of the parochial philistine;
When large, we shudder with proleptic fright
At a new threat to an old human right.

Authors, who eat and drink what they create,
See the prescriptions of a foreign state
As a mere aspect of a threat diffused
Wherever the free-winging word is used.
A book's unpublished lest it may offend;
Published, its tenuous life is at an end
While libel seems to mutter. Books are burned
By activists whose muftis have not learned
The truth of Heine's aphorism: 'Who
Burns books will soon burn human beings too.'
Proscription can be dangerously bizarre.
In Malta, students of the scalpel are
Denied obstetric primers, for within
Are pictures that inflame and lead to sin.
As for the Marxist bloc – despite *glasnost*,
Bourgeois morality must not be crossed
And the whole social structure is so frail
It trembles at a breath as at a gale.
For long, in Britain, censorship has worked
In regions where the dark erotic lurked.
The genitalia, and what they do,
Or have done to them, were pronounced taboo.
No quadrilateral descriptive of
The motions of purgation or of love
Could be allowed. The foul expletive and
The fair descriptive equally were banned.
Obscene – the very word was like a sneer,
Semantically null, a sneeze of fear,

A spurt of shock confronting what was known,
Though glossed as monstrous, in a privy zone.
What decency pronounced should be concealed
Was with a frightful candour all revealed.
Strange that our Western culture should proclaim:
What grants most pleasure also grants most shame.
But the anomaly, the joy-bred guilt
Is, when you think of it, already built
Into our sad condition, for the source
Of ecstasy is also bestial, coarse,
A lowly instrument of base discharge.
Again, note, the disparity is large
Between the exaltations that we bless
And the base agent's total ugliness.
The foul familiar must be rendered strange
– The lingam and the yoni, the whole range
Of Sigmund's symbols before we can start
Accepting sex as matter for high art.
Ulysses and *The Rainbow*, *Lady C.*
Primed act of privy criminality,
Because of shame wrapped in what should exalt.
As for *The Well of Loneliness*, its fault
Lay in its sex invisible but perverse.
Love – bad enough; love between women – worse.
To declare smugly: 'Look, the battle's done'
Is always perilous. Wars are never won.
A truce looks like a peace. It would appear,
However, that what book is published here
Will not be banned for its erotic theme.
True, Kirkup's poem on a soldier's dream,
A gay centurion eyeing the Crucified
As fodder for his gaiety, was denied
The right of print, the poet punished too,
But blasphemy has always been taboo.

A whole new generation flourishes
That does not know what a book-censor is
Except as history dead and buried. Still,
Obscenity is not nor ever will
Be an archaic word. The candid show
Of love, whether heterosexual or no,
Remains a most disputable terrain,
For there is more to sex than Lady Jane,
John Thomas, Boylan, Molly Bloom, et al.
Plain eroticism soon becomes banal;
The stronger gust of sexual cruelty
Begs exploitation. And coprophagy,
Necrophily, paedophily all gape,
Along with sodomy and murderous rape,
To batten on a hard-won liberty.
Is there a limit, then, on themes that we
Submit for the high alchemy of art?
This is a question we may only start
To argue when the frontiers that persist
Between the aesthete and the moralist
Have better signposts or have none at all.
As for the law, it is unwise to call
Upon the jurist's skill to separate
Pornography and art. Let not the State,
Only the aesthetician, work it out
And tell us what the business is about.
The writer's business, on one level, is
Exploiting varied possibilities
In human language. There's a trinity
Of author's ends. We clearly see the three –
The pornographic, the didactic, and
The static or aesthetic, lie or stand
At points upon a wide continuum.
Art's in the middle, at the far ends come

Linguistic modes freed from the artist's aim –
The urge to educate, or else inflame.
At one end the didactic; here we seek
The treatise, large or small, on the technique
Of dice or dance, the neutron's mysteries,
The wide, in contrast, sky's immensities.
Appeal is made to the intelligence,
The reason, the bald brain. In consequence,
{The language must be plain, denotative,
{Transparent. No word anywhere may give
{A breath of the ambiguous, and live.
Extruded is the human tear or laugh.
Seek at the other end the pornograph,
Whose etymology means nothing more
Than this: the simple picture of a whore.
Whores, by tradition, need no other names,
Being mere items in erotic games,
And the desirable anonymous
Who, in commercial artwork, ogle us
With a bared bosom or a silk-clad calf,
Are each themselves a kind of pornograph.
But, by extension, the term covers now
The why, the which, the what, the where, the how
Of naked congress, dual, multiple,
With, if need warrants, such additional
Refinements as the pickaxe and the whip,
A luscious area for censorship.
Cocteau – or was it Gide? I am not sure –
Called pornographs one-handed literature,
A term that could, with justice, be applied
To the effusions of the other side,
For, cooking in the kitchen, we may stand
Stirring a pan, book in the other hand.
What the two genres hold in common is

One-handed, yes, but scarcely literature.
That bright commodity that sits secure,
Or nearly, between genres much preferred
By votaries of the thing and not the word,
Wishes to move, and wishes to inform,
But, more, to keep imagination warm.
{Imagination has no ready role
{In the other two. A total lack of soul
{Marks book-as-tool and not organic whole.
The object of one object is to teach,
That of the other – help the reader reach
A swift purgation, often by himself.
Restore the instrument then to the shelf.
Both types attain their stark kinetic aims
Outside, outside – in action or in flames.
But literature is different. It arouses,
Enflames the Thames, engulfs both men and houses,
Drags at the heart, excites to cathartise,
Purges within its rhythm, satisfies.
The reader, calm of mind, all passion spent,
Closes its pages, cool and near content.
True, pornograph and didact are too near
For verbal art to stay aloof and clear,
And they may, with the unskilful artist, taint,
Pollute his purposes and smear his paint.
Thus, in the fiction of the factive kind,
That fills the empty hour and lulls the mind,
The informative and pornographic meet.
Hero and heroine, beneath a sheet
Made sweaty by their amorous exercise,
Recount the history of some enterprise
Or talk of Tuscan incunabula
(The Encyclopaedia Britannica
Fills up the empty space between their ears);

They quieten the poor fact-soaked reader's fears
That mere diversion may become a bore
By falling to their exercise once more.
The continuum is bent, the two ends are
Made one when linear grows circular.

Condemn the factual when it pretends
To be inspired by true aesthetic ends
And, similarly, literary art
Must be attacked and toughly torn apart
When it essays a propagandist aim
(Teaching again); the artist may not claim
The right to wield the pedagogic chalk,
Throw out the drama and resort to talk,
Hammer a tedious tuneless thesis, or
Endue the laurels of a senator.
And when the pornograph presumes to be
A sort of art, condemn it equally.
Do not invoke morality; your ground
Is an aesthetic one and deals with sound
And unsound literary pretensions. But
The door to moral questions is not shut.
The pornographic – is it bad or good?
It provokes onanism, as it should,
And moral theory or moral fact
Means nothing to the masturbator's act.
Moral prescriptions never may intrude
On the amoral bliss of solitude.
But should pornography refollicate
The social act of sex, induce a state
Of mutual satisfaction, where's the sin?
Keep out morality; let reason in.
Still, if the probing police commit to fire
Those ikons of a desperate desire,

Who will complain? So long as we ensure
The mauler's paws are kept from literature
{Which, of its nature, is no instrument
{To gratify the onanist's intent
{Or fire the rapist, we can be content.
We face another question now. Before
I pose it, let me travel back a score
Of years or more to a most heinous crime
Committed in the great permissive time.
Children were caught and tortured and their screams
Recorded in a montage helped by themes
Drawn from the vapid music of the age,
Then they were slaughtered coldly. Neither rage
Nor vengeance was the motive of the deed,
An *acte gratuit*. One killer who could read
Admitted frankly that he might have been
Infected by a glance at Sade's *Justine*.
A lady, brooding on iniquity,
Let out a scream and screamed: 'If only we
Could save one child from lethal agonies
By burning every book that was or is,
We should not hesitate,' implying thus
The thing we knew – that books are dangerous.
Literature, certainly, is meant to hurt,
Seeking not to confirm but to subvert,
To prick complacency, but not to kill:
Here the perverted, not subverted will
Which, heaven be praised, is rare, can be impelled
To sin by what tradition has long held
To be not evil but beneficent.
Take, for example, the Old Testament,
Root of our culture, bright theophany,
Source of corruption for one man, for he,
Eyes misted by the steam of sacrifice,

Contrived his own sublunar paradise
By knifing children in Jehovah's name.
Even the Catholic mass has garnered blame
For hinting anthropophagy to one
Who sought an intimate communion
By slaying all the women that he could
To drink their blood. 'In God's eyes it was good,'
God being he. We cannot legislate
For the unsullied children of the State
In terms of what will make the bad man worse,
The madman madder. The whitecoated nurse
Sequesters what is clearly venomous
To him but is pure meat and drink to us.
A boy reads *Hamlet* and is justified
In consummating family homicide.
And so let muted *Hamlet* join the banned.
The eye that reads King Lear directs the hand
That pulls a pair of streaming jellies out.
That books are instigators we must doubt,
Along with visual versions of the same,
Since they but copy life. Life is to blame.

The question I postponed I now present:
Does writing have an ethical intent
Even while taking Wilde's prescript to heart –
That art's created for the sake of art?
All right – we know that Pater said it first
Dear Oscar was remiss enough to burst
The shackles of Paterian constraint,
Making repentant Dorian slash the paint.
He would not shatter, even if he could,
The bond that bolts pure beauty to the good.
For art proclaims nobility at best,
At worst a sick desire of being blest.

If its implied morality is not
The one that Church and State alike allot,
This is because it claims a wider scope
And stresses love much more than faith and hope.
No novel ever written praised the bad,
Diminished sanity and raised the mad
Except for some ironical effect.
Creators of necessity elect
{Creation not destruction as their theme,
{Fulfilment of a larger moral dream
{Than waking life is able to esteem.
And this condition is not blemished if
Out of the woodwork should exude a whiff
Of pure diablerie. Our William Blake
Sought to exalt hell just for heaven's sake,
Finding in fire an energy to heat
Cold bottoms stuck to heaven's judgment seat,
Or, if you will, a passion that might thaw
Enmarbled reason frozen into law.
The law must trust the artist: only he
Or she proclaims the human. And if we
Shudder at evil steaming from a page,
Then we must damp our moralistic rage,
Remembering that evil must be shown
Only that good may be the better known.
The battle is engaged. The winning side
Is not foreknown, but victory is implied
Even for the victim, should the victim be
Symbolic of a large humanity.
Art may imply, but not directly speak,
Scorning the straight path, prizing the oblique,
Hinting in elegance, loathing to shove
Us bodily into the lake of love.

Love. Now religion. A much graver theme
Confronts us. To begin, let us blaspheme.
Jesus, the bastard of a drunken brute,
Was gotten on the village prostitute.
His followers were active sodomites
Who dragged in Judas to their dark delights.
The heavenly kingdom was not for the just
But just the devotees of lawless lust.
{Read this, and then re-read it. Having read,
{Do not heap hot damnation on my head,
{But add inverted commas and 'he said'.
I may have written this, but on behalf
Of some fictitious sneerer whose foul laugh
A fictional believer counters thus:
'Your fiction is so vilely blasphemous
You damn yourself to darkness.' The reply?
'Christ was a liar and he taught a lie,
A bastard brat, son of a fucking whore,
His words a drunkard's belch and nothing more.'
Our world is built of opposites. Not strange
That one mind can engender this exchange,
And it's unjust to fasten on to me
The fouler voice of the antiphony.
Imagine death and take the blame for death?
Macbeth is bad, but Shakespeare's not Macbeth.
Turn to a later giver of God's laws
And you may libel him with greater cause.
Mohamed claimed no heavenly origin,
And to defame his essence is no sin.
'This shoveller of camel-droppings who
Craftily married and pretended to
Broadcast the Word from Gabriel's microphone
– We have his word for it, but that alone –
Raped virgins under age and robbed the poor,

Corrupted Arab, Persian, Turk and Moor,
And left a bloody legacy of hate
To doubter, heretic and apostate,
A stinking rubbish dump made white with paint,
A *shaitan* masquerading as a saint.'
These words are mine, their import otherwise.
The gravamen of uttering them lies
With some dim personage who does not exist
Save in the fancy of the fantasist.
{We have this right – to voice the darker side;
{The devil's sneer is there to be denied,
{To hear it lying and to say it lied.

Fanatics live by absolutist laws.
They, at this time of writing, are the cause
Of a free writer's cowering in some den
Out of the reach, he hopes, of murderous men
Ordered to hate, but know not what they hate,
Assassins fed on hashish by a State
That re-instils the wretched image of
A God who raves for blood and not for love,
Who're promised paradise but, better far,
Shekels for one swish of the scimitar.
For a new breed of Censor now arrives,
Equating human speech with human lives.
'Follow our law,' he thunders, 'burn or ban
Whatever terrifies Islamic man,
{Even if he's a tolerated guest
{Of polities where no faith is oppressed.
{He has the privilege of knowing best.
There is no God but Allah. Elohim,
God or Jehovah is a shadowy dim
Dull sketch of our invisibly bright One
Who tells us human revelation's done.

For Nabi Musa, Nabi Isa fall
Before the greatest Nabi of them all.
Mohamed saw the last effulgence. Bow,
You rational future, to the Muslim now.
We hold our paynim hostages and slay
Should you oppose our word and disobey.'
Here's the new foe of liberated speech,
Whose insolent arm presumes to stretch and reach
Beyond the confines of Islamic soil.
Allah alone, whose bounty flows in oil,
Will reign inviolate, unopposed, serene
In lands whose present God is the machine,
And churchbells yield to the muezzin's wail
Should oil-rich Islam strike and then prevail.

Here is a slogan sanity must clutch:
'Belief is dangerous. Don't believe too much.'
When I was young, rocked on a papist knee,
Dense with the dogmas hammered into me,
On Rome's authority I used to dub
The Church of England a mere cricket club,
A genteel congeries of vague belief,
Of veal-consumers scared of bloody beef,
With boyish bishops arguing unvexed
At contrary glossings of a text,
Unsure of heaven, unconvinced of hell:
'He's a good fellow, and 'twill all be well.'
Pragmatic England, working underground,
Contrived a creed doctrinally unsound
But geared to toleration's mental sleep,
A creed of 'Gently dip, but not too deep.'
Sick at the rantings of the Moloch-mouth
Of Muslim East and Baptist-bigot South,
I learn to look at faith with the mild eyes

Of tolerance and tepid compromise.
The mariner learned love of the albatross
And, we assume, the man upon the cross,
With passion bubbling from the self-same spring,
But how could anyone sincerely bring
The loving torrent of a human heart
To enigmatic God, who sits apart,
Permits his bigots to show pledges of
A dire vindictiveness, but not of love?
{That God's removed, that God remains unknown,
{Exacts a lesser love than can be shown
{To larks, to lizards sunning on the stone,
{Our co-inheritors of blood and bone,
{The greater love reserved to man alone.
With humour, modesty, and some good will
Also much tolerance, our life can still
Invite a certain measure of content,
Provided we don't wreck the tenement.
Give praise for pleasure, and to pain submit,
But, for God's sake, let's keep God out of it.
Easier said than done, you will reply,
For Blake's old Nobodaddy in the sky,
Grown tired of spinning his self-spinning globes,
Is all too ready to endue the robes
Of the almighty State (he surely knows
His Hegel, and perhaps inspired his prose).
As ultimate authority is God,
Even the atheist sees nothing odd
In man-made structures growing numinous.
This throws our primal missile back to us –
The leader coughs; the myrmidons cry: 'Hark,
He speaks, Lord Oracle. Let no dog bark.'
The writer's the most canine of the lot,
Though doggedly he digs away at 'What

True logic can exist when party's so
Identified with State, we wish to know.
For party is, by definition, part.
A portion of the total beating heart
Which is the social whole. Through its intent
To be the polity's embodiment,
It naturally lies and, more, denies
The right of speech to those who say it lies.'
And so the final glacial music grips
Each island that forgets its dream of ships,
With censorship the one ship in the bay,
Lies and half-lies unladed every day.

We, in a freer State, may pity those
Who wear an iron muzzle on the nose,
But, seeing man is never satisfied,
The happy censorless revolve inside
A vague nostalgia for the unhappy time
When free expression was a social crime.
In the great age of Queen Elizabeth,
Before rebellious Essex met his death,
His sad revolt was signalled by a play –
Richard the Second. 'Now no playwright may,'
The Council thundered, 'borrow for his plot
A phase of English history.' So what
The cunning artists did was turn to Rome,
To Greece, and shun the chronicles of home,
Able, in fancy clothing, to display
All the preoccupations of their day.
The ingenuity the Russians showed
When Czarist hellhounds blocked the freer road
Let them say more in allegory than
Was audible to forcers of the ban.
In Britain, where a milder writ once ran,

Swift could excoriate his fellow-man
Through the bland gestures of a fairy tale,
And Orwell, his successor, could assail
A monstrous revolution with a tongue
Tuned to the blameless accents of the young.
Loss of plain speaking that decorum cut
Bred cunning. But the door of cunning shut
When the permissive portals opened wide,
And periphrastic skills were set aside.
It is not censorship we deprecate,
Only the axe and scissors of the State.
No artist is compelled to strip things bare
Because the moral right to nakedness is there.
The moral and aesthetic merge to one
In certain areas, and their union
Is given a new name – fastidiousness.
This moans a near-articulate distress
But scorns to call the policeman or the priest
To chain or else to exorcise the beast
Which bears no fangs, only a gamy stink,
A snout for the stopped privy or clogged sink
And, for the voyeur's cash, a hungry maw.
Discretion is a virtue which no law
Enforces. An unforced consensus can
Alone sustain the dignity of man,
A dignity that artists must deride
At times lest he become too dignified.
For men in general do not spend their lives
In copulating with each other's wives,
Crawling in crapulous vomit, plotting rape,
All mindlessly unable to escape
The engine rhythm of the dog and bitch
Or else the tumid thrill of growing rich.
The prosperous low fiction of our time

Stands charged with one unpardonable crime –
That of presenting man all shorn of his
Irreconcilable complexities,
Reduced to simple structure – a machine,
Homo politicus or sexualis, clean
Or filthy but not both. We may deplore,
May even weep, but can do nothing more.
Let indiscretion be the major sin.
The state our hidden novelist is in
He can ascribe to indiscretion, to
Not fully weighing what he had to do.
The murder of the faceless who cried out
On something they were ill-informed about,
The raving of a theocratic state
Which cried 'Assassinate the apostate'
Were all, we think, foreseeable by a man
Raised on the Prophet, fed with the Koran,
Quick to revile the Prophet though, if so,
Sequestered, he could watch his profit grow.
Braving the threatened bomb, the ready knife,
We guard his profits, as we guard his life.
For, deaf to the incendiary sect,
It's hard-won liberty that we protect,
Mindful of Milton and his thunderous plea
That truth and falsehood must alike be free,
For only in the war between the two
Can we learn what is false, and what is true.
'Protect the faith,' the furious Muslims cry,
'Extend the law of blasphemy.' But why?
For Christ's divinity offends the Jew
And this explains the split between the two
Creeds bother propounded once in Palestine,
But where's the British Jew who will malign
The tepid or the fervid faith of those

With whom his wanderings have found repose?
'I vomit out the lukewarm,' Jesus cried,
Yet heat is but a mode of homicide.
Let be, let be – you tepid souls, advance
And please the tepid cause of tolerance.

I write in Twickenham, with little hope
Of inspiration from the ghost of Pope.
His willows yet survive, but not his art.
Our literature is barbarous at heart,
Our palate's coarse, our cooks are all unskilled.
The neat heroic cutlets that he grilled
And seasoned sharply with a seasoned hand
Do not appeal to votaries of the canned,
The frozen, the exotic takeaway.
Untempted to confront an April day,
I skulk beneath a duvet, and I eye
Parabolas of aircraft in the sky
Descending at ten-second intervals
To seek their nests in western terminals,
And wonder which will blossom into fire
To gratify the terrorist's desire.
A book is perilous, a book can slay:
That is the text I ponder on each day,
And, smoking, restless, wonder why I chose
To sell my soul for thirty years of prose.
Banned in Malaysia, burned in Arkansas,
Offensive to the Afrikaaner's law,
Padrino of the punk, a swine who gave
A dialect to the nitwit and the knave,
'Whom did I kill? Whom did I hurt?' I ask,
Reflecting that the writer's only task
Is not to preach or prophecy but please.
But pleasure's fraught with ambiguities,

46

And who am I to plead pure innocence?
Still, I can mildly murmur in defence,
Surveying gloomily my loaded shelf,
At least I played the censor in myself.
Custodiet costodes quis? We know:
We guard the guardian in our souls, although,
Accepting shame and blame, we also call
To vague account the father of our fall,
For books are Adam's children, after all.

April 10, 1989

BELLI'S BLASPHEMOUS BIBLE

1. THE CREATION OF THE WORLD

One day the bakers God & Son set to
And baked, to show their pasta-master's skill,
This loaf the world, though the odd imbecile
Swears it's a melon, and the thing just grew.
They made a sun, a moon, a green and blue
Atlas, chucked stars like money from a till,
Set birds high, beasts low, fishes lower still,
Planted their plants, and said: 'Aye, that'll do.'

No, wait. The old man baked two bits of bread
Called Folk – I quite forgot to mention it –
So he could shout: 'Don't bite that round ripe red
Pie-filling there.' Of course, the buggers bit.
Though mad at them, he turned on us instead
And said, 'Posterity, you're in the shit.'

2. THE EARTHLY PARADISE OF THE BEASTS

Animals led a sort of landlord's life
    And did not give a fuck for anyone
     Till man fucked up their social union
With gun and trap and farm and butcher's knife.
Freedom was frolic, and rough fun was rife
    And as for talk, they just went on and on,
    Yakking as good as any dean or don,
While Adam stood there dumb, with a dumb wife.

This was the boss who came to teach them what
Was what, with harness, hatchet, stick and shot,
Bashing them to red gravy, thick and hot.

He stole their speech too, making sure he'd got
Dumb servitude – the plough; if not, the pot.
He had the last word. Nay, he had the lot.

3. PRIDE BEFORE A FALL

This furred and feathered boss of bird and brute
    Assumed the god, all bloody airs and graces,
    Nor deigned to look down in his subjects' faces,
Treating each creature like a mildewed boot.
He swilled, he gorged, but his preferred pursuit
    Mixed sticking pigs and whipping hounds on chases,
    Marches through arches, blown brass and tossed maces,
With decking Eve, that bitch, in hunter's loot.

The beasts had hunted looks, being forced to make,
    Poor wretches, the bad best of a bad job
And put up with that swine – all save the snake
    Who, spitting like a kettle on a hob,
Weaved at the foul shapes tyranny can take
    And hissed: 'I'll get you yet, you fucking snob.'

4. BACK TO THE ROOTS

A sort of interlude. Let's look at dogs.
    At mastiff, Great Dane, greyhound, poodle, beagle,
    The sausage hound, that yelps like a sick seagull,
Asthmatic bullpups honking hard as hogs.

Now men. Irish in bogs and Dutch in clogs,
 Swarthy as turds, sharp-conked as any eagle,
 The Jew and Turk. Then, trying to look regal,
Tea-slurping English, and French eating frogs.

 Compare some doggy that leaps on to laps
 With a prize wolfhound. Different as cheese and chalk.
In spite of this, our parish ballocks yaps
 About us springing from a single stalk:
One primal bitch for pups, and one for chaps.
Did you ever hear such stupid fucking talk?

5. MAN

If God made man, we've no call to regret
 Man's love of blood and lack of bloody sense.
 God, who's all what they call om ni po tence,
(Meaning he'll piss the bed and prove it's sweat)
Pissed on some clay and sweated cobs to get
 A statue from it, sparing no expense.
 Then he took breath and blew – *Ha Hadam*. Hence
Man's sometimes called the Puffed Up Marionette.

In just one minute he could spout out history
 And write and read great tomes as tough as Plato's.
 He knew it all when first he tottered bedwards.
The names of beasts and birds – no bloody mystery.
 Like a greengrocer sorting out potatoes:
 'This lot is whiteboys and these here King Edwards.'

6. HIS OWN IMAGE AND LIKENESS

Now, Brother Trustgod, Godtrust (never knew
    God had a rupture. Sorry), please let me
    Shove in a word. I just won't have it, see.
God made us all in his own image, did he? You
Are mad. If Paul himself, yes Saint Paul, flew
    Down to agree with you, I'd tell him he
    Was mad. (He was mad.) Why don't you decree
Satan was made in God's own image too?

O bleeding Christ and Christ's own bleeding mother,
    Even if the sanctified three-hatted sod
Says what you say, it's still, my half-arsed brother,
    Mad. Is God's image in greengrocers' shops
Then, in greengrocers? God, he must be a God
    Of cabbages and turnip bloody tops.

7. ALL ABOUT EVE

Give me a woman bare as a boiled egg,
    Who'd think a brush and comb came from the divil,
    Who owns no handkerchief to entrap her snivel,
Or towel or dishcloth hanging from a peg,
Who has no shoe on foot or hose on leg
    Nor any of the Amenities of Civil-
    Ised Life, to use the advertiser's drivel.
No jakes to thrutch in and no pot to deg,

She will sup water but not sit in it
    Nor on a chair nor underneath a roof,
    She'll never see the muckman do his duty.
Picture this little lady decked in shit

From hair to heel, then try to give me proof
That Mother Eve, Christ help us, was a beauty.

8. A REPLY

Scorn not our mother Eve. Remember: she,
    When Adam took her, did not turn her face
    But drank the dreadful fire of his embrace.
Dirty or not, without her where would we
Be? She merits homage. So, with me:
    '*O ave Eva*, though full of disgrace,
    We love thee as the root of all our race;
Thy sap runs in us, leaves of thy living tree.'

Dirty? How do we know? Perhaps her skin
Was laved in a miraculous hygiene,
Just as the second Eve was laved within.
Not that it matters. For myself, I lean
To lauding both her sordor and her sin.
Without those to wash off, who could be clean?

9. THE FIRST MOUTHFUL

Which of the seven deadly sins is worst?
    Pride sneering skyward, avarice shrieking *More*,
    Liplicking lust, or anger, one red roar?
No, gluttony, the fifth sin, is the first.
From Adam burst a famine and a thirst
    For a wormy apple offered by a whore,
    A penny pippin. God has rammed its core
Down all our throats, a canker of the cursed.

That bitch, that blackguard. God, I gape aghast as
I contemplate the greed that could have cast us
    Into the outer darkness – fed us, rather,
To final fire. But our ingenious master's
As quick to cancel as to cause disasters,
    And to this end kindly became a father.

10. ADAM'S SIN

The sceptic beats his brain till dawn's first dapple
    Lights him and all his books to slumber's amity.
    Though he's read all from Moses to Mohamet, he
Rejects the truth of temple, mosque and chapel:
That man brought sin and death and hell to grapple
    His soul in irons, condemning God to damn it. He
    Set up an aboriginal calamity
Or, if you like, munched a forbidden apple.

Why why why? One song, too many singers.
Why *why*? *Why* won't unwrite the bloody book.
    So let them write a new one if they must.
Why why? *We want an answer.* They can look
In Milo Aphrodite's clutching fingers
Or up the arsehole of Pasquino's bust.

11. THE FIRST CLOTHES

Before they yielded to the devil's urging
    And crunched the good-bad apple to the core,
    Bare innocence was all our parents wore,
Like Jesus Christ got ready for the scourging.
After their second gorge they felt emerging

A thing called shame. So rapidly they tore
     Leaves from the trees to cover what before
Had been mere taps for secondary purging.

So good and evil, as we must conclude,
Succeed in making rude and crude and lewd
     The dumpendebat and the fhairy grot.
Else why should man and missis play the prude?
Each knew, however leafily endued,
     Precisely what the other one had got.

12. THE STATE OF INNOCENCE (1)

There'd be, if Adam hadn't sold our stock,
     Preferring disobedience to riches,
     No sin or death for us poor sons of bitches.
Man would range free, powerless to shame or shock,
And introduce all women to his cock,
     Without the obstacles of skirt and breeches,
     Spreading his seed immeasurably, which is
To say: all round the world, all round the clock.

The beasts would share the happy lot of men,
     Despite a natural plenitude of flies.
There'd be no threats of Doomsday coming when
     Christ must conduct the dreadful last assize.
Instead, the Lord would look in now and then,
     Checking our needs, renewing our supplies.

13. THE STATE OF INNOCENCE (2)

I'm puzzled. (Bear with me, Father Superior.)
    If Adam's gorging had not been the means
    Of turning us to compost for the beans
– Nothing more useful, yes, but nothing drearier –
And all who issue from their dam's interior
    Did not end up by pushing up the greens,
    Now what would be finale to those scenes
Which start with bouts of murderous hysteria?

Ah but, you say, along with immortality
    There'd be no urge to sin: remember this.
Thank you. And so – predestinate causality,
And no free will (but Adam had it: yes?).
What puzzles me is: would we incur fatality
If we fell down a bloody precipice?

14. HOLY STARVATION

We sinners have to eat four times a day
    Or, if we happen to be English, five.
    But man unfallen would have stayed alive.
If not a single crumb had come his way.
And even if they'd served him on a tray
    Boiled stones, mashed mud, garnished with poison iv-
    Y, he'd survive – indeed, contrive
To thrive on shit like any flower of May.

Everyone thin, carting an empty belly
    About, knowing no gustatory bliss
In wine or trout or grouse in aspic jelly;
    With jam a joke and fowl farci a farce.

The tongue and teeth for talk – yes; but why this
    Hole, O ye holy buggers, up the arse?

15. CAIN AND THE LORD

'Cain, where is Abel?' Silence. 'Cain, *Cain*, where
    Is Abel?' Silence. '*Cain!*' Then came Cain's cry:
    'Shoving your nose in. How the hell should I
Know where he is? Or, for that matter, care?
Am I my brother's keeper?' Eden's air
    Darkened at this, shuddered at God's reply:
    'I'll tell you where, you killer – done in by
Your knife, he's pushing up those parsnips there.

Out of my sight, start running, up and down
    The whole damned earth, you damned, you cursed; and cry
Through every bloody street of every town.
Howl, you unchristian swine, your dismal tune
    Hurl at the stars, then shiver in the sky,
Weep till you brim the pockholes of the moon.'

16. CAIN'S CRIME

Please don't think, Herr Professor, I intend
    Defending Cain. Better than you, perhaps,
    I know him, but know too the sort of lapse
Drink will induce – how it can blind and bend
And break. See Cain drunk, beckoning like a friend,
    Thick stick in fist, an oiled smile on his chaps,
    Wooing his brother hither. Then he taps,
Raps bone, draws blood, the swine, and makes an end.
Filthy? Oh, yes. Still, it was far from funny

Having to hear God hawking up his phlegm
To spit upon his parsnips and his honey
  But not on Abel's sheep, no, not on them.
  Born of the breed of men and not of mice,
  Cain growled revolt then cut himself a slice.

17. THE SECOND SIN

Reproach him not for bidding crime begin.
  Evil was what he sucked in from his mother.
  The murder of his innocent young brother
Derived from something deep beneath the skin.
As two and two make four, so man makes sin.
  Still, there's a nagging problem tough to smother:
  How did he know when one man cracks another
With force enough he does that other in?

Think now. Before Cain played the bloody brute
  No one had demonstrated death as yet.
This doctrine, then, is murderous to refute:
  That murder is an impulse man first met
When his teeth met inside that juicy fruit.
  What's homicide? A thing your father ate.

18. THE UNIVERSAL DELUGE

God said to Noah: 'Listen, er patriarch.
  You and your sons, each take his little hatchet,
  Lop wood enough to build yourselves an ark
To these specifications. Roof and thatch it
  Like Porto de Ripetta ferry. Mark
  Me well now. Chase each make of beast and catch it.

And catch a male or female that will match it.
Then with your victuals, zoo and wives, embark.

A flood is going to test your wooden walls,
    A world's end deluge. Tivoli waterfalls
    Will seem an arc of piss in a urinal.
Ride it until you sight a rainbow. Then
Jump in the mud and make things grow again
    Till the next world's end. (That one will be final.)'

19. NOAH'S ARK

Elephants, fleas, cows, lions, sheep, wolves, hares,
    Foxes and flies, roosters and stags and stallions,
    Mice by platoons and rabbits by battalions,
Donkeys and pigs and bugs, monkeys and mares.
Meat by the ton, cheese, pasta, worms, figs, pears,
    Maize, clover, hay, whey, pigswill, skilly, scallions,
    Bones, birdseed, bran, melons like golden galleons,
Minced heart for owls and honey for the bears:

These and much more poor Noah stowed in the boat
That God made airtight, cosy, close and dark.
A year and more this barnyard was afloat,
Heady with parmigiano, goat and skunk.
How did he cope, our blessed patriarch?
Ask him. He may respond by getting drunk.

20. THE NEW WINE

Drunk, yes. Near his palazzo, safe on shore,
Noah planted vines and fondly watched them sprout,

And when he saw the luscious grapes fill out
(One bunch weighed ten or twenty pounds, or more),
He crushed the juice in ferment, let it pour
Down the red lane, and gave a toper's shout:
'It's good, it's fucking good!' His drunken bout
First made him high and, after, hit the floor.

That was strong stuff, he was not used to it.
Like all us drunkards, snoring at the sun,
He lay as flat as a five-lira bit.
But – shame – our patriarch had no breeches on
And – but I'd better quote you Holy Writ –
'Displayed his balls and prick to everyone.'

21. THE AGE OF MAN

If it is true, as the priests say it is,
 That every ancient patriarch and prophet
 Took a long time for old age to kill off (it
Was, in some cases, nine damned centuries),
They must have been damned short of maladies –
 No stone, hard chancre, or bronchitic cough. It
 Could be they postponed their trip to Tophet
With secrets still unsold in pharmacies.

Such agelessness would wreck our modern age.
 That lad, see, fifty years in his high chair,
A hundred more at school, would choke with rage
 (Himself a dad now, in or out of matrimony)
Waiting for dad to die and bless his heir,
 Trying to run up bills against his patrimony.

22. THE TOWER

'We'd like to touch the stars', they cried, and, after,
     'We've *got* to touch the stars. But how?' An able-
     Brained bastard told them: 'Build the Tower of Babel.
Start now, get moving. Dig holes, sink a shaft. A-
Rise, arouse, raise rafter after rafter,
     Get bricks, sand, limestone, scaffolding and cable.
     I'm clerk of works, fetch me a chair and table.'
God meanwhile well-nigh pissed himself with laughter.

They'd just got level with the Pope's top floor
     When something in their mouths began to give:
They couldn't talk Italian any more.
     The project died in this linguistic slaughter.
Thus, if a man said: 'Pass us that there sieve,'
     His mate would hand him up a pail of water.

23. ABRAHAM'S SACRIFICE (1)

The Bible, sometimes called the Jewish Chronicle,
     Says, midway between Noah's and Aaron's ark,
     That Abraham played the grand old patriarch
And sacrificed to God, with fine parsonical
Language that all that blood made sound ironical.
     He took a donkey from the donkey-park
     (Chewing up chicory and grass in stark
Lordly disdain, as if it wore a monocle)

And called to Isaac: 'Pack the bags and load
This donkey, get the boy to bring a nice
Sharp axe, then kiss your mother on the cheek.
Bring coats and hats, we're going to take the road.

The blessed Lord requires a sacrifice.
The time has come to teach you the technique.'

24. ABRAHAM'S SACRIFICE (2)

They ate, while day was cooking in the east,
    Some breakfast. When their journey had begun,
    Abraham led them in an orison
That lasted for a hundred miles at least.
Then the old swine or, if you wish, old priest
    Said: 'We've arrived. Shoulder that burden, son.
    And as for you –' (meaning the other one)
' – Wait here. You toom,' he told his fellow-beast.

They started climbing. Halfway through their climb,
    Isaac said: 'Where's your victim wandered to?'
'Wait', said his father. 'All in God's good time.'
    They reached the top, where knife-edged breezes blew,
And Abraham said: 'A victim, yes. Well, I'm
    The priest, son, and there's only me and you.'

25. ABRAHAM'S SACRIFICE (3)

'No, no!' The boy knelt in his innocence
    – The right position for that butcher-dad
    Who raised his axe above the hapless lad,
Ready to do paternal violence.
'Stop!' cried a voice. 'I think we can dispense
    With filicide.' An angel. 'You've just had
    A Godsent test, and passed it, I might add.
Baaaah – here's a sheep. Quite a coincidence.'

To cut it short (I'm sick of the damned story),
The sheep was slain, and all the four went home,
The ass to pasture, Isaac to his mother.
As for the slab he nearly made all gory.
It's a prized relic, hidden safe in Rome,
At Borgo-novo, or some place or other.

26. JOSEPH THE JEW (1)

Some merchants, so it's said, near signed the pledge and
    Gave up the drink when they heard something odd:
    A yell deep in a well. 'A child, by God,'
One said, sticking his chin over the edge and
Peering. They hired a dredger then to dredge and
He dredged up, dripping like a landed cod,
    Howling like hell, a stinking clayey clod,
Joseph the Jew, so goes the ancient legend.

They dried him, cleaned him, gave him fodder and
    Bought him a shirt against the inclement weather,
But didn't want to bring him up by hand.
    Seeking returns on what they'd clubbed together
They sold him off in Egypt, contraband,
    For a few rags and half a trank of leather.

27. JOSEPH THE JEW (2)

Joseph grew up. When he was fully grown,
    The lady that he worked for cast him looks
    Whose drift he thought he'd read about in books,
Sighing, trying to get him on his own.
She ogled him with many a meaning moan,

Carefully careless with her eyes and hooks.
   Her hunger could not be assuaged by cooks,
Only by some raw mutton with no bone.

One morning, bringing the hot water to her,
   He found her naked, the sweet buxom slut,
So damped her with the contents of the ewer.
   She grabbed him by his single garment but
He left it with her, naked but still pure,
   And ran away, the bloody idiot.

28. LOT AT HOME

Two strangers, both with staffs, but one a bit
   Lame from the journey, weary but still wary.
   Arrived at the holy hour of the Hail Mary
(I love anachronising Holy Writ)
Looking for lodgings. Lot, who had just lit
His window lamp, saw them, called them and said: 'You're very
Welcome here.' They smiled: 'Ah, a good fairy.
Such kindness. You'll be amply paid for it.'

These two were angels. The buggers of Gomorrah,
Hearing of their arrival, knew it not,
Else all their hair would have stood up in horror.
Their pricks stood up instead. They yelled out: 'You
Selfish unsodomite, let's have them, Lot.
You don't require their arses, and we do.'

29. LOT'S WIFE

The angels now announced themselves to Lot
    And said 'This town must suffer for its fault.
    No rooftop, cavern, hole or nether vault
Will hide them when the flames leap high and hot.
You and your family leave now. Do not halt
    And look back down Longara Road. *Do not*,
We say again.' But hardly had they got
    Away when Lot's wife turned and turned to salt.

Ah, woman, cursed by curiosity.
If all of our Italian women could
So change, as by that precedent they should,
They'd soon destroy the salt monopoly
And bring the price down, though of course we would
Be forced to live on salt and sodomy.

30. LOT IN REPOSE

God, then, assumed the office of a cook
And baked the Sodomites like salmon trout.
Only the family of Lot got out,
Though his wife suffered for that backward look.
They camped near Zoar, in a stony nook.
Lot's daughters, starved of love, began to pout,
Seeing no sign of penises about,
And, driven by a fleshly need, forsook

Propriety. Here at least was their father.
They gave him wine with a well-salted pasty.
When he was drunk they fucked him to a lather,
Not finding this unnatural or nasty.

No fire rained down. It seems that God is rather
Inclined to incest but hates pederasty.

31. EXODUS

Pharaoh, a rogue in charge of other rogues,
First drowned the Jews then turned them into slaves,
Driven to toil by knaves with stones and staves,
Just where the fertile Nilus disembogues.
But Moses (the humane dictator vogue's
Said to start here), after some narrow shaves,
Led the Jews out between two walls of waves:
The buggers didn't even wet their brogues.

When the Red Sea swung open like a door,
The Jews assumed their journey was near done,
Not having met the love of God before.
But round and round beneath the desert sun
They had to frig for forty years and more –
A fucking waste of time for everyone.

32. BALAAM'S ASS

As ancient Hebrew story tellers knew
The future better than the past, we lack
Proof that when Balaam rode his donkey's back
And, since it halted, beat it black and blue
The poor beast turned on him and brayed: 'Hey, you,
Why did you launch that unprovoked attack?
If you could see that angel there you'd thwack
This ass, or arse, more gently than you do.'

If you believe this, welcome an incursion
Of awe to learn that donkeys can be pat in
High class Italian (English in this version).
Accept the premise and it follows that in
Pointing you out the donkeys that know Latin
(*Aspeeeerges meeeeee*) I cast no foul aspersion.

33. THE BATTLE OF GIDEON

300 Jews knitted their warlike brows and,
Armed with trombones and torches hid in skillets.
Marched in good order on their foemen's billets,
Quiet as a moving munching herd of cows. And
As dancers on the stage taking their bows and
Boos in an endless belt endlessly fill it, s-
O this small troop marched in a circle till its
300 men looked damned near like 3000.

Ta-rah, ta-ray – clash pans, flash torches. Flustered,
And deafened as 300 brass are mustered,
The enemy collapses like a custard.
Such thrift! Today we have our martial brawls,
Our soldiers heed the bugle when it calls
And waste 300 fucking cannon-balls.

34. THE FOXES

The Bible is quite verminous with foxes.
Samson caught hundreds and, with foxy cunning,
Tied torches to their tails and set them running
Through his foes' harvest-fields – thus, with hot proxies,
Saving them sweat. Still, they wished ninety poxes

Upon him and increased their vengeful gunning.
Though vermin then, where are they now? They're shunning
Our hounds, like bishops shunning heterodoxies.

We ought to want them, since they stank of virtue
When Samson used them against naughty men.
But still an eggless henless world would hurt you
More than a foxless. If he came back again
With scores of foxes sniffing round his skirt, you
Would say: 'I'd rather have a fucking hen.'

35. GOD HELPS THOSE WHO HELP THEMSELVES (1)

Of all the Bible stories that they tell,
This one to come is quite the most fantastic.
A sonnet being so damned inelastic,
I'll require two to tell it really well.
Well, now – the exodists from Egypt's hell
Met the mad Malechites who, dreadful, drastic.
Ferocious, tastelessly enthusiastic,
Fell on the Hebrews, and the Hebrews fell.

God made a memorandum. After all,
The Jews pursued the then correct religion.
After four hundred years he called on Saul.
'The Malechites,' he said, 'deserve the axe.
Spit the whole nation; roast it like a pigeon.
Don't leave a feather on their fucking backs.'

36. GOD HELPS THOSE WHO HELP THEMSELVES (2)

So in God's name Saul went and waded in,
Trouncing them in one horrible stampede,
Goats, calves and all. Mercy maybe or greed
Or something made him save Prince Agag's skin.
Samuel now prophesied about Saul's sin!
'Idolater, betrayer of our creed,
A holier Israelite will supersede
Your reign and make a holier reign begin.

Bring me the prince you blasphemously spared.'
Tremulous as a fatted pig, that prince
Stuttered – agagagag aghast, shit-scared.
The holy Samuel did not blink or wince
But raised the butcher's blade that he had bared
And made a mound of Malechitish mince.

37. DAVID'S DUEL

How powerful is God's arm! He sent a boy
To fight Goliath, who was tough and scary,
Who swallowed foes like oysters of the prairie
And thought he'd stamp on David like a toy.
But God wished Israel to yell with joy
To know that every flabby, weak, unhairy
Weed that loves Jesus and his mother Mary
Finds giants rather easy to destroy.

Seeing the stone and sling and stripling shepherd,
Goliath cried: 'You little prick, you've gone a
Mite too far,' and tensed up like a leopard.

But David blessed the saints and the Madonna,
Measured his fireline, fired his pebble up it
And saw Goliath crumple like a puppet.

38. HOLY KING DAVID

King David's later life? The stories vary.
It seems, though, his prophetic eye was sharp,
He spoke with God, he much preferred the bar-p-
Arlour to the coffee-shop or dairy.
Jesus, of David's seed through holy Mary,
For David was a very pericarp,
Had his gab-gift, but could not play the harp
Nor sing like David, King Saul's prize canary.

The Bible gives a fairish bona fide
Account of him, although it's hard to follow:
The story is elliptical, untidy.
You'll learn, however, that he loved to wallow
In love, and frot until his balls were hollow,
From Saturday till pretty late on Friday.

39. THE JUDGMENT OF SOLOMON

Solomon's judgment. So. It makes you laugh.
But could a judge upon a modern bench,
Nose lifted high against the rabble's stench,
For all his wigs and tomes and courtroom staff,
Do better? He, drained like his own carafe,
Hearing one wench scream at the other wench
In language that would make a bargee blench,
Could only say: 'Let's chop the child in half.'

The parish register was plain to see,
You say. He could have checked on her or her name,
The date and place of birth of son or daughter.
Fool. In those days nobody had a surname,
And parish registers came in A.D.,
When Christ had shown a brand-new use for water.

40. THE FAIR JUDITH

The Holy Bible tells how the seduc-
Tive Judith feasted Holofernes, winner
Of the late bloody war. They finished dinner,
She doused the lights. He, leering at his luck,
Leapt on her unresisting. Then she struck
His head off with a sword and cried: 'Foul sinner,'
(His milk still frothing to the boil within her)
'Now he could find some blacker hole to fuck.'

She heaved the head up in her lily hand,
Though it was heavy, horrible and gory,
And did a tour of triumph through the land.

I find two morals in this sacred story:
(a) prove your faith by killing people and
(b) be a bloody whore for heaven's glory.

41. GUESSING GAME

The chaste Susannah – what was she chased for?
Her beauty, yes, but was there something more?
The sort of reputation that she bore?
You said the word, not I: the word is w—e.

Those old men said it too (Aaaarh, nothing's lower
Than watching at a lady's bathroom door).
But Daniel caught them out. His lion-roar
Condemned their heads, not hers, to hit the floor.

Chaste, was she? Hm, perhaps she couldn't bring
Herself to fancy two limp bits of string.
A woman's nature's nature in the spring.
To get to know it, cease your pondering,
Slap on your chest two puddings in a sling
And let your haunches launch into a swing.

42. BELSHAZZAR'S FEAST

Belshazzar, drunk, observed a kind of smoke
Resolve itself to something vaguely manual
Writing upon the wall. He called on Daniel.
'*Many tickle your arse* – What's this – a joke?'
The ambiguous bilge that Daniel then spoke
Made less sense than the yapping of a spaniel.
'Weighed in the balance to the utmost granule,
Found wanting.' Why not just 'You're going to croak'?

All right, that's not a literal translation.
But what came next was no big fat surprise:
Belshazzar didn't live to eat his breakfast.
A prophet, scared of sticking out his neck, fast-
Idious about his reputation,
Ought to be told that riddles are damned lies.

43. THE EIGHTH OF DECEMBER

Serious talk now; let's not arse about.
December eight – what do we celebrate?
Come on, you know. Good – the Immaculate
Conception. When that apple-loving lout
Adam first took it in his head to flout
The Lord's law, angels said: 'Evacuate,'
And firmly locked the paradisal gate,
Keeping his maculate descendants out.

Poor Mother Nature, ever since that ban,
Cannot breed even half a child that's blameless.
There boils within the rising prick of man
The seed of something terrible though nameless.
So praise to Joachim who, with Saint Ann,
Achieved a fuck that was uniquely shameless.

44. THE ANNUNCIATION

You know the day, the month, even the year.
While Mary ate her noonday plate of soup,
The Angel Gabriel, like a heaven-hurled hoop,
Was bowling towards her through the atmosphere.
She watched him crash the window without fear
And enter through the hole in one swift swoop.
A lily in his fist, his wings adroop,
'Ave', he said, and after that, 'Maria.

Rejoice, because the Lord's eternal love
Has made you pregnant – not by orthodox
Methods, of course. The Pentecostal Dove
Came when you slept and nested in your box.'

'A hen?' she blushed, 'for I know nothing of –'
The angel nodded, knowing she meant cocks.

45. THE MADONNA'S MARRIAGE

Only a few weeks after did our Virgin see
The need to make a matrimonial match,
To build a nest wherein the egg could hatch
(Her little belly had begun to burgeon, see.)
It was, therefore, a matter of some urgency.
She didn't seek the freshest of the batch;
The one she gave her hand to was no catch,
But any port will do in an emergency.

The foolish gossips gossiped at the feast:
'She might have got a younger one at least,
Not an old dribbler frosty in the blood.'
But that old dribbler dribbling by the side
Of such a beautiful and youthful bride
Found his dry stalk was bursting into bud.

46. THE VISIT

Mary received, while burning Joseph's toast,
A letter. 'Who the hell – ?' (under her breath),
Aloud: 'Ah – cousin Saint Elizabeth.'
Elizabeth, it seemed, could also boast
A pregnancy, though not from the Holy Ghost.
Still, her next birthday was her sixtieth.
Though travel then was slow expensive death,
'We're coming', Mary wrote, then caught the post.

They went. After a short magnificat,
The women were soon chattering away
Of swellings, morning sickness, and all that.
Joseph decided that he'd like to stay
A month or so, and so hung up his hat
Better than sawing wood all bloody day.

47. EPIPHANY

From a far country – how far? Very far:
It grows, for instance, cinnamon and cocoa –
Three kings, their robes rococo or barocco,
Followed their leader – viz., that big bright star.
Each Magus had, like any czar or tsar,
Guards, steeds, a page, a clown with painted boko,
Coaches, a camel, and in leisured loco-
Motion they swayed towards where the Hebrews are.

They reached the stable with their caravan
One morning, evening, noon or afternoon,
With gifts – incense for God, and myrrh for man.
For Christ as king they had a gold doubloon –
Proper, they thought, for the top Christian.
They were, it seems, some centuries too soon.

48. THE CIRCUMCISION

Our Lady had a painful Christmas Day
And heaven the monopoly of mirth.
Between an ox and ass she brought to birth
A stableboy that stank of rags and hay.
His substitutive dad had to obey

The law, so took the lord of earth
Templewards, to have half a farthingsworth
Of hypostatic foreskin cut away.

Thirty years later saw the blessed Lord on
A journey to the rolling river Jordan
To be baptised by Mary's cousin's son.
A Christian man thus sprang from a prepuceless
Jew. I call most turncoats fucking useless
But make a rare exception for this one.

49. CHRIST'S FORESKIN

That sacred relic, by the way, was hid
And either kept in camphor or else iced.
It grew so precious it could not be priced.
And then one day His Holiness undid
A holy box and raised a holy lid –
Behold – the foreskin of our saviour Christ,
Shrimplike in shape, most elegantly sliced,
At last to profane eyes exhibited.

In eighty other Christian lands they show
This self-same prize for reverent eyes to hail.
You look incredulous, my friend. But know
That faith, though buffeted, must never fail.
The explanation's this: God let it grow
After the clipping, like a fingernail.

50. THE FLIGHT OF THE HOLY FAMILY

Joseph was doing bull-roars on his back,
A dream corrida crowd was yelling 'Toro!'
He slept cut off from coming care and sorrow,
Making the stable shake with roar and rack.
But then an angel dealt him a rough smack
And said: 'You know what day it is tomorrow?
The twenty-eighth. I managed, see, to borrow
A copy of the current almanac.'

Herod announced the Feast of Childermass.
Joseph rushed out and had to pay a pretty
Price (how he cursed) for an old spavined ass:
A carpenter would rather gyp than be gypped.
And so they moved off mouselike towards Egypt,
Missing a lively day in David's city.

51. THE SLAUGHTER OF THE INNOCENTS

King Herod now, to minimal applause,
Ordered the babies to be stuck like swine.
There was an uproar then in Palestine
And not, O Jesus help us, without cause.
Those who had seen this coming did not pause
To hide their babes, but let them croon or whine
As visible as laundry on the line,
While they had masses said to Santa Claus.

Their saviour (saviour?) halfway to the delta
Smelt nothing of the filthy bloody welter
Nor heard the parents curse or ululate.
The troops of Herod smote and did not spare

But with each crack a splinter sought the air
And feebly tapped on heaven's heavy gate.

52. ORIGINAL SIN

When he was old enough for politics
Jesus went splashing on the Jordan's bed.
He ceased to be a Jew and joined instead
The Apostolic Roman Catholics.
Then he went dropping homilies like bricks.
'He who seeks heaven with an unwashed head
Will see the kingdom with his arse', he said,
Shouting the odds, wagging his crucifix.

Only his mother got there unbaptised,
Which proves she waved goodbye to mother earth
A good Jewess, staunch in the faith and steady.
Heaven had got her soul well organised:
Why rub and scrub a thing that came to birth
As white as someone's laundry line already?

53. THE WEDDING AT CANA (1)

The guests at Cana, vinously aswim,
Aroar for more, found every bloody butt
Was empty, and the liquor stores were shut.
The innkeeper, fired by a roguish whim,
Had three casks filled with water to the brim,
Then told each sozzled fuddled serving slut
To lug them where, importantly astrut,
The host was, and to leave the rest to him.

Christ was a guest, dressed in his best apparel,
But the host begged a sort of magic act
Through Mary: 'Make him turn this lot to wine.'
Mary replied: 'I know this son of mine –
Moody. But if I speak to him with tact
You'll get, maybe, a quarter of a barrel.'

54. THE WEDDING AT CANA (2)

And so she begged an instant grapeless wine.
But Jesus, who was hardly yet adult,
Sighed like a stone leaving a catapult
And scowled: 'This problem's neither yours nor mine,
Mother. Permit me coldly to decline
To help these boozers. Easy or difficult
Is not the point. Let the fat host consult
Some other thaumaturge, the smirking swine.

Just so some soak can blurt a drunken toast
Or swill the teeth he's sunk into a roast,
You want me to work miracles and such,
To get a toothcomb and go combing out
The various troubles lurking all about.
I've troubles of my own, thanks very much.'

55. THE WEDDING AT CANA (3)

Jesus, I think (Christ rest his spirit), chose a
Tantrum like that one not to be unkind
But to show off. A young man is inclined
To blow his trumpet oftener than his nose. A-
Las, Our Lady, so says the composer

Of this instructive rhapsody, repined.
She'd had maternal victory in mind
But now became the Mater Dolorosa.

I sometimes wish this story had not happened;
But heed its lesson, if you heed no other:
Try not to be the big loud man too soon.
God heard the answer that he gave his mother,
Determined on a right reproving rap and
Lathered his arse one Friday afternoon.

56. THE HOUSE OF GOD

Jesus forgives all sins – or nearly all:
Usury, anger, greed, the knife thrust under
The ribs, robbery, calumny, lying, plunder
Of land condoned by rogues in the town hall.
Only on one occasion did he fall
Into a rage that tore him near asunder
And made him roar with true Jehovan thunder
And bounce in bloody anger like a ball,

And that was when he saw the Church done wrong to.
He took a whip with many a knotted thong to
The moneychangers preying on those praying at the temple.
This is the only place in Holy Writ
Where Christ is shown as throwing a mad fit.
He aged with righteous rage and started greying at the temple.

57. MARTHA AND MARY

Martha said: 'Christ, I'm full up reet to't' scupper
Wi' Mary there.' She belted out her stricture:
'Rosaries, masses – it fair makes you sick to your
Stomach. Stations o't' Cross. I'm real fed up. A
Carthorse I am, harnessed neck and crupper
While she does nowt. About time this horse kicked you
Right in the middle of your holy picture, Mary.
Go on, now. Say it: *what's for supper?'*

'Martha, O Martha,' sighed the blessed Saviour,
'You've no call to get mad at her behaviour.
She's on the right road, and you're out of luck.'
'The right road, aye', said Martha. 'Why, if I
Went on like her, this house would be a sty,
And she'd not see the right road for the muck.'

58. FIRST COMMUNION

With the Last Supper finished and the waiter
Ready to clear, Christ took a loaf of bread,
Blessed it, then fed it to the already fed,
Making each eater a communicator.
He even gave some to his darling traitor,
Proving his mood was rosy, not yet red
(Judas Iscariot, who lost his head
And went to play at swings a little later).

But, friendly as he was, the Master knew
His passion hour was coming, hot and hellish,
So made a good confession, to embellish
His church with not one sacrament but two.

There then remained one holy thing to do –
To eat himself, with little or no relish.

59. CHRIST'S CROSS-EXAMINATION

After they'd knotted Jesus up with rope,
Judas assisting, damned and dirty dastard,
After the high priest's bullies, who had mastered
The spitting art, had given it full scope,
After the maids and grooms had heard the Pope
Say: 'I don't give a fuck about the bastard,'
They led our Lord to Pilate's alabastered
Hand-washing room, already sweet with soap.

This was a case Pilate could not refuse.
He saw the filth of it but might not shed it –
A swine, yes, but a clean swine, to his credit.
He said: 'You're Jesus, then, king of the Jews?'
Christ sought not to deny, affirm or edit,
But looked him in the eye and said: 'You've said it.'

60. CHRIST AT THE PILLAR

Stripped naked like a candidate for slavery,
Lashed to a post, Jesus, from head to feet,
Beaten by bastards who knew how to beat.
Yielded his skin to graduates in knavery.
No spot was spared. He ended an unsavoury
Blue-green-vermilion chunk of dirty meat,
The sort that's bought for cats and dogs to eat
From fly-buzzed butchers' barrows in Trastevere.

No spot spared? Well, I did some small research
Into that very whipping post, that's placed,
As is well known, in St Prassede's church,
And found it didn't come up to my waist.
So, though Christ's limbs, loins, face, flanks, belly shared
Foul blows, his sitteth-on-God's-right was spared.

61. COURAGE

You've seen a felon in the public pillory
Having his buttocks beaten to a mash,
And much admired his cool disdainful dash,
The muscles firm – both gluteal and maxillary
(Aided no doubt by draughts from the distillery).
But now consider Christ beneath the lash,
Deafened by the incessant crash and slash
Of leather, sticks, the whole damned crude artillery.

Consider how each whipstroke gashes, galls
Ribs, shoulders, flanks, how bits of torn flesh keep
Falling away, as, say, boiled mutton falls
From the bone. But does the victim whine or weep?
No. Though all that is left of him is his balls.
He merely counts the strokes, like counting sheep.

62. ILL-STARRED

How can you think of Christ without a sob?
Dropped like a beast in a foul nest of straw,
Forced, as a boy, with hammer, pliers, saw
To slave away at a woodworker's job,
A youth, he walked the world with grumbling maw,

Preaching the word to a disdainful mob,
A man, he had a price upon his nob,
And Judas sold him to the Roman law.

The spit, the lash, the doom, the thorny crown,
The nails, the cross, the vinegar-soaked rag
Tied to a pole, the diced-for bloody gown:
All burdens fell upon him, sacred bag
Of bones – hence the old saying handed down:
Flies always settle on a spavined nag.

63. THE TWO BREEDS

We come into this world bedecked in shit,
Some of us anyway, including Jesus.
But others are born rich as fucking Croesus,
Mightily proud, mightily proud of it.
The crown, the coronet, the mitre fit
Men for whom earth gushes out gold like geysers,
While we are lemons ready for the squeezers,
Scarred nags for spurs, bare backsides to be hit.

If Christ was one of us, why did he give in
Such plenty palaces for those to live in,
Making us stew in filth and sweat and pus?
Why, even on the cross, in the last flood
Of pain, it was for them he gushed forth blood
But trickled bloody water out for us.

64. GUILT IN THE GHETTO

There's a whole race that seems to merit hell
Because the bloody reprobates refuse
To join the Church of Rome – I mean the Jews.
They let Christ die upon the cross as well.
Still, as some learned Jewish rabbis tell,
There is a circumstance that one may choose,
If one's fair-minded, that can near-excuse
The dozen errant tribes of Israel.

When Christ left home to work his métier,
He knew Good Friday was his destined day:
Death was a big word in his lexicon.
Doomed-to-be slain (put it another way)
Must meet a complementary doomed-to-slay.
Somebody had to take that business on.

65. LIMBO

When Jesus rose triumphant from the tomb,
Defying natural law as well as Roman,
He whizzed down like a shot shot by a bowman
And dragged the saintly souls from Limbo's gloom.
Then Purgatory started to assume
The place of rhubarb in a sick abdomen;
Masses were sold like tickets by a showman –
Twin innovations that are still in bloom.

The angels, after brooding wings akimbo,
Put infant souls, baptised in milk and piss
But not the font, into that empty Limbo.
It wasn't meant to last, of course, and when

The Last Trump offers only blaze or bliss,
Christ knows where the young bastards will go then.

66. CHRIST IN HELL

The Creed says Christ descended into Hell.
What could his Father have been thinking of,
Sending him there? Is that paternal love?
Jesus in Hell. Christ Jesus. Hell. Well, well,
For my part, faith and candour both compel
My stating that the buggers up above –
Not God but government – desired to shove
Christ in that ill-appointed hot hotel.

Jesus in Hell. O Jesus Christ in Hades.
Ever since earth was earth and sky was sky,
A finer gentleman, gentlemen, ladies,
Was never picked to whip and crucify
Than Jesus. Let's believe that when he made his
Trip it was just hello and then goodbye.

67. DOUBTING THOMAS

When Christ rose up, those somewhat timid gentry
His friends kicked up a noise, but one apostle –
St Thomas – sang as loud as any throstle:
'It's an imposture. Obvious. Elementary.
Anyway, how could he pass the fucking sentry?'
Jesus meanwhile, unseen in the Easter jostle,
Was making for their place at a colossal
Speed, and he used the keyhole for his entry.

He cried: 'Poke in your finger, near this rib,
And you'll soon see whether I still exist
Or the whole tale is just a fucking fib.'
St Thomas came and shoved his great ham fist
Into the hole. He then became as glib
A Christian as he'd been a rationalist.

68. WHITSUN

You've seen the cook shove larding needles in
Pork, lamb, beef or some other meaty treat,
While seated on your trattoria seat,
Hungry as hell and anxious to begin.
Fat spits and bubbles underneath the skin,
The very sizzle's good enough to eat,
And while the flame and fat and fibre meet,
Saliva dribbles almost to your chin.

This is one way to cook a fine fat pigeon,
But not the dove of pentecostal peace.
Dressed as a grilled lamb-tongue, this fluttered down
And, to feed hungry bellies with religion,
It cooked the eleven apostles good and brown
Until they spat with holy grace or grease.

69. SPREAD THE WORD

When Jesus died, firm in the Christian creed,
St Peter's party picked up the Lord's load
And, staff in fist, they took the Cassia road
And went about the world to sow their seed.
Some sought – lazy, or fired to feed a need –

Baccano and La Storta; others strode
To Nepi, Monterosi, where they showed
The Christian way of death in word and deed.

Nay, more – to teach the good and ban and banish
The bad, they went to lands where pagans chatter
In Russian, German, English, French and Spanish.
Their message was so simple, strong, unkillable,
The fact they spoke Italian didn't matter.
No one misunderstood a single syllable.

70. THE LAST DAYS

When the long annals of the earth are done
And Christ's creation's melted into shit,
The Antichrist will crawl out of his pit
And preach the dirty word to everyone.
Cursed with a wall-eye that the blest will shun,
A giant body and a face unfit
Even to have tomatoes hurled at it,
A prodigy, son of a monk and nun.

He will be bashed by Enoch and Elia
Elijah too – they'll spring out of a hatch
In St Paul's church, between the nave and choir.
Satan will slither up from hell to snatch
His share, snarling it out with the Messiah.
And earth will be a plucked up cabbage patch.

71. THE LAST JUDGMENT

At the round earth's imagined corners let
Angels regale us with a brass quartet,
Capping that concord with a fourfold shout:
'Out, everybody, everybody out!'
Then skeletons will rattle all about
Forming in file, on all fours, tail to snout,
Putting on flesh and face until they get,
Upright, to where the Judgment Seat is set.

There the All High, maternal, systematic,
Will separate the black souls from the white:
That lot there for the cellar, this the attic.
The wing'd musicians now will chime or blare a
Brief final tune, then they'll put out the light:
Er-phwhoo. And so to bed. Owwwww. *Bona sera.*

72. THE FATHER OF THE SAINTS

Here are some names, my son, we call the cock:
    The chair, the yard, the large or little dick,
    The tool, rod of love, Hampton (Wick),
Syringe, red robin, Brighton (Blackpool) rock,
    The fleshly comforter, the six o'clock,
    And Old Blind Bob, the prover, prior, prick,
    Jack Thursday, my best friend, the penal stick
The old man, knobkerry, Kentish Knock.

The jelif, truncheon, he, the lower nose,
    The cad monocular, the butcher's lad,
Will, bill, asperger, Holofernes, rose,
    The gism-engine, bishop, shagger, shad,

The thruster, monkey, climber without toes,
    The sausage and our bad mad glad sad dad.

But let me add
    That scholars, studying with midnight tapers,
    Use the term *phallus* in their learned papers.
    And one old man I know calls it *Priapus*.
His wife has no name for it but a frown:
A sign that life has somehow let her down.

73. LOCAL INDUSTRY

One day I reached the deepest of the dumps:
    I hadn't got the nicked edge of a shillin.
    I thought of somethin that might work, God willin,
So broke the kitchen shovel into lumps.
Off to the cattle market. There was clumps
    Of tourists millin jabberin and shrillin
    'Dis is de Forum'. Where to make me killin?
Some stupid English fart might turn up trumps.

I found one. 'Sir, just see wot ah dag ap
    In me backyard. It's bin a lawnh tahm id –
    A riw aufentic Roman aunty quitty.'
He flashed his winder on the bit of scrap
    And said 'Bravo' and give me arf a quid.
That's how we skin 'em in the Old City.

74. 'SPANIARDS'

Spaniards believe that tuum's less than meum.
They come to Rome and find each thing inferior –

Temple and castle, inside and exterior,
Obelisk, fountain, column, church, museum,
Even the papal singing of Te Deum,
To anything they have in fair Iberia.
It's hell's own job deflating those superior
Sneerers: ('call *that* thing a colosseum?')

I got a bullock's ballocks once and stowed them
Inside a casket with an ornate lid
Then met a Spaniard, saying as I showed them:
'Adam's, sēnor.' He blanched a bit and did
The homage that he thought I thought he owed them,
Then yawned: 'We have his third one in Madrid.'

75. 'WORK'

Work? Work? Me work? The thought of working puts
Me into a sweat. They never have agreed,
Have work and me. There's other things I need
Than work. No work then, and no ifs and buts.
Before I get some dinner in my guts
I'm much too weak to work,
After I feed
At half past twelve I like to crash my swede.
Work? Stuff it where the monkeys stuff their nuts.

Work's holy? Holy? Work? You twat, you should
Look at our priests. Their boss, I heard one say,
Worked for a week and went on strike for good.
For up above, they're up above such stunts
As work. The saints play with their balls all day,
While the saintesses sit and scratch their cunts.

76. THE BET

Some men were arguing, as men often will,
    About their wives. And each with each one vied.
    Over his beer, with a grim sort of pride,
Saying: 'Mine's ugly.' – 'But mine's uglier still,'
Comparing photographs. 'Ah, but if looks could kill,
    My missis could effect mass homicide.
    Just look.' But Albert, with no picture, cried:
'Ugly? Come home with me and feast your fill.'

A bet, then? Right. The money was not lacking,
    A pound a man. Their winter breaths asmoke,
They homed with him when 'Time please' sent them packing.
    'Get ready, missis.' From upstairs she spoke:
'Am I to hide me face wi' piece of sacking?'
    'Nay,' he called, 'it's a bet, lass, not a poke.'

77. TWO USES FOR ASHES

'The ashes of my dear departed?' said
    The widow, serving tea and cake at five
    Five days after the funeral. 'I contrive
To house them aptly. No, not lapped in lead.
See, they are in an egg-timer instead,
    There on the mantelpiece. Ah, ladies, I've
    Determined, since he did no work alive,
The lazy swine will do some now he's dead.'

One widow took her man's remains as snuff,
    Achieving an orgasmic kind of sneeze.
She said: 'The bugger's appetite was rough.
    He entered, without even saying *Please*,

My other apertures. I've had enough,
But as he's dead I'll not begrudge him these.'

78. 'THE ORCHIDACEOUS CATALOGUE BEGINS'

The orchidaceous catalogue begins
    With testicles, carries on with balls,
    Ballocks and pills and pillocks. Then it calls
On Urdu slang for goolies. Gism-bins
Is somewhat precious, and superior grins
    Greet antique terms like cullions. Genitals?
    – Too generalised. Cojones (Español)'s
Hemmish and too whimsical The Twins.

Clashers and bells – poetical if tame.
    Two swinging censors – apt for priest or monk.
    Ivories, if pocket billiards is your game.
I would prefer to jettison such junk
And give them geoffrey grigsons as a name,
    If only Grigson had a speck of spunk.

79. PRIVY MATTERS

A man sat once, writhing in costive pain,
    For a whole wretched hour, crouching inside
    A public privy. Though he valiantly tried
To loose the load, his muscles limp with strain,
He could not. Yet again. Again. Again.
    But no. He heard a desperate urgent stride
    To the neighbour box. A hefty splash. He cried:
'Lucky.' – 'Lucky? Be damned – that was my watch and chain.'

There is another ending, one that I
　　Have in some scatographic theses met.
The costive heard the urgent feet come nigh,
　　The thunder of release immediate.
'Ah, lucky', was his sigh. But the reply:
　　Went thus: 'I haven't got me pants down yet.'

Foreword 1974

This verse narrative in eighteen chapters (not books: only epic po-
ems have eighteen books) is an attempt to mediate between the
craft of film and the craft of letters. The idea of making a six-part
film on the life of the prophet Moses arose in Rome in 1972, and
Radiotelevisione Italiana put up the money for it. In 1973, in Rome
and New York, Vittorio Bonicelli, Gianfranco de Bosio, Vincenzo
Labella and myself worked out the practical details of the project.
Despite the Italian provenance, the series was designed as an in-
ternational venture with an international cast: an American, an
Englishman, a Greek, a Swede and a Frenchman were assigned the
main roles, but most of the nameless Egyptians and Israelites were
Italians.

The task of hammering out a technique for presenting Moses
on the screen which should not seem to compete with Cecil B.
de Mille's *The Ten Commandments* was a collective one, but the writ-
ing of a script in English was my responsibility alone. In order to
establish a general sense of the narrative movement, and to contrive
dialogue which should be neither archaic-poetic nor present-day
colloquial, I found it convenient to write out the story in the form
of what might be termed a poor man's epic. Out of the completed
narrative, which is what I offer in this book, the six television *pun-
tate* were painfully squeezed.

People who write fiction for a living, as I do, are often embar-
rassed when commissioned to write a film script. So much of what
we primarily enjoy in the composition of a novel, particularly the
evocation of physical sensation and the privilege of looking into

not only a character's sensorium but also his mind, is denied to us. A verbal flow is inhibited by the shibboleth about a film being a visual form that can, at a pinch, do without words altogether. Various costive exigencies are imposed on our tendency to logorrhoea. When Mr Graham Greene was asked to write the original screenplay that was to be *The Third Man*, he found it necessary to give it the primary, or preliminary, form of a novella. Only in this way could he make his characters come to life. I could not make a novella out of *Moses*, since there was far too much material and even more lavish 'passing of time', but I could not write it as a novel either. If I wrote it in prose at all, I would either produce the Books of Exodus, Leviticus and Deuteronomy, which had already been written, or else some wearisome archaeological fantasia in the manner of Thomas Mann.

Since the traditions of fictional realism and naturalism came into being, the novel has been restricted to the chronicle of more or less real life, full of events which we are ready to be persuaded could conceivably happen in our own experience, given good or ill luck. A certain solidity is expected, so that Moses in such a fictional tradition would have to scratch his left ear occasionally, be depressed at the stink of his unchanged clothes, gaze out with narrowed eyes at the purple Goshen landscape. And if characters are physically solid, they tend to move slowly. A scene, once carefully set up in words, is not easily struck. A novel, Flaubert said, is a heavy machine; cameras, whatever the grips say, are much lighter. And since we expect a novel to be filled with rational events, there is not much room there for the miraculous. Miracles are for fairy stories or for science fiction.

Although one of the tasks of a fictional chronicler of the career of Moses is to demiraculise wherever possible (manna was really the resin of the tamarisk, blown by the wind; it is easy to strike water from rock when that rock is porous; you can cross the sea of Reeds when the wind blows strongly from the east – and so on), there are still plenty of full-blown and vindictive miracles in Goshen and the desert. Verse will accept these more readily than prose because in verse anything can happen anyway: it is a matter not only of the Homeric tradition but also of the fact that the very movement of verse suggests a wanton twisting of reality. But verse is useful in other ways. It struck me, when first working on *Moses*, and it goes on striking me, that the techniques of film and verse narrative are very close: both admit economy, ellipsis, rapid shifts of scene. Verse can also give the reader a much clearer idea than prose of the way in which words are actually spoken, indicating, by the crowding of syllables into a line or the thinning of them out, the speed of discourse, making use of the strong initial beat of the line for verbal emphasis, thriving on repetition which, in prose dialogue though not in real-life speech, can seem mannered and wearisome.

Nobody is sure what poetry is. As Dr Johnson said, it is easier to say what it is not. That this work is not poetry there can be no doubt. I am not a poet, though I wrote a novel about a poet and obligingly wrote poetry for him, and I have to emphasise that I have no poetic intent here – no deploying of surprising images, no verbal brilliance and no artful ambiguities. Though poets prefer to work in verse, there is no reason why they should have a monopoly of it. But I am aware that, having used verse, I may well be accused by careless critics of having tried to write poetry. I will go further than a refutation of that and say that I have not even tried to produce literature. This work is too far cliché-ridden, simplistic and didactic to be classified as anything other than a piece of sub-literature, pop-craft. A poem, even a bad one, is usually called a work of art, but people are reluctant to call even a good film anything other than a piece of craft. We have still to hear the word 'art' applied to anything seen on television. I am quite happy to place this book in that sort of no-man's-land where aesthetic classification is hardly worth bothering about, except by the librarian.

In 1890, Mark Twain wrote a letter to Andrew Lang in which he said: 'the little child is permitted to label its drawings "This is a cow – this is a horse" and so on. This protects the child. It saves it from the sorrow and wrong of hearing its cows and its horses criticised as kangaroos and work-benches. A man who is whitewashing a fence is doing a useful thing, so also is the man who is adorning a rich man's house with costly frescoes; and all of us are sane enough to judge these performances by standards proper to each. Now then, to be fair, an author ought to put upon his book an explanatory line: "This is written for the Belly and the Members." And the critic ought to hold himself in honor bound to put away from him his ancient habit of judging all books by one standard and thenceforth follow a fairer course.' This book of mine, then, is written for the Belly and the Members, and I should be grateful for it not to be judged by the standards proper to real epic poets.

A.B.
Rome, April 1974

* *

Foreword 1976

A few years ago I was commissioned, along with Vittorio Bonicelli and Gianfranco de Bosio, to provide the script for a television series on birth, life and death of the prophet Moses. I found collaboration difficult and was forced to work entirely on my own, leaving emendation, addition and subtraction to be more or less improvised – by Bonicelli, Gianfranco de Bosio, who was the director, Vincenzo Labella, the producer, the actors Burt Lancaster and Anthony Quayle – while filming proceeded in Israel. The major aesthetic problem was a linguistic one, as it always is with historical or mythical subjects, and I found the only way out of the problem was to precede the assembly of a shooting-script with a more or less literary production – this sort of epic poem you have now in your hands. To have written *Moses* first as a prose novel would have entailed the setting-up of a somewhat cumbersome mechanism, in which the devices of 'naturalism' would have led me to an unwholesome prosaism both in dialogue and récit. Verse moves more quickly and the rhythm of verse permits of a mode of speech midway between the mythical and the colloquial. Out of this homely epic I made my script, but the poem, such as it is, remains and is here for your reading.

If some of the devices used seem close to the cinematic, that is because I had a film in mind while working on a piece of literature. On the other hand, narrative verse – as you can see from *Aurora Leigh* as well as the *Odyssey* – anticipates the cinema. Perhaps the most ambitious film-script ever written is Thomas Hardy's *The Dynasts*, which was completed before even the first crude film had been shown. John Collier recently showed how filmable *Paradise Lost* is, though his script was, sadly, specifically intended for 'the cinema of the mind'. Novels are heavily set in their chosen time and place and resist cinematic adaptation more than film-makers will permit themselves to realise. Epics have more to do with wings than with walking, just like films.

None of us will ever see a film of *Beowulf* or of *The Ring and the Book*. We will have to put up instead with impossible adaptations of Tolstoy, Proust, even Joyce – all of which will be artistic as well as financial failures. But here at least you have an epic that became a film, and a not unsuccessful one. Of course, I was lucky to have the Bible behind me.

Rome, Epiphany, 1976

I

THE BONDAGE

SO Joseph came to die, in some pain, dreaming he was lying
On a thorny bed called Canaan (drought and famine

And they went into Egypt and in Egypt they prospered),
Being a hundred and ten years old, and they embalmed him,
And he was put in a coffin in Egypt, being a
Prince of Egypt, the Israelite Joseph a prince of
Egypt. So Joseph died, the pain passing,
Smiling on the fulfilment: Egypt the promised land,
Brown tough shepherds and plump laughing wives
And son like swords and daughters like date-trees,
Children tumbling like lambs, the benison of mud.
Not all shepherds and shepherds' wives –
Some rose high, though not so high as Joseph,
Becoming priests of the gods, Egypt having many gods,
Officers with seals of their office, officers
On horseback leading troops, gentlemen,
Ladies, but mostly men and women in the
Good air of the delta, lambs and children frisking.
And the children of Israel were fruitful and increased abundantly,
And multiplied, and waxed exceeding mighty,
And the land was filled with them, filled with the
Tribe of Jacob and of Reuben, Simeon, Levi,
Judah, Issachar, Zebulun, Benjamin,
Dan, Naphtali, Gad, Asher,
The tribes keeping their distance one from another,
But all with a memory of a dead land called Canaan
And of a dead prince of god of Egypt called Joseph.
Now there arose up a new king over Egypt,
Which knew not Joseph
Behold, the people of the children of Israel
Are more and mightier than we.
The great intellectual eroded face of the Pharaoh,
The tired eroded voice, the wasted body in gold cloth,
The ringed claws grasping the sphinx-arms
Of the pharaonic throne, aromatic gums asmoke,
Slaves with feather-fans, effigies, effigies,

All empty-eyed. The councillors listened.
'Their men are bursting with seed. Their women
Are round like fruit. Their encampments are loud
With the bleating of children. They multiply, multiply.'
A councillor said: 'Your divine majesty
Has some immediate danger in mind?' And Pharaoh:
'War. Should there be war
With some alien people, might not these
Aliens in our midst join with our enemies.
Immediate danger. Let danger be always immediate.
It is a sound thesis. Let us defend ourselves
Before we are attacked.' And another councillor:
'Your divine majesty's immediate orders?'
'I specify nothing,' Pharaoh said. 'I say:
Deal wisely with them. Use – immediate wisdom.'
So immediate wisdom, in the dust of hooves
And the shine of metal, thundered into the sheep-shearing.
The pipe faltered and the song ceased and the dance,
Israelite mouths open in wonder and fear
As the captain in metal looked about him, taking his time,
Picking at length on one: 'You. Yes, you. Your name?'
The man drew his wife and son and daughter to him, saying:
'Amram. Of the tribe of Levi.' And the captain:
'Pay heed, Amram, of the tribe of Levi. You,
Your wife, your son, your daughter, your beasts and chattels,
All that is yours, these from this day stand confiscate
And are given up to the power of Egypt. In the name of
Horus the god, ruler of the world of the living
And of the dead.' He signalled abruptly and
The ravaging began: the soldiers, going baaaaaah,
Herding the men and women and children like sheep
While the sheep ran bleating in disorder, foodstores trampled,
Tents fired, garments torn, and Amram cried: 'Why? Why?'
And the grinning captain answered: 'Immediate wisdom.'

Therefore did they set over them taskmasters
To afflict them with their burdens.
And they were set to build for Pharaoh treasure-cities,
And the names of the cities were Ra'amses and Pithom.
Amram was surprised, pushed down the dusty street
Of Pithom with wife and family, that the enslavement
Had already gone so far: Israelites
Of other tribes long-settled, ready to laugh
At a wavering old man, a newcomer, who cried out:
'You can't cram us in here like so many
Dates in a jar. We're shepherds. We live on the
Open plains. Shut us up here and we'll die.' –
'Oh no, not die,' jabbed a soldier. 'Work, you'll work.'
Work, and a whip cracked. The quarters were overcrowded,
Suitable for slaves. Amram at the door, shy, said:
'Jochebed, my wife, and my son Aaron and
Miriam my daughter, and I am Amram of the
Tribe of Levi.' A woman said: 'Woman of the
Tribe of Levi, help me to help yourselves to a
Little space. A very little.' A blind old man
Groped through the noise and smells and dark towards Amram:
Ah, a good fresh smell of shepherd. Share this
Bit of bread with me, take it, go on. I'd say
That Egyptian food is good food, not that I
See much of it, not that I
See much. Near-blind and old, no good as a worker.
The workers get all. Where are you from then?'
Amram: 'From the vale of Shefru.' – 'I'd say you were a
Liar. I'd say the tribe of Levi was
Never in Shefru.' And Amram, patiently:
'My father was Cheat, my father's father was Levi.
Do you follow me? My father's father was
Levi the son of Jacob.' And the old man: 'I'd
Say that was a possible story. Me and my family,

We're from the tribe of Gad. But you'll find a
Lot of the tribes all mashed together here –
Benjamin, Reuben, Zebulon – a lot of tribes and
All slaves. I'd say there was a sort of mystery in it,
The twelve tribes brought together at last. But in
Slavery, as it's called. I'd say that he was
Laughing at us, it, if he exists that is, you know, the
Old one, older than me, the
God of Abraham, as they call him. 'Where the children were
    playing
There was a cry and a rattling of little stones
On the clay floor: Miriam, daughter of Amram,
Had pulled a necklace from the neck of an
Older girl, crying: 'It's sinful. To wear a thing like that.
An Egyptian thing.' Tears and reproaches and the
Mothers and fathers stepping in, but Aaron grinned.
'Grin, then,' cried Miriam. 'Grin in your slavery.
But he –' And she ran to her mother, putting her head
To her mother's belly to hear the heartbeat within.
'He would not grin, he –' A woman nodded and said:
'So that's the way of it. I wondered.' And Jochebed:
'I thought he would be born in Tabris, in the pastures.
We would have been there in three fullnesses of the moon,
At the forest of Nisim.' – '*He*, you said. You seem sure.'
And the blind old man: 'All babies are called
He before they're born. And some of them
Afterwards too.' He did not understand the laughter,
Turning his open mouth, like an eye, to the laughter.
Laughter in a place of slaves but in the place of
Royal divinity no laughter. Aromatic oil-lamps,
Shadows, effigies, a cross-legged scribe
Reading to the Pharaoh, Pharaoh cutting in to say:
'The sons of the men of the sand. The name diminishes them.
But they are not diminished.' Dutiful smiles

From the assembled councillors. 'Continue reading.'
'Majesty. *They came from the land of Canaan,*
Driven by famine and plague. In Egypt sought they
Grain and pasture, and behold they found them both.
Their sons and their sons' sons grow fat and
Multiply in the houses of the lord of the house of
Life, the house of death. They multiply and are become
An immense multitude. In order that they may not,
In the event of war, unite with our enemies …'
The sentence unfinished, the stylus poised. Pharaoh:
'So it is written, so shall our
Posterity read it. But the sentence is unfinished,
The stylus poised. Let me hear,' and he looked at them, 'wisdom.'
There was a pause. The head councillor said:
'This present mode of oppression is clearly
Inefficacious. As I see it, the tribes of Israel,
Mingled together in slavery as they now are,
Lose each its special code of law and restraint.
Constrained from above, they are grown loose beneath.
Lechery, adultery, incest. They grow loose.
They grow. This zest for breeding – it is the mark of
An animal race. They couple like dogs of the desert.'
But the Pharaoh said, and they had to strain to hear him:
'And we – we glory in stability, changelessness, power.
Along comes the god of death and says: Behold,
I am all these things. The sentence stands unfinished.
Let the sentence now be pronounced.' The poised stylus
Dove to the tablet. 'Every son that is born
Shall be cast into the river. But every daughter
Shall be saved alive.' The scribe looked up at that.
So it was rods and whips and the occasional
Salutary thrust of the spear that held them back,
The wailing and cursing, as the farm-carts filled
With wailing babies. It became a game,

On Nile bank, to see who could throw the furthest,
Bets laid, but some of the soldiers were sick,
And not only on a won bet of a jar of palm-wine.
They're *things*, man, no more, go on, *throw*. They threw.
It was a long business. General commanding commanded
A free day and an extra beer ration. They threw,
Some of them, in their sleep. And then calm,
Nile unperturbed, birdsong, a gorgeous day
As the princess came down to the river, a cortège
Of priests intoning:

    Lord of the river and of the quickening mud
    Whence all manner of lowly things are brought to birth,
    Bring to thy servant the gift of fecundity,
    That she may not be despised among the daughters of earth,
    And the worth of her birth be matched by the worth of thy gift.
    Lift her, O river lord, to the ranks of the mothers.

The ritual disrobing: the golden headpiece lifted
To disclose a painful baldness, then the silks
Whistling away from scars, emaciation
On slenderness otherwise comely, framed in
Palms and stonework, royalty unimpaired
By the absurd daubing of Nile mud, the carven
Beauty of the face unmoved, unmoved still
As the filthy rite proceeded, ended, the silks
Were laid to the ulcered flesh, the golden headpiece
Restored, and, to a wordless chant with the rising
Notes of hope in it, the cortège left the river.
The river flowed clear, save for lotus and riverweed,
But then the first of the infant corpses appeared,
Floating downstream.
           There had been no craft,
Or perhaps cruelty had its limit, to snatch out the foetus

And examine its sex. So Jochebed came to her time,
Groaning in their corner of a hovel of heavy sleep,
And Amram kneeling anxious by her, each cry of her pain
Forcing him to stifle it with his hand:
'Forgive me, my love. Forgive me. Someone may hear.
I trust no one.' And some of the sleepers stirred,
Dreaming perhaps of a dead son, then resettled.
One of the sleepers awoke and came softly to him,
And he started, but it was his daughter Miriam.
'There is a sort of shed a little way off,
Full of mattocks and brick-moulds. It must be there.'
He nodded. It was a heavy task, under the moon, dogs baying.
The deformed door creaked. 'A space under that cart.'
Her agony mounted, Miriam looked wide-eyed, and then
He came out on the flood, crying to the world. As in response
The feet of a patrol could be heard on cobbles
Not too far off, soldiers marching in moonlight
And that cry going out, moonlight flooding his sex.
Sing, Miriam prayed and, as in response,
The soldiers sang, and the dirty song was a blessing:

    Here's the way
    We earn our pay
    Who's the enemy we slay?
    Baby Israelites if they
    Have balls between their legs
    That's no way
    To earn your pay
    We would rather any day
    Take their mothers and then lay
    Our balls between their legs

Amram in wonder held the howling child in his arms,
In agony and joy for a second son. And yet, how, how –

'None comes here,' Miriam said. 'I know. And if any comes,
I shall be in the way of his coming. It must be three
Roundings of the moon. I shall sit here and guard
And I shall weave.' Weave? She wove out of bulrushes
And parried queries in the sun. *But where did she go?*
To the house of a cousin, just north of Pithom.
And when will she return? She still has fever.
She sends greeting but begs that none come near her.
The fever is catching. *What is that thing you weave?*
A basket. A cage. A cage for doves. *A cage indeed.*
A cage within a cage. When the cage was finished,
Miriam took it, eager-eyed, to her mother
And the three-month child, milk bubbling on his lip,
And said: 'Listen.' And Jochebed listened in wonder.
But it was in fear, in working daylight, that Miriam
Carried her cradle or ark to the Nile, opening it
Often and often as she sped through the meadows
To cluck at the child, to whisper 'Can you breathe'?
The river's weedy length no longer carried
Human corpses. Rats swam, a fish smote the surface and snapped.
And then a cage of bones, a child's bones. She wept,
Heard an ass bray, started, then was able to smile,
Then to laugh. 'Be brave', she whispered. 'You have much to do.'
The baby cried and she hushed him. Then a voice asked:
'What have you in there?' A man's voice. From her crouch
She saw strong legs, hair, leather, a countryman
With a bag and leather bottle, the face stupid
But not unkind. 'My things', she said. 'My treasure.'
He laughed, and the ass brayed, and the laughter of ladies
Could now be heard, downstream. 'Treasure,' he brayed,
Moving off, then whistled a dog. She, from the reeds,
Watched covertly. Downstream, ladies playing at ball.
And then a deep drum from within the
Palace gardens, it must be, and a male chant

As of some holy procession coming. The ladies quietened,
Made *moues* at each other, then scattered through green.
Then Miriam saw a lady immensely tall,
A gold headpiece, silks liquid in the sun,
Well-attended, languid priestesses, they must be,
And burly priests, coming slowly to the river, intoning:

> You who nourish the reed and tamarind,
> The date-palm and the pepper-tree,
> From whose mud the crocodile breeds,
> Many-toothed, tough as a chariot…

And it was at that moment that Miriam saw a child's corpse,
Ravaged by rats, float drunkenly downstream. It was the
Moment of courage, to answer the dead with the living,
And delicately consigned the bulrush cage or cradle
To the waters. The princess, she must be, said, seeing
In revulsion that bloated and bitten cadaver,
'You address the river as a river of life. Leave me.'
They waited, unsure. 'Leave me, leave me.' And they left,
Save for her, it must be, waiting-woman, maid.
'Live,' whispered Miriam, 'live.' A current took the
Cage, cradle, ark, and swirled it shoreward,
Into the reeds. The lady saw. The ladies saw. The
Princess, it must be, said: 'That. What is it? Go in and
Bring it to me. Quick, before the river
Takes it again.' And it was so. To what or whom,
Miriam wondered, did one pray now? She prayed to the
Infant now passing from arms to arms, yelling hard
Against the melting wall of surprise: *Let them that would kill*
Preserve and nourish. More. The royal river
Gives you to a royal house. A prince in Egypt.
Joseph was a prince in Egypt. They were lost in green,
The child's crying, the ladies' cooing. Miriam's task

Was not yet done. She left the river. In the royal garden
A twitter of ladies (who is he where is he from wellfed
Look at those ringlets of fat why is he here who is his
Mother the Nile is his father anyway) about the arms of the
Princess, hushing him, saying to him not to cry, singing:

> Out of the desert the wind blows strong
> But cool but cool from out of the sea
> The desert burns and the day is long…

'He is hungry.' She stopped, they turned to the source of the voice,
Miriam standing boldly at the fringe of the garden,
An empty vase in her hands (a servant to get flowers,
No questions asked). 'He is good. He only cries
When he is hungry.' And then the flurry of who are you
Who let you in here call the guards. But the princess:
'Wait.' They desisted. 'Come here, girl.' She came,
Uneasy but without deference. 'You know this little child?'
Miriam: 'I am an Israelite. We know no
Men children. The Egyptians kill them at birth.'
'How do you know this child is a boy?' No answer.
'Do you know his mother?' And Miriam said boldly:
'I know many mothers who weep for their sons. Whose
Breasts are heavy with milk.' And the princess:
'You mean you can find me a nurse among the Israelites?'
'Yes. One who weeps and whose
Breasts are heavy with milk.' The princess was eager:
'Bring her. For my son. For he is my son.
And his father is the Nile. His name shall be
Moses. Meaning *my son*.' But Miriam, full of light, said:
'Meaning, in our tongue: *I have brought him forth*.'
And she sped back to Pithom for Jochebed. A royal summons.
The eyes of the other women narrowed. Why? What?
What is this about? Saying more, seeing

Daughter and mother leave and the mother, fevered so long,
So heavy-breasted. But the princess said
(And Jochebed had no eyes for the garden, only the marble,
Effigies, effigies, only for the one she suckled):
'What is your name?'
'Does your breast hurt you?'
'I am sorry that your little boy
Died.' But Miriam, bold, said: 'Was killed.'
And the princess: 'We – mothers cannot easily understand
High state policy. We are the givers of life,
Daughters of the sun. Men turn their backs on the sun
To build labyrinths out of the light. The labyrinths
Breed strange monsters. These become the
Gods of darkness. Men love their dark gods.'
The ladies look at her strangely. Heresy? The leavings of
Some ancient faith, destroyed because inconvenient,
Hence heresy? But the princess said to Jochebed:
'You will come back. In four hours time.
And you will keep coming back until he has
No further need of you. When he has done with your breast,
He shall be wholly mine. You will forget him.
Entirely. Completely. For ever. My son.
You will be paid, of course. One of you, pay her.'
A coin in her unwilling hand, a coin in
Amram's hand, a gold coin in Pithom. And the women said:
'She sold her child to the Egyptians. To save him.
Why should her child be saved and none of ours?
Cunning. What is so special about her son that he
He should be saved? She sold her child for
Money. Whores sell their children,
Whores.' A man said *whore* at Jochebed,
And she said nothing. Another spat in her path.
Amram said nothing. And then he said, to Jochebed:
'What name have they given him?' She shrugged, saying:

'Moses.' *Moses.* Amram tasted the name,
Not liking it much. It was not the name
That he would have given the boy. Miriam said, full of light:
'Meaning, in our tongue, *I have brought him forth.*'
They looked at her strangely, a strange girl, full of
Strange imaginings, not like other girls. Moses, then.
Mouths round on the name, they went in to supper.
Corn mash, garlic, dates, beer. A gold coin
Useless in Pithom. *I have brought him forth.*

2

THE YOUNG MOSES

And she whom he called mother came to die.
During dalliance in a royal garden, close to sunset,
He thought he heard, raising his lips from the
Offered lips to listen. The girl teased:
'You hear bats. You hear fieldmice. You hear locusts.
But you always hear them at the wrong time –'
'I thought,' he said, 'I heard,' frowning, 'my mother –'
'*My mother,*' in mockery gentle enough, and she tried to
Pull his mouth down to hers, he resisted, she pouted.
He rose and ran, she running after, laughing,
Through green mazes, reaching cool stone, effigies,
Effigies, the palace of the princess. The princess
Lay in cool gloom, a jewel, muted by the gloom,
In a bone cage that had been hands, her voice muted,
Saying: 'Give this to her, send her away, you will have
Many jewels, many girls to give them to. But to-
Night there is one girl who must say, must say:
Where is my lord? I am taken from him. She is
Lingering outside. I can smell desire and life.
Take it to her.' So he took it to where she waited,

Plump among the effigies, and she snatched it, saying:
'What is it worth?' And he: 'If it were worth all the
Gold of the king's,' smiling, 'goldmines –'
'I know, I know, it could not be so precious
As our night together. Which we shall not have.'
Pouting, then smiling, fingering her jewel.
'I shall be hungry tonight for your hands.' Thinking already
Of other hands, but then only of his hands,
For there were no hands like his in all Egypt.
He left her, taking those hands to the mother's body,
Hands of a healer, saying as he kneaded kneaded
Gently: 'The body. Is a mystery. Like the heavens.
If we could turn for a moment. The skin.
The flesh. To glass. Then we could see the.
Wonders of the streets. Of the city within.
The streets are sometimes roaring. With evil invaders.
Then we talk. Of a sickness. Here are two roads.
That lead to the. Citadel of your lungs. If I could
Clear those. Infested ways. You would be
Well again.' And she said, lulled: 'They tell me
That you love wisdom, but not all the time. Your senses
Get in the way of thought. You hear bats and fieldmice
Crying. They say that you become impatient.'
And Moses, rapt in the office his hand performed:
'Impatient. Sometimes. They say that the
Wisdom of Egypt is. Complete and sealed. That there is
No new wisdom. To be learned. The death of a
Man. Means more than the. Birth of a. Child.
For what new wisdom. Can the. Child bring to the
World? Egypt looks to the. End. The closure. The
Seal.' And she: 'You do not see things as an
Egyptian does, as a true Egyptian does. They want
Certainty. Death is all too certain –'
'If it is so. Certain why is it not. More simple?

It is expressed though. So many gods. Hawk-faced.
Dog-headed. Crocodile-toothed. It is a. Darkness.
Full of monsters.' And she: 'When I was a girl,
I remember, there were men who taught a simple faith.
A faith of the sun, which it seemed right to worship,
The lifegiver. The men were heard for a time,
Then soon not even heard of.' And he, half to himself,
Lulled by his own hands' ministry: 'The wise men.
Have taught me to see. Beauty in the many. Beautiful.
Death in the many. Forms of death. Could there not be a
Light that is not. The sun. But which the sun. Uses?'
She then, urgent: 'Give me light, Moses. Light the torches.'
'But,' he said, 'the sun is not yet down.'
'Light them just the same. I fear the dark.
I would go to the sun and be consumed in him.
But soon there will be no sun.' So he lighted them,
And she said: 'You came from the water. I must return to it.
Embark on a boat whose pennant is the sun that shines in the dark.
Whose name is the name of the god of the harvest of souls.
Whose oars are the arms of a god whose face I must not see.
And the keel of the boat is truth. Or justice.
I am ferried to the western bank of the river,
For there the sun has his setting. And there I
Find a secret way into the earth.
I am going to the river. And you
Were brought out of the river. The same river?'
So Moses, with troubled affection, stroked her brow,
But the hands had no magic... A grain-city,
In wood and baked clay and wire, a toy for Mernefta,
Crown prince of Egypt, cousin to Moses, only a child
But imperious enough, filled the chamber and he strode over it,
Seeing the whole city from his sky like a god, while a
Chamberlain pointed out this and this, not quite a toy then
But a projected glory of the empire, a torment for the slaves.

Moses came and said: 'You summoned me, my lord.'
And the boy: 'It is *highness* you must call me, cousin.
Your highness. I have searched for you all day
And everywhere. That is not right.' ('Not right.
Your highness.') 'You promised to take me to hunt
Crocodiles.' Deferential, a little amused, sad:
'Ah, yes, your highness. But then. I reconsidered.
Your highness. What would have happened to me.
If the crocodiles had. Snapped and eaten you?
What would have happened. To the throne of. Egypt?'
A child's scowl: 'You, I suppose, would have taken it.
I am angry with you, cousin.' A little bemused, sad:
'Do not be angry. You highness. Not now. I am come.
To tell you sad news.' Then the chamberlain, a man's scowl:
'His highness is not to be given sad news. That is laid down.'
Moses, ignoring him: 'My mother is dead. Your
Father's sister. The Princess Bithiah.
Is dead.' A child's cruelty: 'Dead? Like the
Three thousand men who built the treasure-city,
And the ones who will die building this?' hitting it.
'Yes. Highness. There is only. One way of being
Dead.' But the child was more than a child: 'No.
Those dead will be forgotten. Not one name
Of one of them will be remembered. But
My name will be written there. They will take hammers
And hammer my name into stone. Mernefta,
Fifth king of his dynasty, first of them all for glory.
And the thousands of dead, five or six thousand,
Forgotten. A fine thing.' The chamberlain, impatient:
'Highness, you have forgotten the purpose
For which your cousin was sent here.' And the boy: 'Ah, yes.
You, cousin, are to go and see the workers.
To see that they are building right. I asked my father
That you be sent. It is a punishment, you see.

You should have taken me hunting.' A little amused, sad,
Bowing: 'As your highness says. A punishment.'
But there was a task to perform first. Among the effigies,
In the reek of the holy fires, he stood, watching,
While, with wands of obsidian, the priests and priestesses
Opened her dead eyes and mouth, intoning:

> Your lips I open in the god's name,
> That you may speak and eat.
> Your eyes I open in the god's name,
> That light and sight may bless them.
> But not the gross tastes and speech of the earth.
> But not the insubstantial light of the sun
> That warms the earth. When you awaken
> And depart from the tomb, at the endless
> End of the sacred river underground,
> You will raise your eyes to light eternal,
> Open your mouth in speech
> That is soundless since it is the soul of speech.
> Let all my offences be forgotten dust.
> Let tribulation be as motes in the sun
> When the sun is down.
> Greetings to you, greatest god of the underworld.
> At length my eyes are brought to the
> Witness of your beauty, whose eternal contemplation
> Is my sole care. I know your name at last,
> As I know the names of the two and forty gods
> Who preside in the halls of the eternal.
> I am become one to whom sin is not even a name.
> I am become one who had no eyes for the false path.

And line by coil the winding-sheet rose to the
Neck, the mouth, the nostrils. Then eyes alone
Where uncovered. So Moses took the linen, trembling,

And covered them, saying: 'You who became my mother
Out of your goodness
Who leave me motherless
And yet with a mother
Still to be sought,
Farewell.' And the ceremony was ended. It was time to
Engage the sun, the living and dying, not the dead: duty.
Officers of the court invested him in the
Travelling robes of a prince. A princely horse,
With jewelled caparison, pawed dust out of the earth.
He mounted, was saluted, rode off with officers,
Attendants, a body-servant, towards Pithom, asking:
'Pithom. And what is the life of Pithom?' –
'Slaves, your highness. But sometimes unruly. Enslaved,
But a stubborn people. A very alien people.'
Dust and sun and travel. Birds screaming.
But, in a hovel in Pithom, a woman screaming.
The workers passed to work, shrugging, an Egyptian
Overseer claiming his rights from a woman of Israel,
Wife of a slave, what could they do? Still – *cuckold.*
Always a hard word. But what could the cuckold do?
The cuckold, Dathan, inclining to the side of the rulers,
Hence a foreman of workers, opened his own door
To see himself being cuckolded. Inclining to the side
Of the rulers, but showing truculence. The overseer
Looking up, grinning, from the bed, the frightened wife,
To say: 'You should not be here, should you, Dathan?' –
'It seems not,' said Dathan, 'but I have certain rights.' –
'No rights, Dathan.' – 'Not even the right
To report to my superior official? Officially?' –
Grinning, 'Not even that right. You will report
When you are officially ordered to report. In the meantime,
You have duties to carry out.' And Dathan, truculent:
'Duties to my manhood.' The Egyptian laughed at that,

And rose from Dathan's bed, though lazily, saying:
'Only free men can talk of manhood. What does Dathan
The unfree have to say?' And the unfree: 'Straw.
The straw has arrived.' The overseer: 'Oh,
Use some of your own. Man of straw.' The hands of Dathan,
As of their own, were on to the ravisher,
Slid, sweating, on the tunic near the neck. Teeth gritted.
Teeth grinned: 'An example, little Dathan.
An example is required. Would you not say so? An example.'
On the worksite, where the Israelites slapped mud into brick-
      forms,
All eyes looked up in a sort of relief (relief at the prospect of
Change in any shape, even change for the worse)
At arriving hooves. Gold, snorting horses, Egyptians.
Whips cracked, work you dogs and so on, they were used to whips.
Miriam the woman was bringing water in a jar. She too looked up
And her brother Aaron, a man now, or slave, drinking, too
Looked up at an unknown voice. An Egyptian prince
But not quite an Egyptian, the voice hopping like a bird
Not clanking like endless metal: 'Is not this man
Too ill to work?' And an officer, idly swishing a fly-fan;
'He is not too ill to work he is still working.'
And the prince saw, frowning, the lashed back of another,
Asking: 'What is this?' And the worker replied:
'It is what might be termed an inducement to increased effort.' –
'You speak like a scholar. Are you a scholar?' –
'I was a scholar of sorts. When scholarship was allowed.'
Aaron and Miriam looked at each other. Was it not perhaps
Just possible that – The prince said: 'Their quarters.
I will see their. No. Alone. I will go alone.' So it was
That, alone on the Pithom street between the hovels,
The women looking up curious, the children following,
Moses heard pain and the crunch of a rod. He opened a door
On to a naked man held by two men, grinning, Israelites

All three, and a sweating overseer, panting, punishing,
The man howling, a woman sobbing on a bed. The overseer,
Seeing an Egyptian aristocrat come in, smirked
With an air of virtue and smote hard: Dathan howled.
Moses cried: 'Stop. What is this?' Paused, panting, saying:
'Punishment. My lord. For inefficiency. For insolence.
For insubordination.' And raised the rod. Dathan: 'For
Not. Wanting. To be a.' The rod fell, he howled. Moses:
'You. Assistants. Are Israelites?' And the overseer panted:
'They are Israelites, my lord. This is their foreman.
They naturally have no love for their foreman. Now.
If you will permit me.' And he raised, and the hand of Moses,
To the surprise of Moses, rose and grasped the rod,
And the mouth of Moses, to the surprise of Moses, said:
'I gave an order. I said *stop*. I call that also
Insolence. Insubordination.' And Moses, to the surprise
Not only of Moses, leapt from a rock into a
Gorgeous sea of anger, beating beating, following the
Crawling stupefied beaten about the floor, beating.
The Israelites watched with pleasure different from
Their former pleasure, Dathan bled in pleasure but
Shock crowned the pleasure: this surely was what was the word
This was insanity. Without the door women listened,
Children, old men, young men coming off shift,
Screams and beating but soon no more of either,
Only breath sharply intaken and a desperate sobbing
For breath from one. And, within, that one
Dropped the rod, looking narrowly, saw then about him
Eyes not narrow at all, the women's eyes especially
Wide in incredulity, then found breath to, to his surprise,
Excuse the beast that had possessed and was now departing:
'It was. Too much. But a. Man does not.
Die of a beating. His heart stopped. His heart
Suddenly stopped.' And Dathan, to the two

Who had held him: 'My time will come for you. Friends.
Now back to work. This is none of your concern.'
They shuffled. 'I have things to remember, have I not?
Bloody things. Quick to leave, leaving the door wide,
Shocked faces to look in, elation, fear, feelings
Not easily definable.' Dathan: 'You killed him, you.
You will go away and say that I did it.
They will all say that I did it.' But Moses, calm now:
'No one killed him. His heart suddenly stopped.
But the responsibility. Is mine.' He then, addressing the clamour:
'You see a dead Egyptian in your midst.
But you have no cause. For fear. The
Blame will not. Be visited on you. He was
Killed by his own. Brutality. His heart burst.
Have no fear.' An old man, near-blind, said: 'I'd say that
It was a strange thing to hear an Egyptian lord
Speak against brutality. Who are you, young man, who
Speak of Egyptian brutality?' And at last in Pithom
It was heard aloud at last: 'My name is Moses.'
And he thrust through them, man of authority, yet drawn
In a way he could not yet explain to himself
To these vigorous slaves. *Moses.* The crowd handled it,
Rang it like a coin, tasted it, the corpse bloody on the floor,
The killer at large, the police pushing in: 'Who did it?
Who saw?' 'I saw, I saw, his name is Moses.' 'The prince Moses?'
This is nonsense, an Egyptian slaying an Egyptian
In the presence of slaves. But, in her father's house,
Miriam, ecstatic, spoke: 'Moses. It has come true.'
Aaron, far from ecstatic, carper and doubter,
Said: 'Nothing has come true. Except that
What seems to you a beginning is really an end.
All Pithom talks of him already as if he were
Already the deliverer. You have kept his name
Alive of their lips, though in a whisper, these twenty years.

So now he is an Israelite who has killed an Egyptian.
There is no promise of anything save further servitude.
We must go on grovelling to Egyptian gods for, believe me,
These gods will prevail and will always prevail.' Amram, old now,
Said: 'The voice is the voice of a prophet, my son,
But the words are a slave's words.' Wild-eyed, Aaron:
'I see things as they are. I am not, like my sister here,
Wild-eyed.' And Jochebed the old woman: 'When he
When he walks into this house –' Aaron: 'If, if.
He must leave, or else be a sacrifice to Egypt.
He will have no time for walking into houses.'
But she: 'When he talks into the house of his parents,
I shall be expected to have words, but what words
I do not know. I loved a child I lost.
And now I must expect the pain of learning to
Love a child who is found. And must be lost again.'
But Moses, walking alone, touching and smelling this
Alien race, finding it not alien, exerting authority
That did not seem to him that of an alien, came to a place
Where one Israelite fought another, both bloody from fists,
With a divided crowd making cockfight noises,
And cried 'Stop this' so that they stopped an instant,
But only that one of the fighters could pant out: 'Ah,
The Lord Moses. Are you come then to be our judge?
To strike us down as you struck the Egyptian down?'
And Moses said nothing but felt the tremor of the
Fear of the hunted, wondering why. 'Moses,' the jeer went,
'Our judge and our executioner?' A boy in the crowd
Came to Moses and tugged at the princely robe
And spoke and Moses bent to hear, not understanding,
Not at all well understanding, not at first.
But Dathan, blood washed off, bruised, limping,
But in his best robe, understood well enough,
Going from man to man in authority,

Telling his story: 'I have served well, sir, my lord,
And it is my ambition to serve better.
I would not utter the dirty word *payment*, of course –'
You will be paid whatever your information
Is worth. Do not waste time.
'I had thought of, perhaps, some small promotion.'
Do not waste time. 'Waste time, no. I have witnesses
Outside to testify to the murder of our overseer,
A good just man. A senseless murder, if I may say so.'
Do not. 'The Lord Moses was the slayer.'
He had authority to exert discipline. Go on.
'The Lord Moses, with respect, sir, had no such authority.
He is an Israelite. The Princess Bithiah
(May her soul have rest) took him out of the Nile.
It is a long story which I will be happy to tell.
He is the son of Jochebed and Amram of the tribe of Levi.
He was saved by his sister in the old time of the
Necessary execution of the children.' And then,
Not liking the silence, 'I tell no lie. Sir, my lord,
Gentlemen, I tell no lie.' But the silence was the
Silence of rumination of the delectable bread of
Coming intrigue. There were some who hated Moses.
Something unegyptian about him. Bastard spewed by the river.
Stories, stories. 'I tell no lie.' *Give him some*
Bauble or other. Tell him to wait outside.
And the boy from the crowd led Moses to Miriam,
By a tree near the house of Amram. Miriam spoke,
Moses listened, things coming clear, though in pain.
'You believe?' she asked. 'Believe?' He said: 'I was told
Of a taking from the water. My mother. As I
Called her. Hid nothing. Save for names. And names
She did not know. Perhaps not. Wishing to know.
Said that I was nourished. On Israelite milk. That a
Girl of the Israelites. Found me my nurse.' And Miriam:

'I know the palace, can describe the chamber,
The gardens. There was an inscription said,
Or they said it said, he was to be born in the
House of a king, but a lady said that every
House in Egypt was a house of the king.' Moses: 'Who?
Who?' She said: 'He who was to come, the child of the
Sun they called him. But to me he was to be
More than the child of the sun. Will you come home?'
'You mean,' he said, 'I am to. Find a mother?'
Miriam said: 'You are to find a family.'
Torches, horsemen, heralds positioning themselves
Among public effigies, effigies, the political men at work,
The trumpet and then the proclamation:
'Be it known that Moses the Israelite,
Once falsely known as the Lord Moses,
Stands accused of the murder of a
Servant of the king, a free man, an Egyptian.
Let him be rendered up to authority.
Any who hide him or otherwise grant comfort
Render themselves liable to the exaction of the
Capital penalty. So written, so uttered.'
So the time for shy discovery in the house of Amram,
For the turning of an Israelite into an Israelite,
Was not long. The fine Egyptian silks
Were stuffed in a hollow in the wall, lidded with a stone,
And the Lord Moses was turned into an Israelite,
In a worn grey cloak, with the wanderer's staff
In hands that were not yet hands of an Israelite.
He smiled. 'I will learn to be an Israelite.
But not in. Slavery. In exile rather. Not a
Slave. Merely a. Fugitive.' They wept. Miriam said:
'We shall be together in the time of the setting free.'
But Aaron, bitterly: 'If ever such a time should come.'
But Moses, not yet understanding: 'In the time of the.'

The time that stretched now was the time of understanding,
Trying to learn to understand. With the sun setting,
He set his face to the desert. *Be it known that*
Moses the Israelite. Set his face to the desert.

3

THE BURNING BUSH

IT was not, he thought, if it could be called thought,
This shuffling or churning in his skull,
That the desert was empty. The desert was not empty,
Far far from empty: it was a most intricate poem
On the theme of thirst and hunger, it was a
Crammed gallery of images of himself, suffering,
And it rang with songs that never got beyond
The opening phrase, like: *Went to find an Israelite*
And found himself athirst or *I am baked meat*
I cannot eat. Once in joy he contended with
The collective appetite of a million flies
Over a migratory quail, almost fleshless, fallen in flight.
Twice he found porous rock that, struck with his staff
Though feebly, disgorged a fresh trickle. He lapped, blessing,
Thought what to bless? There was once stone
That he wished to take for some effigy but a
Thought of last night's stars made him ashamed.
The way of Egypt with the stars was to make them
Bow down to the muddy god of the Nile, but here
They were, in a manner, unmolested. Nor, so it seemed to him,
Was it all straight lines up there, joining star to star,
No Egyptian geometry. Curves rather. Seeing that
Egypt was all measuring-rods, squares, cubes, pyramids,
But Unegypt, which could be, might as well be,
Israel, was curves – fruit and the leaping of lambs

And the roundness of the body gloried in not constrained
In geometry. Was he delirious, hearing himself say
God is round? The term meant nothing except that the
Sun and the moon possessed this perfect roundness,
But one day he saw sun and moon in the morning together
And saw more than that, heard himself saying:
Not one not the other but the light that is given to both.
Given, that was it, but by what given? What or whom?
The god of the, the gods of the. Miriam had talked
Of the God of the Israelites, the God of Jacob.
Again the god of the. And you tamed the stars then
And set them to prophesying mud. God. The stars were back
In their firmament, aloof. Words mean what exists.
God not a word then. A cantrip. A device for
Keeping the stars free. At some uncounted dawn
On whatever day it was he saw ahead a mountain,
Must be a mountain, no mirage, with a nap of green,
But that could be mirage, as could as must be that,
Tree in the distance, solitary palm, fronds soon able to be
Counted. Counting, though, was Egyptian arithmetic,
Not apt for the desert. Reality was too royal,
Must be accorded the courtesy of averted eyes,
Not too boldly approached. Tried the cantrip *God*
To hold the tree there, and it held. Too weak to hurry, though.
The song of the daughters he could not yet hear,
Was a real song, royal, more than a first line:

>   What will love bring
>   When he comes?
>   A silver ring.
>   Earth will ring
>   With his tread
>   When he comes.
>   On his head

Kingly crown
When he comes down
From the hill.
What will he bring?
A silver ring
When he comes…

The mountain had a name: Horeb. This was a tree-grown pasture
In a valley, and from the well at dawn,
Jethro's daughters drew, singing. But the song stopped
When the leering shepherds arrived, pushing in their buckets,
With *Away there, bitches, find another well,*
Scratch, would you, if you want to scratch
Scratch this itch. Then he came down from the hill,
Wearing dust not silver, crowned with his second anger,
His staff held high, then he smote like a king,
But after fell for faintness, seeing them run
And calling *Mad, mad, he is mad,* leaving blood in the dust.
Surrounded by round-armed girls, he smiled then
Turned up his eyes, seeing round flesh and green
And after nothing but ringing indistinguishable
Suns and moons. But he awoke in a tent smelling
Sheep's cheese, sheep's milk, new bread, an old shepherd
Smiling over him, a girl named Zipporah
Solicitous with a bowl, bread torn into warm milk.
He ate and gave his name, a man cast out of Egypt,
Seeking a new life. Jethro, set around with girls,
Was all to ready to talk to a man, talking at length:
'I was once a priest of the town of Midian.
But I grew sick of stone idols, grew to believe
That faith was concerned with – well, not with,
If you know the word, multiplicity. A man
Must worship something great and simple. In the desert
Sometimes one sees an image of this. On Mount Horeb there

A man, I sometimes think, might see an even greater
Image of the truth. Out of meditation.
I have seen no visions. Perhaps I am too old.
I am certainly too old to climb it.' Zipporah,
Gently: 'Come to our story, father.' Jethro smiled,
Saying: 'Yes yes, I wander. It is easily told.
I turned against these idols, the people against me.
We are cut off. My daughters must draw water
Before the Midian shepherds leave their beds,
Otherwise they may draw no water. But they come
Earlier and earlier. Depriving us of water
Has become a cruel sport. I am grateful for what you did.'
Moses: 'You have said that. Many times. Already.'
But Zipporah: 'Gratitude is not a word.
It is the desire to keep on saying the word.'
'My daughters,' Jethro said, 'are forward in their speech,
If not in their deeds. How can one man prevail
Against so many women'? Then, after a pause:
'You are travelling further? Perhaps to the town itself?'
Moses said: 'For the moment. My own story.
Ends here. My journey has been. Into exile.
For exile is everywhere. For the exile.'
Jethro asked: 'Can you do shepherd's work?'
Moses said: 'I had always been taught. That work.
Was for slaves. Egypt taught me. Many false things.'
Jethro, urgently: 'Put off that word *exile*.
It is your people who know exile, not you.' And Moses, softly:
'Yes. I must learn. To think of them. As my people.'
My people, lashed to labour under the disdainful eyes
Of a growing prince, and Moses already growing
Into a myth. The time would soon come in Pithom
For a story told by the old to the young: 'Moses.
That was his name. He was brought up a royal prince
But one day he turned against the Egyptians. He

Killed some of them. Oh, I do not know how many,
But there were certainly many. He was strong, you see,
Like a bull or a lion. Yes yes, or a crocodile.
And then he escaped out of Egypt for they wished to kill him.
Some say he will come back. But I believe he is
Dead in the desert, eaten by vultures or something,
Just very white bones now, picked clean.
No no, not eaten by crocodiles, where is your sense?
There are no crocodiles in the desert. It is in the
Water you get crocodiles. They are full of water.
Their eyes are full of water. They cry when they eat you.'
Then the old king died and the prince Mernefta
Rules in his turn, the new Pharaoh, remembering Moses,
But not yet as a myth. 'His accusers,' he said one day.
'Are any of these still living?' And a minister:
'Majesty, the accusation was naturally
Brought by the Crown. The Crown is still living.'
But Pharaoh said: 'The Crown is he who wears it.
I hardly need my father's dusty archives
As part of my inheritance. Is there a
Living accuser who does not wear a crown?'
'Some Israelites,' was the answer, 'who swore that the
Accused was himself an Israelite.' Pharaoh rose
And walked his council chamber among effigies, effigies,
Slaves following with fans. 'I knew him. Moses. I
Remember him with some tenderness – an elder cousin
Who was always promising to take me hunting.
He would listen to bats and the cries of fieldmice.
No one else would hear them – only he. I cannot
Easily see him as a great vengeful lion, striking
Men dead with a rod.' A minister said: 'There
Was a death, majesty. An Egyptian corpse. Very bloody.'
'Men,' said Pharaoh, 'are not, I think, beaten to death.
The beater must die of exhaustion first. So. It was

Officially I who sent him to Pithom and to this
Old accusation. Did I also send him
To death in the desert'? Another minister said:
'There is no certainty of his death. At least
Two caravans have brought back news. News of a sort.
Of, for instance, a hero who came out of Egypt
And into Midian, killed twenty men with a blow,
Married seven or eight sisters – the exact number is unclear.
The name we heard seemed to be some
Outlandish deformation of his true name.' Pharaoh smiled.
'I would prefer him to be back with us. It would be
Good to see him smiling at my triumphs.
His smile was like none else's – no fanfare of teeth.
It always seemed to hold back, to hold something back.'
And the first minister said: 'So, majesty,
The sentence is quashed? The accusation cancelled?'
Pharaoh said: 'Let us have him in Egypt again.'
But not even a king of Egypt could put time back.
Moses, the shepherd, with his, or Jethro's flocks,
Dreaming under Horeb, dreamed of no future other than
A shepherd's future. A husband and a father,
His wife, as was to be foreseen, the eldest, Zipporah,
His son named Ghersom, a strange name, apter for himself:
Stranger in a strange land. And the future? Well –
There was the taking of Jethro's place, when the time came,
And the time could not be long. Problem of girls
Without dowries, a whole family cut off
From the idolators of Midian. He turned now to wave
As Jethro watching him, Zipporah, Ghersom in her arms,
Up there by the tents and the palm, rain-clouds behind them,
This being a place of rare rain, but of rain.
Jethro was saying to Zipporah: 'Now you see how
A good shepherd works. First he takes to pasture
The very young, so that they may eat of the

Tender grass, full of juice, and then the older ones
That they may eat what is fitting for them, and last
The full-grown sheep that can chew the tough grass. All this
I did not teach him: he seemed to know it already.'
The child Ghersom cried, and Zipporah rocked him,
Singing: 'Ghersom – Ghersom – stranger in a
Strange land.' Her father said: 'A gloomy lullaby.
A gloomy name. It rings somehow of his father.
Settled and not settled. Never quite at rest.
But a good son-in-law. An only son-in-law.'
In sad affection he turned his eyes to the other girls,
Washing clothes and squabbling. A good son-in-law,
Carrying a lamb to the desert for sacrifice,
The knife raised, Jethro intoning: 'Unknown of the desert,
Great one, faceless, voiceless, we offer thee this
Fruit of the fertile lands. Accept it of thy goodness,
Eternal unity, whatever, whoever thou art.' But the name
Moses, Moisha, Musa was no unknown of the desert.
The Egyptian patrols heard it among nomads, searching,
As they had been bidden, but long in finding.
Until at dawn, walking to birdsong, smiling he suddenly
Started, and she said: 'What do you hear? I hear nothing,
Nothing but birdsong.' But grasped his robe, rising,
And left the tent to see horsemen on the hill crest,
Egyptians. The daughters of Jethro welcomed them,
With yesterday's bread, pitchers of well-water,
And their leader spoke to Moses, saying: 'You have proof
That this is your name?' Moses smiled and replied:
'A name is merely. What a man is called. I am
Called Moses. My wife is called Zipporah. My son is
Ghersom. And here is my. Wife's father. Jethro.' –
'The documents I hold', said the officer, taking bread
With a desert courtesy, 'are signed by the royal hand.
They attest your right to return to Egypt freely,

To resume your former status, former office.'
'My status. And office. You see. I am a shepherd.
I am an Israelite.' But the leader swallowed and said:
'You are the Lord Moses, cousin to the Pharaoh.
As such, your place and duty are self-evident.
If I may say so. With respect.' But Moses said:
'You are not then come. To force me. Back to Egypt?' –
'I have no such authority. I am but the bearer
Of a royal message.' And Moses spoke his last words to them
(They were welcome to rest. Then let them return to Egypt):
'My compliments. To the Pharaoh. Tell him that I
Too have my kingdom.' He left them, broke bread alone,
Then led his lambs to pasture. But that day
Was to be no common day. Tending his flocks,
He heard a sound from Horeb, a sound as of the
Manifold cracking of twigs in the fire, and he turned
To see the mountain melting, shifting towards him,
Then setting in its old shape: an illusion
Of a more than Egyptian kind, occasioned no doubt
By today's voices from Egypt. But, peering, he saw
What seemed no magic: there on the upper slope
A flame that burned steady. Who had made fire on Horeb?
He left his lambs and, staff in hand, incredulous,
Moved to the mountain. The flame burned steady.
Its reality was somehow fixed in his brain by the
Smell of wool-grease on the hand that he lifted to
Shade his eyes from the light, to see better the
Flame that burned steady on the upper slope. So, slowly,
Driven solely by desire for a strange thing to be
No longer strange, he began to climb, and the climb
Hid the flame from him until, sweating, panting,
No longer a young prince racing over the delta,
He faced at length a boulder on the upper slope
And rounded, panting, the boulder and there he saw a

Flame burning steady but the flame calm as a diamond
And the flame the flame of a bush burning, its leaves
Burning but not consumed, and sound from the flame
As of the noise of some element striving with little skill
To become a voice, then finding more skill and becoming the
Voice of his sister Miriam. 'Miriam!' And, in Miriam's voice:
'Come no closer. Put off your shoes from your feet.
For the place whereon you are standing is holy ground.'
He was slow to obey. 'Miriam? How is it possible?
Miriam?' And the voice: 'I speak through the voices
Of those who are near and yet far. The voice of your father.'
And the voice was of his father. 'Put off your shoes.
For this is holy ground.' And Moses, not without trembling,
His fingers clumsy, clumsily obeyed. 'I speak also
With your own voice, but a voice no longer
Slow and unassured.' And so it was, his own voice,
Saying: 'I am the God of your father,
The God of Abraham, the God of Isaac,
The God of Jacob. And also the God of Moses.
Listen. I have surely seen the affliction
Of my people in Egypt, and have heard their cry
By reason of their taskmasters. For I know their sorrows.
And I am come to deliver them out of the hands
Of the Egyptians, and to bring them out of that land
Unto a good land and a large, a land that
Flows with milk and with honey. Now therefore behold:
The cry of the children of Israel is come unto me.
Therefore I will send unto Pharaoh
You, Moses, charged with the task of
Bringing forth my people, the children of Israel,
Out of the land of Egypt.' But Moses, hesitant,
Stumbling, in his own voice, what there was of his voice,
Said: 'Who am I. That I should. Go to Pharaoh.
And should should. Bring the children. Of Israel.

Out of.' But the voice said: 'I will be with you,
I. And when you have brought them out of Egypt,
You shall serve God upon this mountain.' *God.*
'It is God who sends you. God. The God of your fathers.'
But Moses: 'And if I say. The God of your fathers
Has sent me to you. And they say. What is his name?
What shall I. Say to them?' And the voice replied:
'You shall say to the children of Israel that he is called,
For what he is called he is: I am that I am.
And say too: the Lord God of your fathers,
The God of Abraham, the God of Isaac,
The God of Jacob has sent me unto you. And I am sure
That the king of Egypt will not let you go,
No, not by a mighty hand. But I will stretch out
My hand, my, and smite Egypt with all my wonders.'
Moses said: 'But they will. Not believe me. They will
Say: the Lord has. Not appeared unto you.'
But the voice: 'What is that in your hand?' And Moses:
'My shepherd's staff.' – 'Cast it to the ground.'
And Moses, bewildered, did so, and the staff,
Touching the ground, writhed, hissed, a snake.
A snake. He started back, afraid. And the voice said:
'Put out your hand. Take it by the tail.'
And Moses did so, still afraid, and what he took
Was his own shepherd's staff, no snake. Then the voice said:
'Through this power they will believe. And through this, too:
Put your hand into your bosom.' Moses slowly did so,
Doubtful still. 'Now remove it.' Did so, and his hand
Was white as leprosy. 'Return it your bosom,
Then remove it.' Did so, and the hand was of its
Former colour. 'If', said the voice, 'they will not
Believe one sign, then let them believe the other.'
Moses, now near weeping, said: 'O Lord. I am not
Eloquent. Not before. Not now. I am

Slow of speech. I am of a. Slow tongue.'
The voice was thunder, crying in fire and thunder:
'Who has made man's mouth?
Who makes the dumb or deaf of the seeing or the blind?
Am I not the Lord? For a time, for a time,
Your brother Aaron shall speak for you, and you
Shall put the staff in his hand. But with you, with you
Shall be the power of the Lord.' And the bush burned
But was silent. Burned still, the leaves and branches
Still unconsumed. He believed, he had to believe,
Believed, had to believe, descending to his sheep,
To the evening fire, the meat roasting, to Jethro saying:
'You believe what you saw what you saw, heard what you heard?'
Believed, had to believe. 'And thus a heavy burden
Is placed upon you. So.' Seeing it all. 'It is true.
The one. The great simplicity. The is what he is.
Well, at least I can die in the truth, knowing it the truth.
But for you a heavy burden.' Moses, sighing:
'My shoulders are too narrow. My voice is not the. Voice.
Of a deliverer. Easier to believe. It was a dream.
It was a whiff of magic. Delivered out of Egypt.'
His head fell to his bosom in a sudden sleep.
Zipporah started but Jethro shook his head, saying:
'He does not wish the belief. The belief is a burden
His very flesh rejects. But we must believe, even though
It means we must lose him for a while and, in a sense,
For ever. He was not, as I always knew,
Meant to be this kind of shepherd.' But Zipporah wept.
'It must be with our blessing', Jethro said. 'We must all
Not merely bow but bless, we must will our loss,
For think what we stand to gain.' And he repeated: 'True.
The one. The great simplicity.' But Zipporah wept.
And when Moses woke, bewildered, he sought his tent
Shivering, as though belief were an ague. Sleep now

Would not come, but a storm came, and he went to the tent-flap
To secure it against the rain. In lightning he saw Horeb
And cried in agony to it: 'Who am I?
I am. No judge in Israel. Let the task be given.
To one of the wise. One of the strong. Do not
Place the burden on me. I refuse the burden.'
Wife and son, awake, heard, then they saw in terror
The naked body of the husband, father, hurled,
In another flash, as though taken and thrown
And lie writhing, groaning, then still. The wife cried
Aloud to Horeb: 'Whoever you are, what do you want of him?
Is it his life? For you shall not have his life.'
Lightning showed metal, a blade. In this dark she groped,
Her fingers finding, as though told to find,
A shepherd's knife, his. Over thunder: 'Take the child's
Life, if you must have a life', and raised it.
But with fresh lightning came the right words:
'Not a life. But a token of life. Not the body.
But flesh of the body that the body will not miss.
Will that satisfy you?' And, in an impulse, drew
Taut the child's foreskin and, with the sharp blade,
Cut. The child, maimed, screamed, clutched where blood
Flowed on to the flesh of the father, the loins and his father,
And the father stirred, groaning in air,
While blood dripped on the father. Then the father arose
And the child was in his arms, then in the mother's arms,
Kissed, soothed, while the storm travelled on
And dark hid Horeb. So morning came,
Fresh after rain, with birdsong, and the child was sleeping.
They lay in love awhile, and after, in sad calm,
Zipporah said: 'Today?' Kissing her eyelids, he:
'It has to be today. It has to be. Alone.' She wept,
He comforted, and they rose as the day warmed.
At least it was a known way. Staff in hand, he

Blessed, awkwardly, a family that had done with weeping;
'The blessing of the God of Abraham.
The God of Isaac. The God of Jacob. The God whom
Jethro has long sought. My love. My blessing.
The blessing of Moses. For what it is worth.'
And then: 'We shall be together. In the
Time of the setting free.' He turned and strode
Uphill to the solitary palm, blessing that too,
Then engaged the desert. But he already knew the desert.
It was Moses he did not know.

4

RETURN INTO EGYPT

Aaron dreamed of an eagle made of fire,
Consuming, unconsumed, swooping out of the sun,
Yet this time now, as in the other dreams, in the desert,
But here, in Pithom. And as it swooped, men ran
To hide their own long shadows. He awoke
To a relay of distant cock-crows. His wife Eliseba,
Eleazar his son, slept on. He lay, loving and troubled,
As the light advanced, dreading action, longing for action.
(Alive, at least they were alive, they could live out their lives.
No man could have everything.) Sighing, he arose,
And he took his dream to Miriam's house, but she
Had left her pallet, earlier than he, her children
Undisturbed, happy in sleep. At least the children
Knew no other life. Was it right then to impose
The promise of long agony on them? Troubled, he walked
Down the street of the workers' dwellings, open doors,
Bodies obscenely huddled, flies, ordure.
(Better the long agony, but still agony,
Still long, perhaps endless.) Where the slave town ended,

Miriam the widow cleaned out the bulrush cages
She had woven for doves, and the white doves throbbed around
    her.
Miriam the prophetess, as some called her, prophesying
The long agony, but then freedom, whatever that was,
Vigorous, laughing often, smiling now at her brother,
A question in her smile. 'I saw him again',
Aaron said, sighing. 'This time as an eagle,
Flying almost above us here. No longer in the desert.
I knows what it means. It means he is close to us.
It means I must go to meet him. I know, I know.'
She said: 'You still have too much doubt, like the others.
But for the others there is excuse. None remembers him.
Or, if he is remembered, it is in the wrong way –
A far-off hero who could tame snakes, who could
Strike men dead with a glance. Here once and hence,
They accept or half-accept, may come again.
But *again* is a future so far off as to be a
Sort of past. A past like the beginning of the world.
For us it is different. For our mother and father
It was different, though they had to die with the hope
Not yet bursting into dreams. Your dream is clear.
I have silver hidden in the house. We need to bribe,
Our overseer is bribable enough. You need to go
Over the river.' He said: 'Silver? Where from?'
And she, laughing: 'Theft is too much virtue in you,
Virtue meaning timidity.' Laughing, launching a dove
Into the light. He nodded, troubled, knowing it true:
Why was the long agony reserved for him
Who would have been content with quietness, or with words,
The action left to his son, or his son's son?
So, when the work-day started, he trudged to the river,
The ferry just arriving, loaded with farmers,
A bull-calf snorting at a flutter of squawking hens,

The boat emptied, the ferryman, black, from the south,
His carven face swimming with light, swigged from a jug,
Sour-faced on a mouthful of sour wine. Aaron said:
'Will you take me to the other side?' – 'Double fare.
A lot come into Egypt. Not a lot
Go out, as you see. It's always double fare.'
Aaron said: 'But you have to go back there anyway.' –
'Always double fare. Some are very glad
To be paying double fare.' So it was double fare.
The ferryman was curious: why the journey? And then,
Incredulous: 'A dream? You say a dream? You
Seek somebody because of a dream? Paying double fare too.
A dream?' Aaron said: 'There was a time
When dreams were considered important in Egypt.'
The boatman spat. 'That was Joseph. The old days.
My grandfather told me about him. This is today.
All science today. Nobody follows dreams, not any more.'
Aaron said: 'I do. There was a time
When I did not. But I follow this dream. I have to.'
The ferryman said: 'Then you're mad.' Aaron spoke angrily:
'I see. And the rest of the world bursts with sanity,
Is that it? Mad because I dreamed of the coming of
Salvation? The others sane because they are slaves –
Is that it?' The boatman earnestly said (and would have
Laid a hand on Aaron's arm had not his hands
Been engaged in rowing): 'Never be taken in by
Words is what I say. Say that word slavery
And it sounds bad. Say instead a mouthful of bread
And fish and palm-wine for a day's work and it sounds
A great deal better. Who is this one you're going to meet then?'
Aaron told him. 'Hear that, you fish down there?
He's going to meet his brother and his brother
Is going to save the world. Look.' (Earnestly,
Squinting at Aaron across the blinding river light.)

'If you're going to have salvation, as you call it,
It won't be through your brother or my brother or
Through anybody else's brother. Forget all about it.
You're wasting your time. Nobody's coming from over there.
This Lord God you talk about has forgotten.
He has other things on his mind. Let me take you back.'
But Aaron smiled. 'You seem,' said the ferryman, 'to be a
Decent sort of a man. Touched, a bit, but that may be the sun.
I'll take you back. I'll return your fare to you.
Half of it anyway.' But Aaron smiled. The fight, he saw,
Was a fight against a man who, ferrying from bank to bank,
Believed they were travelling. Good men, no doubt of it.
Given time, they could be fought with words. Words:
Words were a comfort as well as a weapon. So he landed,
Sketched a blessing, smiling, and the ferryman
Offered a swig of sour wine. Then, head-shaking,
He waited for a boatload of the sane, seeking the world,
Egypt. Aaron now left the freedom of slavery
And sought the prison of the desert. Solitary, terrified,
When night fell, of the geometry of the stars,
He spoke to himself, or to someone: 'There is, you see,
The question of convincing them. So set,
All of them, in their ways. Made soft by slavery.
Who is he? Who? Never heard of him. Show us a
Sign. Give us a sign. What signs does he have?
Does he have any signs? Signs are what we need. Signs.
You know what we mean? Signs. Signs. Signs.
Something out of nothing. Miracles,
Miracles is the word. You know the word. Miracles.'
A star shot. The sky swung like a pendulum.
Then day, a mirage of green, mirage of a caravan,
Vultures gyrated, swooped. The corpse of a dog
In the rocks. Vultures swooped. 'Listen, Moses.
Listen, brother. Brother. You know that word?

You know these words I speak now? The joys of
Slavery. The relief at not having to be
Free any more. A terrible word, freedom.
We are degraded, yes. But it is hardly our fault,
Is it, hardly our fault. Only slaves.
We are only slaves. You see, Moses? Do you
Understand the words I speak to you, Moses?'
A black sky, starless, with a dying moon.
'Signs. You know, signs. You know what we mean?
Signs, signs.' Day and a fierce wind and he lay then
Talking talking, half-buried in a sand-drift.
Sand in the furrows of his face, till a hand came
Gently to clear the sand, and he saw the hand,
The arm. It was the eyes, he knew the eyes then,
And the mouth quiet in the beard of one who, he saw
With shock, was no longer young. Said to himself: No word.
And no word. It is the first sign. No word.
For though the word is in him it is I I I
Who must speak the word. And so, together,
With few words, words unneeded, they
Stumbled back into Egypt. And, in black night,
Unseen to Miriam's house in Pithom. Unseen
But heard of, guessed at. There was a morning
When the whip was hardly felt: *Came two days ago
Over the river.* And the children talked: 'Gave signs.
Turned his stick into a snake.' – 'But signs of what?'
'Signs that he is a god. They're always saying
That we're going to have a god. Well, here he is.' –
'But what is a god *for*?' And the old men talked:
'Something about his arm having leprosy on it.
Then he puts his arm on his robe and pulls it out
And the leprosy's gone.' – 'That's an Egyptian trick.
He sounds like an Egyptian to me. Somebody coming
To make us all work harder.' But Dathan, plumper now,

His linen bright, his fingers flashing in the sun,
Spoke of the newcomer not to fellow-slaves
But to the enslavers: 'Moses. Brother of Aaron.
The one who killed the Egyptian and ran away.
He's back now, thinks no one remembers.'
What is all this? What tale do you think you're
'True. Look, sir, I was always a friend of Egypt.
I can give good information. Valuable. This Moses
Is up to no good. I would appreciate,
Sir, a little Egyptian generosity…'
To work. You are drunk. Go on, friend of Egypt.
Young girls spoke of a god, golden-haired,
With a firm strong body, young, bearing comfort,
Making life easier (said the older women).
But to Aaron fell the task of talk, to the elders,
To the young who bore authority: Joshua was one,
Hard-eyed but supple of thought, as though thought were muscle.
'What god'? an elder said, and patiently,
Aaron: 'The God who spoke from the burning bush
On Mount Horeb. The bush burned and was not consumed.'
And the voice said: 'I am the God of Abraham,
Of Isaac, Jacob. I am sending one who shall
Set my people free.' But another elder, doubtful:
'It is the notion of the one god that I
Find tough to eat. What is this god's position
In relation to the other gods? That, I would say,
Is a reasonable thing to ask.' Patiently, Aaron:
'There are no other gods. God is God.
The God of the Israelites is God, the one God.' –
'The one remaining god, is that what you mean?' –
'Our thinking', Aaron said firmly, 'has become
Egyptian thinking. The Egyptians see the world
As multiple, various. Do you understand me?
There are, they say, many things in the world of sense

And, so the Egyptians argue, there must accordingly
Be many things in the heavens, matching, ruling
The many things of earth. We Israelites
Never believed that. In the beginning we knew
That all was one, that All was made by One.
We forgot the knowledge. Now, my brothers, we are
To remember that knowledge. Remember it in action.
It is that knowledge that is to set us free.'
And an elder wavered in doubt: 'Free – you mean
Free to leave Egypt?' Aaron said: 'Just that.' And Joshua:
'Mere knowledge, I would say, sets no man free.
Man, I would say, does not find freedom through God,
But God through freedom.' Aaron: 'And how does he,
How do we find freedom? We cannot fight
These Egyptians with Egyptian weapons. We have no
Battering-rams or crossbows. We can achieve freedom
Only by knowing the power of God and knowing
That one man can call down that power.' – 'Knowing?' –
'You have heard of the signs. Of the miracles.' – 'Heard, yes.
But seen, no.' – 'You will see, will certainly see.
But meantime, you must believe.' – '*Must? Must* believe?'
'A man must believe there is a better life
Than this life of bondage. Our God is not a
God of slavery.' An elder shook his head:
'If you say there is one God, then it is this
One God that has sold us into slavery.' And another:
'Or else one could say that there are at least two Gods –
One to enslave and one to free. And to have two Gods
Is the beginning of having many gods. So we are back where we
    started.'
Aaron cried: 'No. Not that. Cannot you see
That our God may have let the wicked work on the innocent,
The enslavers enslave the enslaved? God will in no wise
Interfere if he sees not fit to do so.

Is this our bondage not perhaps a test,
A proving of our right to be the
Chosen of God?' An elder said: 'Unconvincing.
I am unconvinced.' Caleb, another of the young,
Spoke boldly: 'There are weapons other than
Bows and battering-rams and pitchballs.
There are bricks and mattocks. There are muscles.' –
'Fools, fools', cried Aaron. 'Egypt is the world.
Only the maker of the earth and sun and stars
Can prevail over Egypt. God is our way, God.
And our way to God is through him.' Head-shakings.
'His that is come.' Wistfully one old man said:
'Free to leave Egypt. We are all, I fear,
Growing too old for that kind of freedom.' But Joshua,
A trumpet to that plaintive piping, said: 'We
Will help you to courage. None is too old to be free.
We, the young.' Head-shakings still: 'I am not convinced.' –
'*Nor I. Very far from convinced. Convinced. Nor I.*'
In the house of Aaron, at sunset, a ceremony,
A celebration: the bathing and clothing of Moses
For his visit to the Pharaoh. It was women's work,
And they sang, bringing water from the well, a song of water,
How water would yield to man, but only so far,
Water as flood or river or sea, never yield.
And Moses, smiling in a fodder-trough turned to a bath,
Was laved by his sister, who said, clucking: 'So dirty.
It seems you carry the dirt of a twelvemonth journey.'
And Moses: 'Dirty or not. You knew that. It was I.'
Nodding, 'I knew. I will always know. Remember your name:
It means *I have brought him forth.* And the I means I.' –
'And yet you do not', he said. 'Know me. We have had
No youth together. Have not rejoiced. In each
Other's marriage. Or children. Though I can rejoice in
Your children now. If only I can find out

Which they are. Ah, I know. You are Lia.' –
'No', said the child. 'I am Rachel.' Miriam said:
'There, that is Lia.' And then: 'My husband died
Soon after she was born. Soon after our mother…'
And Moses, sighing: 'Yes. Before I had time. To know them.
Both dead. Too many dead. Before the promise.'
Miriam, brisk to his sudden melancholy: 'When do I meet
Your wife? Your son?' Moses, brightening: 'They will be
Waiting for us. On the way. To the land. A long
Long journey. And we,' in gloom again, 'are not yet even
In the way of being able. To start on the journey.
My first. Door out of Egypt. Is a door into the
Very core and temple and shrine. Of Egypt. Pharaoh
Must be asked. Then begged. Then entreated. Then
Threatened. Then the threats. Must start to be
Fulfilled.' Miriam said softly: 'It will be a hard time.' –
'Ah', said Moses, brightening, '*you* are Elisa.' –
'No', the child said, 'I am Rachel. I
Told you I was Rachel.' Moses begged graceful pardon,
Then said: 'Hard? It will, I fear, be a hard time
For all the innocent. It is always the innocent who
Must suffer first. We sacrifice a lamb.
Not a crocodile. One of the great mysteries.'
Then he turned to women's noises of pride, pleasure,
And saw what they had drawn forth from a hiding-place –
Cleaned but worn, ravagings of moth and white ant
But poorly disguised, that former princely robe,
Robe of a lord of Egypt. The smiles turned to pain
And puzzlement when he thundered 'No' at them.
'No', he thundered, 'I go as an Israelite.
I go. As what I am.' And so he went
In the summer evening, in a pilgrim's jerkin,
His old rough cloak, carrying his staff, to the palace.
At first they tried to beat him away but he said:

'Moses. My name is Moses. Formerly a prince.
And still cousin to the king. I am expected.'
So he was half-bowed in, in puzzlement, and was expected
In the room where the models of treasure-cities,
Grain-cities, were built. A new rich project gleamed
Among torches, candles, gold effigies, effigies,
Rich on the walls. Then Pharaoh entered, softly,
Alone, with the face Moses remembered, a clever face
Though hard (and it must learn, he sighed, to soften),
And Pharaoh said: 'Is it you? Is it really you?'
Moses smiled. 'I fear. I can give you. No
Proof of. Who I am.' But Pharaoh: 'The voice is enough.
Everything else has changed. But the voice, no.
That sudden cutting off between phrases, as if
Speech were sometimes being whipped out of you.
Moses. Cousin Moses. You look,' smiling, 'like a
Very poor relation, if I may say so.' Moses said:
'You summoned me back to Egypt. I did not come.
Now I am come in my own time. But tell me why
You summoned me.' Pharaoh said: 'Simple. I could not
Forget you easily. Others I forgot –
Streams of courtiers, glorying in self-abasement,
Wise men, men who were called wise, sycophants,
Relations, none of them poor relations. A time came
When I felt homesick for you – you, the cousin
Who taught me, against his will, how to hunt gazelle.
The enigmatic prince of my boyhood. I must have been
A most unlikely boy. I was, of course,
Too young to use you.' Moses said: 'And now
You are old enough.' – "Old enough. Also, smiling,
'Master of the world, of the sacred blood of Horus,
Blood that, the poets write, is knitted from the stars.
Divine and holy, wholly divine, cousin Moses.
Gods work through men. And gods need men

Who know what godhead is. Do you still listen
To the voices of bats at nightfall?' Moses said:
'In the desert there are many voices. Voices
I had not. Heard in Egypt.' – 'You did not hear
My voice calling you? Or any voice
That spoke of me?' Moses said: 'Yes. I did.' –
'A human voice?' said Pharaoh. And Moses: 'No.
No human. Not a. Human voice.' Pharaoh fingered
An ornament, gold-chained, dangling from his neck, saying:
'Voices of the desert. That formless shifting world,
Whistling and singing nonsense. There is no
Solidity, no certainty in the desert.
Reality is here, cousin. For a thousand years
We Egyptians have been the masters of reality.
We have an exact and perfect, an exquisite,
An almost painful knowledge of the nature of
Power, power. The means of its acquisition,
Its growth, its maintenance. Power is here and for ever.
This is the real world, and you belong to it.
You, who know reality, have been whoring too long
After dreams of the desert. You are recalled to
Reality.' But Moses, softly, 'Called, not
Recalled.' And his eyes were lost an instant
Among the effigies, and Pharaoh did not
Well, for an instant, understand. But then he
Looked up, showing pleasure, for into the chamber
His queen came, and also a nurse, and in the nurse's arms…
'My son,' cried Pharaoh in joy. 'My first-born.
Is he not beautiful?' Moses nodded sadly. 'Beautiful.'
Pharaoh took the child in his arms, saying in joy:
'My son. He will reign after me.
The unbroken and unbreakable chain of rule.
The strength which sets the desert winds
Howling in impotence. And you, and you

Choose these empty voices out of the dead sand.
This I cannot comprehend.' Moses said:
'It is a simple matter, majesty. It is a
Matter of one's race. One's people. The
Destiny of that people. I have discovered
Where I belong.' The child cried, putting out arms
Towards his mother, and Pharaoh kissed and
Hugged him, handing him reluctantly over,
The queen saying: 'He is ready to sleep,
Now he has seen his father.' And she left,
Looking curiously at Moses, whom she did not know.
'Where you belong?' said Pharaoh. 'You belong to us.
To me. Bemused by the fable of your birth,
You ignore the truth. And the truth is that you are of Egypt.
Of the blood. For the blood is not what passes
From mother to son. That belongs to
The order of the beasts. It is rather what is of the soul,
Whatever the soul is. The woman who
Made herself your mother – she was the substance. She
Remains the substance, even in death. You, Moses
You are of Egypt, and one of my tasks
Is to confirm that truth – in your own life,
In that bigger life called history.' But Moses,
Impatient: 'This is the. Mysticism. I must
War against. The voices of the. Desert spoke hard
Metal. The shifting. Swirling. Insubstantial.
Those are in your words. I reject Egypt.
I embrace my people.' And Pharaoh, harder now,
Metal: 'Your people, as you call them,
Belong to Egypt. They are the tough skin of the
Hands and feet of Egypt, no more, but the
Body does not disown them.' And Moses, urgent:
'Beware of such. Images. The reality is that
We are a. Different animal. We scent our.

Own destiny. We must be free. To track it.'
And Pharaoh, hard, metal: 'Never. Never.' Moses said:
'I know. You will never be. Persuaded by.
Entreaties. Egypt is locked against
Voices from the desert. It must be signs, signs.'
'Signs from whom or what or where?' asked Pharaoh. –
'From the Maker of the World who is the
God of my people. The God. Of what he has made.' –
'Signs?' cried Pharaoh. 'Tricks? The Egyptian conjurers
Know them all. You are being more Egyptian
For thinking of signs. What will you do, cousin Moses –
Turn that stick to a snake? My sorcerers
Can do that yawning. Make your snake swallow theirs?
We must from Moses, must we not, expect
Big magic? I should be appalled if Moses let mere
Magicians, salaried nameless men of trickery,
Beat him at that game.' But Moses shook his head.
'My Lord Pharaoh. Highness. Majesty. There must be
None of that manner of. Commerce between us. No
Ambiguity in your mind. You must believe that the
Signs and the demands. Come from a true. Israelite.'
But Pharaoh could smile, saying: 'You are an Egyptian.
Will always be an Egyptian.' Moses did not smile.
'So you will believe. Until the signs
Persuade you otherwise. Let the tale begin now.
I shall not at first be in it. I am not qualified.
Being so. Slow of speech.' And Pharaoh, smiling again:
'Another of your fallacies, cousin Moses.'
But Moses was troubled at having to hate this man.

5

THUS the tale beginning, the voice was Aaron's.
And all was done, in the beginning to a
Strict pattern of decorum. For, to an official,
An overseer of overseers, Aaron brought the petition
That was partly a lie, but a lie was part of the pattern.
Saying, with proper humility: 'Three days in the desert.
A small request, your honour. We have orders
To sacrifice to the God of our people.' But the official
Stormed, according to the pattern: 'Orders? Orders?
We give the orders. You interest me, little man.
Why in the desert?' Aaron duly replied:
'Since it was in the desert that my brother Moses
Heard the command.' – 'Whose command?' – 'The command
of Him who demands the sacrifice.' The official said:
'You talk round and round, round and round.' –
'Three days in the desert, your honour.' The official said:
'Request refused' – 'What request?' spoke a voice.
It was in the open air, near a half-built wall
Of the new half-built treasure-city, and the voice
Was that of some peacock of the royal household,
Gorgeous, his face already an effigy,
On a horse sumptuously caparisoned. 'My lord',
Grovelled the overseer of overseers, 'this slave here
Asks on behalf of other slaves permission to spend
Three days in the desert. Request refused, my lord.' –
'Who put you up to this nonsense?' His lordship asked,
And Aaron: 'With respect, we do not consider it
Nonsense. We must sacrifice in the desert.
You have your gods. We have our God. Only one.
We make no high pretensions.' His lordship said:

'You have not answered my question.' So Aaron answered:
'It was my brother Moses who in the desert
Heard the word of God.' – 'Why does your brother
Not make the request himself?' And Aaron said,
True to the pattern, 'My brother is slow of speech.' –
'And slow perhaps of understanding. When will you
Israelites realise what you are?' Decorously, Aaron:
'We are beginning to realise, sir.' – 'Take him back this answer.
And deliver it as slowly as you will.' He raised his whip,
Its handle gorgeously patterned, and lashed. The blow was feeble,
Apt for the giver of the blow, but blood came,
Rippling through Aaron's beard, first blood. Aaron bowed,
Humble, submissive to the pattern. But his word travelled
Quickly enough. Israelite insolence, to the palace,
And one day two high ministers sat at a game
Of senet, an intricate, geometrical game, one saying:
'Three days in the desert. How do we construe that?'
The other: 'Israelite insolence, but we know its origin.'
And the first: 'Moses, yes. And what precisely
Is the present position of Moses?' The other shrugged,
Eyes on the game-board: 'The situation between him and the
Pharaoh – forgive me, I have that in the wrong order –
Is that he, of his own free will, has cast himself
Clean out of favour. I gather that Pharaoh
Had an accession of chagrin, something to do with the past,
A kind of nostalgia, but that everything now
Is perfectly clear.' The first one took a piece,
Grinning, and said: 'The fable – you know the fable.
The lion prepared to eat the lamb and the lamb said:
Before I am eaten, sir, let me put my
Affairs in order. I assure you, noble sir,
I will be back in time for dinner.' The other laughed,
Examined the board, then said: 'The Israelites, I gather,
Are buzzing with hope. There is a little device

I have always been interested in trying. Bricks. Bricks.
Have you had any experience of brick-making? No,
Of course not. It is a simple process. Listen…'
So it happened, the next day, at the mudpits,
That the workers stood around, puzzled, and the foreman,
Not Dathan, an honest man, sincerely puzzled,
Went to his overseer, noticing that, usually,
There were soldiers around, and asked: 'Sir. Where is the straw?'
There was no answer but grins began among the soldiers,
A kind of expectant lip-licking. 'The straw, sir, straw.
To make bricks with. We have not straw. The straw hasn't come.
Straw.' An officer said: 'What's going on?
With respect, I mean, sir. Of course we have to have straw.
Mud, straw, water, the sun – that is how bricks are made.
Give us straw and we give you bricks. As always. Sir.'
A scribe sitting by, busy with accounts, said: 'Changes.
There have been some changes. Nobody brings you straw,
Not ever again. You gather your own straw.
Or you do without. Is that clear? Is that perfectly clear?'
The foreman frowned, very puzzled, and the laughs began
Among the soldiers. He took the word back to the workers,
And Joshua, one of the workers, said: 'No straw.
No bricks. A simple enough equation.' Caleb nudged him,
And Joshua saw soldiers with bows and arrows at the ready.
A deputation – Aaron, and Moses also,
But a silent Moses at this stage of the tale,
Joshua, Caleb, others, the foreman leading –
Went to say to what was now a
Grinning knot of officials, well-backed by arrows:
'Sir, sirs, with respect, we do not
Understand. If we get the straw ourselves
That doubles the work. I thought you needed bricks.
If this, of course, is just a way of saying
We don't work hard enough – I mean, you can have more bricks,

If that's what you mean. But give us the straw first.'
The Egyptians said nothing still, but smiles were wider.
Then Joshua cried out: 'New Egyptian injustice!
We have had enough and more than enough!' The smiles went
And the soldiers were on him. He spat
Lavishly into a military face, and then the fists started.
The other workers drew back – they had not meant this –
They had merely wanted to – Aaron looked at Moses
But Moses did, said nothing, abiding to the pattern,
While Joshua was lashed to a whipping-post and
Lashed to near-death. Joshua, when the sun set,
Still there, soldiers around him, guarding, covered with rod-marks,
Dried blood, flies frantic around the
Wounds still open. The foreman spoke to Moses:
'You. You put the rod in their fists. You.
You'll put the sword in their hands tomorrow.
Or tonight perhaps. You and your brother.
This God of yours. I hope he strikes you down.
Both of you. Strikes you dead.' Moses was silent
But the voice within him spoke bitterly to a fire on Horeb:
Why have you done this? Why do you bring only
Evil to your people? Why did you send me back here?
Why could I not be left alone? The sun dipped,
And soon the bats circled, whistling, and then the
Irrelevant constellations, no answer. No speech
At the table in Aaron's house – bread, fruit,
A meagre supper – and eyes averted from Moses,
Moses eating nothing, Aaron little, his eyes
Not averted though very troubled. When Moses left
To look at the stars in bitterness, Aaron followed
And said at one: 'I want no more of it.'
Moses nodded. 'You want to be free of me.' –
'Free of this business', Aaron said, 'Of having to
Speak in your name.' – 'You think it all a lie,

That the voice was a delusion, that I'm
Mad. Or misled. – 'So our people think.'
But Moses: 'They think wrong. The voice spoke
True. It made no false promises. Nothing will be easy.
But the Lord did make. One error. The error of choosing
Me.' They were both silent then and, for a whole day,
Silent with each other. Silent to his face the
People Moses was sent to deliver, but behind his back
Not silent. Children would throw feeble stones
And old men spit in his path, no more. Joshua,
Broken, groaning on his bed with the flies about him,
Was a sufficient witness against him. To the fire on Horeb
Moses spoke desperately: *See, Lord. See what you have done.*
Since the moment of my return there has been
Nothing but sullenness and a renewal of evil ways.
Your people are sunken into a deeper slavery.
You do not wish to set them free. He walked through Pithom,
So speaking, seeing whores offer themselves,
A young man sunk far in disease and neglected,
Children squabbling for a cheap Egyptian toy.
And are they not right to have lost hope?
Lord, why was it I who had to be chosen?
What shall I do? What shall I say to them?
And then the Lord spoke, but in the voice of Moses:
Moses. I begin now. Go to Pharaoh.
Say to him all that I bid you say. But the voice
Must be Aaron's still. He must stand in your place.
But you must stand in the place of the Lord your God.
So Moses stood entranced a moment on the street in Pithom,
Saying aloud: 'The Lord my God.' There were jeers
As at a madman. A stone was hurled, and not by a child.
But he stood transfixed, impervious. 'Lord my God.'
So there came the day, in a day or so, of the petitions.
A royal pavilion, with pennants, a throne, effigies,

Trumpeters, drummers, the whole court in attendance,
On a bank where the Nile narrowed, the water muddy,
Turbulent over a bed of slippery stones.
And on the opposed bank the suppliants,
With petitions for the Pharaoh, waited in the heat,
Swatting flies with palm-fronds. Aaron and Moses
Waited with them. After hours of waiting,
Trumpets sounded, and a herald spoke:
'Whatsoever person desires to present his
Petition to the most sacred majesty of the Pharaoh,
The divine Mernefta, must do so as follows. He must
Step into the sacred waters and be purified.
Thus purified, he may proceed to the royal shore.'
Trumpets, then trumpets, drums, cymbals as
Pharaoh himself, well-attended, came to his throne.
On his throne, he saw many eyes quick to avert themselves
From blinding majesty, but the eyes of Moses
Were not averted. The suppliants entered the water
And, as was foreseen, stumbled, slithered,
Crawled back again, some, to their own bank,
While the court grinned, laughed when one old man
Had to be saved from drowning. Pharaoh smiled,
Perhaps dutifully, but he did not smile
When Moses and Aaron, upright among the slitherers,
Trod the river-bed towards him, Aaron crying:
'Pharaoh... We humbly request... that your majesty
Accede to our...' The king signed to the herald,
And the herald signed to the captain of trumpeters,
And the trumpeters blasted forth, so the words of Aaron,
Save for 'strike' and 'punish' and 'revenge',
Were smothered, and all speech and laughter smothered
When the drums and cymbals added their clamour. The eyes of
    Moses,
The eyes of one who had foreseen all, held steady

And now Pharaoh avoided them. But those eyes turned,
Again as one who had foreseen, upstream where a
Man cried soundlessly, and the eyes of Pharaoh
Followed. The man was as though painted red,
And viscous red ran from him and he shouted.
Pharaoh stilled the clamour of the silver and skin,
And the shout was heard: 'Blood. The water has turned to
Blood.' Laughter, and then not laughter.
For red was tumbling, sluggish at first, downstream,
Then bubbling over the stones, and the smell
Was, without doubt, the smell of blood. Moses and Aaron
Stood as it surged about them, let the others,
Terrified, crying *It's blood blood the water has*
Turned to blood, slither and stumble out, stood till
Pharaoh himself came down to the river-verge and
Dipped his hand in. Blood. His eyes found the eyes of Moses,
And they said, surely: 'Clever, cousin Moses.
But no more clever than my own
Magicians can do.' And then they looked on blood.
Servants rushed with towels, wiping off the blood
From the royal hand, throwing the towels in
Blood, the towels filling with blood, floating sluggishly,
While the cry of *blood blood* went on, and Moses and Aaron
Strode through blood, their backs to Pharaoh,
Back to their bank. And now, all along the Nile bank,
The cry or scream was *blood*, and in the fountains
Blood seethed and frothed, but in the wells of Pithom
Water sang clear. Then, from the waterways
Which were now boiling bloodtides, the frogs came croaking,
Blood on their skin, frogs countless, in droves,
With a deafening croaking, on to the land, advancing.
Water blood, and the land all frogs, then the air
Filling with gnats, beasts and men
Thrashing and screaming, the sky black with gnats.

At the core of maddened Egypt, fires burning
To keep off the gnats, in a gauze tent
In a room of the palace, the chief magician used words,
Reasonable words, to calm the ministers, saying:
'Maintain, my lords, a scientific approach.
Approach by way of reality, by observation,
Analysis, never by way of theory. You ask:
Is it blood? If blood, whose blood? I reply:
That is not to the purpose. The substance, true,
Behaved like blood, smelt, tasted like it.
Whose blood? That is no question for the
Physical investigator. Think now. There are records
Of mud-pollution on the Nile, followed inevitably
By an immediate exodus of creatures that live
And breed in clear water. Swarms of frogs and gnats –
Inevitable. We may expect also flies, locusts,
A murrain on the cattle – all stemming from
The pollution, by whatever cause, of the river.
You ask: is the blood, or whatever it is, a product
Of thaumaturgical conjuration? I say in reply:
The term has never been adequately defined. Miracle,
Magic – what do the words, scientifically considered,
Really mean? But, my lords, we have to remember
That this perverse and defecting Moses is, by upbringing,
Education, an Egyptian. He has had, doubtless, access
To obscure lore which, in this age of stability
And power, has never had to be invoked
Against enemies. To talk, as some are doing,
Of the magical potency of a new god, a god moreover
Of an enslaved people, is, to say the least,
Premature. Again, you ask: how is it that the
Israelites remain immune from these – nuisances?
The reason, my lords, may well be geographical.
Goshen, remember, is some way from the Nile,

Sheltered, removed from the causative pollution.
How dark it is getting.' It was true.
They peer through their mesh at thickening air. Flies.
Thick, black, buzzing irritably, flies.
Clouds of flies. But none in Pithom. There
Aaron addressed the elders, saying: 'The signs are before you.
Can you harbour further doubts? I know, I know
It is hard to take in. The God of the universe
Has chosen a people weak, enslaved, hopeless,
Indolent.' – 'Chosen for what?' said one. And Aaron:
'For the working out of his divine purpose on earth.
So it would seem. We must not ask too much.
What we must rather do is gird our loins,
Prepare for the coming of the day.' But an elder said:
'The day, you mean, of leaving a bondage that has become –
Well, all that some of us have known. We are old.
It is hard to face the new life. It is a hard God,
This God of yours, ours.' But Aaron cried:
'We must learn to think of ourselves as a people,
Not as mere tribes, families, lone beings with
Individual sufferings. Many of us
May be discarded on the way – worn-out, useless –
But the people goes on, the race continues. They that
End the journey may not be those that began it.
We are all one, and the dead and the yet unborn
Share in the common purpose, the common goal.'
And one said: 'I don't like this sort of talk at all.
It's all blown-up, like a sheep's stomach full of wind.
Life is, life is what we see, smell, feel –
The taste of a bit of bread, a mouthful of water,
Sitting at the door, watching the evening come on
With the circling of the bats. The things you talk of
Are only in the mind. We are too old, I tell you,
For this talk of common goals and purposes and journeys.'

And Aaron was angry, shouting: 'You speak thus,
When the Lord your God exerts himself beyond
What may be thought of as proper for a God.
For God has shown himself in the running blood of the
Rivers, in the swarming gnats and flies.
God leaves us unscathed and wholesome while all Egypt
Screams. Does this mean nothing?' And one said:
'It means, I suppose, that we are the chosen people.
Means we must face the desert and dream of the promise.
It means – oh, is it so blasphemous
To wish to be left alone?'
           Then came the locusts,
Stripping the trees, save in the vale of Goshen,
Where Pithom sat. And then came boils and ulcers,
And lancings, and running of pus, the afflicted
Wretched, waiting in line for the lancet, and the
General wonder that things should be as they were.
Had the gods failed Pharaoh? How could they fail
One who was one of themselves? Was it some demon?
But no demon could be mightier than the gods'
Whole army. Pharaoh had done so much
To the glory of the gods – opulent monuments.
He had done for the gods far more than the
Gods might reasonably expect to be done. The pyramids.
Take the pyramids. To count the bricks in
One pyramid alone would take up years. What then
Had gone wrong? 'They wonder', Aaron said,
In conclave in Pithom, 'what has gone wrong. But they know
That we remain untouched, this they know. They fear us.
It is a new thing for the Israelites to be feared.'
Miriam said: 'We were always feared. If the Egyptians
Had merely destroyed us, our memory still
Would have been feared. There are many dead nations
That growl out of their ashes. But they brought us low,

They made us despised among nations. And the fear –
How is it now expressed? They are already beginning
To bribe us into leaving, to skulking out
In the dark.' And she looking at Dathan, who,
In a corner of Aaron's house, gloated over
A little hoard of jewels and gold pieces,
Egyptian bribes. Dathan said: 'I shall be happy
To take charge of all this side of our
Operation. We need such resources presumably.
Nor is there any need to wait to be given.
One may take. Take. There are any number
Of fine villas already abandoned. Death. The plague.
I knew some of the victims well. Through my position.
They're well served now, God curse them.' Now Moses spoke,
Saying: 'The potter has his craft, so has the builder,
So has the maker of songs. The Lord too
Has his craft. And it may be called. A
Dance of numbers. So far he has smitten
Egypt seven times. Rivers of blood.
Frogs. Gnats. Flies. A striking down of their
Sheep and cattle. The curse of the teeth of the
Locusts. Now the plague.' On the mud floor
He marked in strokes with his staff to the number seven.
'The making of the world,' he said, 'was a dance of seven.
The bringing low of Egypt. Will be a
Dance of ten.' They listened. 'For in the heart of
Pharaoh there must be a kind of dance.
It must soften. It must harden. It must
Soften again. Must harden for one last time.
And then, like stone, it must crack. It must
Shatter. And Egypt. Must shatter with it. Delay.
Some of you think of delay and fret. But remember.
The Lord must have his craft. And we need the delay.
We must gather our possessions. Our carts. Cattle.

There is a matter of supplies. Grain. Water.
We must prepare. Our order of march. Think of the
Sick. The unwilling. The cries of those who
Would be left. To last out their days. In Goshen.
Women with child. Many problems. The question of
Unifying the clans. Creating degrees of leadership.'
'The question of arms, defence,' Joshua said,
Eager though battered, scarred, limping. 'The army.
The training of an army.' – 'That too, Joshua.' –
'The treasury,' Dathan smiled.
                    In the imperial palace,
In full assembly, ministers about him, Pharaoh paced,
Hiding his deep agitation, while a scribe
Read figures out: 'One hundred and seventeen thousand
Five hundred and sixty-seven. This is the latest
Computation, your divine majesty.' Pharaoh said:
'I am not greatly interested in numbers. So many dead,
So many lost cattle, devastated fields. It is not
Flesh and bone and possessions we lose,
For these can be replaced a millionfold.
It is the heart of the empire, the central idea…'
And a minister said, in pain: 'With respect, majesty,
You cannot so easily ignore the suffering of
Your subjects. It is an essential in kingship:
The king must see himself as a head, his kingdom the body.
Must not the head feel the anguish of the body?' But Pharaoh:
'It is the heart that feels, not the head.
The head must be clear. The heart clouds and confuses.
Let us hear no talk of feeling. Thinking –
That concerns us now.' But the minister cried:
'If you have suffered – if you had lost –' And another:
'If I may say this, majesty, our friend is distraught.
He has lost both his wife and daughter.' But Pharaoh said:
'He can have another wife within a day.

Another daughter within a year. I do not wish
To listen to womanish laments and improper rebukes.
Let us quieten our hearts. Let the head speak. Listen.'
And they listened. Pharaoh said: 'This empire, Egypt,
Is the greatest the world has ever seen, perhaps
The greatest it will ever see. Our cities
Are crammed with all manner of merchandise, our ships
Sail all the known seas. Our towers kiss heaven,
Our armies shake the earth. We prosper, prospered...
At the very core of our empire lies a truth.
Or shall I say a belief that has long been taken
For a truth – the belief that the ruler of the empire
Has been appointed by the gods themselves,
That the Pharaoh is the issue of their flesh. How then can
The Nile fail to bless the land, the land
Fail to groan with the overwhelming
Blessing of increase? But now the gods
Seem to turn against their own flesh. Starvation.
Disease. Dissension. Fratricide. Distrust of authority.
Why? Why? Can the changeless gods then change?
Can the eternally strong grow weak? Can, from nowhere,
A new god appear to overthrow the
Tables of the eternal?' The chief magician spoke,
After a pause: 'Your majesty has touched upon
An interesting, indeed compelling, theological point.
The gods are the gods, eternal, self-created,
Subsisting out of time. There are no new gods.
But, your majesty, the gods, so we must believe,
Have no essential interest in human affairs.
It is only by virtue of prayer, sacrifice,
The raising of monuments, even the skills of conjuration,
That they can be swirled into the human orbit.
Now, as it seems to me, one god forgotten,
One long removed from the concerns of the state of Egypt,

Has been conjured. You know which god. You know
By whom.' A nerve beat on Pharaoh's brow.
Then he said: 'You take us back to an old time –
A time when the false belief in a
Single god possessed many of the most subtle and
High-placed of Egyptians. You refer to Moses.
This belief has come back and it has attached itself
To a race of slaves.' The chief magician said:
'Logical, majesty, as you will admit. Will the slaves
Willingly embrace the gods of their masters?
These questions, as I said, are of immense
Theoretical interest, but – there remains
The matter of what is to be done. I would, I know,
Be overtreading the bounds of my office if I
Ventured to – ' But the first minister cut in with:
'It is a simple matter, divine majesty.
The devotees of the god ask that they may do
Sacrifice to him. They request three day
Away from their holy work of building monuments
To the glory of the true gods of imperial Egypt.
It would be a mark of a kingly clemency to grant…'
And Pharaoh cried: 'Be forced to grant, impelled to?"
For the slave to cease to be a slave? For the
Power of his God to be recognised, acknowledged?' –
'Only three days, majesty. With guarantees of return.' –
And Pharaoh began to see what was meant. 'Guarantees?'
He smiled. – 'Guarantees, your divine majesty.'
Then the hailstones came, thudding on the street
And roofs and deafening, and, landing,
Spurting out flame. But not Goshen, land of
Servitude but also of sun and clean water. From Pithom
Moses and Aaron came to the palace, knowing it was
Time to ask again, and were admitted to a
Dark chamber full of candlelight, where magicians

Consulted entrails, burned rare gums and powders,
Intoned in an old tongue. Pharaoh was there.
Aaron spoke at once, saying: 'We are come again,
King of Egypt, to ask that we be released
From our labours in order to...' Pharaoh ignored him,
Addressing Moses instead: 'Have you no respect
For our religion, cousin? We are at holy work.
We seek to avert these inexplicable nuisances
From the innocent Egyptian people.' Aaron said:
'Not innocent. Not inexplicable.' Pharaoh sighed,
Saying: 'Our ceremonies are tainted by the presence
Of the unbeliever. Go.' And the magicians
Put out their fires, made obeisance, departed.
'You seem to have reached the limit, clever cousin,
Of your resources', Pharaoh said. 'This magic
Hail of yours can harm no one.' Aaron replied:
'Harm was never intended. Not at first.
It was thought the signs of God's power would be enough.'
But Pharaoh ignored him still, fixing Moses
With a look malevolent, admiring, even affectionate.
And Aaron: 'Do we have an answer, sir? May we
Take an answer back to our people?' Pharaoh still
Ignored him, addressing Moses: 'Are you pleased
With your power, cousin? Does it satisfy you
To have impaired, even part-destroyed, this great
Flower of order? Do you wish me to bow down
To a god who is the enemy of the State?
For, believe me, the State can be hated only by the
Eternal forces of disruption, little of whose power
You have, through your trickery, shown us.
Without the State we are nothing, any of us.
Order, beauty, majesty, the unbroken
Chain of rule. To destroy the state
Is to betray us to those windy voices out there in the desert.

You wish to see Egypt become broken stone,
Lizards sunning themselves on broken stone.'
Then Moses spoke: 'You cannot. Maintain order –'
Pharaoh feigned amazement: 'You have recovered your voice?' –
'Cannot. Maintain order. On slavery.' Pharaoh cried:
'What slavery? Any slavery? Or merely the
Slavery of your people? If you were to be made free,
Would you not have your highest and your lowest?
Would you not build your own pyramid?' Aaron said:
'Sir, we need your answer.' And Pharaoh, in scorn:
'Quiet, little man. I am talking to your better.'
Moses said: 'We will build on the covenant.
On the bond. Freely embraced. The contract
Between man and man.' Then Pharaoh bitterly:
'Your high talk in a land you have turned into a
Charnel. I cannot stand your smell much longer.
You had better go.' Aaron, eagerly: 'May we then
Have a scribe called in? May we have this written
And stamped with the royal seal?' Pharaoh spoke still
Only to Moses: 'The word of the Pharaoh, Moses.
You may go to the desert and perform your sacrifice.
I have, may the gods forgive me, spoken.'
Moses said: 'You have not finished, majesty.
I would rather you had said it now than shouted it
To our backs as we left your presence.' Pharaoh cried:
'What have I not then said?' And then, quieter:
'Ah yes. The men may go to the desert
And do sacrifice to the god of destruction.
The women and children shall remain behind.
As this is a kind of war, cousin Moses,
Shall we call them a hostage?' Aaron was ready to
Rave, but Moses held him back, half-smiling:
'Your heart is still hard, Pharaoh. This must mean
You have not yet had enough signs.

Or enough suffering.' So they left,
And Egypt, as Moses knew, was ready for the
Ninth course. The hail had departed, the sun shone.
And God said to Moses: *Take up a handful*
Of the dust of the earth and hurl it into the sky.
He did so, and blackness fell. Thick, palpable
Dark in a black dark wind that doused all lights.
Nor did the other curses abate – the water blood,
Frogs, gnats, flies, locusts, murrain, plague,
Hailstones that flamed fire. Misery.
Death-carts through the dark. So, as foreseen,
Moses and his brother were summoned again to the palace,
But this time met by a minister, who said:
'The order is that you leave Egypt and go
Into the desert, there to conduct your
Sacrifice.' But Aaron, quickly: 'The women?
The children?' – 'They are to go with you.'
Moses waited, holding Aaron back,
Aaron anxious to leave, so the minister said:
'You expect something more?' – 'Something more.' –
'There is nothing more in the royal instructions.'
'Nevertheless,' said Moses, 'there is something more.
We must wait for that something more.' The minister cried:
'"hat manner of man are you? If you wish something more,
You may have it from me – the loathing of
One who did ill to no man and yet was compelled
To suffer. Who lost two of his dearest – No matter.
You are stone men. You ask something more
That our suffering may be prolonged. Go. You heard the order.
See – it is written clear. Why can you not go?'
And a voice said: 'Yes. Why can they not go?' The Pharaoh
Stood by a door of ornate gold, attended
By torchbearers, cold loathing on his face, saying:
'They cannot go because they know there is something more.

What is the something more? You, Aaron, his voice –
What is it?' Aaron said: 'We are to go
Into the desert for three days, there to do sacrifice
In the middle of our month of Nissan. Men, women, children.
With our beasts, our goods –' But Pharaoh cried out: 'No.
You have eaten of the bread of Pharaoh, drunk his wine.
For three days you shall neither eat nor drink.
You will sacrifice fasting. Then you will return.
Your beasts will bleat and bellow a welcome home.
Your pitiful goods will lie snug, awaiting you.
This is the contract. That the god cease his torments.
That you go forth for three days, three days only.'
But Moses said, 'This, Pharaoh, will not do.
Your covenant with us was broken. Long ago.
There is no bond between us. When we leave this land
It shall be as free men. Taking with us our wives.
Taking our children. Sheep. Oxen. Goods –
Such as they are. Not the paring of a nail
Shall be left in Egypt. Not a hair or a scale
Of the skin of the beast.' But Pharaoh cried:
'You go forth naked. Naked you return.'
'No.' And Moses was not now slow of speech.
'Your heart is still hard against the Lord and against the
Servants of the Lord. The land has suffered,
The king of the land must see the suffering brought home.
There is, Pharaoh, one last trial, the tenth,
And it will still not fall directly on your head.
You will live, whole and free, to see
The Israelites leave Egypt. But the trial to come
Will be the worst trial in the world. Do you now relent?'
But Pharaoh said: 'The Pharaoh is not threatened.'
And then his stone face became flesh, then the flesh writhed,
And the tongue ground out: '*If I see your face again…*'
But Moses bowed to the words, calm, saying:

'So be it. This is the last time, Pharaoh,
The last time you will ever see my face.'
They left the presence, the palace, walking surely through
Howling darkness, until, on Goshen's border,
They walked through howling darkness like a wall
Into sun, clean air, and the song of fresh water.
Moses shuddered. The last thing coming. The last.
The tenth figure of the dance. But Pharaoh had willed it.
Men will even their own destruction. A heavy burden,
Free will, Moses sighed to himself, seeking fresh water,
No torment in the world greater than freedom.

6

THE PASSOVER

Moses, in sunlight, with the whirring of Miriam's doves
And the cry of children about him, sighed and spoke
Softly of the Angel of Death. 'Who shall describe him?
Or her? Or it? Like a trained hound of the hunters
He has the scent in his nostrils. He follows the scent.
He will follow the scent of the first-born.' Miriam said:
'You were told this?' And Moses replied: 'It is the
Last thing. The tenth figure of the dance.
Four days from now on the night of the
Fourteenth day of Nissan. The nose and the teeth of the
Angel of Death will dart straight
For the first-born. Whether Egyptian or Israelite –
It will be no matter to him of the
Separating of the nations. Even the
First-born whelp of a bitch's litter. The
Hatchling of the hen. He will go for the scent.'
And Miriam, in terror: 'For ours? For our
First-born?' But Moses said: 'Have no fear.

We have a secret. We will put him off the scent.'
So Aaron that day addressed the people, saying:
'With your loins girded, sandals on your feet,
Staff in your hand, you shall be ready. So says the Lord.
For the time is with us. You shall eat the flesh of the lamb
Roasted, eat it in haste. And the bread your eat with it
Shall be unleavened, shall be a bread of haste,
With no time for the leavening. And you shall
Season your meat with bitter herbs, that the
Bitterness of the exile shall be in your mouths
At the very door of the exodus. Kill now and
Pray as you kill, for you kill in the name
Of the Lord's Passover.' So the knives came down
On the necks of the lambs, and Pithom was
All blood and bleating for a space. Passover,
Some said, what is Passover? Moses explained
In his old halting way: 'We call it Passover,
And shall call it Passover till the end of our race,
For tomorrow we pass over from death to life.
And this strange supper we take tonight
In a ceremony. We shall have need of ceremonies.
To remind us who we are. What we are.
Till the end of our race. And the lamb we kill,
Each of our households, the lamb we eat
Is an offering to the Lord, who leads us
In our passing over from death to life.' But of that other
Passing over he did not for the moment speak,
Learning fast the beneficent wiles of the leader.
So Aaron said: 'On the lintels of your dwellings
And on the doorposts, you shall daub some of the
Lamb's blood, as a sign.' As a sign of what?
So the bolder asked, and Aaron said: 'As a sign
Of the primal sacrifice, wherein we kill,
And of the second sacrifice, wherein we eat,

Marking the place where 'we eat" [beneficent wiles].
The daubing was done and inspected, and, on the fires,
The tender flesh seethed, while in the ovens
The heard heavy bread was baked. So at nightfall
All were ready to sit, girded, sandalled,
The children excited, and there was laughter,
Even song, for the time was coming. 'The time is coming,'
They said, but not really believing,
For this was a ceremony only of deliverance.
But in Aaron's house where all the blood of Amram
Sat, fingering bitter herbs, 'The time is coming',
Moses said, and shuddered. 'This is Passover,
And will be so till the end of our race, to mark
The hour of his passing over.' Shuddering. 'But it is a
Terrible thing, a terrible burden, and the
Burden is just beginning.' He put his head in his hands,
But Miriam held his shoulders, saying: 'Courage.
Courage.' Then all suddenly listened.
But there was nothing to hear. 'The silence,' Aaron said,
'Strikes like a new noise.' Then Moses heard.
'He is coming. God help them. He is coming. Now.'
Then, from afar, a scream, and another,
And soon the sound of wailing. They sat silent,
The meat grown cold on the table, listening.
Then the noise of a nearing wind at the door,
And the door shaking, but then the shaking ceased,
And the wind passed over.
                              In the imperial palace
They heard the wailing without, even Pharaoh heard,
And his queen, in the innermost chamber, listened dumbly.
The infant prince slept in his cradle, placed in the heart
Of a magical pentacle, and the chief magician,
His assistants all about him, intoned, intoned:
'For the safety of the house and all within it.

May the first nameless, who guards the doors of the eyes,
Be doubly watchful. May the second nameless,
Who sits in the doorways of the ears, be this night aware
Of the rustling and breathing of the malign intruder.
May the third nameless, who lives suspended in the
Air of the nostrils, smell out the evil of him
Who approaches with the intent of evil...' A little cry
From the cradle, and the king froze, and the queen,
But they bent over and Pharaoh said: 'He is dreaming.
It is a good dream – see, he smiles in his sleep.
My precious. See, he holds out his little arms.'
And he lifted the child from his cradle and held him, crooning,
Like any father, then said: 'No harm, no harm,
No harm shall come to him, for he is my precious.'
A sudden scream from afar stopped the magician's chant
An instant, but he continued: 'And the nameless one
Who sits in the cup of the navel...' Pharaoh said:
'Be quiet. What was that?' And a minister, soothing:
'A servant, majesty. The child of a servant.'
Pharaoh whispered: 'Nothing shall. Nothing.
Stand round us with your torches. Burn your incense.
Say your prayer. Say it.' So the magician intoned:
'Gods of the seven worlds, hear, hearken.
Let the word of your servant be sweet in the ear
Of the guardians of the living. Let no evil
Touch your servant this night, let the dark be
Beneficent, and the vapours of the night
Be like the balm of the morning. Let the souls
Of the evil dead lie in sleep, unenticed
By the smell of smoke that puts out the light
Till the morning comes again, and the world is living
And the sun blesses and there is nothing more to fear.'
Pharaoh looked down on his child, cradled in his arms,
Looked and looked and did not believe and looked

Incredulously towards his queen and all looked and
None was in any doubt as a bank of candles
Flickered as in the draught of a great wind,
And from Pharaoh went up the cry of an animal,
Filling the chamber, the palace, spilling into the night,
Spilling into one pair of ears in Pithom, those
That had listened to fieldmice chatter and bats at nightfall.
The palace took up the cry and gongs and drums
Turned it to a geometry of lamentation,
While, like a thing of wood or metal, the king
Carried the child blindly, the mother following,
Choked in pain the gongs muffled, till they stood
Before a god of metal and Pharaoh whispered:
'What do I do now? Beg you to comfort him
On his passage through the tunnels of the night?
Beseech you to remember that he is still
Of your divine flesh, and to restore him to the light
Where he is – needed? Or do I see you already
As very hollow, very weak, impotent, a sham?
Am I born too early or too late? Does heaven
Remake itself? Has the dominion passed over
To that single God who was neither sun nor moon
But the light of both? But in your eyes there is nothing.
Your head is the head of a bird.'
The mother took the tiny body, weeping under the gongs,
And Pharaoh turned his back on the god, looking towards
Goshen, Moses, saying, 'Did you hear my cry?
And the cries of the other fathers of Egypt, mothers
Of Egypt? Go, then. Take your women and your
Unscathed children. Take your cattle and sheep
And your wretched possessions. Leave my people in peace.
Go, serve your God in what manner you will.
And come no more into Egypt.' And said again:
Rise up and go forth among my people,

Both you and the people of Israel, and go,
Serve the Lord, as you have said.
Take your flocks and your herds and bless your freedom
Be gone. And bless me also. Me also.

7

THE EXODUS

Before dawn, with a foredawn wind blowing,
With the blowing of ram's horns, answering
From tribe to tribe, under the moon and stars,
They got themselves ready, hardly able to believe it,
Many sad at leaving the evil known for the unknown good,
Especially as the hovels emptied of chattels,
The meagre good were roped to carts, and
Home, such as it was, dissolved with the
Fading of the stars. There were tears enough
As the cocks crew, answering from
Village to village. The cows were milked in haste
And, lowing, herded for the journey. A choral bleat
Of sheep drowned the horn and the cock-crow. Oxen
Were harnessed. While Aaron marshalled the tribal leaders
And then the leaders marshalled the tribes,
Moses walked among them all, cutting off thought,
For thought was mostly doubt of himself, seeing
The women with child, the children, the champing old
Lifted on to ox-carts. The stars were gone,
The east promised another day of fire,
The desert beckoned. Miriam released her doves
And her doves flew eastward, into the light
That was not yet cruel light. Dathan was a flame
About the cart whereon the treasury was loaded,
Gold, jewels, all Egyptian bribes. Then Moses spoke

To the God within him, saying: 'Be with me, be
With me,' raising his staff, setting his face
With smarting eyes to the east, and so it began,
The ragged exodus, with none to oppose them,
Through the delta land, through scrub, then to the desert,
Already, as the sun warmed, the lineaments
Of fatigue, despair, the promise of rebellion
Among some who, tasting that word *freedom*,
Were ready enough to spit it out of a dry mouth,
Longing sickly for the slave's day, the known evil.
So Pithom was empty. In the empty house of Aaron
A lone dog crunched the paschal bone. In the
Empty heart of Pharaoh bitterness
Found a house, then the house grew to a palace,
Then massive portals of the palace heaved to opening,
After the funeral, one of many, the priests
Giving unctuous comfort, saying: 'It will pass
As a bad dream passes. For the pestilence is gone,
The rivers flow silver not red, the air is
Filled with the song of birds not the buzz of gnats
And the fretful cry of locusts. The land, you will see,
Will be fruitful again, your loins, you will see,
Will be fruitful.' But the bereaved wept.
'The evil,' spoke the priests, 'that visited our land
Was an emanation of an evil people.
But the Israelites are no longer with us: the gods
Gave us a sign to drive them out of our midst.
And lo they are gone…' At Pithom, in the empty mudpits,
A scribe drank palm-wine with an overseer of workers,
His occupation, for the moment, gone. 'Quiet,' said the scribe.
'The silence is a sort of memory of their noise.'
'Not quiet in the other mudpits,' the overseer said.
'He should never have done it. Now all the slaves –
Greeks, Berbers, the rest – want to go to the desert,

To do sacrifice to what they call their gods.
Of course, it could all be a coincidence –
The plague, the flies, the locusts. But the
Blood was real, though. Red, thick,
As any in a slaughterhouse. All against nature.
It was as if nature went wrong for a time.
And these – ' He gestured towards the huge absence.
'These took advantage. They cause it, no.
They pretended to cause it. Cunning.' The scribe said:
'This too is against nature. This not having slaves.
How does one build a city without slaves?
A civilisation – do you know that word? – without slaves
Is totally against reason, meaning nature.
You have to have slaves.' So they drank palm-wine
To protect themselves from the evil emptiness.
In that other emptiness, nearly a day's march done,
The emptiness began to fill with the
First of the new signs: a dust-cloud swirling
And many fearful and talking of being lost,
We're lost already, and look at this evil dust
Enveloping us, I said we should never have left,
At least we were safe there. The words of Moses
Relayed through leaders to tribe after tribe:
'You say we are lost. But we are not lost.
You see this cloud of dust. It is God's sign
That he is with us. See how the wind
Drives the cloud before us. God works through
Everything. Even a cloud of dust. God works
Through the smoke and rain. And dust of the desert.
God works through this pillar of cloud. See –
How it moves ahead of us. It bids us follow.'
Follow, some said, *follow where?* The answer was ready
On the lips of the leaders: 'The promised land.
Where else.' *We shan't see much of it.*

Not with the dust in the way. And then there's night.
What do we follow at night? 'The Lord,' said Moses,
'Will think of something.' And, indeed, at nightfall
A blinding company of fireflies, was it fireflies?,
Flashed into view. *Fireflies? Glowworms?* 'Let's follow,'
Moses said. A pillar of fire, moving ahead of them.
They followed, marvelling some, some grumbling.
How did they know it was not Egyptian magic,
Leading them back to slavery? Ah, slavery, some said.
The word is worse than the thing. But they followed.
And, in the council-chamber, the Lord Pharaoh
Followed his ministers' words distractedly,
His ears still filled with the sobbing of his queen
And his own sobbing. 'The shock of the people, majesty,
Has been, naturally, profound. It is manifested,
So to speak, in a slow numbing
Illness of doubt. Such doubt has not
Previously been known.' And 'The whole concept of the
Monarchy is inevitably in jeopardy,
Since there seems, in the eyes of the commonalty,
To have been a withdrawal of divine power.' And Pharaoh:
'What reports from the worksites, my lords?' They answered:
'Majesty, the recent riots have been contained.
There has been what is termed in this message here
A slackening of fibre, the sense of a
Silent but massive insolence in the face of the
Threat of…' And Pharaoh: 'Yes yes yes, and of course
The great evil is already a great dream.
Except among the bereaved.' So one said:
'Wounds heal, majesty. A truism, but true.' Pharaoh answered:
'Anger does not heal. Hatred. But then of course
Comes doubt – doubt as to the validity
Of the whole ancient system. New modes of justice.
New gods. Can there be new gods?' The chief magician:

'The gods, as I have said, majesty, subsist
Outside time. Only in time is change possible.
There are no new gods. You may, majesty, take that
As an irrefutable fact.' Then a minister:
'History, as our records show, is full of the
Inexplicable. The sudden famine, the muddying of the Nile,
Plagues, storms – Nature is wayward, self-willed.
But this has nothing at all to do with the gods.'
Pharaoh said: 'Vague theology, half-chewed theory.
What is to be done? What practical measures
Offer themselves? There shoring up of a whipped monarchy
With the gods yawning…' The chief magician said:
'With respect, your divine majesty, such cynicism
Is in itself a corroborative of the already increasing
Popular lack of confidence in the…' A minister
Spoke firmly: 'The following narrative is no lie.
The Pharaoh, out of his divine benevolence,
Granted the request of the Israelite work-force
That they be permitted to do sacrifice
To their god in the desert. The period of leave requested
Was three days.' Pharaoh saw. 'How many days
Have they now been out of Egypt? Five, is it not?'
Five, five. 'So', Pharaoh pronounced.
'We bring them back. Nothing could be simpler.'
Nothing simpler. Smiles, but he did not smile.
At the end of the fifth day in the desert, Aaron spoke,
Dissatisfied, to Moses, looking ahead,
Pharaoh and Pithom already far in the past:
'The mistake, I say, lies in the organisation.
Old men, hereditary leaders of tribes and clans –
What true leadership can you expect from them?
They will be good enough at sitting in tents, cross-legged,
Giving judgments on marriage and property. But for a
Desert march…' Moses looked back at Pithom,

Into the sunset, faintly troubled at something
He must wait for time to define, and said: 'I know.
But this is no time to reorganise.' Aaron cried:
'We cannot survive if we do not. Already
Water discipline is bad. Food is stolen,
Selfishly hoarded. We need police, weapons,
A disciplinary court.' Moses said: 'The time is not yet.
We are not yet out of Egypt.' Joshua spoke:
'We're a five days' march out of Pithom. As for Egypt,
It belongs to our past, a past to be wiped out.
We are already living in the future.
Perhaps Aaron is too old to feel the flame of the future.
We organise in a new way – from within.
Not the Egyptian way. He talks of police,
Of disciplinary courts. That won't be our way.' –
'There is only one way', said Aaron hotly. But Moses:
'Not yet. I say again not yet. Nor is the past
To be wiped out. If all others forget,
If even Egypt forgets, we have to remember.
He brought us out of Egypt. Write that in your hearts.'
Then Miriam spoke: 'Many of our women, I fear,
Still have their hearts in Egypt. All they remember
Is gossip around the fountain at nightfall,
The daily baking of bread. They whine for it –
The bread of Egypt.' Joshua said: 'Even the young,
A few of them, talking about going back. To the
Only life they knew – whips and tyranny
As part of the order of nature. But I dealt with them.'
Moses smiled, asked how. 'Talked with them,
I and some of the other progressives.' Moses said:
'A good word, progressive. Progress means
Going forward. No matter to what. Just forward.
Tomorrow we go forward to meet the water.' –
'Water to cross?' asked Aaron. And Moses: 'Hardly.

No boats, no bridging, no fording places.
We have to keep to the western shore, upstream.'
Joshua said: 'Still on Pharaoh's soil. Or sand.
I somehow still feel him breathing down my neck.'
'Let us', smiled Moses, 'now do what must be done –
Go round the encampments. See to the sick.
Soothe the querulous. Put our
Fractious children to bed.' Smiling. They all smiled,
With the first faint lines forming on mouth and brow
Of loving exasperation.
        And Pharaoh said,
From his chariot, in his ornate armour, the lines forming
Of geometrical pursuit, the squadron leaders
Calling out names, said to his chief of staff:
'A minimum of violence you understand.
We are not fighting a war. There are no army.
Threats, however, will be much in order. Hostages,
Especially high ones. As for Moses...' *Moses, sir?*
'No violence, no. He is to be brought back.
Stand trial. A public execution. Formal charge.
Formal arrest. The charge? All the charges in the world –
Blasphemy, disaffection, treason, murder.
Very much murder.'
        In rocky terrain, at sunset,
Joshua sat alone, fashioning a bow. Arrows,
Already fashioned, lay neatly by him. Then he saw,
Out of the sun, a cloud of moving dust,
He peered narrowly, then ran to make his report.
But Moses already had heard, saying to Aaron:
'You hear nothing?' – 'Nothing unusual.' Moses said:
'Pharaoh must know I can hear him. We expected this.'
Joshua running towards them, pointing. 'A cloud of dust,'
Moses said. 'The dust of his chariots. The masters
Are coming to reclaim their property.' And Joshua:

'What do we do? What do we fight with? I always said
That sooner or later it would be a matter of fighting.' –
'Sooner or later, yes,' said Moses. 'But not now.
We do not fight the Egyptians. Nor do we
Go back into slavery. What is left to us?
We progress, Joshua. We move on.' Joshua, gulping:
'I say it with respect, but – ' And Moses: 'Yes, I am mad.
And our cause is mad. And the Lord God is mad.'
But, those miles distant, at nightfall, Pharaoh was saying:
'They will never cease to be slaves. Slaves
To hunger and thirst, no doubt, at this very moment.
At least we can liberate them from that. Slaves
To geographical circumstance. They cannot progress.
They can, of course, go sideways like crabs. But,
Whatever they do, they are certainly pincered.'
At first light, sir? 'Oh yes', said the Lord Pharaoh.
'Their humiliation must be clearly visible.'
But, those miles distant, at nightfall, Moses stood
On a rock, looking down into a swirl of waters.
A wind blew from the west. The voices in his head
Were louder than the turbulent Sea of Reeds.
Why could we not stay in Egypt? At least we were fed.
At least we slept in a bed. Let us go back to
Slavery, as you call it. If that was slavery,
What name do we find for this? Are there not enough
Graves in Egypt? Dathan's words. Dathan,
Truculent with his rebels, crying out:
'Are there not enough graves in Egypt,
Since you bring us into the desert to find them here?
I was well enough off in Egypt. The lords of Egypt
Could be generous to those they knew were their friends.
Are there any ready to return with me to Egypt?'
And then the shame of it, Joshua's discovery:
Dathan and his runagates, stuffing into sacks

The Israelite treasury, then, discovered, crying:
'We were just protecting the treasury, no more.
There are thieves among us. I know what you are thinking.
But we have no such intention. We are all together in this.
We trust Moses. We trust Aaron. We trust you, Joshua.'
Then Joshua and some more of the young progressives,
Hit out, hit. Warm in his cloak, Moses
Reviewed all this sadly, snatching sleep,
Praying even in his sleep, then waking to the
First streak of dawnlight, aware of
Some change that had dawned in his sleep.
The wind was blowing out of the dawn.
'The wind,' he whispered, 'is blowing out of the…'
And then: 'Lord, if it be your will, if it be your will.'
He stood, praying as others came to see
The morning over the waters. They looked down in awe
At the waters ruffled by the wind out of the dawn,
A wind that seemed, oh God, to be parting the waters
As a comb parts hair. 'Look,' Aaron said,
'See what the wind is doing to the waters.'
But they could not see what the wind was doing to the
Vanguard of Pharaoh's army, the pillar of the cloud
Swollen and all about the horsemen, the sand in their eyes,
And in their horses' eyes, hindering the advance,
Nor were their eyes turned to the west. Into the east,
As the sun rose, moved the Israelites, towards
Moses on the shore, making his decision, offering
A wordless prayer, stoutly raising his staff,
Then Moses, first, into the whistling wind,
Into the hair-parting of the Sea of Reeds,
Aaron after, the others after Aaron, timidly at first
But then with confidence growing – men, women,
Children, sheep, cattle, ox-carts, the young
Strong, fearless, astounded at something in the heavens,

Unseen of the others, pointing, then hurried on,
The waters seething on either side of them,
But the channel near-dry and safe.
                              At the water's edge
The cavalrymen of Egypt stood hesitant, seeing
Moses and Aaron on the further shore, helping,
Bidding hurry, the eyes of Moses on the army
About which a dust-storm whirled and howled, seeing
One pair of eyes for the last time. And there were the eyes
Of Pharaoh, seeing trickery, not more, evil magic,
Pharaoh calling: 'Why the hesitation? Why the delay?
The way is open. Go for them.' So the charioteers
Went hurtling into the channel, seeking the further bank.
Some of the old and feeble were slow in reaching.
(A donkey grew stubborn, a cart-wheel broke). But the wheels
Of the chariots did not break, rather mud and reeds
Clogged them. Then the wind changed.
The wind changed and the water tumbled in,
And Pharaoh did not think now of mere magic,
Seeking men swimming but trapped in mud and reeds,
The horses struggling, the chariots overturned,
Dumb cries in the tumult of water. The eyes of Pharaoh
And the eyes of Moses sought each other, but in vain…
So the crossing was accomplished. The Israelite camp
Was joyous that night with fires and wine,
The flute, the harp, the drum, and Miriam
Led the maidens in song and dance, singing:

    The Lord is our captain,
    His helmet the sun, the moon his shield.
    The night sky is pierced by his arrows.
    Halleluiah.
    The hands of the Lord were with us.
    They pushed the water aside and aside

Like the hands of the farmer dividing grain.
Halleluiah.
The horse and his rider were cast into the waters.
The Lord is just, quick to smite the tyrant,
Quick to heal the oppressed, comfort the afflicted.
He dips his sword in honey, in balm his spear.
Halleluiah.
We have seen the wonders of the Lord – in fire, hail,
Plague, famine, in the parting of the waters.
He leads us to a green abode, bursting like a pod with richness.
Praised for his name for ever and ever.
Halleluiah halleluiah.

But there some who listened to the tale of a child,
The child repeating and repeating to the questioners:
'It was heaven, I say. I saw it. God was there.'
How do you know? Who has ever seen God?
'It was God, I say. A beast with a man's face.
And he was all made out of gold.' *What kind of beast?*
'Like that one there with a cow, his mother.'
'It's the children that see heaven', said someone drunk,
'That's well-known. That's written down in books.' –
'I saw it, I tell you,' said the child, 'crossing the water.'
Eat up your cake and go to bed. 'I saw it.'
Moses grave amid the revelling, spoke to the elders:
'You must make it clear to the tribes. That the worse is to come.
It is good to rejoice now. If we are truly rejoicing
In the Lord. His goodness. His omnipotence.'
And he looked with stern sadness on a
Passionate embrace in the shadows, the lurching
Of three men full of wine. 'Tomorrow,' he said,
'Will be a hard day. Especially for some.' An elder spoke:
'The worst is to come, you say. It would be, surely,
Unwise to speak to the people of that. Is it not enough

To live for the day, hoping that the next day
Will bring sight of the land we are promised?
The day's march is enough, the repose at nightfall.' –
'No,' said Moses. 'We enter on our inheritance
In the knowledge that freedom is a bitter gift.
It will bring many days of hardship. Shortage of
Water and of food. Sickness. Death. Cursing and grumbling.
Your task is to teach. The agonies of freedom.'
Another elder said: 'It is hard for a man to keep
Authority with such a slogan.' But Moses, with energy,
With bitterness: 'Must we build on false promises?
It is dangerous to think in terms of the day.
If we eat and drink what the day sends
We shall have nothing for the morrow. The day is for
Slaves. Slaves. There is a bigger time for men
Who are free. Let us begin by thinking of the
Week. The week.' And with his staff he traced
Seven strokes in the earth. 'The Lord took six days
To make the heavens and the earth. On the seventh day
He rested. We shall follow the Lord. The seventh day
Shall be called the Sabbath. On that day we shall rest.
Think of the Lord. Drink in the new strength from the Lord.
And this this this shall be the law.' *A law?* 'And those who
Break the law must be punished.' A third elder said:
'Punished? How punished?' Moses smiled a little,
Saying: 'I will start to think of punishments later.
It is for the present enough to think of the
Lord's displeasure. There will come a day
When that will seem punishment enough. Punishment enough.'
Dathan came with his friends to the assembly, drunk,
A bowl of palm-wine in his hands, saying, slurring:
'Moses, we have come to express our
Complete confidence in your leadership.' Moses said:

'You will always have confidence, Dathan, when these things go
    well.' –
'No, no,' said Dathan. 'Well or ill, we
Acknowledge you as our undoubted leader.' And Moses,
Sternly: 'I am not your leader, Dathan. The Lord God –
He is your leader. I am but his instrument.
Never forget the Lord.' But Dathan said, tottering:
'Oh, this is a night for rejoicing, not for
Thinking about the Lord. We ask you, Moses,
In token of our amity and awareness of our confidence,
To drink wine with us.' To which Moses replied:
'I have but a weak head, Dathan. But I am
Sincerely grateful for your confidence.'
Then, with a drum-thud, a flute-skirl, and a
Sweep of the harp-string, the evening came to an end.
You must make it clear to the tribe that the
Worst is to come. The worst. Starting tomorrow.

8

MIRACLES OF THE DESERT

Sand-caked, sweat-blind, inexpressibly weary,
Through the scorching wilderness, Aaron panted:
'Do you know where we are?' And Moses, squinting about him,
Not showing weariness, upright, said: 'The tribes
Called it the wilderness of Shur. We cross this wilderness
To reach Elim, Elim.' And Aaron said: 'What
Is at Elim?' – 'Palms. Tamarinds. Water. It will be a
Hard climb.' And Aaron: 'Can they make the hard climb?
They need water in order to reach that water.'
'They drink too much,' said Moses. 'The tribal elders
Are too old to set a good example there.' –

'As I said,' cried Aaron, 'as I always said.'
I'd give all his Promised Land to be
Coming home from work in Goshen. Water.
A bite to eat. More water. So they were all saying.
They came to rock, a rocky land, and Moses,
Showing no weariness, comforting the snarling weary,
Saw two young men, not of his tribe, but of Joshua's tribe,
Wresting from a wailing group of the old a water-skin,
Then drinking thirstily, spilling wantonly in the sand
Much water in their haste and greed. The old wailed.
And Moses said: 'Theft, my brothers, theft.
We will have no theft. They have prudently saved their water.
You have imprudently used up yours. Now you steal.'
An insolent youth said: 'Moses, this is the law.
The law that this desert of yours has taught us.
God made them weak. God makes us strong', water
Dripping from his insolent young mouth. And Moses said:
'The strength of the body is nothing. Is a crocodile
Better than a man? Men, my young brothers,
Are strong in a different way. What a man has
He has through foresight and prudence.
You shall not take from him what he has.' And the other youth:
'What will you do to us, Moses?' Sneering. 'Send down
Another plague? You would do far better to
Lead us to water. Including these weak and
Prudent snivellers here.' And Moses said:
'I will lead you to water. In time. But now I tell you
That you must not steal.' Grinning: 'No more than that?' –
'No more,' said Moses, 'for the moment. The time shall come
When we will try a man for stealing. Will exact
On the common behalf just punishment. But that time
Is not yet. For now, think that you are
Displeasing to the Lord. And that the Lord
Could strike you down if he wished. But that the Lord

Would prefer you to learn how to be men.
Not crocodiles.' And he passed on. And they sneered.
But did not sneer at Joshua, the young, the muscled
Progressive. So the thirsty journey continued,
Until, in that rocky wilderness, under a copper sky,
The sun all burning bronze, they came upon
A spring, a feeble spring running through rock,
And they feebly cheered, limping with their
Pots and cups and water-skins, while Joshua
And Caleb and the young of the tribe of Levi
Watched grimly, keeping guard, letting the old
To the stream first, trembling with relief and joy as they…
And then the old man screeched feebly: 'No. No.
 Nobody can drink this. Salt. It's salt.' Groans
And spittings and the mutter of anger, then more than a mutter.
The sneering youth: 'He said he'd lead us to water.
But what kind of water he didn't say.' And Dathan:
'You said you knew this place like the back of your hand.
Every rock and spring you said you knew,
Every tree and stone. But you were lying.
Lying, weren't you? *The Lord* was lying too.
If he exists, that is. What now, great one,
Do you propose to do?' Moses, wearily,
Humbly even: 'One cannot always. Be exactly sure.
We have been taken. So much off the path. That I knew.
Strayed sheep. Stragglers. I promise you, promise.'
Faltering. But Dathan cried: 'All promises.
Promised freedom, promised land, promised
Milk and honey, promised, promised. We can
Do without the milk and honey. We want water.
Water.' That one word taken up – *water water
Water water*. And later, to the night sky,
Moses spoke, wretched, solitary: 'Lord Lord,
What shall I do with these peevish children? Lord,

Tell me what I must do. Man is strangely made.
Fill him with bread, or water, and his spirit
Comes alive, ready to brood on heaven, on you, on
Human freedom. But let the meanest of your gifts
Elude him, and he croaks like a fractious frog.
Tell me, Lord, tell me. What shall I do?'
And what the Lord said or seemed to say,
Not from the silver and empurpled firmament
But from some dank small room in the skull of Moses,
Even in sunlight, the dead tree-trunk in his arms,
Ready to hurl. 'Throw,' said Moses. 'Believe.'
And Aaron hurled the trunk into the salt stream,
Unbelieving. 'Now,' said Moses, 'let them drink.
Let them at least taste it.' Some tasted,
With sour faces of unbelief, then, believing, drank,
The wonder of thirst satisfied occluding
Simple wonder. Joshua, Caleb, others policed
The thirsty, screeching their joy, while Aaron said:
'How much longer will they have to be given miracles?
They cry like babies, expecting the breast
Always ready to be bared to them.' But Moses:
'They must be led easily. Easily.
They have to be weaned into freedom.' And the water
Bubbled in preternatural clarity and sweetness,
In potability, never-ending, and Dathan grinned,
Sleek with water, in forgiveness. 'Weaned, weaned.'
So the weeks passed, the days notched by Moses,
And the Sabbath observed, though not clearly understood,
With the cries of *water water* renewed, the journey
Upwards, over rocky land, the old and sick faltering,
The young learning to help the old and sick,
And Moses as weary as any, showing his age,
Till at last they reached a summit of rock and looked down,
And Joshua opened his mouth in joy and a cry:

'Elim?' They looked. Mountain beyond, but below
Springs, tamarind, palm, green grass like a
Torrent of emeralds. 'This,' said Aaron, 'this
Is the true miracle.' So they descended and encamped,
Some thinking that this was already the promised land,
The sheep and cattle going hungrily to grass,
The young bathing, playing in the springs,
The hungry eating dates from the date-palms,
Sheltering under the palms. 'The promised land?'
But Moses smiled and shook his head. At night,
Under the incredible heaven, the flute sounded,
The drum, the harp, there was song and dance,
And Moses, walking, came across love in the shadows,
A couple starting guiltily as the shadow
Of Moses came upon them, Moses saying,
Gently, always gently: 'You, my brother,
I do not know. The woman I think I know. Sister,
Are you not the wife of Eliphaz?' She nodded,
Dumbly, and the man was ready to speak, truculent.
'Eliphaz', said Moses, 'is old, near-blind.
He is content to play with his children, yours.
Youth is drawn to youth and to the
Lusty pleasures of the bed. I know, I know.
But it is a sinful bed.' The man replied,
Truculent: 'There is no sin in pleasure.'
'Nor', said Moses, 'should there be pleasure in sin.
For good or ill, a family should not be broken.
Your husband, sister, if he knew, could
Rightly put you away. And the children would grieve,
Lacking their mother. It is a bad business.'
The woman spoke. 'He knows nothing. We have been careful.' –
'Not careful enough', said Moses, 'to prevent my knowing.
If I know, others know. He will know. Soon, if not yet.
We face the hard task of building a nation.

The bricks of that edifice are the families.
If the families crack the whole structure totters.'
The man said: 'We are a very small crack. In a
Very small brick.' But Moses: 'Never think of yourself
As an exception that makes no difference to the whole.
For why should not everyone, if he so desires,
Be an exception? Only God is above the law.
But God works through the law. You, my children,
Are breaking the law.' The woman said: 'What will you do?'
And Moses: 'I have done all that I wish to do.
For the moment. But remember – in your bed
Another lies, a third. He parted the waters.
He killed the masters who enslaved you. And already
You destroy what he bids you build.' And so he left them.
The woman said to the man: 'Does he have a wife?' –
'He's old', said the man. 'He's beyond passion. Love.'
And so they fell once more to their embrace,
But she started, uneasy, thinking she heard
One of the children crying, and though he tried
To imprison her once more in his embrace,
She resisted, rose and left him. In an embrace
Wholly sanctified, Aaron and Eliseba,
She of the smooth brow and sweet tongue, lay,
Quiet after love, the children sleeping,
Fruit in a bowl, water in a pitcher near by,
And Eliseba said: 'Why then not here? Here
Is everything.' But Aaron said: 'Because the promise
Is to be fulfilled elsewhere, not here. Simple,
Simple as that.' But she: 'Will we live to see it?' –
'If by *we*', said Aaron, 'you mean our people –
Yes, I believe so. If by *we* you mean yourself,
Myself – I am not sure. But I believe our children
Will see it.' She said: 'We could settle here
Very comfortably. Fine pastures. Much water.

The whole place laughs and rings with water.' He:
'No. We have to have more than a mere oasis.
We have to build a city, build a temple.' – 'Have to?' –
'Have to, yes. Call it the fate of a nation.'
She mocked gently, smiling: 'Those big words.'
Aaron said: 'I do not, I think, believe
There is anything after this life. We die alone
And go alone into the dark. Us – you, me,
Each and all of the others. But all of us
Made into a nation – that is different. Here is a
Man called Aaron and a woman called Eliseba.
There is a new kind of human being we call Israel.' –
'And where' she asked, 'is this new kind of human being?'
'Trudging through the desert,' Aaron answered,
'Seeking the appointed place. And still being made.
It is a formless lump so far – it has to be moulded,
Kneaded, like bread. But when it is made,
This new being, when it lives and breathes and follows
The laws that sustain it, there will be no end to it.'
She thought and said: 'There have been others, nations.
They died. You told me once that Egypt is dying.'
Aaron said: 'We are different. We cannot die,
Because, for the first time, the nation will not be
Greater than the smallest within it. It will live for ever
While men and women will dies, but it will not live
By eating the flesh of those within it. Not like Egypt.
Do you understand?' She grimaced, saying: 'No.
We had better sleep. Did he tell you all this?' –
'Some of it,' Aaron said. 'Some of it
I worked out for myself.' She said: 'Poor Moses.
Alone. No wife. No children. Does he even know
If they are still alive?' Aaron said: 'He does not doubt it.
Nor do I doubt it. They will be there, waiting,
Under Mount Horeb. That,' he smiled, 'is one reason

Why we hurry. Why we leave early tomorrow.'
But so many left with regret, some weeping,
Some loud in anger at once more engaging the desert,
When here were date-palms and springs and rest and pasture.
Soon hunger and thirst, under that metal sky,
Sand and sand and sand beneath, raised voices:
Good fish and meat and bread, onions, garlic,
In Egypt, Egypt. Why did you take us from Egypt?
We were happy there. And some spoke of the oasis
As a home they were wrenched from, till Moses rose and cried:
'Will you never cease to complain? Why God chose you
From all the peoples of the earth I do not know,
Will never understand. Did you not have your chance
To fill your store-bags in the oasis of Elim?
You were careless, wasteful, improvident. Ill-disciplined,
Selfish, totally ungrateful. You say you lack bread.
You say you lack meat. Well, believe me –
You shall have flesh to eat this evening and
In the morning bread to the full. You have the
Lord's promise, through me, that this will be so.
And now you smile, changing the set of the face
Like a child that howls to be picked up and then sees
Its mother come running. Ah, I am sick of you',
Seeing the petulant, scolded children's faces,
Adding: 'But, God help me, you are all I have.'
But there was no petulance, only relief and wonder
When, at nightfall, a monstrous cloud of quails
Was thrown out of the sky. Joshua, Caleb,
The provident young, schooled by foreknowing Moses,
Were ready with the nets they had improvised,
And they caught the quails, and the quails were spitted
And roasted and eaten – another miracle,
And they were ready, picking the bones, to grow used to miracles.
Miriam said to Moses: 'You take credit for

A miracle when there is none. You told me
About the migration of quails when we were in Pithom
And I was scrubbing the dirt off you.' Moses smiled.
'I never take credit for miracles. Yes, the quails.
They rest at night in the scrublands. They are easily caught.
A miracle, I suppose, is the thing we need
Happening when we need it. I suppose now
They would like bread to sop up the drippings.' –
'Will they get their bread?' she asked, and Moses said:
'I said *in the morning*. I did not say which morning.
Have you heard of manna?' – 'Bread', she said, 'from heaven.' –
'True, it comes from heaven, even when it is the
Resin that falls from the tamarisk tree. I have tasted it.
It is blown by strong wind, lying like a gift on the ground.
A fine flakelike thing, fine as hoarfrost,
White as coriander weed, and the taste of it
Is the taste of wafers made with honey.' She smiled.
'A poem?' – 'A song', he said, 'sung by Jethro.
He taught me the song and I sang it to Zipporah.
I sang it about the body of Zipporah.' –
'How soon' she asked, 'shall I meet her? And see Ghersom?'
'Oh,' he answered, 'there will be more days of grumbling
And days of short-lasting joy. And, God help us,
There will be a time of bloodshed.' He brooded, but she
Asked no question. He, brooding, looking into the fire,
Saw enough blood in it. But one thing at a time,
For soon the tamarisk resin came blowing in, another miracle,
So many miracles, bread from heaven: they crammed their
    mouths,
Their baskets. There seemed no end to it, soon
No urgency in the gathering: it was always there.
But one day a family was manna-gathering blithely
And Caleb came to them, stern, to say: 'Come.
You must come with me. And bring your baskets.'

'What is this?' said the father. 'Why? Who are you?' –
'My name is Caleb, not that it matters. You,
Do you know the law of the Sabbath?' – 'What law? What
    Sabbath?'
The elders, sitting in judgment, were patient enough.
'The law', said the presiding magistrate,
'Has been clearly laid down. The Sabbath is for rest,
For thinking of the Lord's justice and goodness.
No journeying – so it is enjoined. No work.' But the father,
Spluttering, indignant, said: 'But we were hungry.
We were not working. We were gathering food.' –
'You must have your food ready on the eve of the Sabbath.
We make no distinction between kinds of work.
Shear the sheep, mend a tent, gather food –
It is all work, and it all fills time that should be filled
With the contemplation of the Lord. Work must not defile
The Sabbath of the Lord.' – 'Mad, it's madness!' –
'Oh, can you not see', the chief elder said, 'can you not –'
But Aaron, silently arriving, completed the sentence
And added more: 'Can you not see, you fool,
That if God rested from his work on the seventh day
Then man, made in God's image, must rest too?
That only to slaves is every day the same –
Toil, toil and again toil? That man, God's image,
Is not just toiling flesh but contemplative mind,
And for contemplation there must be leisure?
That leisure must not come capriciously,
Irregular, but in a known rhythm?
That leisure must be total?' And the elder added:
'Thus saith the Lord. Have *you*, friend,
Anything now to say?' And the man mumbled that he was
Sorry. 'This is a first offence? Very well, then:
Discharged with a solemn warning. And, ah yes –
Go hungry till tomorrow.' The father, mother,

Children looked glum at that. But Aaron smiled,
Saying: 'Tomorrow begins at sunset today.'
So they smiled and got them gone. The rule was mild
In those early days of the journey, the children of Israel
Truly children in the knowledge of the blessing of freedom,
The harshness of freedom. The blessing would be long delayed
In the eyes of the many, but the harshness they had known
Was nothing to what was to come: it was coming.

9

THE MOUNTAIN

They struggled through the wilderness of Rephidim,
Where there was no bounty of quails or manna,
And soon, with their bags and water-flasks long empty,
They yet found strength to stone Moses, stone him,
For there was no shortage of rock. Aaron, Joshua, Caleb,
Even Miriam were swift to protect him,
The whole tribe of Levi, stronger-hearted than the rest,
Was a jagged fortress about him, but even there
Despair rose and the old cry of *water water*.
He could only raise his face to the burning sky
And cry: 'What shall I do with this people?
Tell me, what shall I do?' The answering voice,
His own voice, was angry and strident, saying:
'Stride forth to the rocks. Strike the rocks
With your rod. They shall have their fill of water,
My thirsty people.' So he struck and struck,
Rock after rock after rock, and it gushed out,
Silver water, and bellies and vessels were filled with it.
There was little gratitude: miracles were their due.
And Dathan was even ready to doubt the miracle,
Saying to his cronies: 'See. Anyone can do it.'

He smote the rock with his cudgel, saying: 'See.'
And water trickled forth. 'Porous, you see.
This rock holds rain like a sponge. You hit it,
No more. The Lord God, indeed.
Cunning, cleverness. Anyone could have thought of it.'
So they went about, hitting out trickles. The Lord, indeed.
It seemed certain to many that the Lord was not with them,
Never more so than when, one night among rocks,
The night fires burning out, on the verge of the encampment
Rods struck, knives struck, rocks rained,
And where there had been night quiet was shrieking,
Cursing, bellowing, bleating, and the
Laugh of triumph in a strange tongue. A raid,
With the carrying off of cattle and women,
Men lying brained in the sick dawn. Moses saw
And said: 'The Amelekites. This is their territory.'
Joshua cursed: 'We are weak. We have no weapons,
None except these wretched arrows and bows.
I always said we should be ready for this.'
A tremulous elder kept saying: 'It is the Sabbath.
By my computation it is the Sabbath.
We need a ruling. Do we fight on the Sabbath?'
And Moses: 'Oh, yes. We fight on the Sabbath.'
Aaron looked on the crude weapons
Joshua had made, Joshua and some of the other,
And said: 'When did you make these?' Joshua answered:
'In my leisure hours, such as they are, and, of course, on the
    Sabbath.
There was nothing else to do except contemplate God,
And this, surely, does not count as work?' There was silence,
A rather embarrassed silence. A young man named Koreh
Broke it by saying: 'I have no experience of war,
Nor have any of us. Slaves are not warriors.
But I think I could suggest a simple strategy.'

Moses said: 'We are listening.' So they listened.
When the next night raid came they were ready with
Lambs laid out as decoys, temptingly bleating,
And, when the Amalekites appeared, Joshua and his
Warriors rushed out of the rocks with rocks and arrows
And killed and put to flight, killing with daggers
Dropped by the put to flight. 'Next time,' Koreh said,
'It will not be a little matter of a night raid.'
Nor was it. When, in strengthening light,
The Israelites, with goods and flocks and cattle,
Were ready at the mountain foot for the march,
Hidden among boulders on a high slope Moses stood,
With Aaron and Koreh, watching. He watched and saw,
In dust, the entire tribe of the Amalekites
Approaching in the distance. He raised his staff.
Joshua and his warriors, on a lower slope,
Hidden among rocks, armed with rocks, saw the sign.
The raiders came nearer, bold, seeing only
Tired wanderer and cattle and flocks,
And greed quickened their pace towards the prey.
So Joshua signalled and shocked them with a quick fire
Of arrows, till all the arrows were spent.
Then came the hurling of stones, stone after stone
After stone, for there was no shortage of rock.
They had not expected this, the Amalekites:
Howling, they turned tail, in spite of the
Howls of the leaders, their retreat thickening and growing.
And now was the turn of the hidden reserve,
Lurking behind the non-combatant Israelites,
Rushing on the rear, busy with rocks and daggers,
Picking up daggers. Carnage, delectable spoils
Of swords and spears, breastplates even, helmets,
For the Amalekites were a warlike people.
So as the Israelites trudged on their way,

There was a breastplate on Joshua, and a helmet,
And a dagger in a sheath – the general Joshua,
Close to Moses, and Aaron some way behind,
The office of Aaron somewhat less clear than it had been.
They trudged towards Midian, and the heart of Moses
Beat painfully as he said to himself: 'Thick and strong
It beats, the desert blood. In the women,
As much as in the men. What law prevents her
Yielding to some young red mouth of Midian,
Black-bearded, a storm in the pulse? And, if she has waited,
Believing me still to be among the living,
There begins the double burden – that of a man
With two families, two.' There it was, then,
At least, old territory, loved, fateful –
The solitary tree on the hill, the sacred mountain,
The wells of Midian and, yes, a group waiting,
Waving. Moses ceased to be a leader,
Breaking with an unwonted speed from the van of the progress,
Becoming the husband and father. Joshua smiled,
The Israelites waited in wonder. And so – Zipporah,
Ghershom grown, Jethro old, the sisters
(Some married, one dead), embraces, tears,
And embraces and tears in the tent of Zipporah
In the following dawn, Moses saying: 'My love,
It will take time for me. To be again what I was.'
And she: 'You have grown thin. You have lacked
Too long the roasted firstlings and the broths
Of herbs and mutton I cooked for you. Also the love.
You are very thin.' – 'Also old? Also very old?' –
'I did not,' she smiled, 'say that. But you need time
And rest to make those eyes lose their fierceness,
Those hard lines round your lips melt to tenderness.'
So they embraced, but a voice outside called: 'Moses!'
And Moses wearily smiled: 'So it will always be.

Israel lying in bed between us.' He donned his robe
And left the tent to hear news of fighting.
'Reuben and Judah?' he said. 'Impossible.'
'All too possible,' Joshua said. 'Tribal war.
It was some matter of a woman.' Bitterly, Moses:
'A woman. A woman of Reuben and a man of Judah.
Is that the story?' Joshua said: 'A man of Reuben,
Single, and a married woman of Judah.' –
'So,' said Moses, 'they've developed a taste for war.' –
'We shall all', said Joshua, 'need to develop that taste.' –
'But.' Moses cried: 'this is not a matter
Of repelling invaders. It is brother against brother.
Do not the followers yet see that we must be one,
One, one, not a loose parcel of tribes?'
Joshua said: 'To be truthful, the possession of weapons
Drove to the use of weapons.' – 'It is always so',
Sighed Moses. 'You must construct an armoury.
You must keep our weapons clean and locked away.
If we are to fight with nations – then, so be it.
But we are not to make war amongst ourselves.
How many are dead? – 'Only one dead,' said Joshua.
'A very small war. Caleb and I soon stopped it.' –
'Brother killed brother', sighed Moses. 'Cain and Abel
Back to life, or death. And was the man…?'
'The man,' Joshua said, 'was the single
 Man of Reuben, no longer able to love the
Married woman of Judah.' So they walked through the camp
And saw the adulterer, pitifully broken and rent,
Lying on the ground, and assembly fearful
As Moses spoke: 'This is no war but murder.
The law says that you shall not kill, but we
Make an exception to the law. For if the enemy
Seeks to kill you, then you may justly,
And out of the need of nature, kill him first,

If you can. But what is your enemy?
He is someone remote, of strange tongue, of evil intention.
You will meet many such enemies, believe me,
Before you cross to the land of the Lord's promise,
And even thereafter there will be enemies enough.
But we are one, of common custom and speech,
And – note this, note it well – chosen together,
As one people, as one family, for the special favour
And the special chastening of the Lord our God.
Therefore I say this to you: that the deed
That was done was no brave deed of warfare
But a foul act of murder. And if there was a murder,
There must of necessity be one accused of murder.
Let him come forward.' There was silence for a space,
And eyes turned to the ground, and the eyes of Moses
Saw that dead man as he had once been, alive,
Embracing lustily, and remembered his own words,
Gentle, warning, in vain. Sly, shamed eyes
Fixed on one young man, who now came boldly,
And Moses said, gently enough: 'What have you to say?' –
'I acted under order,' the youth said.
'We were ordered to attack the enemy.'
Moses said: 'There was no enemy.
A man killed a man and that is murder.
And what is the punishment for murder?
Let us hear from the heads of the tribes concerned.'
These came forward, doubtful, and Moses asked again:
'What is the punishment for murder?' The head of Judah
Said, full of the old way: 'The washing out of
Blood by compensation. Let the young man
Or his parents make good the loss of
An able-bodied member of our tribe.
Let us then have a warrior or a slave.
Or cattle. Or sheep. We can discuss the details now.'

But Moses cried: 'No! No! We cannot and must not
Value human life in terms of possessions.
For human life is precious and irreplaceable
And cannot be treated as a kind of money. So I say again:
What is the punishment for murder?' The leader of Reuben
Said, cunningly as he considered: 'If we cannot
Put a value on human life, then we cannot
Compute the punishment.' And Moses answered: 'That is
Right. And yet also wrong. For human life
Can be valued only in its own terms. So I say:
A life for a life. Which means: a death for a death.'
The silence was full of fear, and Joshua spoke
To break the silence, resolve the fear: 'How shall the
Murderer – What I mean to say is: how
Is it to be done?' Moses answered, sighing:
'Joshua, Joshua, to think of that now. Did you suppose
I intended his immediate execution for
His life is still a precious life.
The judges of his guilt must, as I see it,
Learn to revel in their own confusion, thinking:
Did he do it or did not? Can the witnesses
Be trusted? Did not perhaps the dead man
Drop dead in fright when he saw the knife approaching?'
And he looked on the butchered body and trembled, saying:
'You have hardly begun to conceive, any of you,
Of the preciousness of a human life.' Of this he spoke
To Jethro, in the pasture below Horeb,
Soothed by the old shepherd's trade, and Jethro said:
'Give them the law, then delegate, delegate.
Change now, now. This will not do,
This wearing out of one poor brain and body
In the service of so many. Organise, delegate.
And first, get rid of your hereditary chiefs.
Heredity is not enough, it does not of necessity

Qualify a man to rule. Then remember this:
The basis of good government is the ten,
The ten, the ten. Good junior officers –
Each one in charge of ten. Then senior officers,
Each one in charge of fifty. Then you climb
The ladder – very good men charged with a hundred.
And then at last the cream – the superb, the
Incorruptible leaders of a thousand.
God-fearing men, trustworthy, humorous,
Preferably young men. There is no great virtue in age.' –
'Men like Joshua, you mean,' Moses said.
'He is one who carries the new fire.
But first I must tend his fire for him. Also,
Warm my own hands by it.' – 'Joshua?'
Jethro said. 'Is he married?' Moses said not,
And Jethro sighed with a faint hope. 'All this,'
Moses said, 'will strike them as – subversive.' –
'Good,' said Jethro, 'good.' – 'Something like the
Organisation of an army.' And Jethro: 'So it is. You
Are an army. But an army of human souls:
Let none forget that. You will be fighting
Your way towards this land of milk and honey.
The zest is all in the fighting. It will be a long time
Before the cows and goats are born that will yield that milk,
And for that honey – the bees must gather. A bland diet,
Very bland.' And then the mountain shook,
As out of sleep, and Moses said: 'It sounds
As if I am to be summoned. Ah, God help me.'
Jethro smiled. 'That, my son, is a prayer
You will be able to deliver in person.' And Moses smiled,
And looked towards the rumbling of the mountain.
That day, with pain, he climbed it, saw the bush
That had once burned, but this time heard the voice
Come from the very peak, saying: 'Say this

To the house of Jacob, this to the people of Israel.
Say: If if if you will obey my voice
And keep my covenant, you shall be to me a
Kingdom of priests and a nation of holiness.
But the choice is theirs, the choice, I say, is theirs.
And if they choose this covenant with me,
Then let them spend two days in the holy rites
Of purifying themselves. On the third day
I will come in a thick cloud on the mountain top.
What I speak with you the people shall hear,
And may also believe you for ever. And the words of the covenant
Shall be set down on stone imperishable,
That they may be beheld by the eyes of men.'
The peak was silent, and so Moses descended
To the world of his waiting people, bidding craftsmen
Prepare two tables of stone for the covenant, speaking
Patiently, but with no hesitation,
No sense of the words being whipped from him, to his leaders:
'Thus I leave to you the duties of
Administering, of ordering, or judging.
The task which will long absorb my time,
My energy, and such poor brains as I have,
Will be the task of making the law of our people,
The law you will administer. The law
Is like the blood-channels of the body, or shall I say
That first there are the great trees of blood,
And then the numberless branches and twigs. It is the
Trunks that we must think of first, the solidities
Which even the weak of sight can see. The branches
And twigs can come later. First, we must remember
That the great laws come from God. They are the laws for all men,
And yet they are laws the world has not seen before.
But I say this to you, that so long as men shall live –
In freedom, unoppressed – it is on such laws

That their lives must be based. They must know that
These laws are sanctified by the Lord himself,
And they must see the ground from which the great trees spring
As the godhead that sustains them. God is not a
Demon of the rivers, or of fire or air.
He is not a stone idol – he is a spirit,
And it is as spirit that men must worship him.
So there shall be no making of gods of stone
or wood or iron or silver. Nor shall the name of God
Be thrown in the air like a ball or kicked like a pebble.
The very name is sacred and its use shall be sacred.
The day of rest, which is God's day, shall be sacred –
Given to the contemplation of the eternal,
While the body rests from labour. It shall be a day
For the family, and the family itself
Shall be seen on that day as sacred. Nay, the family
And the bond of marriage, and the children that are
The fruit of that bond – shall always be bound in a garland
Of love and honour. And what a man owns shall be sacred,
Since it comes from God – be it his goods or his life.
Both are inviolate – no killing, no stealing. Nay, more:
No coveting of the things our brothers possess,
For sin begins in desire. Above all, we are free,
Free beings, copies of that God
Who is the first and last free being – free
Even to choose to enter the covenant
With him, with him who made us. And now I ask:
'Will you accept the covenant?' And again he asked
Not the leaders alone but all the people:
'Will you accept the covenant?' The word bounced,
Echoed – *covenant covenant* – and the reply
Echoed and bounced all along the valley.
The tablets in his arms, the graver's tools
In the hands of Joshua, who was to be with him

The long climb of his absence, Moses began
To climb the mountain, slowly, Joshua after,
And the Israelites watched him leave – for how long? – their lives.
But Aaron was with them, Aaron still, in Aaron's hands
The rule, in Aaron's head the law, on Aaron's
Tongue the word. They watched, and Aaron watched,
Till Moses was lost to view, then turned to their lives,
Their grumbling wives, the cow in labour, sheep
With foot-rot, work and sleep, the common lot,
Thinking of God and Moses and the covenant
But not too much, having other things to do.

10

A RESTIVE PEOPLE

Up high on Horeb, with the evening coming on,
They looked at the rolling cloud that, somehow, beckoned,
And Moses nodded slowly, saying to Joshua:
'I must enter now. Do you understand? I must be
Entirely alone with the voice of all things. Make you
Camp somewhere down there, in the rocks' shelter.'
And Joshua asked: 'How long will it be?' Moses smiled.
'The world and the seas and the stars were made in
Six days. To make laws for the Israelites
May take somewhat longer. A good deal longer.
But I think we are well enough supplied.' Joshua said:
'It will be a bread and water matter.' – 'Bread and water
Will suffice me. At dawn and at sundown.
But you are a young man. Hunt by all means,
But do not wander too far. Remember – if all this
Should be too much for me – if –' But Joshua said:
'You are not to talk in that manner.' And Moses: 'I
Grow aware of my age. The laws of living and dying

Will not be suspended for a mere
Instrument of the Lord. There will be others.
Already this one shows signs of wear. Remember,
I say, that you are the next chosen.' – 'No,' said Joshua,
'There must be others before me – your brother –'
'Aaron,' said Moses, 'grows old too. And – I may say this –
The faith wavers in the old and the ageing. They
Dream too much of the past, a past of old gods.
I must look to the young. To you. And now –'
Joshua saw the solemnity of the moment
And sank to his knees. Moses blessed him, saying:
'May your body be washed in the waters of the eternal.
May the eternal dwell in muscle, nerve, sinew.
Be near, Joshua, near, for you too are called.'
So Moses entered the cloud and was lost to view.
But Joshua, in moonlight, tending his fires, hearing
Owls and the bark and squeal of hunter and hunted,
Heard also a voice, and it was not the voice of Moses.
'It is true', he whispered to the fire. 'All is true.'
So time passed, and a time passed below
Among the Israelites, neither exciting nor exacting,
Feeding their flocks and their children, baking bread,
Loving, quarrelling, sitting at night around fires,
Talking of the past not the future. One such night,
Aaron and Koreh strolled among the tents
On an informal patrol when a voice hailed them
With 'Any news from up there?' It was Dathan,
A little drunk, stepping out of the shadows.
'News?' said Aaron. And Dathan: 'I apologise.
A very homely and earthly word. What news
Of the cow in calf? What news
Of the woman stoned by the well for alleged adultery?
I merely wondered – well, when he is returning to us.
It seems to be already a long time.' –

'Two Sabbaths,' said Koreh, 'if you would be precise.
One of which, you will recall, you neglected to keep.' –
'I forgot,' said Dathan. 'You will remember that I said I forgot.
You will also remember that I said I thought it was nonsense.' –
'And that you were rebuked for blasphemy,' said Aaron.
'The Lord's Day is not to be termed nonsense.' –
'I thought we were all free men now,' Dathan said,
'All entitled to a free opinion. Rebuked, indeed,
For blasphemy, indeed. Who says it's blasphemy?
You? Him?' And Koreh: 'You should be sleepy, Dathan,
Not ready for argument. Go to your bed now.'
And Dathan: 'When I wish, sir. When I am ready.
Or is there a law about going to bed?' Aaron answered:
'Do not sneer at the law. The law is your
Tent and your blanket. The law watches over you
While you sleep.' – 'Pretty words,' Dathan sneered,
'But tell me this: where is this law you sing about?
Is it written in books? Is it engraved on stone?
I hear much of the law but see nothing of it.' –
'All in good time,' said Koreh. 'You will see
All that you wish to see. The law on stone
Will soon come down from that mountain. Then, Dathan,
You can pore over the law to your heart's content.' –
'I wonder,' Dathan said. 'Is that blasphemy too?
Blasphemy to wonder whether he'll ever come down again?
He's growing old and weak: the wolves could get him.
His heart could stop. He may have received new orders:
Go down, Moses, to the other side. There are
Other slaves to bring to freedom.' Aaron frowned.
'Have a care, Dathan. You do not know what you are saying.' –
'Ah, more blasphemy, is it?' Dathan said.
'More law-breaking? I'd be glad to see that law
Written down somewhere. And now I shall go to bed,
Like a good law-abiding citizen. God watch over you.'

And he stumbled off in the shadows. Aaron and Koreh
Looked at each other. Aaron shrugged. The two
Continued their patrol. The next day came
With the things it had to bring – sheep to pasture,
A cow calving, a human child brought forth
And, that night, to the blowing of bull's horns
And the plucking of the harp and the breathing of the flute,
A celebratory song from Miriam, a dance from the maidens,
Extolling their God of life:

    His strength is the strength of the bull that charges in thunder,
    His wonder is in the flow of the seed of men.
    Again and again, above in the skies and under
    The skies, in the gold noon and the moon's gold,
    His power and his wonder are told.
    Halleluiah, halleluiah.

Outside their tent, in fireglow, Eliseba,
The wife of Aaron, spoke to Aaron: 'So no news.' –
'As I have said before,' said Aaron, 'we do not
Talk of news.' – 'I thought perhaps Joshua
Might have come down – with news, or whatever I am to call it.' –
'Joshua has his orders.' – 'And you have yours.' –
'And I have mine,' said Aaron. 'Orders to give orders.
My order was to keep order. Which I am doing.' –
'Yes,' said Eliseba, 'which you are doing'. –
'You have some strange thought in that head of yours,'
Aaron smiled, and she said: 'No strange thought.
A very natural thought. You keep order
Until Joshua is ready to come from that mountain.
Then Joshua keeps order.' – 'But this is nonsense',
Aaron said. 'Joshua has his work. I have mine.' –
'Whatever it is,' she said, and he: 'I am his voice.
Joshua is his right arm. That has been understood,

Clearly, ever since the war.' – 'War?' she said,
In feigned puzzlement. 'Oh, the little desert skirmish
With those unwashed desert people. General Joshua.
Joshua the great warrior.' – 'Joshua' Aaron said,
'Is a good man and good leader. Believe me,
We shall need good military leaders before that time comes
When we settle down in peace. What have you against him?' –
'Nothing,' Eliseba said. 'I just wonder sometimes
How I fit in – How you, I mean – ' He was stern, saying:
'What you mean, I think, is that you have not been
Accorded the respect you consider your due.
You want the deference you consider owing
To the wife of a great man. The *consort*
Of a great man. Did I ever pretend to be
A great man? There are no great men here,
Believe me. Not even my brother. He is under orders
More than anyone. He is thrown into that position
Against his will. Against his will, do you understand?
We ask very little. To build our nation. That means
Law, law and more law. What we are doing
Is waiting for that law to be hammered out,
Painfully. When we have law we will have judges.
I shall be a judge – is that great enough for you?
Eliseba, the judge's wife. Will that do?'
But she said: 'You misunderstand me. You
Misunderstand my meaning. Ah, I am not even sure
I understand it myself. But, let me say this:
Once there seemed so much to look forward to.
Now there seems to be nothing.' – 'Nothing?' he cried.
'Nothing to come out of Egypt a free people,
Free, I say. Nothing the wonders, miracles?' –
'Miracles,' Eliseba echoed. 'Or is it trickery?
There are some who are saying it was trickery,
His trickery. That he knew a strong wind

Would blow back the waters. It's happened before, they say.
And the water in those rocks, and the quails, the manna.
Cunning, clever – but it was all supposed to be
The power of this God. His God. And where is this God?' –
'You forget,' said Aaron wearily, 'the miracles in Egypt.
God was in those, God is in everything –
In the strength of the wind and the lightning and the sea.
And now he talks to my own brother, gives him the law,
Makes a covenant with our people. Beware,
Beware of blasphemy, woman.' Eliseba, unabashed,
Said: 'You say that to everyone. And now you say it
To your own wife. Blasphemy blasphemy blasphemy.
But what I say is this: What comes next?
We move on to some other place full of sheep,
After General Joshua has kindly won more battles for us,
And then we obey the law, smelling of sheep-dung.
Is that life?' Aaron said: 'We are the builders.
We are the beginners. We will make kingdoms
Greater than Egypt when the time comes. But
That time is not yet.' And Eliseba answered:
'We will look up at the sky, pretending we see
A God who is not really there – who only lives
In the mind of your brother Moses. Have you ever thought
That your brother may be mad – that he'll starve to death
Up there, brooding on his God? And that we have to wait
While he starves to death or wanders away on the
Other side of the mountain, forgetting us,
All the big promises. Not that they are so big,
Those big promises. Looking after sheep
And bearing children and having lots of laws
And an invisible God grumbling all the time.' –
'I think,' said Aaron sighing, 'we should go to bed.' –
'Bed,' said Eliseba. 'Bed and work and bread
And goat's milk. And occasionally, if we are good,

A song and dance from your sister Miriam. Life.
At least in Egypt there was – ah, it is no matter.' –
'In Egypt', Aaron cried, 'there was misery,
Whips and pyramids and filthy stone idols. Misery.' –
'Also', she said, 'baked Nile fish and palm wine.
What are you going to do, Aaron –
Aaron of the golden mouth, what are you going
To do? The people are unhappy, Aaron.'
'They have no right,' he muttered, 'to be unhappy.
They must be patient. Patience, the great thing is patience.' –
'And where did patience,' she said, 'ever lead them?
What did patience ever get them? They want to live.
He may never come back, Aaron of the golden mouth.
What are you going to do? This is your kingdom.'
So she left him alone by the fire and he looked
Bitterly after her. *They want to live.*
Next day a strange thing, a new thing, though small.
One of the idle appeared before the children
With little figures of stone, crudely carved,
And a crude platform of wood, and he set the figures
Acting on that stage, lending them his voices,
One voice a mouse-squeak, the other heavy, solemn,
A *bearded* voice, which rumbled: 'Tell them all
That nobody is to work on the Sabbath, the Sabbath
Being my day, my day.' – 'Why not give us that day
And you have all the others? Then we should be able
To rest nearly all the time.' The children laughed.
'Because', in thunder, 'I tell you. And you tell them
That if they do wrong I will punish them, punish them.' –
'How will you punish them?' – 'I'll swoop down from on high
Like a mountain-lion. I'll crash like a thunderbolt.'
And one of the bolder children grasped the God-effigy
And chased the weak with it, crying: 'Go on,
On your knees, bow down, bow down or I will

Clout you on the head.' And a sickly child,
Grinning, abased himself to joyful laughter.
But then a voice of true anger, Koreh's crying:
'Stop! Stop that!' Surprised by unabashed,
The puppeteer and the children: what wrong had they done?
Here came some official spoilsport. Koreh said:
'You know the law. You know that there is to be no
Worshipping of graven images. And that means also
The pretence of worshipping –' The puppeteer cried back:
'Are there to be no children's games then any more?' –
'I admit,' admitted Koreh, 'that the line is
Hard to draw. It will be drawn firmly when
He comes down. Meanwhile remember
What you have already been taught that there is
Danger even in children's play.' And he took the
Crude God of stone and hurled it, hurled it,
And the children looked at him with open mouths.
The law was a problem everywhere, on every level,
As Aaron found with the thieves arraigned before him,
Saying, calmly, clearly: 'I am saying
Not that you stole as men steal in the
General way, the old way – from other men,
From this man or from that man – do you follow me? –
But that you stole from us all. The gold and silver
And jewels that the Egyptians gave to us,
Gave us to go away – do you follow me? –
Are the wealth not of one man, of one family,
Of one tribe, but of the entire people,
Of what we now call Israel.' And the first thief,
Wall-eyed and hulking, said: 'What you're saying then
Is that we stole from ourselves. But how can people
Steal from themselves? Answer me that.' And Aaron:
'Listen carefully. Listen. A whole nation
Can own a thing in common – do you follow me?

Perhaps some public monument, some statue –'
'Some god, you mean?' said thief, a youth
Golden, angelic. And Aaron: 'I did not say that.
Some fine piece of craftsman's work, shall we say,
That is set up in a public place, that would be
Seen and enjoyed by the whole people. It would be theft
For one man or three men to remove it. Now do you
Follow me?' But the first thief said: 'That gold,
Silver and stuff was shut away in a wagon,
And not very well guarded, if I may say so.
Anybody could have taken some, but it happened to be
Us. And it happened that one of these Midianites
Didn't keep his mouth shut.' Aaron turned to Caleb:
'Not very well guarded, do you hear?' And to the thieves:
'What have the Midianites to do with it?' The third thief said,
An upright clipped man, like a warrior:
'They wanted to sell us palm-wine. As for us,
We wanted to buy it. We had nothing to buy it with.
Except sheep. But they said they had plenty of those.' –
'I see,' sighed Aaron. 'Caleb, sequester the palm-wine.
It belongs to the community. There may some time
Be occasion to celebrate something. As for you three –'
And then he cried out in impotence: 'Punishment, punishment –
What punishment can we give? By rights you should each
Have a hand cut off at the wrist. But who would be so
Foul as to order such bloody execution
And who so depraved as to do it? Nor can you be
Cast into prison. We are not a township –
We have no prisons. Throw you back to the wilderness?
That would be death, and theft hardly warrants it.
All I can say is that you must abide the
Coming of the covenant, the return of the
Ordained lawgiver. Be warned. You are free to go.'
So they went, and the voice of the clipped and upright

Warrior-looking thief could be heard some way off,
Mimicking Aaron, while the others laughed.
'If I may speak,' said Caleb – 'Speak by all means,'
Aaron said, and Caleb: 'We have here a nation
Of town-dwellers who have almost forgotten
That their forebears were herdsmen. It is hard to turn them so
    quickly
Into tenders of sheep again. They think of enslaving Egypt
As a land of fair cities. What have they, after all, here?
Goat's cheese and sheep-fat, and that useless glittering hoard
Out of a fair land of fine craft and richness.
Melt it down.' And Aaron started at that.
'Melt it down,' said Caleb. 'We have men here wasted –
Men who have learned the crafts of smith and carver,
Brought down here to be mere shepherds. Melt the gold
And melt the silver and give them work to do.
Some effigy of skill and beauty that shall
Stand in the midst of the encampment. Some symbol of
The unity of the people.' Aaron shook his head:
'But this is no time for that. We are still waiting
To go to the lands we are promised, there to build our
Cities and fill them full of the craftsman's work.
This is a time between times, it is not yet
Even an era of making. Except for the law,
The law comes first. We build first with law
And then out of stone and marble and metal.' –
'A very long time of waiting,' Caleb said.
To many it feels that this is to be their life.
A life full of toil with nothing at all to look at
Save that sky and that mountain. He has been
A long time up that mountain. If, of course, he is
Still there.' Glumly, both looked up
At the mountain. *If he is still there.*
'Even he said that,' said Aaron to Eliseba,

The following dawn, as they lay hearing the cock crow
And smelt the baking of bread.'Even Caleb.
The people are wavering, full of doubt. Some of them
Talk with regret of leaving Egypt. They forget so quickly.
They forget Moses. *If he is still there*, he said.' –
'Whether he is there or not,' Eliseba replied,
'You are here, you. The time is come, I think,
For you to rule.' – 'I do what I can', said Aaron. –
'And what you can do is to say either *no* or *wait*.
No more. Have they been asking you for gods?' –
'For what?' Aaron was startled. 'For gods, gods,'
She said. 'Not some big bearded father
Up the mountain or in the sky. Gods such as
The Egyptians have. Gods they can touch and speak to
And chide and beat if they do not behave well.' –
They are 'fools', Aaron said. 'They do not realise
How far we have come. We, of all the people of the earth,
Know what God is. Not gods – God –
The one containing the many. It is staggering.
Too staggering. Yes, they have been asking for
Gods.' – 'And what,' said Eliseba, 'do you say to them?
Wait, I will tell you. You thunder and use big words.
You talk of the big invisible God who has brought us
Out of Egypt and into the bondage of sheep-dung.
And they don't understand.' – 'He will make them understand,
My brother.' She said: 'You used to be the great explainer.
He was supposed to be slow of speech. Well, talking
Is not enough now. What are you going
To do?' Roused, he cried: 'Will *you* understand
What I say now? I will show them what God is,
Not talk and explain, but show. They need an
Image for their poor minds to cling to. They must
See the strength of God. He carries the sun and the moon
On his brow. He has the power of all the

Beasts of the earth and yet he is gentle, loving.
But that is not God: it is but a picture of God.' –
'Time to get up,' she said. 'You have ruling to do.'
So that very morning the treasure hoard swung open,
And the gold and silver and jewels of the Israelites
Were brought in baskets joyously while Aaron explained
To the craftsmen and artists what was to be made. One art,
The art of song, was fired while the kiln was built
And the fire puffed within it, and the song was sung
By the people, joyous, their eyes at last to be fed
With something other than promises:

> His head is the sun,
> He carries the moon on his brow,
> His limbs are the north, the west,
> The east, the south,
> And his breath the winds thereof.
> His coat is speckled with the stars.
> He strides in power over all the world.
> Halleluiah halleluiah.

II

THE GOLDEN CALF

Out of the fire came an indeterminate lump
Of fused gold and silver, but mostly gold,
And the craftsmen worked on it: it became
An indeterminate beast with a crescent moon
On its brow like horns, so that a certain child
Cried: 'That's it – that what I saw that time
When we walked through the water – up in the sky it was,
A baby bull.' The father said: 'A calf, you mean,
A bull-calf. I see. Like that, was it? A heavenly bull-calf.'

And the parents smiled at each other: *Children.* Soon
On a rough tumulus the image was ready to be raised
And blocked into place with stone. Aaron was there,
And Aaron spoke to the people who watched, saying: 'Listen,
Children of Israel, you have asked for gods.
You were wrong to do so, sinful indeed, but the sin
Sprang mostly from ignorance and from inability
To grasp what great thing has happened to us.' (The craftsmen
Polished the back, the horns, the blunt muzzle.) 'For what has
    happened
Is this: we have been chosen by God himself
– Not by gods, not even by a king of gods, but by God,
The one true indivisible God who made us
And made everything. At this moment my brother Moses,
Our leader, our giver of laws, is in converse with the
Voice of God on the mountain top. The voice he hears
Is perhaps his own voice, animated by God,
For God has no voice as a man has a voice. God
Has no body, God is in no one place.
God is spirit, and spirit is unshackled by the
Chains of time and space. God is everywhere.
The image you see before you is not God –
The very idea is absurd. But it will serve
To remind you of God, each day as you pass it. God
Is strength, and this is an image of strength – its head
The sun, the moon on its forehead, its limbs the four
Corners of the world. But it is a loving strength,
A mild strength, the strength of an eternal being
That will never use its strength against us.' The child cried:
'A bull-calf, that's what it is,' and the people smiled
And Aaron smiled, saying: 'It is not what it looks like
That is important. What is important is that you
See in it an image of our unity as a people
Chosen by the one true God. At last the silver and gold

Of the Egyptians who enslaved us have been put to
Holy use – the profane made holy, remember that.
What was hidden away is now here to be seen by all
– The richness of a people's unity – (And now there were jewels for
    eyes)
And the ultimate unthinkable richness of God himself,
Whose silver is the moon, whose gold the sun,
Whose jewels the eternal constellations of heaven.'
He smiled at the applause, but Miriam,
Standing near with her children, did not smile,
Nor smiled when, in huge moonlight, the young danced about it,
Singing:

> Where will our wedding breakfast be?
> Up in the fronds of a dikla tree.
> What will we drink? What will we eat?
> The moon for wine and the sun for meat.

As the old sat by, approving, a bit of life in the evening
Now. 'It has become the centre of life,' smiled Aaron.
'A gathering place for talk and play. It is as if we were
Building a city.' But Miriam said: 'Not for long,
Not for that long. I saw some old men this morning
Touching it for luck, as they said. And there was a
Young man giving thanks.' – 'It is good to give thanks,'
Said Aaron. – 'Thanks to an image?' Miriam said.
'His wish had come true, something to do with a girl,
And he said that thing was magical.' – 'Harmless, Miriam,
Harmless. A simple people needs something simple
To feed its senses.' – 'Wait,' said Miriam. 'Wait.'
And one evening, the moon still huge, Dathan and his wife
Sat drinking palm-wine, the three thieves with them, and he said:
'Can you get any more of this stuff?' – 'What do we buy it with?'
Said the wall-eyed one. 'That chunk of gold up there?' –

'Risky,' said the angelic one. 'I somehow doubt
That you'd get away with it.' – 'Well,' Dathan said,
'I'd rather drunk this than drink that smoke that the
Young ones drink, snuff up rather, that grass that grows
By the wall. Visions of golden cities,
That's what it's said to give you. Men of my age,
It makes us sick'. Dathan's wife tipsily sang:
'Where will our wedding breakfast be?' – 'I'd rather,'
Dathan said, 'drink this than take that smoke stuff'. –
'Some of the tribe of Judah,' said the soldierly thief,
'Mash up dates and add honey and water. It bubbles,
Bubbles you know.' – 'I suppose it's against the law,'
Said the angelic thief, his gold hair moon-ensilvered. –
'Nothing,' Dathan said, 'is against the law,
Because there is no law. It has to be written down,
Then it becomes law. Not that anybody can read it,
Except those that pretend they can. The bondage
Of unintelligible signs. That is well put,
Remember that.' And Dathan's wife went: 'Unin-
Telligibubble.' – 'He's coming down soon',
Said the soldierly thief. 'Still, I suppose it's
Time we knew where we stood. Then we get the law.' –
'We ought to have a sort of celebration,'
Dathan said, 'not when he gets here, but before.
I suppose he'll have a law against celebrations,
All nicely carved out.' – 'What will we celebrate?'
Asked the angel. – 'Oh', said Dathan, 'we'll think of
Something or other' – 'Rother,' giggled his wife.
But it was not till the new moon that something or other
Got into the people, helped by palm-wine, date-wine.
Some drunken women were singing Miriam's song
About the effigy:

His strength is the strength of the bull that charges in thunder,
His wonder is in the flow of the seed of men.
Again and again, above in the sky and under
The sky, in gold noon and the moon's gold,
His power and wonder are told.
Halleluiah halleluiah.

Some of the young sang their marriage song, and others
Drank smoke, while some of their elders kept to date-wine,
Date-wine. All very harmless: the young dancing about
The effigy, the old clapping their hands
To the rough music. Harmless enough perhaps
The fixing, by drunken women, to the effigy's loins,
And Dathan swinging grinning with a pair of pomegranates.
But then the calf was jerked, to cheers, from its plinth,
Brought down to strong young shoulders, carried about
In song, while the tremulous old touched it, praying
For an end of the journey, for all to go well. Song
And a claw-buttock dance behind it, one young girl
Shedding her garments one by one in the dance,
Then by two young men, screaming and laughing.
Aaron and Miriam were far from all this, tending
A sick child in a distant tent, Aaron saying
(And the child was the child who had had the vision) to the
    mother:
'The fever must come to its height. And then, we hope,
He will grow cool again. Give him nothing to drink
But bathe his forehead.' – 'Listen,' Miriam said.
He listened, both listened. 'So', she said, 'it is come.
God help us.' They hurried, meeting on the way
Grave members of the tribe of Levi: *We can do*
Nothing. We always knew it was a
Grave mistake. Graven images. Aaron saw,
Miriam saw a woman, near naked, on the ground,

And the calf's phallus in pretended hammering rut,
The calf in strong arms, and cheers and cheers,
The old, clawing buttocks, dancing, men and women,
Men and men, in a dance mime of sodomy,
The young, mad on the smoke they had drunk, dancing
Crazed dances of their own, a hugely corpulent
Sot draining, to cheers, a carboy of palm-wine,
And Caleb, crying for order, sense, near-trampled,
And other Levites brutally stricken with staves.
'God help us,' Miriam said. 'You see what it is –
They are back to the worship of – Wasted, all wasted.'
'I will speak to them', Aaron said. 'Let me mount the
Plinth.' (Was that woman Zipporah, was that
Zipporah?) An obese matron, naked,
Pig-squealed, pleasured by a skeletal youth. Aaron smote,
Smote with his stave, mounting. 'Listen,' he cried.
'Listen.' And a few turned and groaned and cheered.
'Brothers and sisters – children of Israel – listen.
Return to your dwelling at once, under pain of death.
Sin, sin – the Lord sees – the Lord will strike.' Cheers,
And many were swift to drag him down, drowning his shouts,
Stripped him, thrust a jug of wine to his
Shouting mouth, dragged him into the throng.
(Far above, on Horeb, Joshua,
Tending his night fire, thought he heard revelling,
Riot, war. He turned to the cloud, heard a
Stronger noise of hammer and chisel on stone,
And a kind of – or did he imagine it only? –
Disheartened thunder.) Dancing, rutting,
The disrobing of a screaming boy by men who
Slavered in lust. Lust, drunken fighting,
And Dathan, drunk, screaming ecstatic: 'There has to be
A sacrifice, the god wants a sacrifice' pointing
Among cheers and growls to a trembling girl. Miriam

Stood in Aaron's place, hardly heard: 'Cannot you
Understand? This is another kind of
Slavery. God, the true God, sees all and will punish
Terribly. Turn away from your sin before it is
Too late.' A cloud covered the thin moon,
And some, in slow fear, looked up. 'A sign,' she cried.
Then the cloud passed. 'Cease your wickedness.
God will forgive, God will understand.' But they
Dragged her down, stripping and beating her, lifting
The battered dull gold effigy to its old place,
Holding the terrified naked girl beneath
A jagged slab, while a gross lout as priest
Prayed gibberish to the calf – *O guk O guk*
Bondage of unintelligibubble. Gaaaaaar!
And he raised the knife and plunged, plunged
Till he was tired of plunging. Horror, awe,
Joy. He covered his arms and head with blood,
He daubed the loins of the calf in it, and now
The calf surged about, dripping in blood,
Anointing their own loins. They brought a boy,
Already stunned with a sharp rock, and rent him,
And some drank the blood and chewed and spat out
The rent flesh. (A drunk made slobbering love
To a woman equally drunk, and, equally drunk,
Another man wrestled with him in jealousy
And then took a stone and spilled his brains.
All brains and blood about them, he and she
Made slobbering love.) The dull gold effigy
Was everywhere daubed with blood and brains and seed
And, like red seed, blood dripped from its loins.
Battered and sobbing, Miriam crawled to her tent
And found Eliseba there, and the children, safe,
But where was Zipporah? The moon was setting.
The faintest dawn-streaked flushed. And high on Horeb

Moses emerged from the cloud, under his arms
Two tablets, intricately carved, grim, growing gentle
As he bade the sleeping Joshua awake.
Joshua looked up, saw the tablets, saw
A kind of white light about the head of Moses,
And, seeing, knelt. 'Rise, Joshua,' he was told.
'We have mischief below. We must go down to the mischief.'
So they descended as dawn grew, till at length,
From a ridge above the encampment, they saw enough:
A beast of metal drunkenly on a plinth,
Daubed with dried blood, some of it flaking off,
A naked body, too mauled to show its sex,
Men and women sleeping naked, corpses,
Bloody everywhere, odd whimpering cries
From sources unseen, half-devoured whole sheep,
The flies already at their work, shattered wine jugs,
Blood. 'Call', said Moses quietly. 'Call, Joshua.'
So Joshua put his hollowed hands to his cheeks
And called a long sound. He called and called.
Some stirred, then slept again, moaning. Some
Stirred and listened and wondered, dazed, then saw
Dried blood in the sun. Miriam heard,
Ceasing to sob, and Aaron, bruised, dry blood on him,
Heard. Many heard, looking in fear, wonder,
Seeing bones, spilt wine, soon, silent in the camp,
Two men walking. Zipporah, lying alone,
Blood on her garment, saw: light from his head,
His, shining, and behind his head an instant
The battered horns. He did not seem to see her,
Then Aaron stood before Moses, saying nothing,
Having nothing to say, then fell down in tears,
And Moses said, in sadness: 'Not enough knowledge.
Never enough. And out of ignorance, evil.
The work wasted. All the work wasted.'

In his arms were the stones, painfully chiselled.
'The covenant is broken. We must start again.'
And soon to an assembled nation, weeping and fearful:
'The covenant is broken. We must start again.
You said you would accept the covenant.
But you had no faith, a frail and ignorant people.
And now the tablets of the law, so lovingly,
So painfully inscribed, must be smashed to dust.
For what was accepted in freedom was rejected in freedom.
Men are born free to do good and free to do ill.
You chose the latter way. You must suffer for that,
Suffer, since freedom always has its price.
You must suffer for that, in modes of suffering
That soon you will see, hear, smell, taste, feel in the
Very nerve and the very marrow. But first
We must perform the rite of the breaking of the covenant.
So be it.' And he threw the stones to the earth.
Aaron and Koreh took stones and broke the stones,
Ground the stones to dust, sweating. The words
Were released to the sphere of the spirit, but the stone
Was dust. 'We must start again,' said Moses.
'Once more I ascend the mountain, there to take
Once more counsel of the Lord our God, but first –'
It was evening, and a great fire was being blown
To white heat. 'What you worshipped,' Moses cried,
'Must be your bane. The thing you took unto yourselves
In the spirit you must now in chastisement take
Unto yourselves in the flesh. Not all, but some.
For you are all one people, and it suffices
That one limb, tooth, nerve, eyeball be enforced
To shriek out for the entire body to know
Pain. Pain. I have appointed officers
Of the tribe of Levi to see that mouths which cried
In obscene ecstasy shall now, in a diverse mode,

Cry out. Not all but some, the grosser sinners.
What you kissed you now must eat and drink.'
The calf on it plinth was dragged down by the Levites
And cast into the fire, there to dissolve
To a scalding broth. 'This,' he cried, 'was your God.'
It was mingled with water and thrust down the sinners' throats.
Nor was this all. The grosser sinners were stoned,
Hanged, pierced by arrows, hurled from the slopes
(But not Dathan, whose destiny lay otherwise,
Whose potency of grossness was, as it were,
Decreed as a thorn for Moses). The masons chose
New stone and shaped it for a new covenant.
And Moses, before he sought the peak of Horeb
Once more, Joshua with him, asked the people:
'Will you remember that this is the Lord your God,
Who brought you out of Egyptian bondage? Will you
Promise to worship no other God but Him,
Nor to make images of things that are on the earth
Or in the sky or rivers or seas for profane
And sinful worship? Will you keep the Sabbath holy,
Preserve the holiness of the family, honour your parents,
Respect the sanctity of the bond of marriage? Do you
Promise never to steal, never to murder,
Never to lust after that what is another's? Will you
Keep the covenant the covenant will you
Keep the covenant?' *Will will we will.*
The valley rang with shamed affirmation.
Yes hurtled through the air as the last of the
Condemned hurtled from the slopes. So Moses and Joshua
Climbed Horeb for the second time, leaving below
A chastened nation burying its dead,
Burying much else. So time passed, with the covenant
Unbroken, the covenant the sacred body of the law
Inscribed not in the riddling signs of the priests

They had known in Egypt but in a new way, a way
Apt for a covenant, with signs for sounds of speech
That all might read if they would, but the sacred stones
Had to be housed in a sacred place. The craftsmen
Built an arc of wood, with beauty and cunning
Spent on it to the utmost, and here the covenant
Was tabernacled. Moses said Aaron:
'It is in your keeping, Aaron. *Aaron the priest.*' –
'The priest,' Aaron said. 'How must I take that?
In a manner of a punishment?' But Moses said:
'A priest is God's voice. Could any man wish
To be higher than God's voice?' – 'Once,' Aaron said,
'I was your voice.' – 'And so,' his brother replied,
'Take this not in manner of a punishment but in
Manner of a promotion'. They looked at each other,
A curve unreadable on each other's lips,
And Aaron said: 'Well then – to my first office.'
And Moses: 'God be with you, man of God.'
So Aaron was enrobed and he walked to the ark
And reverently shut the covenant within,
Improvising a ceremony: 'Hereon is inscribed
God's law. The very stone shall be accounted
Sacred. Behold our God is a just God.'
Stiff-jointed the people knelt. Then Moses knelt.
And Aaron the priest prayed: 'God, who art a just God,
Be also, we beseech, a forgiving God.
For men are weak, being made but of earth's clay,
Quick to transgress. If, Lord, we have sinned once,
Will we not sin again? If we were perfect,
Would we not have need of thee?' Moses, kneeling,
Was thoughtful (*weak – forgiving*). After sunset,
Zipporah, his wife, preparing Ghersom, his son,
For sleep, heard Ghersom's question once more:
'Is he still very busy?' – 'Yes,' she replied, 'busy.

He has the whole of Israel to look after.' –
'When' asked Ghersom, 'will he be with us again?'
But, before she could answer, a shadow stood between
His bed and the lamp of sheep-fat. Ghersom said:
'You had better not stay too long, sir. Israel needs you.'
And Moses smiled and wept and took his wife
In trembling arms. 'Who am I', trembling, 'to reproach,
Even to talk of sin or weakness? To forgive
If forgiveness is needed – enough. Forgive me too,'
As she sobbed in his arms. 'We all have to start again.' –
'It was little enough', she sobbed. 'Wine in my head,
A pair of young arms in the dance. But it was too much.' –
'Learning is heard,' he said. 'We all have to learn.
And now we can start again.' There were family embraces,
Sobs, even laughter as Ghersom said once more:
'Israel needs you. How long will you stay?'
But the time of staying under the mountain in the valley
Of Jethro was now to end. An order of march was worked out,
Moses drawing with his stave on the sandy earth,
Saying: 'There in the midst the ark of the covenant,
With its own bodyguard drawn from the Levites. No enemy
Shall take it, no infidel defile it. It is our hub,
And, as twelve spokes, the fixed and changeless posts
Of the tribes,' showing – Dan, Reuben, Benjamin…
'A battle order,' Joshua said. And Moses:
'You may call it that.' Then Caleb: 'When do we march?'
And Moses pondered. 'Miriam,' he said to Aaron.
'How is she?' Aaron said: 'Very sick. But ready.
Ready to go to the land.' *She will not see it,*
Moses told himself. *But it is better thus,*
To die striving forward, in others' hope.
'So,' he pronounced, 'we move tomorrow at dawn.'
There was weeping at the well when they took their leave of Jethro
And his daughters, some now married, some not. Weeping

Of many over many graves, brethren buried,
Much else buried. Miriam, pale, wasted,
Lay in rugs on an ox-cart, Eliseba tending her.
Just before the raising of the staff as signal, incorrigible
Dathan rooted in the ashes of the punitive fire
And came up with a thumb-nail fragment of the gold, holding
That nothingness up to the sun; the sun swallowed it.
They took their last look of Horeb, its peak no longer
Enmisted: eagles circled there. Towards rock,
Desert, thirst, hunger, the law in their midst,
They moved.

12

DEATH AND THE LAW

At the next oasis Miriam's end drew near.
Moses wiped her fever, in the coolness of a cave,
And Miriam shuddered painfully, hearing from without
That marriage song of the young: 'It will happen again.
Again.' But Moses soothed her, saying: 'This
Is a different excitement: they already smell
The air of our promised land, or think they do.
The hope lies with the young. The old, alas,
Are more than ever set in the old ways.
They have learned fear but not yet understanding.
And you, my sister, how is it with you?'
She murmured: 'I lose blood. I am weak. But feel
Little pain. I shall be glad to move on.
Move on. No more. Towards something even if we
Never reach it.' – 'We shall reach it,' he said.
'There's a hunger to build – especially with the young.
To build, say, a temple and then a city
To hold the temple.' She said: 'I will not see it,

But it matters little enough. My work, the work
I was ordained to do has been long done.
You were my work. My name perhaps will be known
For that. Girls given the name of Miriam.
It is something. I rescued a child from murderers.
And if I had not rescued that child –'He said:
'You were ordained to. It was all laid down.
We are all in God's pattern.' But she, distressed:
'Was that too part of God's pattern? Is then evil
Part of God's pattern?' – 'We must believe it,' he said.
'If evil is in man it must come from his maker.'
'And it goes on', she said. 'It will go on.
Law will not quench it. I see much evil to come.
Law will not contain it. Nor will punishment.' –
'But men,' he insisted, 'learn from their own transgressions.
There will be no more building of golden calves.
Other things perhaps – man is ingenious.
He gets his ingenuity from God.'
And then she wept. 'They had ceased to be men and women.
I could do nothing.' Later her mind rambled
Or grew prophetic. 'I heard the soldiers singing
Their dirty song. And God surely was there,
For if they had not been singing they would have heard,
Heard him crying. A new-born cry, very loud
In the night. But God made them sing their song,
Which was filthy and evil, and so they did not hear.
Little floating cradle. Meant to live,
He was meant to live. Girl girl, they said,
Who are you, girl, can you get him a wet nurse, girl?
And I did. Poor mother. But he lived, lived.
A pretty baby. They made him an Egyptian.'
(The moon showed Passover, the angel passing over.
'Will he pass over tonight?' the children asked,
Making sour faces over the bitter herbs,

The hard dry bread.) 'They would not see it,' said Miriam.
'Many gods, like bits of pottery,
A housewife's pride, but not the one true God.
So simple, and so many thousands of years
For it to come to the light. And still they will not
See it. And when they see it they will always say:
What good is it, what good? For the pains of life
Will not be easier. Truth makes nothing easier.
But truth must be sought.' Eliseba, hiding tears,
Said: 'Rest my dear, rest.' But Miriam said:
'Oh, there will be no rest. And when it is built,
The city, it will be knocked down, and the temple
Destroyed with the city. And it will go on and on.
They will wander and be made to wander further.
For there is no abiding city. Only the dark.
I must speak to my brother Moses.' Moses said:
'I am here, Miriam.' She said: 'You will not see it.
You will be forbidden to see it. It will take a
Long time to be made clean.' Then they waited
For Miriam to say more, but she said no more.
Her eyes were open, but said no more. And Aaron
Closed her eyes, and then the wailing began.
The angel, it was shuddered about the camp.
Aaron said: 'Let the soul of this thy servant
Go calmly to its haven, where is no pain,
Where the mill of the heart grinds no more
Of the bread of tribulation.' Moses touched her face.
'Rest, Miriam, rest.' Then left and went
Into the dark to weep. So they buried her –
Another grave to mark their journey. Buried her,
With rites according to the law of Israel.
Nothing stayed, but there was always the law…
And Moses was administering the law one day
When Caleb appeared to speak of a monstrous serpent

Voided from a child's body. 'A bad omen.
That is the general feeling.' But Moses said:
'Let us hear nothing of omens. Let us hear rather
Of foolishness. What has the child been eating?'
So the story came out: some of the Israelites
Sick of their diet of mutton, traded a sheep
For a pig from a wandering tribe that herded pigs.
'The pig,' said Moses, 'is not like other beasts.
It harbours worms in its gut and gives the worms
To those who eat it. Call it an act of revenge,
Though posthumous.' Nobody smiled. Loudly he said:
'Does it occur to no one that this serpent
Is a consequence of eating forbidden flesh –
Not a sign from heaven, but the passing on
Of a disease from beast to man? Can they not *think*?
Are they to be treated for ever like children?' Caleb said:
'There is no instruction about this. What is the law?
It seems not to be covered by the basic ten.' –
'More laws,' said Moses. 'No food from now on may be eaten
Without some act of supervision, God help us.
We need priestly intervention even there.
The body of the law must wax fat
Because the brain of the Israelite is small.
They cannot eat, God help us, without being
Told what to eat. Shall we put the spoon to their mouths?'
And, on another day, when Aaron was called
To see a sick child, its loins inflamed,
And its parents applying some filth of fat and spittle,
He saw that the child was uncircumcised. 'Dust,' he said,
'Dirt has been trapped there.' The father: 'We did not think.' –
'You did not think,' said Aaron. 'And yet Zipporah,
Wife of our leader Moses, herself gave to God
As an offering the foreskin of her firstborn.
Was she not at that moment divinely inspired

To do what was for the child's good? We are, above all,
A people of cleanliness. Remember that.
We are not disease-ridden rats of the wilderness.
Your son shall be circumcised.' But the mother said:
'I am not Zipporah. I could not take the knife
To my precious.' Aaron sighed. 'It shall be done for you.
So God be with you.' And wearily he left.
But there was yet another day when Moses
Sat with his problems, in the cool of a cave,
And a tribal leader came with another problem,
A violation of the law of the Sabbath.
'What were they doing?' Moses wearily asked. –
'Gathering palm fronds to feed a fire. It seemed
Harmless enough, but, knowing that the covenant
Is strict on the matter, knowing that you yourself –'
'Yes?' said Moses. ' – Set great store by the
Punctilious observance, as you term it
Somewhat grandiloquently, is of the very
Essence of the law. It is to do with man's duty,
Duty, not right, to abstain from labour
That the body may be at peace and the spirit
At one with God. With God. One day in seven –
Can we not spare that day to honour our God?' –
'This,' said the tribal leader, 'is generally
Recognised and accepted, but – after all,
The gathering of a few palm fronds' – 'Yes?' said Moses.
'Wel,' said the leader, 'we were somewhat unsure
Of an appropriate penalty. The men in question
Were, naturally, rebuked. But they did not seem to be
Truly repentant. And then what happened was –'
'Yes?' said Moses. – 'What happened was that one of them
Was discovered later looking for dry sticks –
For tinder. The rebuke had been of no avail.' –
'So now?' said Moses. – 'Now I seek instruction.

As to the appropriate mode of punishment.'
Then Moses felt the wrestling within
And the curse of his leadership was sour in his mouth,
But, wearily, hopelessly, he said: 'The holy rest
Of the Sabbath must not be defiled. Let the miscreants
Be stoned to death.' The tribal leader did not
Think that he... 'Forgive me, I do not think that I
Quite.' And Moses: 'My sentence was, I fancy,
Clearly enough articulated. Let the miscreants
Be stoned to death.' The leader: 'With respect and deference,
I do not think that my people could at all
Possibly accept such a harsh, a disproportionate –
Forgive me. Sir.' And Moses stood and said:
'Can you or your people think of
An alternative punishment? More rebukes? Torture?
Turn them into living martyrs? Imprisonment?
We are all imprisoned until we reach the land.
Best be bold and have done with it. The law is the law,
One, indivisible. To kill another man
Merits death. To kill the Lord's day,
The living breathing peace that belongs to the Lord,
Can that be accounted a lesser crime? The Lord God
Is thus blasphemed against. Blasphemy,
A sneer, a gob of spit in the face of God.
Let them be stoned to death.' He said no more,
Returning to his rock seat and his problems,
But the tribal leader was aghast. That very day
The penalty was exacted – a wall-eyed thief,
A thief whose hair shone gold in the sun, transfixed
With twisted ropes to tree trunks, the crowd around
Murmuring, and soon doing more than murmur
When the muscles of the executioners
Glistened in the sunlight. They took, in an easy rhythm,
Rock after rock from the pile and hurled,

Hurled. The one died quickly, faceless, but the other
Lasted till there was not much of the human about him,
And then his head dropped to his shoulder. Not murmurs,
But yells of anger before the cave of Moses,
And stones thrown. The armed guard held steady.
Justice not murder to hell with your commandments
Break your stones again murderer your laws are
Nothing but murder. Grim, he came out. The stones flew.
He bled from his brow. The guard hit back with staves.
Many dispersed, yelling, but Dathan and the
Third thief, the soldierly one, held their ground,
And, inside the cave, Dathan spoke of barbarism.
'Barbarism?' Moses said. 'You talk to me
Of barbarism? When you, to my certain knowledge,
Were one of the leaders of the most filthy display
Of barbarism known in the annals of all the tribes.
Count yourself lucky, Dathan, that you were not chosen
For the ultimate punishment after that abomination
Which stinks still in God's nostrils.' Dathan replied:
'Very well, Moses. If I was a sinner,
I was unenlightened. What excuse can you show?'
And Moses cried: '*Excuse*, Dathan? Must we
Have excuses to sustain the law,
The law that sustains the life of man? For I
Am in the service of life, while you are
All given over to death. You, the nay-sayer,
The sneerer, the denier, you still live,
While better than you could ever be granted a dream
Of becoming are struck down by your sneers,
Your greed and your lust.' The soldierly thief said:
'It is a strange way of serving life,
Killing men. It was my brother you killed,
Do you know that? A man who had his faults,
Like all men, but meant to harm to any, dead

And dead like a dog beaten to pulp by children.
Dead because of some nonsense about the Sabbath,
For nonsense it is, and all the world knows it for nonsense.' –
'All the word', said Moses, 'the little world
Of the stupid who disdain the vision. Your brother, you say,
On your head and the heads of the evil like you
Lies my sister's death. Ah, but it is no matter.' –
'Ah, it comes clearer now,' Dathan said, in glee.
'It is not the law that drives you – it is revenge.' –
'No, Dathan,' said Moses, 'not revenge.
Vengeance is not for me. Vengeance is for
The Lord God, in his own time. There is for me
The law and the enforcing of the law –
Yes, by murder if need be, since you hold
That just execution is murder – until men
Cease to be ignorant and know that their own good
Is the good of the commonalty, and that that good
Is enshrined in the law. You will learn, be made to learn.
Perhaps you are already learning, you,
Dathan, the most obdurate of my children.' –
'Oh yes,' sneered Dathan. 'I am learning one thing:
Remember thou to keep holy the Sabbath day.'
In torment of spirit, Moses walked the night,
Addressing bitterly the torrent of stars
And the silence of the wilderness. 'My people,' he said.
                              'Your people.
They are a stiffnecked people. They are a people
Who savour their ignorance like manna. Why why,
O Lord, am I set above them? Why, of all the
Men that walk the earth, was I chosen
To lead them to a fair land that is
None of their deserving? Why, Lord, was I chosen
To bring them to the law they despise and spurn?
They speak harshly of me, spit in my shadow,

Cast stones at my son, send my wife home weeping.
Am I not a man like any other,
Deserving of peace – deserving of wine at sundown,
A glowing fire to dream into under the stars?
Was I not better off as a prince in Egypt,
Jewelled with office, wearing the perfume
Of the respect and the worship of men? God, my Lord,
I speak from the heart and I have ever done.
I am sick to death of the burden of rule I bear.
What will you do if I renounce it now –
If I pass it to Aaron or to Joshua
Or to any of the young who promise richly?
You can do little more than strike me down
As you have struck down others. Well, it may be
That I am willing to be struck down – lie at peace
In the earth, where is no more trouble, pain
Or oppression of the wicked. I defy you, then,
Or am willing to do so, as others have.
Am I not free to do so? Am I not a man
Like other men, clothed in the garment
Of liberty of choice? And yet I have not forgotten
The humility of the servant before the master.
In humility I ask – let your servant
Go, let your servant go.' But there was no answer
From the array of the stars or the night's silence.
So he went to his bed, finding his wife asleep,
His son happy in a dream, and tried to sleep.
Then he heard a voice, his own, grown old,
Speak slow and tired: 'Moses, my servant Moses,
I will ride you as a horseman rides a horse.
You will always know my weight at your back,
My spurs in your flank. I will never let you go.
You have doubted, and will doubt again and again,
 But in spite of your doubts, you will bear the burden

To life's end. You will lead your people to the land
That is promised, since that is my will. You will lead them,
But you yourself will never eat or drink
Of the fruit of the fulfilment of the promise.
I will never let you go, but I will never
Let you enter. Nor will any one
Of your generation, sick with the doubt
Of the Lord's promise, ever enter that land.
The milk of my beneficence and the honey
Of my jealous love – neither is for you
Nor for the generation that is yours.
Those will flow in a land you may see from far
But whose soil will never bless your foot, whose air
Never delight your nostrils, and whose sun
Never warm your grey head. I have spoken.'
Ghersom lay silently awake now, listening
In wonder to a sound he had never heard:
The sobbing of his father.
                              So at daybreak
They addressed themselves to the march, with Moses grim
In the vanguard, and the young, guarding the tablets,
Sang with a hope they had a right to feel:

    We go to the land
    Where the hand of the Lord
    Showers blessings, and
    The sun fails not, nor the soil
    And man's toil is a prayer
    Of thankfulness to the Lord.
    There it lies, beyond our eyes
    And yet within reach of our hand.
    We go to the unknown land.

Lustily singing,
The young, guarding the Ark of the Covenant.

13

EVER UNREST

The wilderness of Paran. Wilderness
After wilderness, and now this wilderness.
Sand, rock, distant mountain. A copper sun
Riding a wilderness of bronze. Thirst,
Their close companion in the wilderness.
Here? Here? they cried. *We camp here?*
A wife said humbly: 'I should think there must be
A good reason for it. I have a feeling –'
What feeling, woman? 'There must be a reason.
What are they doing up there?' Pointing
Into the distance, and they squinted into
The distance, to the mountain range,
To two lone figures, high up, scanning the distance.
Moses pointed afar. 'Is that Canaan?'
Aaron asked. 'It is what I saw in my dream,'
Said Moses. 'I heard the name.' What Aaron saw
Was wilderness and mountain. 'Now,' said Moses,
'We must spy out the land. There will be a long
Time of waiting still. Set up the tabernacle.
Our symbol of permanency.' Aaron groaned:
'Permanency. What do we live on?' *What do we live on?*
They asked that question down in the wilderness,
Setting up their tents. One man said to another:
'Can *you* see anything beyond there?' –
'The same as lies beyond *there* – the way we came.' –
'Then what is all the fuss about?' – "He says

We're near it. But we've been near it
Ever since we left Egypt. It's always the same.
Sand sand sand and more sand." –
'Be reasonable. We have rocks as well, sometimes.'
And, in mock solemnity, the other intoned:
'Beyond there, O my people, lieth Canaan.
And what is Canaan?' Another growled: 'It's a word
Meaning a dry throttle and an empty glut.
And sand, of course.' He spat towards the sand.
The sun and sand wrestled for the moisture
And the sand won. In the midst of the encampment
The ark of the covenant, magnificently adorned,
(*Nothing too good for the law*, they growled) shone out,
And artists still worked on its adorning. Aaron
Called out the names of those who were to spy
Into the wilderness ahead, one from each tribe:
'Shammua, son of Zaccur, from the tribe of Reuben.
Shaphat, son of Hori, from the tribe of Simeon.
Caleb, son of Jephunneh, from the tribe of Judah.
Igal, son of Joseph, from the tribe of Issachar.
Joshua, son of Nun, from the tribe of Ephraim.
Palti, son of Raphu, from the tribe of Benjamin.
Gaddiel, son of Sodi, from the tribe of Zebulun.'
And so to the end of the twelve. Moses addressed them:
'Over there, my sons – the land of Canaan.
Yes, the promised land. But a land so fertile
That it is doubtless inhabited by men
Of rich flesh and strong bone. Yet remember:
Whoever now possesses the land possesses it
Not by God's promise. You will find people wild, uncircumcised,
Worshipping idols. The land is ours,
But not ours for the easy taking. Your task
Is to spy out the land.' They listened, alert.
'Get you up this way southward and go up

Into the mountain, and see the land, what it is.
Whether it is fat or lean, whether there is timber
Or not. And be of good courage, my children,
And bring of the fruit of the land.' In his tent, near dawn,
Joshua lay with a girl, who said: 'How long?' –
'Who knows?' he answered. – 'But will you be back?' –
'Again, who knows? But you will be a good reason
For wanting to come back,' embracing her.
'Why,' she asked, 'is it you who have to go?
I thought you were learning to stand in his place'. –
'He would go himself', said Joshua, 'if he were younger.
He's as curious as I am.' The girl pouted:
'That is the trouble with me. Too much curiosity.
Never at rest.' He kissed her. – 'You are my rest,
You are my heart's ease, my soul's tranquillity.' –
'But curiosity comes first', she said. – 'Alas,
Daybreak,' and he gave her a final kiss. She said,
Sardonic: 'You had better blow your horn.'
He smiled, strode out, and blew it. They assembled,
The eleven others, armed for adventure,
Hearing, as they went, with Joshua leading,
Words Moses had spoken: *See the people*
That dwell therein, whether they be strong or weak,
Few or many. And what cities they dwell in –
Whether in tents or in strongholds. Search the land
From the wilderness of Zin unto Rehob.
You will come, so says the Lord, to Hebron,
Where Ahiman, Sheshai and Tamlai dwell,
The powerful children of Anak. Be of good courage…
So time passed and the spies did not return,
But the men of Israel said: 'It is always the same.
He starts something off, and then we wait.'
The women: 'Like laying dishes for a meal
When you know there is nothing to eat.' And the men, impatient:

'Is anything being *done*? Magic, that is.
Spells, anything, to get something *done*?'
But other men said: 'That is against the law.'
What was against the law appealed to Dathan,
Who lighted a fire and seasoned it with nitre
And addressed the coloured flames: 'Tell us, we beg you,
O spirits of the desert, when these twelve
Are going to return.' There was no reply.
'What do they say?' asked the credulous. Dathan said:
'They say they do not know.' – 'Try something else.'
Dathan drew charcoal, sulphur mixed with nitre
And raised a flashing spurt. 'They say,' he said,
'Never.' But over mountain slopes in the sunlight,
Under stars, standing on hilltops, seeing
Distant night-fires, and soon – ah, blessed – hearing
Tumbling horns hurtling down rocks, dauntless the twelve
Fared on. One day, from behind bushes, some saw
Huge-limbed laughing men, bathing in a spring,
Speaking strange language, laving metal muscles,
Tough of sinew. Ahimen? Sheshnai? Tamlai?
If so, God help the Israelites, muttered Joshua.
While, back there in the encampment, the Israelites,
Mercifully shut off from future troubles,
Pondered present agonies, as they called them.
Dathan said: 'Manna, nothing but manna. How about some
Flesh to eat, as in the old days?' chewing his manna
With a sour face, and his wife said: 'Kill a sheep.'
'A priest has to do that for you,' Dathan said.
'And no priest will do it. We have to, *he* says, *he*,
Conserve the livestock. God help us, or somebody.'
His wife dreamed, looking into their fire, of Egypt:
'Remember the fish we used to eat, and the melons,
The leeks, cucumbers, onions, garlic?' – 'Don't,' he cried.
'You make me thirsty. Not till tomorrow midday

Does he strike the rock, his twice-weekly miracle.'
No miracles in Eshcol, or all miracle,
The crystal plashing down, the pomegranates,
The grape-clusters heavy on the vine,
While the spies stared incredulous before
Their thirst and hunger growled at idle fingers,
And then the fingers tore, cluster after cluster,
And the noon was a riot of juice. Juice-stained, they heard
What greatly qualified this juicy heaven,
Mouths open, dripping juice, listening to
An undoubted war-chant. Some, from hill-slopes, saw
A distant dust of an army, armour and swords
Catching the light, heard drums and horns and shouts,
And at each other, dismayed. *Be of good courage,*
So he had said. Much good would good courage do them,
Strong-limbed armies barring the way to Canaan
Of a people weak and weaponless, a people now
Cursing Moses: *Worker of miracles, work*
A proper miracle, give us proper food,
Or at least let us slaughter some of the sheep and kine
That we may fill our bellies with meat. He cried:
'Is there no end to your complaining?
Is not the Lord God looking after your needs
Have I not told you till my very teeth
Are shaped like the letters of the words, that we are
Here but for a space? The antechamber of your inheritance,
I call it that, and soon the doors will open
On Canaan, where you will feed fully of its richness,
Be clothed in suet like the kidney of the ox?
I warn you now – if any of you shall seek
To eat flesh meat against my will and the will
Of the Lord your God, it shall be accounted a curse.'
And then the lifting of rocks and pebbles began,
The regular stoning of Moses who, angrily,

Shouted: 'Fools, can you not understand?
We have no Egyptian gold or silver now.
We have only our flocks and cattle – the wealth
We take with us to Canaan. If we start killing –
Even a ram, even a bullock – all too soon
We shall have nothing.' But still they hurled their stones
Till the troops hit back, and then they hurled only curses.
That evening, in proper furtiveness, a ewe was slain,
Some said by Dathan: Dathan was certainly one
Of the greasy tearers and munchers about a fire
Spitting with fat in the small hours. When arrest was made,
It was Dathan who smiled: 'Very well, do your worst.
At least our bellies sing and roll with meat.
Would you gentlemen of the law care for a kidney
Or a hunk of haunch?' Moses, sitting in judgement,
Sighed, said: 'I believe that some of you
Would eat your own mothers.' Dawn was coming up.
'Meat meat – is there no other thought in your heads?
The gravity of the crime must be matched by – O Lord help me –
Must I go down in their annals as the hard man,
Moses the cruel?' Dawn mounted, higher. He heard,
Or thought he heard, jubilant noises from the sun,
And then he turned and, striding through the dew,
Twelve men seemed to be singing. Aaron said:
'The punishment – what is the punishment?'
And Moses said: 'Not now, Aaron. Let us not talk of
Punishments now. See, they return, all twelve,
Singing and bearing poles, and on those poles –'
Soon they could see jostling pomegranates,
Figs ready to burst with sweetness, grapes,
All tied with vine-ropes to poles borne on shoulders,
The poles sagging midway with the weight,
And the cheerful faces of the spies. 'You see,' Moses said
To his people, whose eyes were eating the promise

Of sugared juice in the distance, 'that land, as we were told,
Is flowing with milk and honey, at least with fruit,
You wretched grumbling ingrates.' Some ran out,
Not listening, to greet the approaching twelve, cheering,
And soon they were approaching with them, munching,
Dripping with juice. It was Shammua spoke first:
'We entered the land, Moses, as you instructed,
And it bursts with richness. These grapes and figs and pomegran-
    ates
We gathered by a brook that we call Eshcol.' –
'Well-named, Eshcol,' Moses smiled. 'A grape-cluster.
So we have planted at least one name of our own
In the land of Canaan. See, you foolish children,
The wealth of that land. And that land is ours.' –
'The land is not ours,' Shammua said. 'We saw the people.
They dwell in walled cities and are warlike.' –
'Giants,' Shaphat said, 'the children of Anak.
We saw them. Hittites, Jebusites – who were the others?'
Igal said: 'Amorites, the mountain people.
And by the sea the Canaanites. It is not ours,
That land. We could not possibly prevail.' –
'True,' Shaphat said. 'We have not the numbers.
We have not the weapons.' Caleb spoke up at last
To cry that this was foolish and feeble talk.
'We are strong enough. We can strike now. *Must* strike now.'
Moses turned to Joshua: 'What do *you* say?'
And Joshua said: 'I am of Caleb's mind.
We can do it. We have certain advantages.
They do not know our numbers. We can strike from the moun-
    tains.' –
'And what' asked Moses of the others, 'say the rest of you?'
At once a protesting babble: *There is no comparison*
As to strength we saw them on parade
Huge armies we lack the power we lack the training

The weapons. But Caleb cried aloud: 'It is
Strength of purpose you lack.' Shaphat said:
'Look, we have been through all that land, a land
That would swallow us as a toad swallows a gnat.
The sons of Arak are giants. Compared to them,
We are as grasshoppers are to us.' Then Dathan,
With whom Abiram stood, Abiram, a man
Who had suffered but said little, also Koreh,
Koreh, that strong upholder of the law,
Spoke in no loud voice, not at first. He said:
'Listen to me, Moses. We have borne much trouble
With hardly a murmur.' Moses smiled at that.
'We were given a promise, and that was that we were to
Walk into this land of yours – without trouble,
For we have not had enough and more than enough
Of that? I say this now to you and think I say it
On behalf of all: I would to God
We had died in the land of Egypt. I would to God
We had died in the wilderness. Why, tell us why,
We have been brought towards this land to fall by the sword,
To see our wives and children cut to pieces.
What strong plan does this God of yours have in mind?'
Abiram spoke. 'I vote we choose a new captain –
One who will better consult the people's interests –
One who will lead us back to Egypt.' And he
Looked at Dathan, who looked modestly
Down at the ground. Moses spoke now to Koreh:
'You, sir, were the rigorous upholder
Of God's law. Do you then join this new party?'
Koreh, embarrassed, said: 'I have to confess that –
Well, my confidence in your leadership (with respect)
Has long been wavering. I am of the people,
For the people. The people with me must come first,
And if the law turn sour and if the people

Cease to see good where no good is to be seen,
Then am I not right to waver? There is a feeling
That we ought to return to Egypt.' Moses said:
'Never waver, Koreh. Ever be firm
For one thing or another. Never waver.'
But now, spilling grape-pips, fig-sap, many mouths
Began to cry scorn for Moses, and for Abiram,
Dathan, Koreh, strong sounds of support.
Till Joshua cried: 'Listen.' But they would not.
So he took his horn from his side and blasted loud
And, taken by surprise, they listened. He said:
'The land we passed through – it is a good land.
It is *our* land. If the Lord delight in us,
He will bring us to that land. He will give it to us,
Against the opposition of mere giants.'
Moses looked towards his own tribe of the Levites,
Saying: 'The sons of Levi have no word
Either against or for me.' Indeed, they stood
With blank sad faces, shut mouths. 'Decide', he said.
At least *decide*. But they stood there, gnawing their lips.
'Milk and honey,' sneered Abiram. It was taken as a sign
For the throwing of stones. Joshua cried again:
'I say this – do not rebel against the Lord.
Do not fear the peoples of that land.
We can chew them up like bread, for our teeth will be
The Lord's teeth. Their defence will melt like
Honey in the sun. The Lord is with us, not them.
Do not be afraid. Follow me. Fight.'
So they threw and threw, there being plenty of stones.
And then a sharp-sided flint caught the brow of Moses
And he cursed the people, or tried to: 'God's curse
On you who curse the Lord.' He was struck again
And this time fell, though at once found himself standing
In a crystal desert, looking at a tabernacle

That was twenty suns, unflinching, hearing a voice:
'How long will this people provoke me?
How long will it be ere they believe me,
For all the signs which I have shown among them?
Because all those men which have seen my glory
And my miracles, which I did in Egypt and in the wilderness,
And have tempted me now these ten times,
And have not hearkened to my voice,
Surely they shall not see the land which I
Promised unto their fathers.
Their carcasses shall fall in the wilderness.
They shall wander many years in the wilderness.
None now living shall come into that land,
Save Caleb the son of Jephunneh
And Joshua the son of Nun. But your little ones –
Them I will bring in, them,
And they shall know the land which ye have despised.'
So Moses in the spirit stood erect,
But in the body lay stricken on his pallet,
While Zipporah wept and tended his wounds. Without,
In the place of assembly, Abiram spoke to many:
'He is about to die. I have this, friends,
On the best authority. He is only a mortal man.
You have now the choice of living or dying yourselves.
Who will lead you to life, if it is life you choose?
Egypt is far. Beyond these mountains there
There is hope that is near – food, water, life.
We do not seek a kingdom. We seek a place
Where we can enter quietly, live in peace –
In slavery, if need be. Slavery –
Is slavery worse than this life-in-death?' Doubtful,
Divided, the people knew now which way to turn.
Dathan had counselled Egypt, so had Abiram:
Now they tugged different ways: a choice of enslavements.

But when Moses, weak but beyond fear of dying,
Lay awake in his tent, Aaron came in to say
That now they had various kinds of revolt on their hands.
Some had gone over the mountains. Moses rose,
Helped by his brother, to look afar and saw them,
A band of climbing Israelites. He wept and raged,
Though feeble: 'The Lord is not with them.
They enemy will see them – the Amalekites,
The Canaanites. Ah, the fools. The foolish children…'
By the Ark of the Covenant, Levites, some with packs,
Already ripe to move, still strove in
Justification of their timid revolt:
We are the tribe of Moses, brothers, yes –
But are we not also the chosen of God?
Is it not of God himself we must seek counsel?
At least we find that God does not speak against us.
Has perhaps the Lord God forsaken Moses?
In Canaan, Ahiman and Sheshnai looked,
From the stream where they were bathing, up in wonder
At a strange horde, unarmed, on the mountain-top,
With sheep and goats in plenty. They ran in glee
And wetness the sun drank to speak of it,
To summon the drums and trumpets. And all too soon
The fugitives looked down, panic dawning,
Ripening, to see a dusty army flashing,
And many began to scramble back, ready to curse,
When they had breath, the plan of Abiram.
Some held out longer, then fled, having seen things
They later were to unlade in front of Joshua:
Cut to pieces. My own father. They started
With chopping off his ring-finger. They could not
Get the ring off so they. Horror, sobbing.
They are coming. They're getting their army together.
The Israelite camp filled with weeping, cursing,

The fluttering of fowls at the scent of the fox.
Joshua blew his horn, brought order, order,
Order of a sort. 'Let no more try to leave.
You are all under my orders.' At least forewarned,
Seeing in no surprise the flash of weapons
Coming over the mountain, the army, such as it was,
Had not time to arm and assemble under Joshua.
A small armed guard, under the command of Aaron,
Guarded the tabernacle, rich gold in sunlight,
The enemy's, without a doubt, prime target.
So down they came, yelling, with drum-thump,
With bray of horn, in dust stabbed with points of silver,
To the Israelite plain. The women screamed and scattered
While Joshua raised his spear. In the first skirmish,
The enemy was surprised – these were, then, after all,
No enfeebled people sucking goat-teats. Joshua smote
Hard and hard. Caleb killed a giant.
But the enemy drove in to the centre, seeing gold.
Aaron was pierced in the thigh, but the inner guard
Fought the more for his scream, beating them off,
The dirty defiling fingers. Within his tent,
Moses prayed, tried to rise, was held down
By Zipporah and Ghershom, so prayed again:
They may not prevail. You, O Lord God,
May not suffer them to prevail. And the earth shook,
But it may have been a natural fault of the earth,
Or the shaking of the armies. He heard a trumpet
Crying retreat. Joshua, wiping the sweat away, saw it –
Retreat. But it was the retreat of an army
That had had enough for the day, driving before it
Herds and cattle, also women. (They would return:
Rich fields for reaping here.) Among the women
Was the wife of Dathan, but Dathan did not weep,
Rather blew his rage to a white fire.

14

THE DEATH OF DATHAN

There were three of them, then, all in a sort of accord
Hammered out of necessity, as they saw it,
And, adorned like men of partition, with men behind them,
They marched on Moses and Aaron. Moses, weak still,
Lay pale on the bed, seeing three princes approach –
Abiram, Koreh – and, ahead of them, Dathan.
Dathan's rage was in check. 'If I may speak –'
'You do not look like a man who seeks permission,'
Moses said. 'Speak by all means, Dathan.'
So Dathan spoke. 'What I say I say
On behalf of my peers. What I say
I do not lightly say. What I say I say
After grave and long consideration.' –
'And' said Aaron, 'What is it that you have to say?'
Dathan said: 'This. That we have reached the limit
Of endurance of your tyranny over us,
Prince Moses. You made promise of milk and honey
And silver and gold and a land over which our people,
The children of Israel, should rule.' Moses said:
'The milk and honey were certainly promised, Dathan.' –
And what', said Dathan, 'have we been given instead?
Starvation in the wilderness, death in the wilderness'.
Moses said: 'You, Dathan, have avoided
Both starvation and death with exemplary cunning.
Now will you come to your point?' And Dathan said:
'My point is that your day of rule is over –
Or soon will be. We have support in all the tribes.'
Moses said: 'I see. And what then do the
Usurping princes seek to do with their power?
Koreh is one of them, I see. At least he is no longer

Wavering.' Dathan cried out: 'You have failed.
The whole expedition has been a failure.
With your tricks and talk of an all-powerful God
You've swollen yourself to an imitation Pharaoh,
Forcing your failure upon us.' Moses sighed.
'You forget much, Dathan. You forget that I
Was once a prince of Egypt, laden with gems,
Stuffed with sweetmeats, suffocated with the
Perfume of courtesans. This is a strange power
I have taken on, is it not? – The burden of rule
Without its comforts: my palace a tent, my kingdom
A wilderness. I ask again: what is your policy,
Prince Dathan?' And Dathan replied: 'To lead the tribes
Back to Egypt, but not into slavery.
To make, out of a sufficiency of power,
A treaty with the Pharaoh. To demand
That the God of the Israelites be of equal status
With any of the gods of Egypt.' Aaron smiled
Frostily: 'At least at last you believe in a
Sort of God of the Israelites. It is a beginning.' –
'A true beginning', Dathan said, 'will be to
Show your impotence by wresting this thing away –
This ark you use for holding the people down.
We can provide our own priests –' Aaron said:
'For holding the people down.' And Moses: 'Dathan,
Dathan – I confess my failure as a teacher.
It seems I have taught you nothing. God chooses man.
Man does not choose God. God shows how he chooses
Through signs – signs. What signs do you have?'
Dathan said: 'If by signs you mean trickery –'
And Moses: 'I see you all carry your rods
Of potential rule. Those are a kind of sign.' –
'Those sticks,' said Dathan, 'stand for the confidence
Of the twelve tribes in our mission,' raising his.

'We are delegated to speak for them all.' Moses said:
'Aaron, cast your rod to the ground.' He did so.
'Now, let the rest of you contend
With the priestly power of Aaron. Signs, signs –
What have we, any of us, but signs?' Then Dathan:
'More Egyptian trickery. Foolishness.
An old man's foolishness.' Moses said to him:
'Indulge an old man's foolishness a while longer.'
So Dathan, sneering, cast his rod down, and the others,
Abiram, and Koreh, cast down theirs.
'What will you do with Aaron's?' Dathan grinned.
'Turn it into a serpent? That's an old trick.'
But as he spoke he ceased to smirk: the rod
Of Aaron put out leaves and flowers and fruit.
The others stayed but rods. Then Moses said,
Wearily: 'I have warned you often enough
In my time, Dathan, and now I swear to you
That this warning shall be final. Hear me, then.
Seek not to rise against the Lord your God.
To you all I say this – bear back my word to the others.
Tempt not the Lord your God, lest the ground
Open under your feet and swallow you.'
But Dathan and his fellows strode away,
With no further word, while Aaron
Picked up his rod, smelt at a budding rose,
Saw the rose fade, the fruit wrinkle, the leaves
Drop, become nothing before they reached the earth.
That night, in torchlight, Moses spoke to his people:
'Keep, I warn you, away from the tents of the wicked.
Touch, I warn you, touch nothing of theirs, lest ye
Be consumed in all their sins. Pay heed to my words.
You shall now know, once for all, that the Lord chooses,
That men do not. And if these men – pay heed –
Die the common death of all men,

Be visited after the visitation
Of all men, then the Lord has not sent me.
But if the Lord your God makes a new thing,
And the earth opens her mouth and swallows them
And they go down swiftly to the pit then, pay heed,
You shall understand these men have provoked the Lord.'
But Dathan, Abiram, Koreh blasphemously
Attired themselves like priests, scoffing at his words,
And they stood before the tabernacle like priests,
And Dathan spoke out strong: 'So, we stand here
By the tabernacle to tell you that your God,
The God of the people, speaks through the people
By means of the voice of them that the people have chosen,
That what the people have chosen as prudent and wise
Will be confirmed by the God the people. We,
The people, choose to return to Egypt, there
To live in peace and fatness. Will our God
Say nay?' And that word was caught up: *nay* and *nay*
In the torchlight. So Moses shut his eyes
That he might not see what he knew must follow,
Hearing only thunder, the jolting of the earth,
Cries of terror, opening his eyes to see
What he knew he must see: dust and enveloping smoke
About the tabernacle, and the three false priests
Not there, but the people on their knees in terror.
Dathan no more: the earth had eaten Dathan.
And Moses spoke to himself: *Yet mercy is infinite.*
At least let us believe so. Dathan, Dathan,
I shall miss your thorn in my side …
Now, by a different way, skirting the mountains
And the fierce foes beyond them, in a new unity,
But wretched, they fared on, leaving behind
Carcasses in the desert, as foretold,
Seeking Mount Hor. Jolted in a cart,

Attended by his wife and sons, Aaron lay,
The wound on his thigh grown green, in great pain,
With nauseous ointments lapped by the blowflies. 'So',
Eliseba his wife said, 'your reward
For protecting that tabernacle of yours'. She wept.
'The pain', he said, 'grows less. The wound will sleep.' –
'But not the fever. The fever is very much awake.'
Aaron said: 'I will be better at the oasis.
Trees and running water. Fruit.' She wiped his lips
With a towel, and he spoke to Eleazar,
His son, saying: 'You know what you must do
When we reach Mount Hor?' And the son replied:
'I must become a priest.' – 'A priest,' said his father.
'You must take over my office, wear my garments.
Eleazar the priest. Your mother will be proud.'
But she said: 'Do not talk like that.' And Aaron:
'It is never too soon to prepare him for the task.
It is the task and the glory that his sons
And his son's sons must fulfil till the end of our race.
A task and a glory he will take with him into Canaan.
It is he who will perform the rite of thanksgiving.'
But Eliseba said: 'You will be well soon.
You will be there in all your robes and glory.'
But Aaron replied: 'The journey is by no means over.
We cannot enter in peace. Bitter enemies –
Those are to be faced. Oasis to oasis,
Skirting the promised land, seeking a way in
That is not to be granted so easily. Eliseba,
You have known a hard life.' – 'All life is hard,'
She said. 'It is the nature of life
To be hard. But there have been – Well, shall I say
The hardness has made the pleasures more pleasurable.
I do not complain. Try now to sleep a little.'
So she laid his head in her bosom, and he slept.

But slept less, raving, as the fever raved,
And ceased to rave when they came in sight of the mountain,
Speaking strange words softly, and soon no words,
No breath for words. She shut his eyes for ever.
He was borne on a litter, in his priestly robes,
Up to the mountain-top. Gently, Moses
Took off the priestly garments, and invested
Eleazar, the son of Aaron, in them,
And Eleazar led the chant, against the morning,
Blessing all, finally blessing his father
Who lay in the morning for ever. Moses spoke:
'I speak of him as my brother first – faithful,
Unwavering in his faith. My very voice,
My other heart. And of the house of Israel
None was more brave, more steadfast. His mouth was of gold,
The spirit of the Lord burned in him. Now we see him
Gathered to his fathers. God grant him rest.
God grant that his spirit ever animate
The race he so adorned, lending it
Something of his strength, of his faith.
So be it.' But to himself he said:
And how long will the race last? We are dying,
The old men are dying. Can the young
Survive? Can they keep the fire alight? He foresaw
A desert of corpses, foreheard travelling voices:
Dead so long ago. So much time passed.
That body there   that could be my father's.
A powerful people – at least a numerous people.
Have they disappeared? Are they gone for ever?
The end of them, the end of them, I'd say.
It would be a kind act to bury these dead.
But they are already buried. Already forgotten.
Just dead bodies. Without a name.
Without a race. He shook the voices away,

And turned again to the task of quieting
Real voices, living voices. So they moved towards Edom,
Living bodies, with a name, with a race, moved.
And one day, in the palace of the king of Edom,
A crude barbaric throneroom, eating grapes,
Handmaidens about him, the king sat
While a chamberlain spoke. '*Ganas voti,*' the king said.
So in they came, dusty, travel-worn, bowing,
Joshua and Caleb: 'May we speak, sir king?'
The king nodded, spitting grape-seeds. Joshua:
'You will have heard of our nation. Israel.
We have been in bondage to Egypt for many years,
Not only our generation but generations
And generations before us. We cried out to the Lord
And the Lord brought us forth out of Egypt. Now we are in
Kadesh, on the border of your kingdom.
We are sent to ask leave to pass
Peacefully through your country.' The chamberlain
Translated into the dialect of the kingdom:
The king showed little interest. Caleb said:
'We promise, majesty, not to pass through your fields,
Or through your vineyards. We promise not to drink
Of the waters of your wells. We promise to go
Only by the king's highway – yours, majesty.
We will not turn to the right hand nor to the left,
Until we have passed your borders.' The king listened,
Spitting a fig now, and at length said: '*Nor vah.*'
'I am instructed', said the chamberlain, 'to inform you
That the answer is no'. The king spoke a longer sentence:
'*Go nadi daya, goro mi nadi nadi in vebu.*' –
'His majesty's words are these: if you try to pass,
We will slay you all with the sword.' Regretfully.
'That was sufficiently plain,' Joshua said.
'I am instructed to add that if our people

Or their cattle drink of the water of your kingdom,
Then we will pay for it.' The king waved a violent fig:
'*Garata karvol. Nor vah nor vah.*' The chamberlain
Began to translate, but Joshua said:
'We understand.' They looked at each other wearily.
The king offered grapes, figs. They refused.
Handmaidens. Regretfully, they refused.
So Moses sought another road, young men about him,
Men even younger than Caleb and Joshua,
While he traced a map in the sand, saying: 'Yes,
We are ready to *progress*, Joshua.' They smiled.
'But not by the northern road. We are, thank God,
Much better warriors than we were, but hardly
Good enough yet to face those northern armies.
So we have to think of another road.' But all roads
Led, it seemed, to war – skirmishes
With dirty desert people, formal battles
With men in armour, their trumpets sweet and polished,
Encounters with barbarous hosts that spoke a language
Of growls and coughs. But, as time passed, the Israelite banners
Prevailed more. A matter of training. Stolen arms.
Even a matter of silver trumpets. There was a night
When the Israelite warriors, proud of being warriors,
Feasted and listened, full to a blind harpist
Who sang of their strength: 'Woe to thee, Moab.
Thou are undone, O people of Chemosh.
We have shot at them. Heshbon is perished
Even unto Dibon. We have laid them
Waste even unto Nophah.' Caleb, wine-flushed, said:
'And yet there was a time, not long ago,
When we couldn't win a single battle.' Joshua,
Wine-flushed, said: 'Discipline. Generalship.
Youth. New methods.' The blind bard sang:
    'And we turned and went up by the way of Bashan.

And Og king of Bashan went out against us.
He and all his people, to the battle at Edrei.
And the Lord said unto Moses: Fear him not,
And thou shalt do unto him as thou didst
Unto Sihon, king of the Amorites.
So we smote them and his sons and all his people.
Until, halleluiah, none was left alive,
And we possessed his land.' Warriors listening,
Scarred, patched, amputated, reminiscent,
Not above tears, cheering the end of the song.
'Discipline', Joshua said. 'Generalship.
And God, of course. God is on our side.'
Wine-flushed, scarred, tough in the flare of the fires.

15

BALAAM

Woe to thee, Moab. That was a proleptic phrase.
They were hearing, in Moab, of a tough, scarred people,
Young, with a leader so aged as to be mythical
And hence unaging. In the royal palace at Moab
The king, Balak, listened to a minister saying,
In loud agitation to another minister:
'Have I ever denied it? I said all along
They were, are a dangerous people.' The king said:
'Where are they now?' The second minister pointed
To a crude map on sheepskin: 'There. You see.
The side of Jericho. By Jordan river.
They have set up their tents on the plains of Moab.'
So the king cried: 'My territory. Do you mark that?'
And the first minister: 'As I said before,
They were, are, a dangerous people. Also they are
A *breeding* people. Babies scarce out of the cradle

Doing arms drill, or so we are told. And look what they did
To the Amorites.' The king said: 'What did they
Do to the Amorites?' The second minister said:
'Your majesty is presented with a comprehensive report.'
King Balak said: 'Yes, yes, mass castration or something.
I know.' And the first: 'With respect, your majesty.
Slaughter, yes. But no atrocities. They are not a
Castrating people.' The king said: "Slaughter is enough.
Slaughter will do very well. They'll lick us up,
As the ox licks up the grass of the meadow. Eh?
Eh?' An apt simile, they all agreed.
'How many men can we put in the field?' said the king.
'Not enough', he was told. 'It's a matter of numbers,
Not of courage or organisation. No,
Certainly by no manner of means enough.'
King Balak thought and at length said: 'How about a curse?'
A curse, sir? 'A curse, a malediction. Scare them off.
A religious people, are they? Very well,
They will know all about curses. Potent weapons.
Also economical. A curse.' The second minister
Smiled wanly, and said: 'Ah, Balaam. Balaam.' –
'Balaam, Balaam, a very powerful blesser
And an equally powerful, if not more so, curser.
Where is Balaam these days?' The ministers knew.
'In Pethor, your majesty. You know – by the river.'
Balaam was fishing happily in the river,
Singing a song of his youth. As he grew older
His youth grew clearer. A song of his childhood.
A fat short man, amiable, a powerful curser,
This being his profession. Fishing in the sun,
He scowled when he saw a shadow come over him
And yet the sun still there. Looking up,
He saw that the shadow was of four men, gentlemen,
Of high rank certainly, standing there. He said:

'Ah, gentlemen. You I know, I think.
I am afraid the other gentleman – 'Two elders from Moab:
These he knew. The others? 'Greetings, Balaam',
Said one of the Moabites. 'We are come from the king.
These gentlemen are from Midian. We bear you word
From the court of Moab. The gentlemen of Midian
Wish to be associated with our mission.'
Balaam said: 'Ah, come, come then, got you,'
Landing a carp. Then: 'Mission? Message?' A fine one.
The elder Moabite read aloud from a tablet:
'Behold, there is a people come out of Egypt.
Behold, this people covers the face of the earth
And abides over against me. Come now, I pray you, therefore:
Curse me this people, for they are too mighty for me.
Then perhaps I shall prevail, drive them out of the land.
For I know well that he whom you bless is blessed,
And he whom you curse is cursed.' Balaam heard that,
Complacent, then he said: 'The king's own words?'
The elder said: 'You will recognise the style.'
Balaam rose and said: 'Lodge here tonight.
Plenty of fish, as you see. I have to consult –
I must – You understand there are certain things
I shall have to do.' They understood. 'And in the morning
I hope you may take back word to – How is his majesty?'
Distressed, they said. Very fine carp, they said.
They ate them that night, sucking the bones,
And drank the thick black wine of Pethor. Balaam,
Expansive, told tales of cursings. 'Ah, yes, gentlemen.
That was one of my better curses. It was
Extremely efficacious.' The eldest Moabite:
'I hope you can provide an even better one.
One worthy of this accursed people.' – 'Accursed?'
One of the Midianites said. 'That is surely
A little premature.' They laughed, finished the wine,

And Balaam said: 'Now, I will go to my sanctum
And brew up my curse. Excuse me, gentlemen.'
In what he called his sanctum, reeking of mould,
Fish-glue, asafoetida, by a fish-oil lamp
He muttered over signs of old sheepskin, a skull,
A dried crocodile for company. Then the skull spoke.
Out of the sempiternal grin of the skull –
Or was it the crocodile's? Words came,
Gentle enough: *Who are those men with you?*
Balaam gaped, gaped again, then answered:
'Balak, the son of Zippor, king of Moab,
Sent them to me. But who are you, who *are* you?'
The voice said: *With what word?* 'Who are you?' gaped
Balaam. 'Who?' *With what word?* Balaam took the
Tablet and read from it, shaking: 'Behold,
There is a people come out of Egypt, which
Covers the face of the earth. Come now, curse me
Them, then perhaps I shall prevail –' The voice said:
Listen, Balaam. You shall not curse this people.
For the Lord has already blessed them. You hear, Balaam?
'Lord Lord what is the Lord?' *The Lord God,*
Balaam. 'But I have an instruction, an order –
From the king himself. What is this *Lord God*?'
The voice said, quietly still: *I am the king*
Of your king and all kings that ever were
And shall be. Therefore, Balaam, I say to you:
You shall not go forth and curse the children of Israel.
So the skull or crocodile was silent. Balaam sat,
Gaping. A dream? No, not a dream. Nor wine,
Not wine, he knew the effects of wine.
The emissaries snored. He sat there, gaping.
In the morning, at first light, as they smacked dry mouths,
Squinting for the wine-jug, he told them, spluttering,
Saying: 'You understand? You understand me?

It was the voice of the *Lord God,* so he is called.' –
'And not,' said an elder, ringing the taste of the wine
On his morning mouth, 'some devil of your own conjuring?
Some devil that consults your interests? I'm empowered to say,
On the king's behalf, that he had thought of some
Highly tangible reward.' But Balaam cried:
'If Balak should give me his palace crammed with silver,
Gold too, rubies, I could not go
Beyond the word of this Lord God, as he is called.
I fear him. It was a quiet voice.' The elder said:
'And if Balak should, say, order decapitation,
Preceded by certain ingenuities
Of torture?' Balaam stoutly said: 'This Lord God
Would intervene, of this I am sure.' The second elder,
Not much of a talker, spoke, rasping, saying:
'Why not call on him now for assurance, Balaam?
Are you certain, by the way, that he exists?
That he was not a phantom induced by carp-flesh
And the damnably heavy wine of Pethor?' Balaam,
Distressed, said nothing. And the first elder smiled:
'Come then, O Balaam of my heart, let us go.
There is work to be done, if cursing
Can properly be called work.' Balaam gulped, saying:
'Where do I have to go?' The elders told him:
'To the plains of Moab, the tents of the Israelites –
There to do your cursing. You have cursing to do.'
The road they took, Balaam ahead on his ass,
Led to a narrow way between two vineyards.
Balaam with servants behind, behind four elders,
Riding an ass, which he preferred to a horse,
Being easier, for one of his bulk, to mount,
Found that the ass responded with a bray of fear
To something she saw, something he did not see.
And she tried to get from the way of what she saw,

Thrusting towards one of the walls. He whipped her, while
The emissaries behind expressed impatience, anxious
To get the cursing over. So she took the road
Again and again brayed fear, thrusting towards the
Other wall. Balaam yelled and beat her,
But, taking the path again, this time she fell
And Balaam fell with her. He rose, his anger was great,
He whipped and whipped, panting. And now she spoke.
Now she spoke. She brayed: 'What have I done to you?
Why must you beat me three times?' Balaam cried:
'Who said that? Who spoke then? Was it you?
You? If I had a sword I'd thrust it straight
Into your faithless flank.' So the ass brayed:
'Kill me? Faithless? Am I not your beast?
Have you not ridden me every day?' He said,
Panting: 'You mocked me. Do you hear? You mocked me.'
And the ass said: 'Did I ever mock you before?'
Balaam wept (he is drunk, he is old, he is mad,
The emissaries said to each other). 'No.'
And he turned to them and to his servants. 'Did this
Animal really speak? Am I going mad?'
An elder from Midian spoke. 'A touch of the sun.'
And on that word light brighter than sunlight struck
Balaam, him only, and he fell flat on his face,
Hearing the voice of last night out of the sky:
Your beast saw me and turned thrice from the path.
The Lord God is no figment of man's mind
But very reality which even the beasts may know.
Your ass has saved you by turning you from the path.
For, Balaam, if you had ridden into my path,
Then surely I would have slain you. Balaam sobbed,
Raised his terrified head towards the light,
Then lowered it, blinded. 'I have sinned, O Lord.
I have displeased you. I will go back again.'

No, said the voice. *Go to the court of the king*
And speak there what I shall put in your mouth to speak.
Then the great light faded, leaving the little light,
Birds singing, the ass cropping vineleaves
And Balaam said, trembling: 'We must go to the king.'
The eldest elder nodded, saying: 'Yes.
The king must see you. You are obviously
In no fit state for cursing.' So, in the palace of Moab,
The king was loud: 'Why? *Why?* You had your orders.
Your orders were clear. You were to put a curse
On the hosts of Israel. And now you come babbling
About the *Lord God*, whoever he is.
Are you now in the pay of the Israelites?
Have they cast a spell on you? Are even their
Magicians more potent than ours?' But Balaam said:
'I have no power to curse the Israelites.
All I may speak is what the Lord God
Puts in my mouth to speak.' The king cried: 'God?
God? You mean the god of the Israelites?'
Balaam said, humbly enough: 'It seems to me
That such language is foolish. I speak with respect.
No, I do not. Respect and disrespect
To kings and men in high places – what do they mean
To me now? It seems to me that there is only
One God, and though the Israelites
May have found this out before other men, yet this
Does not make him merely a God of the Israelites.
But certainly this God will not curse the Israelites.'
King Balak cried: 'We have a god of our own.
It seems to me that you have wronged our god.
Ba'al has turned against you. Reparation,
Sacrifice is called for.' But Balaam shook his head,
Saying: 'There is only one God,
So this Lord God said to me. And idolatry

Is an abomination before the Lord.'
He seemed ready then to fall into a trance.
The court was shocked at this blasphemy, the king
Outraged. When night fell, Before the idol Ba'al,
With flares and aromatic gums burning, priests
Despatching a ram with knives, then firing the flesh
On the altar, an abomination before the Lord,
Balaam was dragged, under guard, forcibly enrobed
And ordered by the king himself to curse, but he could not.
Now, Balaam. Beg of our god what I beg of you.
A curse on the Israelites. But he could not.
Instead he spoke, as it seemed, for some not present:
'Balak the king has brought me to this high place
Before the idol Ba'al. And he has said:
Come, curse Israel, curse the blood of Jacob.
But how shall I curse whom God has not cursed? How
Defy whom the Lord has not defied? From the top
Of the rocks I see him, and from the hills
I behold him. Let me die the death of the righteous
Before I curse Israel and the God of Israel.'
The king wept aloud: 'What have you done to me?
I took you to curse my enemies: behold, you bless them.'
And Balaam said: 'The Lord God is not a man,
That he should lie, neither the son of man,
That he should repent. Has he said, and shall he not do it?
Has he spoken and shall he not make it good?
Behold, I have received commandment to bless and I cannot
Reverse it.' At the king's sign he was led away,
Crying out: 'God brought them out of Egypt.
His strength is the strength of the unicorn. Behold,
The people shall rise up as a great lion,
And lift themselves up as a young lion.' They imprisoned him,
Manacled him to a wall, with serpents about,
Toads and scorpions, and thonged whips ready.

The king, troubled, said: 'If you will not curse them,
Then at least do not bless them. Let us have you
Neutral in the fight that is to come.'
But Balaam said: 'I shall see him, though not now.
I shall behold him, but not nigh. There shall come
A star out of Jacob, and a sceptre
Shall rise out of Israel and shall smite
The corners of Moab and all the children of Midian.'
The king struck him in the face, twice, thrice,
But Balaam cried: 'Moab shall be a possession,
And Israel shall do valiantly.' The king, in disgust
Said: 'Loosen his chains. Let the madman go.
Send him out into the wilderness,
On that talking donkey of his.' And they did so.
The Israelites in the their tents woke at sunrise to hear
A voice raised to the sky, speaking their own tongue:
'How godly are thy tents, O Jacob,
And thy tents, O Israel. As the valleys are they spread,
As gardens by the river's side, as the trees
Of lign aloes which the Lord has planted,
And as cedar trees beside the waters.' Balaam
Had come riding ecstatic into their camp,
His ass placid beneath him. He cried aloud:
'He shall eat up the nations his enemies
And break the bones, and pierce them through with arrows.'
Moses came from his tent to see and hear
This prodigy: a fat old man on an ass,
Declaiming to heaven: 'He couched, he lay down as a lion,
And as a great lion. Who shall stir him up?
Blessed is he that blesses thee, and cursed
Is he that curses thee.' Moses said:
'Whoever he is, he needs to be looked after.'
So gently Balaam on his ass was led
Towards the tents of the high. 'She spoke,' he cried.

'She was fired with the fire of the Lord, and behold she spoke.'
The ass was led to grass, and Balaam laid
Gently in Joshua's bed. They listened to him,
Joshua, Caleb, Eleazar, Moses,
With grave attention, while the younger children
Spoke to the ass, saying: 'What is your name?
Where do you come from?' And the ass said nothing,
Finding the grass good. But Balaam cried:
'Behold the great truth is come upon me.
He is a God of all things, halleluiah.
To one of the uncircumcised, a son of Moab,
He shone like a great light and so shines still.
Halleluiah. And the vessel of the Lord,
Which is Israel, shall prevail, and God shall prevail.
Halleluiah, halleluiah.' Moses spoke to Joshua,
Quietly, half-fearful, half-unwilling to believe:
'So – the Lord God spreads his dominion.
Slowly. Almost cautiously. And the days of bloodshed
May soon be at an end. Our land may fall to us
Like a ripe pomegranate. Without a struggle.
Without the snipping of a single lock of hair
Or the bruising of finger.' But Joshua knew
He spoke too soon. Balaam cried on and on:
'Strong is the dwelling-place of the most high.
Thou puttest thy nest in a rock. And ships shall come
From the coast of Chittim, and the enemies of the Lord
Shall perish for ever and ever. Halleluiah.'
And the ass, without raising her teeth from the grass,
Raised her voice and brayed. 'It was Amen.'
The children said. 'It sounded like Amen.'

16

ZIMRI

So that, and they praised God for it, was all behind them:
The Dead Sea stretching in sunlight like a living one,
The boys diving into it for coolness
Shocked at not sinking, borne up by the hand
Of hidden water giants. They had shrieked, splashed,
Splashed, tasted. *Salt*, they had cried, *salt*.
Salt indeed, a salt lake set in a saltscape
Glooming with crystalline menace in the sun.
All we need is something to eat with it.
Salt salt salt. Remembering grandmothers' stories,
The women saying: 'The wife of Lot must be here
Somewhere.' And the men: 'She could be anywhere.'
Zipporah moaning: 'Salt. Salt in my throat.
Soon surely we shall meet the fresh springs.
Why do we move so slowly, Ghersom?' They were not
Moving at all: the tents had been set up
In the salt desert, salt under a salt moon.
But now the plain of Moab, with Moses saying:
'You think we can travel safely?' Joshua replying:
'We can never travel safely. The strength of Moab
Is still an unknown, and Moab has many friends.
Do not take Balaam as a sign of the weakening of Moab.'
Moses smiled sadly: 'Driven mad by the word of the Lord.
Poor Balaam.' (Happy Balaam rode on his ass
Through the Israelite encampment, crying to the sky:
'For the Lord of the Israelites is all things.
Behold, he is in the creeping worm of the earth
And in the fiery lioness that is the sun.
He is the unicorn and tiger and his name
Shall be blessed for ever and ever. Halleluiah.'

And a sardonic Israelite: '*Halleluiah.*')
'Caution, then,' said Moses. 'We must send patrols
To learn about their defences. And the general attitude
Of the Moabite population. We need them friendly.
We need their wells and pasturelands.' Joshua said:
'But we must push on. Time is short.' Then Moses:
'You were never a discreet man, Joshua. My time
Is certainly short, but do not remind me of it.
I shall see the Jordan before I die – fear not.'
Joshua said: 'I did not mean that. I meant
That the patience of our people can hardly be
Tried much longer. They are sick of wandering.' –
'Oh, the young are patient enough. As for the old –
Well, there are few of us left. Aaron gone,
His poor wife Eliseba. And, soon, very soon –'
He sighed. 'None is exempt, Joshua. The earth
Is hungry for us all. But that is what I meant
When I said we must stay here a little while.
I do not think she can very well be – moved.'
Wasted with fever, Zipporah cried: 'Tomorrow.
We shall see him tomorrow, then?' And Ghersom:
'Who, mother?' – 'My Father, of course. And my sisters.
Those that are left. But not those wicked men
Who keep beating us away from the well. He took his stick to
    them.
He ran down the hill and trounced them and they ran off howling.
He was very strong in those days.' And Ghersom said:
'Is still. Is still very strong.' (Very strong
In the synod, explaining the law at that very moment:
'The line must be drawn wide, very wide. It is the margin
That is the essence of the law. Thus we condemn
The eating of the flesh of swine, and why?
It is not enough to say that it is unclean.
If you eat the flesh raw you will, as we know,

Contract disease: you belly will writhe with serpents.
If you eat it well-roasted you will be safe,
Since great heat kills the eggs of the serpents within
The body of the beast. Now who is to draw the line
Between well-roasted and ill-roasted? Who, indeed,
Is to draw the line between the roast and the raw?
It is safer to draw the margin too far out
And condemn the eating of swine's flesh altogether.
And so with marriage – always the safe margin.
Marry your brother's daughter; soon enough
Others will marry their mother's sisters, even
Their sisters, even their mothers. Draw the line
Far out, always far out, remember that.')
And Zipporah rambled more. 'It will be pleasant
To sit by the well and talk. And sing. And play
Games with the ball as we used to. Waiting still
For the strong man from the strange land over the mountains
To come and fight the bad men by the well.
He will come with sunrise. Is it sunrise yet?'
Not waiting for an answer. 'Sunrise. There is a
God in the sun, did you know that? And a god in the moon.
But the god of the sun is made out of fire. He has a
Beard of fire. And he eats fire.' Then she cried out:
'Why do you give me fire to eat? Why do you
Keep pouring fire down my throat? Cold water –
From my father's well. Give me that, give it to me.'
Moses stood, sad, resigned: a matter of waiting.
He went out into the sunrise. Joshua said:
'The patrols are leaving now. It would be good
If you could give them a word of encouragement.' –
'I cannot give her water from her father's well',
Sighed Moses, 'but I can always give encouragement.'
The patrols were assembling now. Moses saw
A young man he though he knew, one tall and clean

And upright. 'Zimri' he said. 'Zimri, is it not?'
The young man held himself stiff, answering: 'Sir.
The son of Salu. Of the tribe of Simeon.' –
'I knew your father,' Moses said. 'He was brave.
I trust his son takes after him.' *Sir*. And then,
Raising his voice in the sunrise, Moses spoke
To the entire parade: 'What you have to do
Is to find out what chance we have of passing
Through Moabite territory in safety. You may find
That the people are friendly. Do not be afraid
Of admitting you are Israelites. Watch out
Less for fights than for snares. The king or his princes
May arrange a feast and soak you in Moabite wine.
Then, while you are snoring, your throats may be quietly cut.
See what amenities are available: wells, pasture.
Avoid their women. This is a pagan people.
They worship a false god. Do not be drawn in.
They practise all manner of abominations.
Do not be corrupted. Go, with my blessing.'
Zimri, presenting the shiny face of one
Who is incorruptible, said, firmly: '*Sir*.'
And so they passed, in their several patrols, to Moab –
Gentle pasture, gentle people, pagan though,
Hence corruptive. Igal and Shaphat entered
A pleasant town, seeing a market-place
Where fruit and roots and sheep and goats were chaffered for,
Seeing a troupe of acrobats perform,
Seeing women, veiled but giggling,
Wagging provocative haunches. At an upper window
A lady sat in indolent enjoyment
Of the admiration of the street, fanned by a girl.
They sought and found a town office and, to a clerk,
In their own speech, slowly, said what their mission was.
The were understood and led to an inner room

Where an elegant officer sat but rose when they entered,
Offering cushions to sit upon, offering wine.
But they refused the wine, said who they were
And what they wished. 'Yes. I understand you.' –
'We naturally undertake to respect all property
As well as human life. We will certainly pay
For damage inadvertently done.' And the officer:
'How will you pay?' – 'In sheep. In cattle.' –
'I see', he said. 'Not in slaves? Or women?'
Igal said: 'We do not sell our women.
And we do not keep slaves.' Shaphat added to that:
'We have ourselves been enslaved – to the Egyptians.
Or so they tell us – it is rather a long time ago.'
The officer said: 'The story of your people
Has travelled even to our cities. So. Now I see
Real live Israelites in the flesh. Not very much flesh,
If I may say so.' Igal said: 'We are a lean folk.
That comes, I would say, of not living in cities.'
And Shaphat: 'A chosen people has to be
A lean people.' The officer smiled. 'But has also
To beg occasionally of the unchosen – and the fat.' –
'Oh, we do not beg, sir', said Igal. 'We merely request.'
The officer said: 'With an army behind you? I do not
Think we can very well refuse your request.
We like to think of ourselves as *hospitable*.' –
'And the wells?' said Shaphat. 'The grazing lands to the north?' –
'You have, I hear, been living off salt,' said the officer.
'It would not be *hospitable* to send you back to it.
Salt is good, but only in moderation.'
And so the Israelites moved into the kingdom of Moab.
But Moses said to Joshua: 'Towns. Towns.
Very corruptive places.' Joshua said:
'We shall, we hope, be building towns ourselves.'
But Moses shook his head: 'Market-towns perhaps,

Full of sheep-dung. Call them disposable towns.
I am thinking rather of the cities where the citizens
Amass possessions – jewels and golden bedsteads.
Compromise, fatness, wavering in the faith.
Corruption. Even our short time here is dangerous.
The religion of Ba'al is seductive, Joshua.
We must watch our people.' Caleb said: 'We know that.
Zimri is watching. He has appointed himself
A kind of moral spy.' And Moses said:
'A young man of good family. Reliable.'
(Zimri walking watchfully in the evening,
Passing signs of corruption – laughing girls
Selling themselves for an hour or a night – swine flesh,
Drunken singing. He walked watchfully.)
'Oh yes,' Caleb said. 'Very reliable.'
But Zipporah lingered at death's gate. In the night,
Moses spoke to his God: 'Let her go in peace.
I shall have no power over her final agony.
Then, soon, there will be very few of us
Left over from the old days. And Joshua and Caleb –
They alone of the old days shall enter the land.
Not I, because of my sin of doubt. So be it.
But what then is left for me now? Let the day come soon,
For all things are ready – a people in a good heart,
A people that learns to know its God. Let me see then
The river and the land from the high places,
And then be set free.' He heard wailing
From the tent where Zipporah lay and bowed his head,
Though dry-eyed. *What then is left for me now?*
Zimri in daylight, walking the streets, observed
A public monument depicting men
Half-beast half-fish, engaged in contorted acts
Of love unknown to the Israelites. He saw
A woman, all brown blubber, laden with jewels,

Being carried on a litter, on her lap
A silver sweet-dish piled with powdery sweetmeats,
Powder and sugar about her mouth. Two flunkeys
Whipped beggars and children out of her path. He saw
A blind man, in the final stage of some pox
Unknown to the Israelites, being led by a boy
In the first stage of some pox unknown to the Israelites.
He saw a vendor crying his works of art:
A frank act of sodomy in silver,
A man eating a cat alive, an image
Of Ba'al both foul and seductive, the rarest modes
Of love on wood or copper. And then he came
To an open-air feast, a table loaded heavy
With strange dishes. Beggars hungrily watched
But were beaten away by men with staves. Odd scraps
Of odd-looking meat were thrown at them: they gnawed
At bones like dogs. And Zimri, horrified, saw
Two Israelites at the feast, wearing the apparel
Of the Army of Israel. Their host, a gross Moabite
With a moon-belly, urged them to eat and swill:
'Nothing like this in the wilderness, my boys –
Lobsters fresh from the coast – crack one, crunch one,
Sausages – try one, try several. And this dish
Is one of my cook's great prides: an unborn calf
Cooked in its mother's milk. Fall to. Eat, eat.'
Zimri waited, collected a patrol,
And drove the drunken offenders, bellies taut,
Back to the camp and judgement. Joshua raged:
'Why not? I will tell you why not – because it is
Expressly forbidden by the food laws: that's why not.
Ten days on fatigues: you'll soon learn why not.'
Zimri in night town, walking amid torches,
Music, dance, passed a man and a woman
Embracing naked and frankly in the shadows.

He shuddered, then grew angry when he observed
An Israelite he knew – Gaddiel, son of Sodi? –
Mounting steps to a temple, or what seemed to be
A temple, its front carved with contorted bodies
In acts of love unknown to the Israelites.
He followed but had already lost him in the shadows
When he entered a chamber leading off the porch of the temple,
Lighted by torches and splitting oil-lamps, gross
With pagan effigies. His heart thumped, he looked about him,
And then a woman emerged from the shadows, a Moabite,
In garments he took for those of a priestess, ugly,
Obscenely so, appallingly, seductively so.
She spoke honey: 'You sir, are a stranger.' –
'An Israelite,' he answered, his voice not
Well in control, and she said: 'Ah a follower
Of the new god we are hearing so much about.
The god of vengeance which is called justice.' He:
'A God of love, we are taught. Of love. A God.'
But she said, smiling: 'So – not a new god, then.
You are interested, stranger, in our faith?'
Stiffly he said: 'My own faith is enough
To keep my organ of faith fully occupied.
Other faiths are an abomination, so we are taught.
Many gods – all of them unclean:
The way of the Moabites, we are taught, much like
The way of the accursed Egyptians.' She said:
'The Egyptian gods are gods of death – so *we* are taught.'
He said: 'Madam, you have been well instructed.
I must tell you that I am here officially.
Are Israelites frequenting this temple? I thought I saw
One enter now.' She said: 'Israelites, Moabites –
The names mean nothing. Servants of Ba'al
Come to the temple to worship. I do not enquire
Beyond the faith, beyond the willingness

To embrace the faith.' – 'And what' he said, 'is the faith?'
She said to him softly: 'Look about you.' He looked
At effigies, paintings, showing modes of love
Not known to Israel, she talking the while,
Holding a torch to light the effigies:
'The faith is love, but not perhaps love
As a desert people will know it. You desert-folk
Live in wide space and feel a desire to fill it.
You are a nation, so I hear, that is desirous
Of being great among the peoples of the earth.
You breed, you fill your tents with children. With you
The coupling of man and woman is to that end.
You do not talk or dream of the ecstasy of love –
Only the seed's flow, the setting of the seed to work.
To you, the act of the man and the woman is like the
Sowing of a field. To us, it is not so.'
Zimri gulped at some of the effigies.
'Whatever it is, this love of yours, it is an
Abomination before the Lord.' – 'Which Lord?' she asked.
Zimri said: 'There is only one – our God,
The creator and sustainer of the world,
The God of Israel, the God of mankind.'
She smiled 'The God of a madman on a donkey –
That is how he appears to the Moabites.
But you must see what we mean by love. Come with me.'
He cried out: 'No. Blasphemy. Filth.' She said:
'It is blasphemy and filth to know that ecstasy
Which divides men from the beasts of the field? It is
Blasphemy and filth to know oneself
In the very living presence of the god?
The ecstasy is sent by the god: it is blasphemy
To reject it. The cleanness of the spirit,
From which all earthly dross is purged away –
To reject that is the sin of wallowing

In the filth of animals.' But Zimri cried: 'No. No.'
But he suffered himself, saying *no no* the while,
To be led to the inner temple, drawn there
In his own despite. The priestess ordered, with a gesture,
Two servants to open the portal. Then he saw.
He saw, before an effigy of Ba'al
As god of love, votive lamps burning. He heard
Flutes and a harp, incense-boats clanging, smelt
The richness of roasting herbs. Above all, he saw.
His eyes throbbed at the sight of the men, exalted
In a kind of holiness of lust, prostrating themselves
Before the prospect of love, before the flesh
Of the temple houris. He saw them, evil beauty,
And saw eyes on himself. They stood there, naked,
Before unseeing Ba'al. Zimri moaned, fled, blinded.
And the priestess said, as he fumbled at the portal:
'Well, Israelite – are you prepared
To become not an Israelite but merely
A worshipper at the shrine? You are heartily welcome.'
But he cried out: 'No. No.' Blindly stumbling
Down the steps of the temple, jostled and jostling
Along a street of the city (*no no*), followed by laughter,
Obscenity, out of the city by its gate,
Back to the camp, hearing ring in his head
Moabite voices crooning about love.
He lay alone in his tent, writhing (*no*
No), and, pale in the morning, went to Joshua
To render a report. Joshua said:
'Filthy pagan rites. Any evidence
Of our people indulging in filthy pagan rites?'
Zimri said: 'I thought I saw – but no matter.
Nothing as yet really to report.
Wait. I am watchful.' – 'We know are watchful, Zimri.
We call you Zimri the incorruptible.'

Was there a sneer in the voice? He went again,
That night, to the temple. The priestess greeted him:
'The Israelite. Is this more official business?'
Zimri said: 'I come with a warning.
Any of our people – engage – in your rites,
You yourselves will be in danger.' She smiled:
'You mean the Israelite god of love and justice
Will wipe us all out with the sword?' Zimri said:
'Admit none of our people. You who talk of love
Should not desire to see love followed by pain.
But they will be punished, I warn you. I am watching.'
She said: 'Well, if your priests and priestesses
(Do you have priestesses? I am somewhat ignorant
About your faith) – if, I say, they are willing
To persuade us of the superior attractions
Of your god, then we will be ready to listen.
Conversions are made in men's hearts and men's loins.
They are not easily enforced with armies and thunder.'
Zimri said: 'I warn. It is a warning.'
From out of the temple two men came with obeisances
To the priestess. They recognized Zimri, being Israelites,
But he had his eyes to the ground, unwilling
To meet hers, despite his 'Warning, a solemn warning'.
The Israelites rushed away, and Zimri, emerging,
Saw men running, but did not know who they were.
So, watchful Zimri, he wandered the town in torment,
Not knowing his feeling – anger, lust, envy –
Not knowing what he felt but knowing its violence,
And he came to a tavern and drank of the wine of Moab,
Hearing song, drank of the wine till a girl came
To ask if he would drink yet more of the wine,
Of the wine more, more of the, Moab the wine of,
More. But no. He shook his head and could not
Stop shaking it. No. *I warn. A warning. Solemn.*

'So' the priestess said, 'you are very persistent.
Another solemn warning?' For he was back there,
His tongue thick, tottering, shaking his head,
Not able to stop shaking it, hearing laughter,
Then hearing the laugher cease, hearing himself
Fall to the floor, hearing, feeling nothing.
Servants came forward, solicitous to raise him.
He was helped away to a bed somewhere, and the priestess,
Smiling with the sadness of long knowledge,
Said: 'As so often happens, he finds his way
Through the little god of wine towards the great god:
Blessed then be the little god,' seeing him there,
Smirking on the wall, crowned with vine-leaves,
The great god waiting apart, master and servant,
Humbly on Zimri's awakening. *Most blessed be he.*

17

ABOMINATIONS BEFORE THE LORD

Zimri emerged from the cave and saw bright morning
Beyond the casement – a fountain, oleanders –
And flooding the chamber, wondering where he was
And then remembering the waking in the night,
Her beside him. She now, with eyes laughing,
Poured from a pitcher into a cup. She said:
'You have slept long and deep. Take this', bringing it.
'Take. It is no poison.' Herbs, achingly pungent,
View with dried rose-petals on the bed where he lay.
He drank, tasting herbs and petals, seeing the cup
Cunningly embossed with arms and bosoms,
Then probed in his mind for shame but found none. She
Lay by him in a loose robe, her eyes laughing,
Her hair loose, a torrent of bronze. 'Your name', he said.

'I forget your name, or did I hear your name?'
She told him he had heard it – Cozbi, daughter
Of a minor prince of Moab whose name did not matter,
Servant of Ba'al. 'Daughter of a prince',
He said, 'and you are here.' – 'But this is holy work',
She told him. 'We are not street-girls. What we do
Is in honour of the god. We call it holy work –
To bring men closer to the god.' She kissed him then,
Holy work. 'We are the chosen ones.
Not every woman can take her place in the temple.
Today you are specially blessed, I also,
For today is a feast-day of the god. You came to us
On the eve of his feast-day: it was as if you knew.'
Ba'al, genially ferocious, in a hammered bronze,
Was carried about the town that day, drums beating,
Trumpets and shawms braying, flutes cooing,
Some of his votaries drunk, all half-naked,
Honouring the god. Two Israelite officers,
Biting their lips, watched the procession,
Looking for – 'An abomination,' said one.
'Look at them – look at that couple there.' – 'I see them',
The other said, seeing them. 'But what can we do?
The Moabites are not our responsibility.' –
'But those are', said the first, pointing. 'Look at them.'
Israelites, drunk and gay, dancing along.
'Some of ours', said the other. 'I see what you mean.
But can we make an arrest? Now?' The first one gloomed,
Envy perhaps in his gloom. 'I see what you mean.
They'd tear us to pieces, man.' As night fell,
The Moabites set up their bronze Ba'al high on a plinth,
And the revellers danced about, in contrary circles,
A contradance, singing something filthy and ancient,
Ending exhausted on the sward, any with all,
Man with boy with woman with man with, not too exhausted

To frot away, very holy work, while the god grinned.
But in daylight, in the garden of the temple,
Jasmine, oleander, fountains, birdsong,
Zimri saw holiness of a different order,
Walking, fingers entwined, with Cozbi, saying:
'Why was I so slow in learning?' – 'You were not slow.' –
'I mean, I mean, why did it never occur to me,
Or to any of our people, that truly we worship
A god of misery, a god who hates all joy?
I see the truth clearly now. A god descended
When first we lay together, and it was not our God,
Not the God of the Israelites. Yet this god,
Or goddess as it may be, is a true god,
Laughing, benign…' – 'The god will descend again,
Any time we call on him – or her',
Cozbi said, 'for Ba'al is both she and he,
Mother and father, taking a lover's lineaments,
All things to us.' He embraced her lovingly,
Saying: A new misery torments me.
You will leave me. You will give yourself to others.'
She said: 'That may seem strange to you. To us
It is a sacred duty.' – 'But, beloved, might it not be
A duty more sacred to be my love, my one love?
If there is a god of love, there must also be
A god of marriage.' – 'The gods' she said, 'do not
Concern themselves with marriage. Marriage is for
The making of children, the fixing of – what is the word?'
He said: 'Inheritances. Land. Wealth. Cattle.
Maintaining the power of a family. That is true.
But I have seen with my own eyes a god shine out
From the bodies of girls and boys who have entered marriage.
She said: 'For how long? The god yawns after a time
And then departs. Or he reveals himself
As a god of bitterness. In our temple

There is only the ecstasy.' – 'But you,' he said,
'You are not just the vessel of the ecstasy.
You are yourself – you are my one dear love.
Love is not something out there, not a passage of joy,
Between people who have no names. Love is ourselves.
Love is a word invented for us and us only.
The god is alive when you and I
Lie embraced, alone, the world shut out.'
She said: 'Our high priestess would call that heresy.'
But he: 'Yet she would smile when saying the word,
As you are smiling now.' So they embraced,
And his eyes watered with love, his limbs trembled.
While *out there*, in the city, a great banquet
In honour of Ba'al proceeded – spitting roasts,
Wine spilling. 'Eat,' cried the host. 'Eat ye.
For this is the very flesh of the god Ba'al,
Whose name be blessed in the ten worlds for ever.
Eat, eat, and do homage, for he is here
In the flesh of the lands and seas, in the birds that sing,
In the beast that grunt, in the armoured fish of the waters.
Eat, eat: do homage to his greatness.'
And they ate and belched their praise. Moses heard of it,
Moses heard all from the moral patrols and cried:
'Every abomination that defiled them
With the worship of the golden calf – worse, you tell me,
Since they are eating of filthy forbidden flesh –
Scavengers of the sea, filled with dirt,
Pig-flesh, milk and flesh-meat in the one vessel.
Who has allowed this to happen? Speak. Who?'
And he looked at Joshua, Caleb, Eleazar,
The patrol-leaders, but none said anything,
And their silence was in manner of a rebuke.
Sighing, he said: 'It is, at the last, myself –
The bad shepherd who has let the lambs go astray.

I have had a bereavement to suffer, a black season
Of mourning and solitude. But Joshua, my son,
You who must take up the rod of office, you
Who must bear the burden of leadership, Joshua,
How is it possible?' Joshua spoke softly.
'There were reports of particular transgressions.
Action was taken. As for the recent events –
Information was slow in coming. We had no
Word from Zimri. We understood all was well,
More or less well. Odd acts of delinquency.
But nothing that seemed to require major action.'
Moses said: "Where is Zimri?" – 'No one knows.
We surmise that he may have been killed, because of his zeal.
They are an unruly people, the people of Moab.'
Moses said: 'He was of good family.
I knew his father well. Honest, steadfast,
Pious. Now, Joshua, what do you propose?'
Joshua said: 'Some of our erring people
Have already come home, ashamed and sick.
Ready for punishment. I suppose we must march in,
Ferret out the others. Or perhaps show
Our power and our righteousness. Punish the whole town.
Massacre. Set fire to it. Though, to speak truly,
We have had enough of such wholesale slaughter.'
Moses said: 'The time for a judgement on Moab
Must come later, come in the Lord's own time.
Meanwhile, our punishments for our erring sons
Must be', he said, 'exemplary.' – 'Exemplary – how?' –
Moses said: 'The word will come to me.
I fear it will be a harsh word.' Harsh word, harsh,
And more than a harsh word. Cozbi was weeping
In Zimri's arms, in the room of a squalid inn.
He said, not unhappily: 'Punishment
For loving too well. Or it may be a reward.'

She said: 'I was always told,' then she wept again,
'It was not for the weak of heart.' But he said: 'Strong,
Strong of heart. Is not this love of ours
Better, holier, than all that nonsense of the temple,
That wickedness of the temple?' She spoke of dishonour.
'You do not understand the dishonour.' Harsh words
From the high priestess. 'How can I show my face
Again in the streets, in my father's house? The god
Has turned his back on me.' Zimri kissed her tears.
'You have found out in time, through the grace of some other god,
That you were not meant for that service. And yet, of course,
It was that which brought us together. The world is strange,
God is strange.' She said: 'Which god do you mean?'
He said: 'Who knows? Perhaps the God of my people.
What kind of,' he said, 'malediction
Did your high priestess pronounce on you?'
Cozbi sobbed again. 'She said that I had
Disgraced the temple, but then she admitted
Her own share of the blame. After all, it was she who
Encouraged me to to...' Zimri smiled:
'Seduce me to a religion of love? There, you are smiling.
And you, my love, a princess among your people,
Shall be an ever higher princess among mine.
So all shall end well.' They kissed and then she said:
'Where is this promised land you talk about?'
He said: 'Beyond the Jordan. Even now
The work of parcelling out the land goes on.
To my tribe comes a great tract of rich soil,
Rich grass. We shall build a fair palace of stone
And live in love for ever and ever.' Then she said:
'You must know now – but surely you already know –
That I may not have children. The temple of love
Was given over to joy, not fertility.'
But he cried: 'What does it matter? Israel

Can grow and flourish with no need of our help.
We shall be a new twin star in its sky.
That word – it is meant as a word of shame,
But the moon is barren and its light shines on the earth
With a beauty that the sun does not know. As now.'
He embraced her tenderly. 'We are the moon lovers.'
She said: 'We must leave early. Put out the light.'
So he doused the lamp, saying however: 'The light
Can never be put out.' And the moon
Embraced them who embraced each other. *Never*
Be put out. In harsh sunlight Moses
Addressed the multitude: 'You, children of Israel,
Have committed whoredoms with the daughters of Moab.
You have sacrificed to their gods, you have eaten
Of foul flesh and bowed down to Ba'al.
The anger of the Lord is a burning torrent.
For he is the one God, the God of mankind,
Who made mankind and all the earth and the heavens,
And he is a jealous God.
And his word has come to me, and this is his word.'
The sinners waited, rightly apprehensive,
The troops stern behind them. Moses said:
'His word is this: *Take all the heads of the people*
That have sinned, and hang them before the Lord,
Up against the sun, that the Lord's fierce anger
May be turned away from Israel. Judges,' he cried.
And the judges, shocked but ready, looked towards him.
'Judges, you have heard the order of the Lord.
Let justice be done.' So Moses turned away
While justice was done, shutting his ears to torment
And curses, the terrified voices that cried:
The God of Jacob is a God of butchers
And Moses is the chief of butchers, saying:
'I spoke too soon when I said the work was over.

I see now that the work is never over.
But, Lord God, may my work soon be over.'
The lovers stood, puzzled, when they came to the encampment,
Finding weeping and rending of garments by the tabernacle,
Then they looked up and saw. 'Is this what they do?'
Cried Cozbi in fear. 'Is this the kind of
Thing that the Israelites do?' Zimri said: 'Justice',
In a weak voice. 'They have been seeking justice.
For what crime?' Cozbi cried: 'Let us go.
Back to the city.' But Joshua was upon them,
An armed squad behind him, saying: 'So.
You came back to us, Zimri. With, as I see,
One of the whores of Moab.' Zimri cried out:
'Guard your tongue. The *whore* to whom you refer
Is the daughter of a prince of Moab, head
Of a great house in the kingdom. She is also my bride.' –
'Your *bride*,' Joshua said. 'That is a stage
Further than whoredom. You are both under arrest.'
Zimri said stoutly: 'On what charge?' And Joshua:
'Abominations before the Lord our God.' –
'Wait' Zimri said: 'was I not sent to the city
On your instructions? What proof do you possess
That I have committed *whoredoms*, as you call them?' –
'The proof,' said Joshua, 'stands beside you.' Zimri,
In a voice that rang out, said: 'Ah, Joshua,
You who love the law so much that
Severed heads must grin in the sun for it,
You shall have the law, but she and I
Will have it too. For which of our law forbids
The converting of a pagan to the faith?
What law forbids the marriage of an Israelite
To the daughter of a foreign people?' Joshua,
More doubtfully than before: 'The situation
Is, at best, highly suspicious.' – 'I see.

Suspicion is enough for arrest, for threat'
For insult?' – 'The judges,' now said Joshua, "must decide.
In the meantime, you are both under arrest.
On suspicion which, to a people at war, is enough.
And, if you will accept the word of our leader,
Which is also enough, the people of Moab,
From newborn child to doddering greybeard, are
Defined by him as an unclean people, source
Of disease of body and of spirit.' Zimri said:
'Do not talk to me of uncleanness, Joshua.
You smell of blood, blood, which, I fear,
Will not easily be washed out.' – 'No more talk.
Place them in the guard tents. Separately.'
But Zimri countered: 'Wait. I claim, by right,
The protection of my own tribe.' Joshua: 'No.
The law of the whole people cancels out
The laws and customs of the tribes.' – 'Is that then
Written on the tablets? I think not.
The ancient custom of wedlock with the Simeonites
Demands that the bride be brought before the people
To be approved of the people.' Joshua said:
'Go, then. I am heartily sick of this matter.
It shall be left to the judges. But, Zimri, there will be
No escape. The perimeter guards have their orders.'
Now it happened that a new priest, freshly appointed,
Spoke that night to the people: 'My name is Phinehas.
I know I am the youngest of your priests,
But the fire of faith burns the stronger therefor,
Nor is authority nor wisdom thereby abated.
I speak to you of the primal vessel of sin,
Woman. Sin and impurity. Of woman.'
But some of the women hearing hardened their faces
At his words, and at the words that followed:
'It was Eve, the mother of all mankind,

That brought sin into the world, and that sin rests
With all her daughters, sin made manifest
In their uncleanness – filth of the mensal courses,
Of the very process of birth. Far more than men,
Women are lodged in the flesh and cling to the flesh,
Are rarely aroused to climb to the pure spirit.
If all women be unclean, how much more so
Are the women of the pagan peoples, in whom
Dwells the active devil of disruption –
The desire to draw men down from their purity
Into the stinking pit.' Moses said
To Caleb: 'I think he goes too far.' But he listened:
'Within our very gates still lies the stench
Of foreign idols and all their abominations,
Reeking from a vessel of pagan filth.
I demand that the vessel be shattered.' A woman cried:
'You spit on your own mother.' And Moses said:
'He does go too far.' But Phinehas, inflamed,
Cried out: 'The curse of the all highest fall
On all who shut their ears to the voice of holiness.
May they who hearken not to the words of their priests
Be thrust to the bottomless pit of the fires that fail not,
To the eternal dungeons of divine damnation.'
There was much more of this, but Cozbi,
Impure pagan vessel, and Zimri lay
In the peace of their after-love, but a troubled peace.
'Believe me', he said, 'beloved, all will change
When we have crossed the river. There will be no more
Suspicion, hatred, panic. Our people tremble
With fear and disordered nerves.' But she: 'Your people –
The members of your tribe – they like me?' Zimri:
'Did they not show as much? We talk of nation,
But the reality does not lie out there –
With armies, flags, and tablets of the law.

It is in the tribe, which is but a family.
You are become a part of it.' A shadow
Crossed them at that instant, obscuring the moon
An instant. Zimri said: 'Who is there?' And Cozbi
Whispered: 'Are they setting spies on us?'
A voice was over them, in their tent, shouting:
'A spy of the Lord God. Prepare you, woman,
To join your stinking idols in the abode of blackness.' –
'Who are you?' Zimri cried, rising aghast,
Arms out. Then there was a knife to be seen. 'And you, too –
Son of the prince Salu and foul shame
To the tribe of Simeon.' He lunged, Zimri fought,
The strength of the fanatic prevailed. Struck down,
Blood welling, he lay. Cozbi, in fear and horror,
Cried to the moon. 'And now', Phinehas panted,
'Whore of Moab –' A scream through the sleeping camp,
Unheeded, some beast or bird of the night. At daybreak,
Phinehas spoke with pride of his work. *Zeal, zeal –*
The zeal of them who love the Lord 'Your zeal',
Cried Moses. 'Yes, your sacred zeal, as you call it.
But sacred zeal can go too far. I am sickened
By your sacred murderous zeal.' But the priest, surprised,
Said: 'We are an embattled people. Are not those your words?
The speck in the fruit corrupts the whole basket.
The accursed of God may be stricken down by the priests of God.
That is laid down in the law.' But Moses said:
'The law is written on stone   hard, unyielding
But the law may still be as flexible as a song.
Examine your own heart, Phinehas. You took pleasure
In the slaying of that innocent woman.' – 'Innocent?
Innocent?' – 'Yes, she knew no better.
She was not one of the chosen. But perhaps
She was being drawn towards the light and the truth. Yet you
Took pleasure in slaying her perhaps because she was a woman.

You fear women, hence you see them as vessels of sin.
But I say this to you, Phinehas: that it is the women
Who will carry our faith when the men waver. Strength
Is in the woman and not in the man. Men dream,
But the divine vision is no dream. It is as real
As the sweeping of the hearth, real as the beaming of children.
The bones of women are strong to bear. Has the Lord
Spoken to you since your act of religious zeal?'
Phinehas said: 'The Lord has sent dreams of sin
And dreams of killing. Then I wake howling.' Moses
Shook his head: 'You were not meant to be a priest.
A warrior perhaps. Well, you may soon be able
To plunge your steel into flesh less yielding. The news
Of your *zeal* may already have reached the divan of Balak.'
But Phinehas: 'She was a whore and a foul whore.' –
Moses spat. 'Go from me, little man.
What do you know about whores?'

                              The apportioning
Of the land that they were yet to see went on.
Caleb read out the figures of the census, for the grant
Was to be by numbers. 'The sons of Benjamin –
Forty-five thousand and six hundred. The families
Of the Shuhamites – sixty-four thousand four hundred.
Asher – the return is not yet in.' Moses said:
'Not one who was with us in the desert of Sinai.
Not one who remembers Egypt. Except Joshua
And you. And Me, but my day is over. The word
Of the Lord is fulfilled.' Caleb, impatiently:
'Yes yes. The families of Naphtali – little difference
In their numbers from the numbers of Benjamin – two hundred.
One might as well give them the same apportionment.'
Clerks were at work on a planed board. Eleazar,
The son of Aaron, supervised, marking proportion,
Location. Then women approached, and Caleb said:

'Women? What can women want?' Five women,
Making with purpose towards Moses. Eleazar frowned:
'This is irregular. Women should stay with their children
And with their pots and pans.' Moses said:
'You have been infected by the misplaced zeal
Of your former colleague. Where is he now, by the way?' –
'Phinehas?' Eleazar frowned still. 'Out with the army.
He has a gift for fighting.' – 'He will enjoy it'
Moses sighed, 'slaying the Midianite women.
God help us, when shall we ever be at peace?'
Eleazar said: 'The holy war goes on.
Slay them, said the Lord. Feed the earth
With the blood of the idolator.' – 'Enough, Eleazar,'
Moses said, and then: 'Welcome, daughters.' –
'This is highly irregular,' cried the priest.
'Many things are irregular', said one of the women.
'Including what we are about to speak about.
If it is permitted.' Moses said:
'It is certainly permitted. You are, are you not,
The daughters of, the daughters of – Forgive me,
An old man's memory, or lack of it.'
The woman said: 'I am Mahlah. These are my sisters:
Hoglah, Noah, Milcah, Tirzah – daughters of
Zelophehad, now dead.' – 'Ah yes', said Moses.
'Slain in battle, was he not?' – 'Slain.
With his sons, our brothers. Thanks to your holy wars
We are without menfolk. Though how a war can be holy   '
Eleazar said: 'Have a care, woman,' but she:
'Killing, killing, killing. Will your God
Strike me down because I cry against killing?
Well, let him. He is made in the likeness of a man.'
Gently Moses said: 'God is a spirit.
His voice has come to me in many forms,
Because a spirit lacks a voice of its own.

The voice has sometimes been the voice of Miriam,
My own sister.' Mahlah said: 'Be that as it may,
Your God seems fond of killing. A woman brings forth
With pain, high priest, that few men could truly bear –
Only that her sons may be killed in some holy war.
But that is not directly to my purpose.' –
'What', said Moses gently, 'is your purpose?'
Mahlah said: 'We are women without menfolk.
The name of our father has disappeared from your record.
What will happen to his portion of the promised land?'
Eleazar said: 'Woman, it is clearly laid down
That the sons alone shall inherit. If there are no sons,
There is no inheritance.' But Mahlah cried:
'Injustice, man's injustice.' And Eleazar:
'It is the law.' – 'That is always the answer:
It is the law. And how if the law be unjust?'
Eleazar said: 'You merit the Lord's malediction.
One does not question the law.' But she, in anger:
'High priest, I am questioning it.' And Moses:
'Daughter, you are right to question it.
Peace, Eleazar. And my response is this:
If a man die and leave no son, then the father's
Inheritance shall pass to the daughters.' Eleazar
Seemed ready to burn. 'Heresy?' Moses said.
'An abomination? The Lord, as you see, high priest,
Has not yet offered to strike me dead. Nor will he.
Daughters of Israel, you have your inheritance.'
But still in the future, always it seemed, in the future.
Across the plain, soon, advancing armies,
And Joshua said: 'They are coming for revenge.
Or shall we call it a pretext? You, priest,
Are certainly in the fight', addressing Phinehas
Who, stripped of his sacerdotal robes,
Arrayed as a somewhat puny warrior,

Sweated as he heard drums. Moses said:
'Is this the last battle, Joshua?
For all the kings of Midian will join Balak
Evi and Rekem and Zur and Hur and Reba.' –
'The last fight', Joshua said, 'this side of Jordan.
How do the words go? Speak the words again.' –
'The false gods crushed under the feet of Israel.
And you shall take the spoils of all their cattle
And all their flocks, yea, and all their goods,
And burn all the cities wherein they dwell
A holy war, but we have not provoked it.'
Joshua said: 'You are tired. Stay in your tent.
I will send word.' And Moses: 'You will prevail.
The blessing of God go with you, Joshua.'
So banners, trumpets and drums proclaimed to the sky
The going forth of the Israelites to war –
While Moses prayed: 'Let there be an end to war –
An end, O Lord', but little hope in his words.

18

JORDAN

Moses half-slept in his lonely tent – Ghershom,
His son, gone with the army, Zipporah, his wife,
Dust; himself soon to be dust. He heard
His own voice, or the voice of the Lord, or of Israel:
And you have taken the spoils of all their cattle
And all their sheep, yea, and all their goods,
And burnt all the cities wherein they dwelt,
And all their goodly castles with fire and
All their goodly castles with fire and all their
Goodly castles with fire and he saw a
Castle innumerable cubits high falling

In flames and heard the screams of men falling,
Women and children. He came sharply awake
To sense a presence not a dreaming presence
And said: 'Is it you, Lord?' And the presence said:
'All is fulfilled. The slain lie like leaves
In the fall tempests. Over those fallen leaves
You may fare forward. But first the sheep need
A new shepherd. Take Joshua, son of Nun,
A man in whom the spirit burns like a fire,
And lay your hands upon him.' So Joshua, from the wars,
Scarred and ready for wine and a handmaiden,
Was told these words and at once was hushed and solemn.
Before the tabernacle Moses laid his hand
On the warrior's head, saying: 'You are not exalted
To any priesthood. You need no robes, no chrism.
You are become that humblest of beings – a leader
Accountable to the people and to the Lord,
With duties and no rights.' He raised his arms
Before the assembled nation, bidding them
Acclaim their new shepherd, hearing however
Beneath the acclamation the growls of the restive,
As was to be expected. He smiled with relief
At being allowed the guerdon of fatigue,
Old age at last. Under a star-filled heaven
Their caravan moved in silence, under the sun,
Moses at rest in an ox-cart, Joshua ahead,
Until one day Joshua came and pointed
Ahead at a certain mountain. Pisgah? Pisgah.
So in the plain they set up the tabernacle,
Pitched their tents, the people in good heart,
The young singing and dancing about the fires,
Moses fulfilling his last duties. He said,
To the tribal leaders round a fire, plain words
About the necessity and beauty of the law

Or laws: 'Too many laws, some will say –
A huge web woven of many webs – but remember
This, this: that the law is our city,
Complex, cunningly woven – many streets,
Buildings, rooms – yet a city we may carry
About with us, wherever we go. Remember
This: we are the chosen, and this means
Many enemies among the unchosen. Enemies.
They will slay us and pursue us. The unchosen.
And we may never finally be at rest.
But wherever we go we will carry our city with us.
The law. Break one single stone of the law,
However small, and a part of the city falls.
Soon the temples and palaces and dwellings
Will crash about our ears. And we shall be lost.
Keep the law. Teach the law. *Teach it.*'
Phinehas, a subdued man, lacking an arm,
Stiff with scars, taught the children, asking:
'What are we allowed to eat?' *The ox*
The sheep the goat the roebuck 'If you were asked
What kind of animal?' *Animals that have the*
Hoof parted in two 'Like the pig?'
No no no 'Why not like the pig?'
Because the pig does not chew the cud
'So the animal has to chew the cud. So we may
Eat the camel, the rabbit, the hare?' *No no*
No no no 'Why not?' *Because they do not*
Divide the hoof in two 'So we can
Eat beasts that divide the hoof and chew the cud,
But not beasts that just do one and no both.
Yes, my son?' *Why?* 'Well, let me put it
This way...' Eleazar taught older boys,
Saying: 'Well, let me put it this way.
Without the past the present can mean nothing.

Without the past a man is a sort of ghost
Trembling on the brink of a future
He cannot understand. So we remember
The past in ceremonies, force ourselves to remember.
In our promised land we shall remember
Our long exile, tribulations, thus
Becoming aware of our qualities as a nation,
A fighting nation, a law-abiding nation,
A proud nation.' *Rabbi* – 'Yes, my son?'
Why isn't Moses going with us? 'Well now,
Let me put it this way…' Moses was saying,
Addressing the priests and elders: 'Because of my doubt
Of God's promise, because I cried out on my trust
And sought to reject it, I may not enter. You
Shall cross the Jordan, Joshua leading you,
But I – full of years, at the end of my journey –
Must await my end here. But I have taught you
The song I have written. Teach it. Remember it.
Remember me.' So they taught it, and one day,
The whole of the people sang it, the song of Moses:
'Give ear, O ye heavens, and I will speak.
And hear, O earth, the words of my mouth.
My doctrine shall drop as the rain,
My speech shall distil as the dew,
As the small rain upon the tender herb,
And as the showers upon the grass.
The Lord is the Rock, his work is perfect.
Rejoice, O ye nations, with his people:
For he will avenge the blood of his servants,

And will be merciful unto his land,
And to his people.' And they danced to the flute, the harp,
The shawm, the trumpet, to the air of his song:

And Moses said: 'Beloved, keep the commandments.
Love justice and mercy. Love the Lord our God,
For his ways are the ways of justice and mercy.'
And he saw that the time was coming for his people
To pass over the river and take up their inheritance.
So he bade the whole of the Israelite nation kneel,
And they knelt, and then he blessed them, saying:
'Happy art thou, O Israel. Who is like unto thee,
O people saved by the Lord, the shield of thy help
And the sword of thy excellency. There is none like unto your God,
Who rides upon the heavens. The eternal God
Is your refuge, and underneath
Are the everlasting arms.' Then the Israelite Army
Saluted his greatness with shouts and with the clamour
Of drums and silver trumpets. So he moved
To the mountain, and Caleb and Joshua tried to help him
In his climb to the summit, but he waved their help aside.
He climbed and they watched him, thinking: *Strong as an ox,*
With the eyes of an eagle, but it was not true,
Not true any longer. The Israelites, shielding their sight
Against the sun, watched him long and long
Till he reached the top of the mountain. There he rested.
And after a time of rest he heard a voice,
His own voice, young again, saying to him:
'Now, Moses, I will show you their inheritance.'
He said: 'But not mine', with his old boldness,
The boldness of a prince. 'You are a hard
And unforgiving God.' The voice said: 'Unforgiving?
If you but knew, if you only knew. But I

Have sworn and made my covenant with man.
I shall not again destroy him for his sins.
Yet I shall torment him with dissatisfaction,
For only in me shall he be satisfied.
Look now – all the land of Gilead, unto Dan.'
And Moses stood to look, seeing the river,
And all the lands beyond the river, fair,
Rich and fair. 'Look. And all Naphtali
And the land of Ephraim and Manasseh,
And the land of Judah, unto the utmost sea.
And the plain of the valley of Jericho, city of palm-trees,
Unto Zoar. This is the land which I swore
Unto Abraham, and Isaac, and unto Jacob,
Saying: I will give it unto thy seed.
Moses, I have caused thee to see it with thine eyes,
But thou shalt not go thither.' Moses did not
Weep, but he said again, with a princely boldness:
'You are a hard and unforgiving God.' –
'Go down now. Return to the valley of Moab,'
Said the voice. And Moses said: 'To die.'
And the voice said: 'What else?' So he went down
And waited, willing death, which was not long,
For when a man's work is done there is only death.
The women closing his eyes, wailing, but Joshua
Was dry-eyed. Eleazar made an obeisance
To the leader of the Israelites, and said
'You must give the instructions as to his burial.'
And Joshua said: 'Here in this valley of Moab,
This side of Jordan.' And then Eleazar said:
'You must now give instructions as to the gravestone
And what shall be written thereon.' But Joshua said:
'It is better that no man know where he is buried.
It is better that he be thought of as –
Not lying in one place. For he must not have

Idolators at his shrine. He is with us
In the water we drink, the food we eat. We breathe him.'
Eleazar said: 'Will you make up the words
That shall be spoken to the people?' But Joshua:
'I have already made them.' And so he spoke to the people:
'There will never arise again in Israel
A prophet like unto Moses, whom the Lord
Knew face to face. In all the signs and wonders,
Which the Lord sent him to do in the land of Egypt
And in all that mighty hand, and the great terror
Which Moses showed in the sight of all Israel.'
The muffled drums beat, and the body of Moses
Was borne away on a litter. Most of the people
Wished to follow, but Joshua forbade them.
The body of Moses was carried none knows whither
And rests now none knows where. *And Joshua*
The son of Nun was full of the spirit of wisdom.
For Moses had laid his hands upon him,
And the children of Israel hearkened unto him,
And did as the Lord commanded Moses. Joshua
Raised his blessed hand, and they fared forward,
Coming at length to a river. Caleb said:
'At last.' But Joshua: 'We still have to cross it.
God will provide. This is only a river
Once we crossed a sea. Well – we have our orders.'
He smiled, and Caleb smiled, and so they marched.
And then at last, the voice spoke to Joshua:
'Moses my servant is dead. Now therefore, Joshua
Go over this Jordan, thou, and all this people
Unto the land which I do give them. From the wilderness
Even unto the great river, the Euphrates,
And unto the great sea toward the going down
Of the sun. And as I was with Moses,
So will I be with thee: I will not fail thee,

Nor forsake thee. Be therefore not afraid,
Neither be thou dismayed, for the Lord thy God
Is with thee whithersoever thou goest.' The wilderness
Held a grave, but none would know the grave.
Not from the grave but from the living air
And the beating blood of Israel the voice
Of the living Moses echoed: *For the Lord*
Thy God is with thee whithersoever thou goest.

Rome,
March 9, 1974

'And If There Be No Beauty, If God Has Passed Some By'

WINEFRED:

    And if there be no beauty, if god has passed some by
    In beauty giving, what then? Hare lip, wall eye,
    Limbs shrunken? Beauty's giver will be blind to them,
    Will cast them to the pit. What then?
    Beauty is in the doing, beauty is not being
    As for what you speak of – shining hair, feel of primrose skin,
    For what they are, for what I have of them,
    Were they but in my gift, you should have them freely.

'Talk is Easy. Easiest for One Who'

OTHER WOMAN:

    Talk is easy. Easiest for one who
    Would madly shut them away,
    Consign them to darkness
    You speak of beauty in the ghost!
    I would have beauty in the flesh.
    I am not yet a ghost.

'Thank You. Enough, Brother Teryth'

BEUNO:

    Thank you. Enough, brother Teryth,
    Please no ceremony.
    My Lord Bishop to the world I may be.

Here I am back to being a boy with you.
In this farm of our father's, the smell of that burning pearwood
Burns the years between – cancels Rome, Paris,
The learning that has bent my back – the laying on of hands,
the pastoral crook and mitre.
Am come home for ever, but – alas –
Only by proxy. Dirwan stays for the building of a chapel,
A centre for holy mass.
No more long trudging to Caws.

'I Choose No Tail or Toy!'

WINEFRED:

I choose no tail or toy!
Truth – a light that outdoes this sun.
You will not understand –
You do not believe.

CARADOC:

I believe what I see, touch, grope, wrestle with,
What I possess, what I propose to possess
By a man's right –
You are my right.

'Say Nothing, Priest, Father, Mother'

CARADOC:

Say nothing, Priest, father, mother.
I have said all, done all.
This is Caradoc –
A chieftain of this valley.

THE PET BEAST

Pasiphae would pacify a lust
Grown beyond questioning.
In Daedalus she knew at length she must
Deposit trust:
This was a thing she durst not tell the king.

A wooden cow, she ordered, queenly. *Why
Not*, the pared artisan
Said inly, only bowing else. *It is my
Part to comply.*
He gathered tools and plywood and began.

*Why not a maze made from a ball of string,
Why not a clockwork bird,
Or birds wrought of stale breadcrumbs that can sing?*
Beyond questioning
A royal statue, statute, though absurd.

Minos the cold judged cases in his dreams.
Awake, lithe at his task,
The other whistled, sawing pliant beams.
Law is what seems,
The craftsman's place to act and not to ask.

The queen was to be bedded and then shut in
(This was the queen's idea)
A box she might confess unholy rut in.

The artist cut in
A door there with a small foramen here.

The king snored, a treeload of raven-calls
Cried fear. The painted cow
Was carried to the plain outside the walls.
Mobled in shawls,
The queen trod after, shivering somewhat now.

She crouched darkling waiting enwombed in wood,
Awake, asleep, adoze.
Moon rise on empty grass. She started, could
Through the eyed hood
See pleniluned the distant dust that rose.

She racked then on a sea whose spume was dust,
The sea began to bleed,
Its waves were snorts and roars. The white beast's lust
Rent in one thrust
A womb grown sudden hands to grasp the seed.

Moonset. And from the ruin hoofed apart
She wanly signalled Come
To slaves whom not that act but prescient art
Hot as her heart
Had rendered cruelly and coldly dumb.

They bore her sleeping whither she must sleep
Next to the snoring king.
Daedalus had seen all, Daedalus must keep
Silence asleep
As dumbness. Daedalus had not seen a thing.

She was a queen of cautions. Covertly
Had seized his only son
Who, walled beyond the feasibility
Of recovery,
Would be a hostage till her time was done.

Or till no time. As human deeds were shut,
Dried flowers, in books of law,
So human will and love and pain were but
Raw stuff to cut
To the gods' templates. That's what men are for.

She had done the gods' will anyway. And now
The royal days went on,
The king his cases, queen her casing how
She, calving cow,
Would fare if he observed she was far gone.

Myopic Minos, though, in books his eyes,
But dry each nether eye
After two daughters and no son. But wise
To recognise
Signs, changes, moods. And always spies to spy.

After three moon-rolls she announced she would
Spend winter in the south.
He nodded, nodded, said he understood.
The cold here. Good.
The thing within shot acid to her mouth.

SIGNS (DOGS OF PEACE)

Earth remains. The ancient houses of men
Stand or crumble, and then stand again,
But always with blind windows, slow to start
To bid goodbye to the young men who depart
Into the world, the world where now I lie
Smelling flower-smells and hearing from the sky
The vapid news of birds, repeating We
Can see the sea, can you too see the sea?
Nonsense. Still sea remains, the jagged teeth
Of hills beyond, the leagues and leagues beneath
Of frond and fishlife and, above, of men,
Who stand or crumble, and then stand again,
Building a little life of talk and wine
And wine and talk, wives, children. Come, a sign,
Give us a sign. And what shall it signify?
Nothing. Men must just signal or else die,
Erecting signs, ejecting signs, in stores
Purchasing signs and selling signs. Their pores
Sweat signs. But signs of what? Ah come, resign
Ourselves to this: a sign's a sign's a sign.
Or, if you will, signs lead to other signs –
Signposts mean signs lead to cities. See, the sun declines
From his high noon on this – a southern town,
The somnolence of afterlunch falls down
Gentle, like dust, on young, old, and young-old.
Cars move in stupor. Stories that are told,
Ideas put forward, all allophones
Of yawns. Unwilling as trundled stones.

The great dead and the little living move
Down time, down streets and prove – what do they prove?
That signs are signs and signs are signs again.
And dogs are as significant as men.
Men move, and women move, beneath the groin
Of passages where quick and dead conjoin
Looking for signs to sign some cosmic letter.
Accept the universe – by God, you'd better.
Accept this town, *cede victoriam*
To horns that honk and honking cry *I am*.
To clanking girders, trufflings in the earth
To bring some new enormous sign to birth.
Signs ride the streets, unnoticed in the shouts
Of streetlife, see the daffodils put out
Their signs, the fruit upon the barrows too.
Be drunk with signs – what else is there to do?
Yet, if you would ask, ask what colours mean.
We mean ourselves no more, say red and green.
But try this – take us all, the flame, the sky,
The hue of flesh, the flash of the cat's eye.
Mix all these colours even and, how odd,
The end's a blank – or the white light of God.
Any word, any image, will do
To begin with. In the beginning was God.
Why not Dog? In other language God ought to be
Dnuh, enac, but it doesn't
Work in the other languages. But in English, yes.
You can begin with God seen from the rear –
That strange view vouchsafed to some prophet or other –
Dog. Polytheism, polycynism – dogs. Looking up
Down, unable to separate the Godmade from the manmade
Artifact – all things equal – rooms, carpets, air,
Water, gravel, piano, curtain, dogs.
What makes men different from dogs? The hindleg habit,

So that forepaws may hold drinks, the hebetude of the
Sense of smell. A longer ritual before the act of
Coupling. Dogs mark out territory through
Golden libations. Men make cities.

'AUGUSTINE AND PELAGIUS'

He came out of the misty island, Morgan,
Man of the sea, demure in monk's sackcloth,
Taking the long way to Rome, expecting –
Expecting what? Oh, holiness, quintessentialized,
Holiness whole, the wholesome wholemeal of,
Holiness as meat and drink and air, in the
Chaste thrusts of marital love holiness, and
Sanctitas sanctitas even snaking up from
Cloacae and sewers, sanctitas the effluvium
From his Holiness's arsehole. On the village road
Trudging, dust, birdsong, dirty villages,
Stops on the way at monasteries (weeviled bread,
Eisel wine), always this thought: *Sanctitas.*
What does thou seek in Rome, brother? The home
Of holiness, to lodge awhile in the
Sanctuary of sanctity, my brothers, for here
Peter died, seeing before he died
The pagan world inverted to sanctitas, and
The very flagged soil is rich with the bonemeal
Of the martyrs. And the brothers would
Look at each other, each thinking, some saying:
Here cometh one that only islands breed.
What can flourish in that Ultima Thule save
Holiness, a bare garment for the wind to
Sing through? And not Favonius either but
Sour Boreas from the pole. Not the grape,
Not garlic not the olive, not the strong sun
Tickling the manhood in a man, be he

Monk or friar or dean or
Burly bishop, big ballocks swinging like twin censers.
Only holiness. God help him, God bless him for
We look upon British innocence.
And the British innocence.
And the British innocent, hurtful of no man,
Fond of dogs, a cat-stroker,
Trudged on south – vine, olive, garlic,
Brown tits jogging while brown feet
Danced in the grapepress and the
Monstrous aphrodisiac danced in the heavens
Till at length he came to the outer suburbs and
Fell on his knees *O sancta urbs sancta sancta*
Meaning sancta suburbs and…

But wherever he went in Rome, it was always the same –
Sin sin sin, no sanctity, the whole unholy
Grammar of sin, syntax, accidence, sin's
Entire lexicon set before him, sin.
Peacocks in the streets, gold dribbled over
In dark rooms, vomiting after
Banquets of ostrich bowels stuffed with saffron,
Minced pikeflesh and pounded larkbrain,
Served with a sauce headily fetid, and pocula
Of wine mixed with adder's blood to promote
Lust lust and again.
Pederasty, podorasty, sodomy, bestiality,
Degrees of family ripped apart like
Bodices in the unholy dance. And he said,
And Morgan said, whom the scholarly called Pelagius:
Why do ye this, my brothers and sisters?
Are ye not saved by Christ, are ye not
Sanctified by his sacrifice, oh why why why?
(Being British and innocent) and

They said to him cheerfully, looking up
From picking a peahen bone or kissing the
Nipple or nates of son, daughter, sister,
Brother, aunt, ewe, teg: Why, stranger,
Hast not heard the good news? That Christ
Took away the burden of our sins on his
Back broad to bear, and as we are saved
Through him it matters little what we do?
Since we are saved once for all, our being
Saved will not be impaired or cancelled by
Our present pleasures (which we propose to
Renew tomorrow after a suitable and well-needed
Rest). Alleluia alleluia to the Lord for he has
Led us to two paradises, one to come and the other
Here and now. Alleluia. And they fell to again,
To nipple to nates or fish baked with datemince,
Alleluia. And Morgan cried to the sky:
How long O Lord wilt thou permit these
Transgressions against thy holiness?
Strike them strike them as thou once didst
The salty cities of the plain, as though
Phinehas the son of Eleazar the son of Aaron
Thou didst strike down the traitor Zimri
And his foul whore of the Moabite temples Cozbi
Strike strike. But the Lord did nothing.

He strode in out of Africa, wearing a
Tattered royal robe of orchard moonlight
Smelling of stolen apples but otherwise
Ready to scorch, a punishing sun, saying:
Where is this man of the northern sea, let me
Chide him, let me do more if
His heresy merits it, what is his heresy?
And a hand-rubbing priest, olive-skinned,

Garlic-breathed, looked up at the
Great African solar face to whine:
If it please you, the heresy is evidently a
Heresy but there is as yet no name for it.
And Augustine said: All things must have a name
Otherwise, Proteus-like, they slither and slide
From the grasp. A thing does not
Exist until it has a name. Name it
After this sea-man, call it after
Pelagius. And lo the heresy existed.
Pelagius appeared, north-pale, cool as one of
Britain's summers, to say, in British Latin:
Christ redeemed us from the general sin, from
The Adamic inheritance, the sour apple
Stuck in the throat (and underneath his solar
Hide Augustine blushed). And thus, my load,
Man was set free, no longer bounden
In sin's bond. He is free to choose
To sin or not to sin, he is in no wise
Predisposed, it is all a matter of
Human choice. And by his own effort, yea,
His own effort only, not some matter of God's
Grace arbitrarily and capriciously
Bestowed, he may reach heaven, he may indeed
Make his heaven. He is free to do so.
Do you deny his freedom? Do you deny
That God's incredible benison was to
Make man free, if he wished, to offend him?
That no greater love is conceivable
Than to let the creature free to hate
The creator and come to love the hard way
But always (mark this mark this) by his own
Will by his own free will?
Cool Britain thus spoke, a land where indeed a

Man groans not for the grace of rain, where
He can sow and reap, a green land, where
The God of unpredictable Africa is
A strange God.

Augustine said: If the Almighty is also Allknowing,
He knows the precise number of hairs that will fall to the floor
From your next barbering, which may also be your last.
He knows the number of drops of lentil soup
That will fall on your robe from your careless spooning
On August 5th, 425. He knows every sin
As yet uncommitted, can measure its purulence
On a precise scale of micropeccatins, a micropeccatin
Being, one might fancifully suppose,
The smallest unit of sinfulness. He knows
And knew when the very concept of man itched within him
The precise date of your dispatch, the precise
Allotment of paradisal or infernal space
Awaiting you. Would you diminish the Allknowing
By making man free? This is heresy.
But that God is merciful as well as allknowing
Has been long revealed: he is not himself bound
To fulfil knowledge. He scatters grace
Liberally and arbitrarily, so all men may hope,
Even you, man of the northern seas, may hope.
But Pelagius replied: Mercy is the word, mercy.
And a greater word is love. Out of his love
He makes man free to accept or reject him.
He could foreknow but refuses to foreknow
Any, even the most trivial, human act until
The act has been enacted, and then he knows.
So men are free, are touched by God's own freedom.
Christ with his blood washed out original sin,
So we are in no wise predisposed to sin

More than to do good: we are free, free,
Free to build our salvation. Halleluiah.
But the man of Hippo, with an African blast,
Blasted this man of the cool north…

THE PRINCELY PROGRESS

To nubile Charles yet unennobled James
Presents this specimen of Higher Games
Assured though of at least an O.B.E.
Sooner or later for well let's just see –
Skill in the dour destructive witticism
His services to television criticism?
Besides as is well known our Royal Family
Loves digs against Itself however hammily
Delivered. And again (let it be muttered)
The colonially bred must be well buttered.
Though unrelated to the Sage of Rye
And Lion of Lamb House, James trains one eye
Upon the intolerable pinnacles of Style,
Terse verse not poofter mandarin the while
He steeps the other in the pail of crystal
He weekly shatters with his fist or pistol
Nor is this Clive of India. He hails
From Empire's shoddier jewel, New South Wales.
Where penal memories still rawly rankle:
Observe the chain-mark round the loose-socked ankle.
Though Cambridge-sleeked and London tamed, at times
He plonks an Aussie phoneme in his rhymes.
Like *martyred/started* on Page 96
Of this new Hudibrastic instant mix
That mocks and makes the royal congeries
No more fantastic than it really is.
His epic subject is the Prince of Cymru
And all the flaming flim and flam and flummery

That have oppressed our future king's career
From when he first cocked his cup-handle ear
(The image is from Marc on the dust-jacket)
In wonder at the loyal London racket
Which warmed the Arctic day that distant June
Whereon our second (*Vivat!*) mortal moon
Became state welfare's onomastic bastion
And head of two *ecclesiae* – Erastian
And Presbyterian (both, in fact, Pelagian),
Through schools submissive to the harsh contagion
Of SS training camps commando courses,
Through mastery of ships, tanks, aircraft horses
(Though there his sister Anne carries the banner),
The uncondescending condescending manner,
Indeed the whole damned tough *Encyclopaedia
Monarchica* to bludgeons from the media –
Smiles of a playboy, morals of a monk:
One cherry brandy made the whole press drunk
Now *nota bene*: James's spleen is shown
To the dirt-throwers never to the Throne.
Approving of the monarchy, its *semper
Eadem*, out of temper with the temper
Of Irish, wops and polacks in Australia
Who think the crown an old hat and a failure:
And can't equate corruption with republics,
Demos, thinks James (here is his poem's nub) licks
The dictatorial arse when kings and queens
Don't give demotic lips and tongues the means
To kiss blue veins in dreams or, waking, cry:
'God save the…'. James is right and so am I.
Funny enough, his book. You'll meet them all:
Lady Jane Wellyboot, Lord Butterball,
Lord Nikon and Dame Helen Gardenome,
Esther Hotpantz (who's she when she's at home?),

Mark Pillocks, Shirley Whirley, Lord Lambchop,
AJP Tailspin, the whole butcher's shop
And Lady Diana Seethrough-Spiffing 'belle
Of the ball... no iced Pom sheila', she as well.
A nice poetic tribute to the Prince.
Little to make Cape's libel lawyers wince.
And there's another rhapsody to come –
The Laureate's epithalamium.
Though, since John Betje is a thrifty man,
He may retread the one for Princess Anne –
'Glow white lily in London –' No, not that:
Charles is no flaming lily. And that's flat:
At least one dinkum digger makes it clear,
So up with schooners down with the pig's ear,
Rejoice with James and for Prince Charles a cheer.

FIVE REVOLUTIONARY SONNETS
From the novels *Inside Mr Enderby* and *Enderby Outside*

I

Sick of the sycophantic singing, sick
Of every afternoon's compulsory games,
Sick of the little cliques of county names,
He let the inner timebomb start to tick –
Beating out number. As arithmetic
The plot took shape – not from divided aims,
But short division only. Then, in flames,
He read: 'That flower is not for you to pick.'
Therefore he picked it. All things thawed to action,
Sound, colour. A shrill electric bell
Summoned the guard. He gathered up his faction,
Poised on the brink, thought, and created hell.
Light shimmered in miraculous refraction
As, like a bloody thunderbolt, he fell.

2

Bells broke in the long Sunday, a dressing gown day.
The childless couple basked in the central heat.
The papers came on time, the enormous meat
Flowered in the oven. On deep carpets lay
Thin panther kittens locked, in clawless play –
Bodies were firm, their hair clean and their feet
Uncalloused. All their wine was new and sweet.
Recorders, unaccompanied, crooned away.

Coiled on the rooftree, bored, inspired, their snake
Crowed in Black Monday. A collar kissed the throat,
Clothes braced the body, a benignant ache
Lit up a tooth. The papers had a note:
That act may mean an empire is at stake.
Sunday and this were equally remote.

3

A dream, yes, but for everyone the same,
The thought that wove it never dropped a stitch.
The Absolute was anybody's pitch,
For, when a note was struck, we knew its name.
That dark aborted any urge to tame
Waters that day might prove to be a ditch
But then where endless growling ocean, rich
In fish and heroes till the dredgers came.
Wachet auf! A fretful dunghill cock
Flinted the noisy beacons through the shires.
A martin's nest clogged the cathedral clock,
But it was morning – birds could not be liars.
Keys cleft an age of rust in lock and lock.
Men shivered by a hundred kitchen fires.

4

They lit the sun, and then their day began.
What prodigies that eye of light revealed!
What dusty parchment statutes they repealed,
Pulling up blinds and lifting every ban.
The galaxies revolving to their plan,
They made the conch, the coin, the cortex yield
Their keys, and in a garden, once a field,
They hoisted up a statue of a man.

Of man, rather: to most it seemed a mirror:
Augustus on a guinea sat up straight
Proud of those stony eyes unfilmed by terror.
Though marble is not glass, why should they care?
Later the time for vomiting the error.
Someone was bound to find his portrait there.

5

Augustus on a guinea sat up straight
The sun no proper study but each shaft
Of filtered light a column: classic craft
Abhorred the arc or arch. To circulate
(Blood or ideas) meant pipes, and pipes were straight.
As loaves were gifts from Ceres when she laughed
Thyrsis was Jack, but Crousseau on a raft
Sought Johnjack's rational island, loath to wait
Till sun, neglected, took revenge so that
The nodding columns melted, and were seen
As Gothic shadows where a goddess sat.
For, after all, that rational machine,
Granted to Jack's tribe by the technocrat
Chopped logic, hence became his guillotine.

TO VLADIMIR NABOKOV
ON HIS 70TH BIRTHDAY

That nymphet's beauty lay less on her bones
Than in her name's proclaimed two allophones,
A boned veracity slow to be found
In all the channel of recorded sound.
Extrude an orange pip upon the track,
And it will be a pip played front or back,
But only in the kingdom of the shade
Can diaper run back and be repaid.
Such speculations salt my exile too,
One that I bear less stoically than you.
I look in sourly on my lemon trees,
Spiked by the Qs and Xes of Maltese,
And wonder: Is this home or where is home?
(Melita's caves, Calypso's honeycomb).
I seek a cue or clue. Just opposite,
The grocer has a cat that loves to sit
Upon the scales. Respecting his repose,
One day he weighed him: just 2 rotolos.
In this palazzo wood decays and falls;
Buses knock stucco from the outer walls,
Slam shut the shutters. Coughing as they lurch,
They yet enclose the silence of a church,
Rock in baroque: Teresan *spados* stab
The Sacred Heart upon the driver's cab,
Whereupon, in circus colours, one can read
That *Verbum Caro Factum Est*. Indeed.
I think the word is all the flesh I need –

The taste, and not the vitamins of sense,
Whatever sense may be. I like the fence
Of black and white that keeps those bullocks in –
Crossboard or chesswood. Eurish gift of Finn –
The crossmess parzel. If words are no more
Than *pyoshki*, preordained to look before,
Save for their taking *chassé*, they alone,
And not the upper house, can claim a throne
(Exploded first the secular magazines
And puff of bishops). All aswarm with queens,
Potentially, that board. Well, there it is:
You help me counter the liquidities
With counters that are counties, countries. Best
To read it: *Caro Verbum Facta Est.*

THE SWORD

De Kalb, De Kalb, Flatbush Avenue: there, that bright March
    Saturday, I stood
With sclerotic toothache in kalb or calf, heavy on my cane,
A third leg, a British sword sheathed in cherrywood
For passive support, no tool or weapon. Wind, pain

Toothached in from East River. Well then, I thought, here you are,
Middleaged, claudicant, ignominiously propped
On a sheathed sword, wanting a cab, while car after car
Grinned by under the sun, Saturday gift for those who shopped.
    No cab stopped.

So I claudicated to the subway, wanting Brooklyn Heights (Clark),
But, instead of the Tunnel train, I caught the one for the Bridge:
Miles of metal and river and light, no expected comfortable dark
Fit for a middleaged Saturday with, at the end, the hermitage

Of the warm apartment and time to make myself seem younger
Or, at least, less middleaged and put that sword away,
At least for the evening. Canal (Centre). The cabless street, the
    hunger
To bury sword and myself out of the shameless Manhattan day

Increasing to worse toothache, though I am sure it was the wind
That mocked-up wet self-pity. More and more angrily I waved
The sword at the mocking full cabs. But then a sepia-skinned
Cabman responded and stopped. I entered, I was saved.

Back to Brooklyn. The driver, Alvin Lewis, found the street
And I found my key, but, to my incredulous shock,
The apartment door would not open. In bathrobe and flat wet feet,
The woman below came up: no good: something wrong with the
    lock.

So what could I do but do the rounds of the bars –
Harry's, the Golden Rose, Jed's Bar and Grill
And the nameless others? Martinis, cheap cigars,
The nameless others, underwater caves with the shrill

Radio the voice of up there, the TV images like divers
Looking in on this mouthing world, fish, drinking like fish,
Lonely men glass-twirling, making it last, and truck-drivers
Swilling one down, then away, and no matter how much I would
    wish

To clean off the middleage for the evening and her, I had to accept
    my dirt
And the dirty brown taste of my mouth, unanaesthetised
By the ice, my flat wet feet and limp wet shirt
And earwax in my oxters, and brain that was only surprised

Out of its boredom by each radio chime
Showing it was earlier than I'd thought it could possibly be.
But time, as we know, must in time get the better of time,
So time came for slurred and claudicant me

To know I might be late, and, as the lights came on all down the
    river,
Brandish that snugly latent sword at the cabs with lights
Until Jack Greenbaum contracted to deliver
The sclerosis and the cane and the gin of Brooklyn Heights

And, somewhere inside, me, not claudicant but palpitant now.
Hundredth-and-tenth Street, the pay-off, the elevator,
Her door, she, in in quick, with 'I can't allow,
I can't really, it won't do, you know it won't do'. And she: 'Later:

Time for that later. Be calm, be calm.' But I'd gotten into the way
Of thrusting that hidden steel, and I thrust, to protect her youth,
To protect me from her youth. She grasped, and it came away,
Sweetly, the cherrywood, and there, like attenuated truth,

The sword flashed. I said: 'It's only to lean on, to strengthen the
      cane.'
'Yes', she said, 'yes'. It flashed, strong and straight. 'Well', she said,
And she felt the edge, the point. I tried to sheathe it again,
But she said: 'Lay it there on the bed,

In the middle.' So there it lay,
Virtue's protector in the old courting custom. Still, it flashed.
      I washed off the day
And middleage. Clean and hungry, I breathed
More calmly now, and while she brought food, I looked at it
      unsheathed,
At least it was unsheathed, at last it was unsheathed.

O LORD, O FORD, GOD HELP US, ALSO YOU

A New Year's Message for 1975

Unhouse that calendar: her dates are done,
Her whorings over. Get another one,
Try to pretend that a new year has begun,
The diary, blank, apes sinlessness. This is
The most pathetic of all fallacies –
The springs-eternal hope of a 'fresh start'
In the core of winter of, down under, heart
Of summer (the same season, after all:
Both lack the sharp élan of spring or fall,
So very and oppressively much *here*).
The church is realistic: its new year
Does not begin until Easter. New Year's Day
Is part of Christmas time, roughly halfway,
Marked by the Circumcision – snip and bless
And bow half-heartedly to cleanliness.
But we, who groan from drink or, showering, sing,
Believe the first of January can bring
Regeneration magically about
Both in our psyches and the world without.
On Jan 6, 10 – in other words, a bit
Later, we will, we vow, get down to it.
Nonsense – it can't be done: that's definite.
Spring brings the true new, nature's statements are
Simple enough: all the change is circular.
The firm ascending straight progressive line
Is dream geography, that's all. In fine,

This Nineteen-Seventy-five will see us still
Churning in Seventy-four's Satanic Mill.
Has any twelvemonth fed us more with fear?
Was ever a more salutary year?
At least we're learning and no more pretend
That history moves to a Hegelian end.
Utopia spells Erewhon, the earth's
Resources are not infinite, a birth's
Another burden in a hungry world,
Man's gobbed up the soil and also hurled
His poisons in the water and the air,
Hell is a fact and no mere Sunday scare,
America as Eden's dead and gone,
The Devil rides, and so on and so on.
Men we thought big are now revealed as little,
Conniving and contriving, mean and brittle,
Power-hungry merely, greedier than us,
Vindictive, vulgarians, and ugly too
(Truth's beauty, and the antithesis is true).
I gawped at New York television while
Your Ford, unflawed by an ironic smile,
Announced to the whole world: *Truth is a glue.*
O Lord, O Ford, God help us, also you.
Half a millennium has gone by since
Great Niccolò penned precepts for a Prince.
But in those unregenerate days at least
A prince, however hard he played the beast,
Saw statues hovering over him and read
Plato and Aristotle: the huge dead
Were still alive. But now, alas, it looks
As if the drughead's *Nothin', man, in books*
Infects the castles where our rulers sit
(*History*, that other Ford once said, *is sh—t*).
The men that British rotten boroughs sent

To hector in a venal Parliament
Fulfilled no democratic precepts, yet
Saw that their own mean times were soundly set
In an unfolding swathe of destiny;
Man was, and had been, and would always be
What Homer, Seneca, Thucydides,
Xenophon, Cicero, and more like these
Had limned. They saw their legislative task
As somehow philosophical, would ask,
As Jefferson and Lincoln once did, the one
Sound question: *What is man, what must be done*
By government, man's servant, to fulfil
The deeper longings of his higher will?
For politics was metaphysics, art,
Eloquence, knowledge of the human heart,
That is now sunk into a disrepute
Shameful and shameless, all too absolute.

This year will pose the question once again:
Where shall we go to seek superior men?
Superior in what? – a voice asks then:
The answer: In no more than being men.
The great technician's no superior man –
Only a larger type of artesan,
Extensive of his system or machine.
We need philosophers, not men who've been
Exalted through their skill at shyster's tricks
Who shell out shibboleths, who fox, who fix,
Committed to the timocratic view
That wealth is power, and neither is for you.
Add wealth and power to vulgar ignorance,
And you can tune up for our *Totentanz*.
The worship of the base is here to stay:
I heard a British union leader say:

'They brought the plain men where they are today,
The great men: let them sleep, their task is done.'
Exactly. Let your son, and your son's son,
Inherit demo-ethics, demo-art,
And learn this demo-decalogue by heart;
First, order your instructors what to teach,
Since a man's grasp must not exceed his reach:
Spit on the higher values when you can,
Unsanctified by democratic man;
Permit free speech, though, since it can't effect
A blasting of the walls of the elect:
To slay – what is it but to put to sleep?
Computers cost much, human souls are cheap.
Lie all you wish, for who knows what truth is?
Play games among the ruined languages,
Jettison *why* and concentrate on *how*;
Assign a prime reality to *now*;
Deny responsibility for *then*;
Consume and damn posterity – amen.
To opt out of this midden into dreams –
Communes or opiates – to many seems
The desperate one solution. I say: turn
Once more to the necessity to learn,
Not make a *tabula rasa* of your head,
But cram it with philosophy instead;
Leave inarticulacy to the loathed
Nude apes up there: let us at least be clothed,
Attack from knowledge and not just from rage:
Reject from reason. In another age,
Your fathers spoke thus, and did not the grey
Poet on Paumanok cry out: *Obey*
Little; resist much – let those four words be
A lasting slogan for the polity?
Love man the social animal, but hate,

On principle, the engine called the State;
Burn out the evil centre, and resolve
To flaunt a banner blazoned with *Devolve,*
Devolve. Then, last, remember Maynard Keynes:
People alone have virtue in their veins;
All governments are evil. This he knew.

Comparatively, things go well for you,
America. I know – smog makes you cough,
Too many citizens are badly off
(Meaning, by Asian standards, millionaires),
The story of West 77th Street scares
The living daylights out of us – but still
Shocked citizens attempt to work their will
(Devolve, devolve) despite the apathy.
Your dreams, like ours, revolve on bankruptcy,
Moral or fiscal, both, inflation and
Entropy. Here, in Italy's sad land
(Gorgeous December sheens Bracciano's lake,
Clear as a bell beyond, my tired eyes take
Soracte in, that Horace used to know,
All candidly nival, tipped with snow),
Bankruptcy sits beside us, walks the streets,
Takes coffee in the café, chats and eats,
A trusted friend, which never lets you down.
Bankruptcy blows and petrifies the town,
Shuts the museums, spares the mailman's boots,
Blanks out the teevoo, clears the roads, recruits
Spray-gunning thugs who scrawl *Death* on the plinths,
Chokes up the bureaucratic labyrinths,
Hides oil and salt, makes impotent the laws,
But places truncheons in the policeman's paws.
Inflation? Ah, we beat all records here –
A 20 (minimal) % per year.

England, my country, mother of the free,
Is crammed with paper money too. You'll see
Financial columns crammed with reasons why:
The petromoney of the sheiks, the sly
Printing of empty paper by the State,
The blackmail of the unions, some great
Cryptoconspiracy all bloody red
That loves to strike and, striking, strikes us dead.
So England shivers, and the coal's undug,
Darkness abets the murder and the mug,
And light and heat assume definitive
Value – i.e., more than one has to give.
'The oil is Allah's,' yodels the bilal,
'Therefore the Peoples of the Scriptures shall
Learn who the Chosen People really are.'
So freezing people on a cooling star
Envy the Indians, who rarely freeze
But die instead from other maladies.
We're all in this – you there and we back here –
Seeing fresh millions added every year
To swell the hordes of those ordained to starve.
The rich man has a juicy joint to carve,
But no joint's big enough to palliate
The hunger of the hundreds at the gate.
Hinc illae lacrimae. A single penny
Is indivisible among the many,
So is a dime, a quarter, dollar – hence
We justify our modest affluence.

Courage! Though life is feeble, life persists
(Persists? Increases, cry the pessimists).
The Orinoco cannibal affirms:
Better for friends to eat you than the worms.
As you believe that men have reached the moon,

Believe that anthropophagy will soon
Solve all our problems, justifying war,
Since here's a noble cause to wage it for.
The fighting young, the flower of every land,
Will fall in battle and will then be canned.
Try this, the supermarkets will proclaim:
Munch MANCH or MONCH or MENSCH, or some such name.
Meanwhile, although the demonstrator cries:
'Each time you laugh, another Indian dies';
Let's greet old two-faced Janus with dry eyes.
'Whatever the year brings, it brings nothing new,'
Wrote Rose Macauley. True – it was always true.
Walk on the sidewalk's edge, avoid the dark,
Watch out for pederasts in Central Park,
Read Plato and not *Playboy*, cease to try
To see life as a thing to quantify,
Cherish the gunman, guardian of the door,
And you'll come through. You came through '74.

PERSONAL VERSE, VIGNETTES, AND OTHER
SHORT WORKS

A SONNET FOR THE EMERY COLLEGIATE
INSTITUTE

Temerity – to launch into a sonnet
All unforeknowing what it will contain,
Or whether it will rhyme – whether, again,
Enough rhymes are available – not bonnet.
Upon it (they've been used before). I con it
(Five lines complete already) with less pain
Than I anticipated. Don't disdain
The rhyme that's coming. Is it? Yes. Doggone it.
Whatever that may mean. Advice: don't read

A Clockwork Orange – it's a foul farrago
Of made-up words that bite and bash and bleed.
I've written better books beside this *Iago*
Bracciano. So have other men, indeed.
Read Hamlet, Shelley, Keats, *Doctor Zhivago*.

'ADVICE TO WOULD-BE WRITERS?
SIMPLE. DON'T'

Advice to would-be writers? Simple. *Don't.*
Any profession's preferable to this.
Exhilarating, true, the Muse's kiss,
But inspiration's accolades just won't
Pay rent, buy groceries. To grieve, to groan, t-
-o search for the *mot juste*, to aim, to miss

The scene or image sought, to brave the hiss
Of critics, feel in bowel, brain and bone t-
-orment and terror – this, my friend, is writing.
Then add to all the public's crass neglect,
And fellow-authors' sneering and backbiting.
This, and much more, the tyro must expect.
To launch a book, you'd think, would be exciting –
But ship and builder are too quickly wrecked.
Neglect and poverty have rocks in wait to wreck us.
Writers in general are a wretched sect.

'I SEND THESE LINES TO YOU IN AGINCOURT'

I send these lines to you in Agincourt
(The right place for Bucannon) and regret
I cannot send a photograph. Any yet
Why should I sell myself so beastly short,
Bestowing transience – the porcine snort
And not the porcine esculence? To let
My ugliness, irrelevant, beget
My lasting image? – No, I'm not that sort.
A man is what he does, not how he seems,
And what he does is what he bids survive.
The voice that booms, the radiant eye that beams
Are nothing – not the honey but the hive.
Faces are things one shudders at in dreams:
The work is what attests the man alive.

THE LAST DAY (TO THE EDITORS, YALE NEWS)

End of the world – cosy, something thrilling
    Read in a boy's book, heard on the radio:
    Wells or Welles, apocalyptico-
Cathartic, buildings crashings, voices shrilling,
And me outside the frame, clutching the shilling
    Shocker, in an incandescent glow,
    Knowing this the ultimate *frisson*: below
The cindered earth, me saved somehow, God willing.

It will not be that way: no Gabriel's horn
    Over the snarled traffic. A whimper, rather,
Long-drawn and boring. Ravaged earth, forlorn
    With crops parched, seas a polluted lather.
        A man says: This is the end, for days. But never
        Sure. The end could linger for ever.

LATE AS I AM, BUT BLAME THE MAILS, NOT ME (TO MR SELWYN C. GAMBLE)

Late as I am, but blame the mails, not me,
    In haste I send the one thing personalised
    That I can find – a piece, unpriced, unprized,
Of what I call my talent. As you see,
I roll a sheet in the machine: my free
    Fancy is summoned, though weak and undersized
    These days, and, prosodically supervised,
Groans in the toils of sonneteering. Be

Assured, O Selwyn Gamble, as you sit
    With papal cufflinks there in Mississippi,

Sinatran toupees, even exquisite
    Silks from the famous bosomy or hippy,
    Socratic pearls, or pisspots from Xanthippe –
This gift's sincere: don't wipe your ass with it.

FORGIVE THE LATENESS, PLEASE, OF THIS REPLY (TO MR ALAN FOX)

Forgive the lateness, please, of this reply:
    The Italian postal services, alas,
    Exist no longer. Should it come to pass
That you receive this, no one more than I
Will be astonished. Hopelessly, I try
    Believing that there'll be a great *en masse*
    Breakthrough, flood of mail. But, patient ass,
I bear the burden still, and wonder why.

Thanks for your praise and thanks for your request.
    A photograph? Elizabeth the First
Threw out her mirrors, and I think it best

To avoid the camera. Ugly, also cursed
    With only being by my work oppressed,
I've no extraneous liquor for your thirst.

'SOME CONSIDER LOVE IS GREAT'

Some consider love is great
Greater than human hate,
Greater than we estimate.

TO CHAS

If God (if God exists) deliberated
Long on the framing of the human frame
Surely the product would not be the same
As this we have – it's far too complicated.

God would, presumably, have fabricated
A simple substance, unattacked by shame
(defecation, micturation: home – the horror)
or by illness decimated.

Moreover, there's no tinge of godly justice:
You, sir, and I have kept it fairly clean,
Whereas the lout whose life is loot and lust is
Looked after like an opulent machine.
We'll beat the bastards yet – by God, we must. Is
Life, is love, meant only for the mean?

'WHAT CAN I SAY? I'D BETTER TRY A SONNET' (TO MR PETER BRULE)

What can I say? I'd better try a sonnet
    (Verse, anyway, is easier than prose),
    Humility its content, I suppose,
And gratitude, like icing, troweled upon it.
The writer's craft is difficult, doggone it,
    And all too often, so it seems, and he knows
No more of it. Some new-confected bonnet

Its maker-milliner at least may see
    Flaunted in public, publicly admired,

But forgers of less useful goods, like me,
    Know our angelic choirs are not required,
And that is why it's heartening to be,
    As now, with some sense of usefulness enfired.

'FORGIVE MY WRITING VERSE: I GET SO BORED' (TO MR S. G. BYAM JR)

Forgive my writing verse: I get so bored
    With prosing for a living. I did write,
    I think, some effort to throw light or night
On English, in the *New York Times*. My sword
Was not, however, raised that there be gored
    Offending flanks: there wasn't any fight.
    For my commission from the dear *N. Y. T-*
Imes was to write on English – nothing more, d-
ealing out data on the differences
    Between American and British. You,
Dear Mr Byam, bless, since *bless* it is,
    Me with a thing I never did. It's true
    I do deplore some downward tendencies
But someone different wrote about them. Who?

'DEAR CHRIS, THE TROUBLE IS, AS YOU MUST KNOW' (TO MR CHRIS MAHON)

Dear Chris, the trouble is, as you must know,
    The getting over there, the getting in:
    Into the States, I mean. They probe past sin,

The immigration hounds of heaven, go
Probing and prising, peering high and low
    For evidence of redness, pinkness. Win?
    One cannot win, even, indeed, begin
To win against these engines. Even so,

As I am likely to be there next March,
    In the U.S., I mean, doing a little
Lecturing (they desiccate, they parch,
    Those lectures, make the bones grow thin and brittle),
I'll try to march beneath N.D.'s proud arch
    And dole out something, just a jot or tittle.

HAPPY BIRTHDAY TAE ANDREW

Mony happy returrrns o' the day!
May ye hae a' ye'd wish yersel'
Wi' aye guid whiskey on your shel',
Ane haggis on the board forbye
An' griddlecakes a' reekin', ay!
Lang may yer lum reek!
May Scotland feocht for freedom aye
Ah' rin the Sassenach awa'
An' see aince mair ane glorious day
Wi' her ain sun flame 'oer a'.

'SO WILL THE FLOW OF TIME AND FIRE'

So will the flow of time and fire,
The process and the pain, expire,
And history may bow
To one eternal now.

A BALLADE FOR THE BIRTHDAY
OF MY DEAREST WIFE

Various things have sabotaged the making
    Of this my birthday proffer. First, the fear
Of leaving a warm spot and coldly shaking
        The key like teeth (not mine, alas), the sheer
        Middleaged indolence that, year by year,
        Grows with my fat. But still, the urgent truth
        Demands expression. Celebrate, my dear,
        Another anniversary of youth.

I take on, and regret the undertaking,
    Too many things, and mostly out of mere
Inertia. Projects in the oven baking,
        Irons in the fire crowd time. Time comes and we're
        Overcommitted. One big time draws near
        Then leaps or paws – though gently, not uncouth:
        Then I'm all unprepared to clap and cheer
        Another anniversary of youth.

But take this, in the time of sun's forsaking
    The glum earth, in an era of flat beer
And watered gin, when anger in its waking
        Is much too tired to wake and blast the drear

World that our rulers build, when eye and ear
Survey the blazed corn like exiled Ruth.

But hope chose a November to uprear
Another anniversary of youth.

Envoi

Dearest, although the signs of age appear
    In me, in greying hair, deciduous tooth,
You work your yearly miracle. Lo, here:
    Another anniversary of youth.

WHISKY

Double you aitch aye ess kay ee wye spells
Irish and, without an ee, speels Scotch.
Saxon stupidity has made a botch
Out of the Celtic *uisgebaugh*, which tells
The truth about it. *Uisge* flows from wells,
But *baugh* means life – the seed within the crotch,
The thudding heart, tough as a cheap tin watch,
And flowing bowls, and balls, and bulls, and bells.

Whisky will do – ah, liquid sun and thunder,
Rich as the sea that beats the unnumbered pebbles.
But look at the damned tax it labours under.
One year it doubles, in the next it trebles,
Quit or sextuples. Is it any wonder
That whisky-loving men are bloody rebels?

A BALLADE FOR CHRISTMAS

Great Julius Caesar through the British race
    Was despicably weaky, weedy, weeny.
And so it was and is. It's lost all its pace,
    Its morals are as brittle as grissini.
    Still, in this season, greyish and ungreeny,
Something revives, survives, the thinned blood thickens.
    The heart's strings start to throb like Paganini.
I wish you all a Christmas out of Dickens.

A brandy glow irradiates the face,
    The air grows soft, an aria from Puccini,
The stolid London streets attain the grace
    Of a prolonged crescendo in Rossini.
    The holly berries cluster, sharp and sheeny,
And Scrooge, whose heart is smaller than a chicken's
    Learns what to do with money, the old meanie.
I wish you all a Christmas out of Dickens.

Nutmeg's a spice and so, once more, is mace,
    And Christmas cake goes well with capuccini.
With luck, frost will festoon like Brussels lace,
    And circuses please all, just not Fellini.
    The Ulster troubles, hymned by Seamus Heaney,
Will briefly ebb, like everything that sickens
    (Take etiolated Eliot's Apeneck Sweeney).
I wish you all a Christmas out of Dickens.

ENVOY
Principe, Principessa, Principini –
    You'll be abroad when the green season thickens,

But in Long Island's opulent confini
We wish you all a Christmas out of Dickens.

JANUARY 1

1.

Last night, before the death of the old year,
   I got the catalogue of my year's sins,
   Chronic sins really, hurled at me, mere pins
To this habituated cushion, mere
Eveish swipes at the old Adam, sheer
      Archetypal wifedom that begins
      And ends with ego, ego. Still my shins
Winced at the barking. It was not nice to hear.

You'll have to change. I've head such words before.
   Next month, with luck, I score my 68,
And do not think to knock on a new door.
   Change, at that age, is easy to translate,
And so I'll spill my egos on to the floor
And water them and watch them germinate.

2.

The four French télé channels were all smiles,
   Like grand pianos waiting to be struck
   At midnight. Mitterand wished us good luck
And looked as though he'd found a cure for piles.
Cartesian digitals displacing dials,
   We waited for Debussy harps to pluck
   Nouvelle Année, for even time is stuck
On the French culture cake, like cats on tiles.

New Year in England was a whole hour later
    And, naturally, seemed more genuine.
Big Ben throbbed twelve and drowned the Russians' data

    On the same waveband. Noon: I ovened in
A steak and kidney pie. Would that act rate a
    Slight remission of at least one sin?

SONNET À L'HÔTEL LE CLOS VOLTAIRE

Leman's for lovers, still, though Thomas Stearns
Eliot wept a Waste Land out, alone.
Careers (flotations foreign on) the Rhone,
Lapping a thousand banks. Servetus burns,
Or Calvin. Under bald Alps, a city learns
Salvation may be palpable as stone.

Leman's for lovers, still, though Thomas Stearns
Eliot wept a Waste Land out, alone.
Lapping its banks, the incremental Rhone
Out-ticks all purely temporal returns.
Swiss skills from Alpine skulls; Alps carve dead bone.

Virtue's in tolerance, not vaults or clocks
Or Institutes. Voltaire, your surgeon's quill
Lanced Europe's boil. Your knife-eyes rayed their will
To tyrants there. We yet feel these made shocks
And here you went to earth, old friend, old fox.
I seemed last night to hear you breathing still,
Reposeless. Rise, take up your trumpet shrill,
Excoriate our wolves, our bleating flocks!

'THE VERSES OF E. LUCIE-SMITH'

The verses of E. Lucie-Smith
Must not be dealt sneeringly with.
They're not just belle-lettric
I wander on any road under my moon,
Careless of glory, indifferent to the boon
Or stuffed up with rhetoric;
They're full not of wind but of pith.

'YOU WERE THERE, AND NOTHING SAID'

You were there, and nothing said,
For words were dead and dust in the air.
But I was suddenly aware, in the split instant
Of the constant, in a sort of passionless frenzy –
Trees, table, the war, in a fixed relation
Of your calculation, their *primum mobile*,
But that you were there really was all I knew.
What the blood purposed you to be.
Among the things that I bequeath
That safety razor. Stock up with
Blades, particularly the brand
The name of a notable swordsmith.

CATULLUS I

Who shall I give this pretty new
Dry-pumice-polished booklet to?
To you Cornelius, for you

Used to declare: By God, there is I think
Merit in these nugacities.
When you alone of Italy's
Historians had the guts to write
The world up in three volumes, quite
A job, weighty, and erudite.

So take this book for what it's worth.
Hecate, help its birth,
Grant it a hundred years on earth.

CATULLUS 2

Sparrow, my lady's pet,
In play upon her lap,
Her fingertip you get
To peck or sharply snap.
When she my shiny one
Bids sharper pain grow weak.
And pain is only fun
Delivered from your beak.
Sicker in love than she
I wish you'd play with me
Pecking my pain like crumbs
Till the heart's numbness comes.

'HEROES ARE DEAD TO US'

Heroes are dead to us,
    We worship filmstars.

Deep drinking and thinking
  Give place to milkbars.

'MY FATHER, HIS WIFE'

My father, his wife,
Too old to make decisions,
Yet plotted their revisions
Of their life.
Nor could this hope be
More vain for
It was left to me
To open the oven door.
She at least, the mother.
He in his apprehension
Cut the knot of tension.
She thought of other
Uses, seeking a flame
Stronger in her
The instinct came
To start the Sunday dinner.

THAT THE EARTH ROSE OUT OF A VAST BASIN
OF ELECTRIC SEA

Rolled, rolled, rolled,
And all being fills in it,
Where fire flies, sparks gay with gold,
Wash the lot, the tide swills, spills in it.
Tying all, oh with what strings

It binds, binds earth and air to all
It shews and knoes, meets all, leaps and sings
Its way through the spray of it, the misty caul.
Womb of all, tomb of all, the mass
Where mighty fingers beat now, kneed and mould,
With a curling of tongues, a laugh and a mocking to pass:
It ceases note, rolling in wash and glint of gold.

SONNET IN ALEXANDRINES

Whether windowed a greycold welkin or a dawn that mounts and
    breaks
In a roseflush wave each day arises the working man,
Heavy maybe but never for a thwarted life's plan
Seen shaped to the pounding day:- for the day's round he awakes.
He shakes sleep away. Day warms. He leaves and takes
A snap of sullen cheese, hunked bread, a brew for his can,
And thrives in the air, strives, spits, swears. His breastcares span
But Saturday's care or bet; naught deeper rankles or aches.
When the violet air blooms about him, then at last he can wipe
His hands sheerfree of swink, monarch of hours ahead;
Hearty he eats and, full, he sits to pull at his pipe,
Warm at the kitchen glow. The courts and sports-news read,
He argues, sups in the Lion vault; to a plate of tripe
Or crisp chips home returns, then climbs to a dreamless bed.

A RONDEL FOR SPRING

(*from the French of Charles d'Orléans*)

The earth has cast her winter skin
Of warping wind and driving rain,
And garbed greenery again
With fretted sunlight woven in.
No bird or beast but does begin
In its own speech to swell the strain:
The earth has cast her winter skin
Of warping wind and driving rain.
The floods vast, the streams thin
Spin in the source or sweep the plain,
Flaunting a sun-bespeckled train
To swell the wild and waking din.
The earth has cast her winter skin.

WHEN IT IS ALL OVER

One can only deplore
The devastated fields,
And check the fire-spread,
And do no more.
And after it is all over,
And the voices fall in the hoarse
Throats, and rubber truncheons rot under glass covers,
And dream blows are struck without force.
There shall be 'Nazi' lipsticks,
'Gestapo' cigarettes
And children shall cuddle toy
S.A. men in their beds.

WIR DANKEN UNSREM FÜHRER

We thank our Führer for redeeming us
    From the ignoble sluggish slough of peace;
For striking down the sleek, insidious
    Serpents that choked us; working our release
From the semitic bondage of our race.
    Sun symbol held aloft, we climb still nearer
    To the pure sun, the one God-granted place;
    We thank our Führer.

We thank our Führer as the reasoning head,
    We the blind limbs to function and obey,
Content with that. God-like he harvested
    Wheat from the chaff of his own Judgment Day.
God-like our shepherd feeding us aright
    Not in the flesh, what to the soul is dearer,
Our everlasting arms, sheen of our might.
    We thank our Führer.

We thank our Führer that he prophesied,
    Yours is the kingdom. You shall inherit the earth.
Fulfilling that, men will have starved and died
    Gladly with pride in death through pride in birth.
Shadowing space our fylfot will have told
    History's spring and end to the eager hearer,
    Our earth's first blood, our titles manifold.
    We thank our Führer.

GIRL

She was all
Brittle crystal;
Her hands
Silver silk over steel;
Her hair harvested
Sheaves shed by summer;
Her grace in repose the flash
Of the flesh of a river swimmer.
That was not nature's good;
She nothing understands.
Horrible now she should
Use to her own ends.

TO AMARYLLIS AFTER THE DANCE

Semitic violins, by the wailing wall
Weep their threnody
For the buried jungle, the tangled lianas;
Or say that was before, in the first flush,
And say that now
A handful of coins, image and milled edge worn,
Is spilled abroad, and determines
Our trade of emotions. Over this background are imposed
Urges, whose precise nature it is hard
To etch out, to define.
(Shells, shaped by forgotten surges).
One never gets to know anything really, having no word
To body forth a thought, no axe
To reach flagged soil, no drills
To pierce living wells. It would tax

My energies overmuch now to garner you
Cut of worn coins, worn shells.

ORPHEUS AND EURYDICE

Well, my Eurydice, that was pain enough
Having only your name to call on, day and night.
Both day and night were long enough;
Now I lead you laboriously to the light.

Hell played at forfeits. On a swivel of the head
Rested your return; as one might stab a pin
Idly at a fly for its irrelevant end.
The world was plunged into original sin.

That was not in the pattern of our lives,
Whose miraculous fabric has for every strand
Accounted. Wantonly the Destroyer unweaves,
Just as He hides time's secret in His hand.

But it is true I would have been destined then,
Climbing alone back to the light, to have met
The deserved logical end. The tree that has been
Fruitful, only stays to be fruitful yet.

Life's undergrowth of laws that see no light,
This I believe in, as much as anything.
He would have seen you no Proserpina
Nor sent you back to wither up the spring.

'ALL THE ORE'

All the ore
that, waiting, lay
for the later working
I melted before
its time
to make you ornaments for a day.
And all else, too
I drew out, there is no more.
For between man and man at the last
there rests at least shame.

A HISTORY

Anyway, there emerged from his mind's cellar
The forged stamp of the image of goddess,
And it fell upon her,
Almost, as it were, *per accidens.*
And with it a pitiful dual approach,
Half Shelley, half Flaubert.
He broached and broke the hymen of her lips
After three weeks' work, and was pre-occupied
By the technique, art for art's sake, of his kisses.
It was an attempt, having carved her pedestal,
To raise himself, almost by a metaphysical
Conceit, and to conduct love
On the level of Ideas, out of the clogs of time,
Seeing ethereal virtues in the bones
Of a paradigm.
O granted it was to become a grammar of love,
Yet who might construct the language, the vibrant speech

Sprung out of earth, from what had shed
All but archetypes, supposing the language dead?
Anyway, they reached complete intimacy,
And it was all on this level, carved out cleanly in time.
A fulfilling of all parts of the act, except
That it was playing from score, that a pattern was imposed,
That there was no growth out to become the pattern.
And he at least was amazed at the futility,
Thought the whole thing overrated; out of mind
Were the sweat and the labour to compass an ecstasy.
But with her an unpurposed external heat
Had achieved the loosening of the icefloes. A late spring
Became a wonder in her. Her body began
To flower in its own right.
He saw that its opening to man
Was what he had done, that that was the accomplished fact
That had to be greater to her than their personal history,
The released woman more than the melted she.
Stricken, he escapes to the war.
In absence her image reverts to that of the goddess crystallised
About his longings; not before
Might she impartially have watched his spasm worked out
In her the instrument. But to-day
He is outside his handiwork, the unpremeditated lord
Of creation, and that one connecting cord
Shrivelled away.

THE LOWDOWN ON ART
OR ÆSTHETICS FOR THE SCIENCE STUDENT

Art and Science have this in common: they both = man + nature.
They both imposed an ordered scheme on nature.

Science, in its applied state, for a useful end.

Pure science and pure art for a useless end.

(Oscar Wilde said, "All art is perfectly useless.")

You can decorate a wall with a Da Vinci.

You can use part of a Haydn string quartet for national anthem.

That is making use of art, but that is not the essential purpose of art.

Pure science is seeking to discover and manifest Truth.

Art is seeking to discover and manifest Beauty.

These are called Values. Their discovery and
	manifestation are considered to be valuable or
	worth while.

No that Truth or Beauty exist.

There are only true things and beautiful things.

So no one should think that Science is on the trail of Ultimate
	Truth.

Or Art on the trail of Ultimate Beauty.

Both these quests are the job or Religion.

* *

What is Beauty?

One says that the colour of a flower or the note of a
	bird is beautiful. This, however, cannot be
	the sense in which we are to take the beauty
	that art creates.

Because this beauty is natural, not created by the artist.

It is beautiful in that it is pleasing to the senses.

A church father called St. Thomas Aquinas said
	that those things are beautiful the appre-
	hension of which is pleasing.

So the beauty that art creates is also pleasing, but not only to the
	senses.

This beauty is a beauty of form, not of texture.

The business of the artist is to create new forms.

The artist's job is not purely a decorative one.
Wallpaper has a pattern,
But the pictorial art has form.
The pictorial art takes over the raw material, the forms found in
　　　nature,
And disposes them into a new and original form which is not
　　　found in nature.
Which is pleasing and significant.
(The artist does not copy nature. That is the photographer's job.)
In what way significant?

* *

Our minds are full of images, sounds, thoughts, and
emotions which we never use.
Which are chaotic, undigested, unarticulated.
Art digests and articulates these.
Makes them have meaning by giving them a form,
Which has such balance and unity that the effect strikes us as
　　　beautiful.

* *

A poem takes over the emotions which we feel
　　　Vaguely but cannot express complete.
It expresses those emotions in words completely,
　　　using everything that speech can give to attain
　　　that completeness.
It binds words and balances them to a unity to
　　　Attain that completeness.
Then we feel that the emotion has been mastered
　　　by being expressed,
Objectified, separated from ourselves.

* *

And music makes something organised, new and
   original out of the chaotic rhythms and sound
   intervals of nature.

* *

So that the more we know about art and the more
   we learn to appreciate it, the more we feel
   that we have mastered nature and enriched our
   own experience through making something o
   nature's into something of ours.

* *

Now you may read Shakespeare,
Listen to Mozart,
Look at Michael Angelo.

DEAD LEAVES

Lonely as the last batch of swallows that swing
Desolate on the aerial, and taut
With unthought memories, we bring
Four figures only to the melody,
And leave the dead note dead.
We are not those whose life is blown away
By the omission, not those for whom
Normality is formal now, each day
An exercise in self-control, but yet
We feel regret for the abrupt

Manner of going, cannot quite forget
The lull when conversation for a moment stopped:
We turned, with a remark half-said,
To find a room grown suddenly dark,
And you – fled.

SONNET ON EXAMINATIONS

Hard thing it is to sweat and strive and aim
And feel the very task within consume
All that is best in us, as the blown bloom
Waits for full summer, but the blasts proclaim
(Being like weak old men, feeble and lame,
Yet envious and powerful) clouds to gloom
And darken long, till like the crash of doom
They burst, and these laugh loud and love their game.

So it has been with us (seems for an age)
And darken on us thoughts of high-born rage,
Avenging anger lest we sink i' the scale,
It's Judgment's show and shadow: sot and sage,
We build a narrow home fast in this cage
And our on one song then 'Is it pass or fail?'

SIXTH-FORM TRIOLETS

I.

All agonies that torture us
Find fast their home in H. S. C.
The aching arm, the fevered fuss –

All agonies that torture us.
Words that won't come and (what is wuss)
Though learn'd with labour, thought that flee,
All agonies that torture us
Find fast their home in H. S. C.

II.
The strain of waiting for results
Is really more than man can stand,
It ages children to adults,
The strain of waiting for results.
'Mention, or space that just insults?'
Turns in the mind on every hand; –

The strain of waiting for results
Is really more than man can stand.

III.
Regrets, those spectres faint and pale
Were surely born in this exam.
They see the truth too late and wail –
Regrets, those spectres faint and pale.
They prompt us, when we fear a 'fail'
To cry 'what a – – I am!'
Regrets, those spectres faint and pale
Were surely born in this exam.

JACK'S STORY

Browning made haunches, Rupert Brooke made branches stir,
Both seeking rhymes for names of towns that rhyme,
Though Grantchester could not be less like Manchester,

Which city, in a rather distant time
My muse invokes. Stir, Muse! Come, stir! Why can she stir?
She's bogged down, as a bird is bogged in lime,
At the sheer prospect of our setting forth
To engage the smoke and the vowels of the North.

'PRUDENCE! PRUDENCE!' THE PIGEONS CALL'

'Prudence! Prudence!' the pigeons call.
Serpents lurk in the gilded meadow.
An eye is embossed on the island wall.

The running tap casts a static shadow.
'Caution caution' the rooks proclaim,
'The dear departed, the weeping widow
Will meet in you in the core of flame.
The running tap casts a static shadow.'
'Act! Act!' The ducks give voice.

'Enjoy the widow in the meadow.
Drain the sacrament of choice.
The running tap casts a static shadow.'

FISH AND HEROES

A dream, yes, but for everyone the same.
The thought that wove it never dropped a stitch;
The absolute was anybody's pitch
For, when a note was struck, we knew its name;

That dark aborted any urge to tame
Waters that day might prove to be a ditch
But then were endless growling ocean, rich
In fish and heroes, till the dredgers came.
Wachet auf! A fretful dunghill cock
Flinted the noisy beacons through the shires;
A martin's nest clogged the cathedral clock,
But it was morning: birds could not be liars.
A key cleft rusty age in lock and lock;
Men shivered by a hundred kitchen fires.

'NYMPHS AND SATYRS, COME AWAY'

Nymphs and satyrs, come away.
Faunus, laughing from the hill,
Rips the blanket of the day
From the paunch of dirty Will.
Each projector downs its snout,
Truffling the blackened scene,
Till the Wille's lights gush out
Vorstellungen on the screen.
Doxies blanch to silverwhite;
All their trappings of the sport,
Lax and scattered, in this light
Merge and lock to smooth and taut.
See! The rockets shoot afar!
Ah! The screen was tautest then.
Tragic the parabola
When the sticks reel down again.

'AND IN THAT LAST DELIRIUM OF LUST'

And in that last delirium of lust
Your image glows. Love is a blinding rain,
Love crow all the cocks, love lays the dust
Of this cracked crying throat whose thirst is pain.

'EPITHALAMION'

The cry in the clouds, the throng of migratory birds,
The alien planet's heaven where seven moons
Are jasper, agate, carbuncle, onyx, amethyst and blood-ruby and
bloodstone.
Or else binary suns
Wrestle like lions to a flame that we can stand,
Bound, twisted and conjoined
To an invertebrate love where selves are melted
To the primal juice of a creator's joy,
Before matter was made,
Two spheres in a single orbit
Swollen with cream or honey
The convalescent evening launches its rockets,
Soaring above the rich man's gala day,
In the thousand parks of the kingdom
Which radiate from this bed
Anoint the ship with wine! On ample waters,
Which always wear this ring, that the earth be humbled
Only away from cities, let it dance and ride
And you whose fear of maps
Set buzzing the long processes of power,
Resign your limbs at length to elements

Friendly or neutral at least,
Mirrors of the enemy

And even the dead may bring blue lips to this banquet
And twitter like mice or birds down their corridors
Hung with undecipherable blazons
For two at least can deny
That the past has any odour. They can witness
Passion and patience rooted in one paradigm; in this music
    recognize
That all the world's guilt can sit like air
On the bodies of these living.

TO TIRZAH

You being the gate
Where the army went through
Would you renew the triumph and have them decorate
The arch and stone again?
Surely those flowers are withered, the army
Now on a distant plain.

But some morning when you are washing up,
Or some afternoon, taking a cup
Of tea, possibly you will see
The heavens opening and a lot
Of saints singing, with bells swinging.
But then again, possibly not.

'YOUR PRESENCE SHINES ABOUT THE FUMES OF FAT'

Your presence shines about the fumes of fat,
    Glows from the oven-door.
Lithe with the litheness of the kitchen cat,
    Your image treads the floor
Ennobling the potato-peel, the lumps
Of fallen bread, the vulgar cabbage-stumps.
'Love!' cry the eggs a-whisk, and 'Love!' the beef
    Calls from the roasting-tin.
The beetroot blushes love. Each lettuce-leaf
    That hides the heart within
Is a green spring of love. Pudding and pie
Are richly crammed with love, and so am I.

'THE DRAGON'S MOUTH WILL CONSUMMATE OUR SEARCH'

The Dragon's mouth will consummate our search
For pillars of the borough and the Church,
Whose bar-side stance bespeaks their propping function.
There stands the Vicar who, with extreme unction,
To flesh and blood will transubstantiate
The cups that Sunday abstinents donate.
This generation, wiser than the luminous,
Thus gains vicarious contact with the numinous.
Here ruined farmers, in new hacking-coats,
Pour Scotch and ram fat bacon down their throats;
And children, obdurately red and flaxen,
Proclaim the crass inbreeding of the Saxon.
Observe the maidens who, with brawny arms,

Gush the seductive fragrance of the farms.
They feel the body should be mainly meat,
That ankles have no function and that feet,
Disdaining shape and glorying in size,
Should shout a curious kinship to the thighs.
But lest with so much weight the streets should rock,
The desiccated matrons of good stock
(Though not for soup) tune their patrician tweeds,
Then hog the pavements with their barking spouses
Before they seek their deathwatch-rotting houses,
Where flies die in the port and rabbit, stewed,
Provides for dog and man a basic food.
The manor gates are down, the past is dead.
American police patrol instead,
Save there, where feudalism's greasy scraps
Still touch the villagers who touch their caps
To soap king's lady or to upstart lord
Who licked the party's boots or swelled its hoard,
Trimming like mad or clinging like a louse
To be translated to the Upper House,
Whence now he comes to dogmatise and hector,
Sway the church sycophants and hound the rector.

'WHERE SWEAT STARTS, NOTHING STARTS.
TRUE, LIFE RUNS'

Where sweat starts, nothing starts. True, life runs
    On in a way, in rings of dust like Saturn's,
    And creating is creating arid patterns
Whose signature prove, always, the arid sun's.

'LAND WHERE THE BIRDS HAVE NO SONG, THE FLOWERS'

Land where the birds have no song, the flowers
    No scent, and time no movement; here
The rhythms of northern earth are frozen, the hours
    Set like ice-cubes; the running of the year
I stopped and comma'd only by the moon's feasts,
    And the sun is Allah, never an avatar;
In sight of that constant eye life crumbles, wastes
To the contented champing patterns of the beasts
    Which live in day's denomination. Far

The life of years and works that yet a day's
    Flight can restore…

'CRACKS OPEN THE LEADEN CORNCRAKE SKY WITH CRASS, ANGELIC'

…Cracks open the leaden corncrake sky with crass, angelic
Wails as round
as cornfruit, sharp as crowfoot, clawfoot,
Rash, brash, loutish gouts of lime or vinegar strokes
Till the crinkled fish start from their lace of bone
But loss, too, is at least a thing which, in the dark,
We can hold, feeling a sharpness, knowing that a knife
Is a double-edged weapon, for carving as well as killing.
The knife in the abattoir is also the knife on the table,
The corpse becomes meat, the dead stone heart the raw
Stuff of the sculptor's art.
In moments of crisis hunger comes, welling
Up through the groaning tubes, and feeding-time

Is the time of waking of perhaps the time before
Night settles on the land, endless night.
Light, whether of dawn or evening, turns
The river to glow-gold syrup, the trees
To a fairyland of fruit.

'THE AFTERNOON HOUR HAS STRUCK FOR YOU TO'

The afternoon hour has struck for you to
Enter, become your body, pay
The forced grin of affection due to
What is now you. That is to say:
You are this pate and mouth of missing teeth.

You are these sagging bulbs and bags beneath,
And the leering social face in that far mirror
Recognized with sock (but no, no error) –
That is you, too.
Youth was a knife and lakes and air,
Metal and glass; you could bestow
Your body as a gift of swords to spare.
It was different then. It was not you –
Be patient. I will learn to be concise
Again, the hot room shrinks to austere ice.
The silver will evoke a salmon's leap,
And bone-rungs strong enough for a single step
Will make a one-way stair.

'RICE-PAPER LAND, O LOTUS-FOOTED'

Rice-paper land, O lotus-footed,
Whose tiny trees are tiny-rooted,
And cherry-blossom bells tingle over the lakes
And old Fujiyama shakes and quakes.

'YOU TAKE MY HEART WITH SUCH UNFORMED GRACE'

You take my heart with such unformed grace,
One, at times, with the heartbreak earth
And its children, fur or bone – fawn, mouse,
Palpitating duckling, stumbling calf.
In touching you, silk, silver, I touch half
Of the whole dreadful mystery of birth.
I dread you faring forward into the world,
Carrying your beauty like an innocent gift
Among the grown beasts. I am appalled
At the scratching of hungry fingers at the door,
Already. Two handfuls of years, no more,
And what of this heartbreak changeling will be left?

'BERYL IS THE DAUGHTERLY DAUGHTER'

Beryl is the daughterly daughter:
The rankest filial piety oozes
From the flesh that she washes in greasy water
And the pallid pie that the cat refuses.
Mother and womb must come to dust;

The gone, what else can compensate?
In sheer devotion then she must
Inherit the entire estate.

EPIGRAPH ON A PRINTER

He, who did not originate the Word,
Yet brought the Word to man when man was ripe
To read the Word. But that ill-bound, absurd
Book of his body's gone. A mess of type
That death broke up reads greater nonsense now.
Now God re-writes him, prints him, binds him, never
To fail or be forgotten: God knows how
To make one copy that is read for ever.

THE MUSIC OF THE SPHERES

I have raised and poised a fiddle
    Which, will you lend it ears,
Will utter music's model:
    The music of the spheres.

By God, I think not Purcell
    Nor Arne could match my airs.
Perfect beyond rehearsal
    My music of the spheres.

Not that its virtue's vastness –
    The terror of drift of stars
For subtlety and softness

My music of the spheres.
The spheres that feed its working
Their melody swells and soars
On thinking of your marking
    My music of the spheres.

This music and this fear's
Work of your maiden years.
Why shut longer your ears?
Look how the live earth flowers!
The land speaks my intent:
Bear me accompaniment.

'NOT, OF COURSE, THAT EITHER OF US THOUGHT'

Not, of course, that either of us thought
We were too good for this world. No such thought
Had ever entered heads lacking in thought.
But shall I say there was a sort of hopelessness, a sort of
Sickness which further living could not cure,
Aggravate rather. We started off with those certain loves
Of desires for love which men have, such as,
Being English, a desire to love England.
But we saw England delivered over to the hands of
The sneerers and sniggerers, the thugs and grinners,
England become a feeble-lighted
Moon of America, our very language defiled
And become slick and gum-chewing.
Oh, and the great unearthed and their heads
Kicked about for footballs. We saw nastiness
Proclaimed as though it were rich natural
Cream and the fourth-rater exalted

So long as her tits were big enough. Alas
For England. England is not an England
We would wish to stand and see defiled further –
We've all betrayed our past, we've killed the dream
Our fathers held. Look at us now, look at us:
Shuddering waiting for the bomb to burst,
The ultimate, but not with dignity, oh no.
Grinning like apes in pointed shoes and grinning
National Health teeth, clicking our off-beat fingers
To juke-box clichés, waiting
For death to overtake us, rejecting choice
Because choice seems no longer there. But to two at least
Choice shone, a sun, a gleam of Stoic death.
Better out of it steak and kidney
Steak meets kidney and asks to dance
KNOCK KNOCK
The band strikes up with one-er two-er three
It might as well be steak and kidney pie I can always
Boil some potatoes no need for a second
Vegetable
KNOCK KNOCK KNOCK

'IN THIS SPINNING ROOM,
REDUCED TO A COMMON NOUN'

In this spinning room, reduced to a common noun,
     Swallowed by the giant stomach of Eve,
The pentecostal sperm came hissing down.

I was nowhere, for I was anyone –
     The grace and music easy to receive:
The patient engine of a stranger son.

His laughter was fermenting in the cell,
    The fish, the worm were chuckling to achieve
The rose of the disguise he wears so well.

And though, by dispensation of the dove,
    My flesh is pardoned of its flesh, they leave
The rankling of a wrong and useless love.

'PERHAPS I AM NOT WANTED'

'Perhaps I am not wanted then', he said
    'Perhaps I'd better go',
He said. Motionless her eyes, her head,
    Saying not yes, not no.

'I will go then, and aim my gun of grief
        At any man's or country's enemies.'
He said. 'Slaughter will wreak a red relief.'
        She said not no, not yes.

And so he went to marry mud and toil
    Swallow in general hell his private hell.
His salts have long drained into alien soil,
    And she says nothing still.

'TOMORROW THERE WILL BE LOVE FOR THE LOVELESS, AND FOR THE LOVER LOVE'

Tomorrow will be love for the loveless, and for the lover love.
The day of the primal marriage, the copulation

Of the irreducible particles; the day when Venus
Sprang fully armed from the wedding blossoms of spray
And the green dance of the surge, while the flying horses
Neighed and whinnied about her, the monstrous conchs
Blasted their intolerable joy.

Tomorrow will be love for the loveless, and for the lover love.
The swans, with garrulous throats, crash through the pools
In a blare of brass; the girl that Tereus
Forced to his will complains endlessly
Among the poplars, desperately forcing
The heartbreak message through, but only forcing
More and more ironic sweetness till
The ear faints with excess of sweetness.

Tomorrow shall be love for the loveless, and for the lover love.
The scrubbing and dusting, the worry about what to eat,
The stretched elastic of wages and housekeeping money
Ready to snap, the vertigo vista of debt
Shall no longer seem important; the housewife's fingers
Shall love their creases of grime; the husband's hair,
Receding, will give him a look of Shakespeare. Honey
Will flow from the lips that meet in perfunctory greeting;
The goodnight kiss will suddenly open a door,
And sleep then will be a bouquet with lights and music.

Tomorrow shall be luck for the luckless, and for the lucky luck.
The luckless punter will have unbelievable luck
And the bookmaker doubt his vocation. Houses will echo
With a fabulous smell of frying onions, steaks
Will be feather beds of salivating thickness.
Beer will bite like a lover and prolong its caress
Like cool arms in a hot bed. And clocks
Shall, in the headlong minute before closing time,

Not swoop to the kill, but hover indefinitely,
Like beneficent hawks.

Tomorrow shall be love for the loveless, and for the lover love.
The bed will be no monster's labyrinth,
But spirals winding to a blinding apex,
Sharp as a needle, where the last shred of self
Is peeled off painlessly, and space and time are bullied
Into carrying their own burdens. Tomorrow
Shall be love for the loveless

And for the lover love.
The map of love, spread on our knees, disclosing
The miraculous journey, shall not terrify
With lack of compass points, with monstrous patches
Of terra incognita. Every sea-lane
Leads us home to each other, and always home
Is a new continent, of inconceivable richness.

'TO ENDYMION'

The moon awaits your sleeping: fear to be kissed.
Tepid her light unblenching, but will twist
Your features to strange shapes; though blind, those
Beams
Get in the mind's slime monsters for dreams.

'THE STOAT'S CRY'

The stoat's cry tears long slivers of the night,

And, luminous, the owl in the rustling fruit
Draws up the sweating lovers by the root;
They warm in water-blankets worlds of fright –

'AND HIS HOOVES HAMMER ME BACK INTO THE GROUND''

And his hooves hammer me back into the ground,
The four gospel hammers, till, in that corn death,
I am promised to be queen of the bellied wheat.
I pray a last thanks in my killing breath,
Glad to be ripped, torn of the panting hollow,
While his one eye glows, the angels carry away
The suffocating forge to become the sun,
Who throbs in waves to suck the fainting day.

'PIGS SNORT FROM THE YARD'

Pigs snort from the yard.
Above, gulls mew and heckle.
Memory's shadows speckle
The blind, with its swinging chord.

'GASPING IN THE DUNNY IN THE DEAD OF DARK'

Gasping in the dunny in the dead of dark,
    I dream of my boola-bush, sunning in the south,

And the scriking of the ballbird and Mitcham's lark,
    And bags of the sugarwasp, sweet in my mouth.
For here in the city is the dalth of coves,
    Their stuff and their slart and the fall of sin,
The beerlout's spew where the nightmort roves
And the festered craw of the filth within.
God's own grass for the porrow in my tail,
    Surrawa's lake for this puke and niff,
Prettytit's chirp for the plonky's nipper's wail,
    And the rawgreen growler under Bellarey's Cliff.

'DRAGGED FROM HIS DOINGS'

Dragged from his doings in the roar of youth,
    Snipped like the stem of a caldicot flower
    Snarled time's up ere he'd quaffed his hour,
Tossed to the tearing of the dour dog's tooth.
Bye, my brad, let the bright booze pour
    That is suds of stars in the Milky Way,
    And its door swing open all the joylit day
And the heavenlord landlord cry you time no more.

'ARCHANGELS BLASTING FROM INNER SPACE'

Archangels blasting from inner space,
Pertofan, Tryptizol, Majeptil,
Parstelin and Librium.
And a serenace for all his tangled strings.

'BELLS BROKE IN THE LONG SUNDAY'

Bells broke in the long Sunday, a dressing-gown day.
The childless couple basked in the central heat.
The papers came on time, the enormous meat
Sang in the oven. On the thick carpets lay
Thin panther kittens locked in clawless play –
Bodies were firm, their tongues clean and their feet
Uncalloused. All their wine was new and sweet.
Recorders, unaccompanied, crooned away –
Coiled on the rooftree, bored, inspired, their snake
Crowed Monday in. A collar kissed the throat,
Clothes braced the body, a benignant ache
Lit up a tooth. The papers had a note:
'His death may mean an empire is at stake';
Sunday and this were equally remote.

'USELESS TO HOPE TO HOLD OFF'

Useless to hope to hold off
The unavoidable happening
With that frail barricade
Of week, day or hour
Which melts as it is made,
For time himself will bring
You in his high-powered car,
Rushing on to it,
Whether you will or not.

So, shaking hands with the grim
Satisfactory argument,
The consolation of bone

Resigned to the event,
Making a friend of him,
He, in an access of love,
Renders his bare acres
Golden and wide enough.
And this last margin of leaving
Is sheltered from the rude
Indiscreet tugging of winds.
For parting, a point in time,
Cannot have magnitude
And cannot cast shadows about
The final kiss and final
Tight pressure of hands.

CURTAL SONNET

And so the car plunged in the singing green
Of sycamore and riot-running chestnut and oak
That squandered flame, cut a thousand arteries and bled
Flood after summer flood, spawned an obscene
Unquenched unstanchable green world sea, to choke
The fainting air, drown sun in its skywise tread.

But the thin tuning-fork of one of the needs of men,
The squat village letter-box, approached, awoke,
Call all to order with its stump of red;
In a giant shudder, the monstrous organ then
Took shape and spoke.

'SHREWSBURY, SHREWSBURY, ROUNDED BY RIVER'

Shrewsbury, Shrewsbury, rounded by river
    The envious Severn like a sleeping dog
That wakes at whiles to snarl and slaver
    Or growls in its dream its snores of fog.

Lover-haunted in the casual summer:
    A monstrous aphrodisiac,
The sun excites in the noonday shimmer,
    When Jack is sweating, Joan on her back.

Sick and sinless in the anaemic winter:
    The nymphs have danced off the summer rout,
The boats jog on the fraying painter,
    The School is hacking its statesmen out.

The pubs dispense their weak solution
    The unfructified waitresses bring their bills,
While Darwin broods on evolution,
Under the pall of a night that chills –

– But smooths out the acne of adolescence
    As the god appears in the fourteenth glass
And the urgent promptings of tumescence
    Lead to the tumbled patch of grass.

Time and the town go round like the river,
    But Darwin thinks in a line that is straight.
A sort of selection goes on for ever,
    But no new species originate.

'I SOUGHT SCENT'

I sought scent, and found it in your hair;
Looked for light, and it lodged in your eyes;
So for sound: it held your breath dear;
And I met movement in your ways.

'THE URGENT TEMPER OF THE LAWS'

The urgent temper of the laws,
That clips proliferation's claws,
 Shines from the eye that sees
 A growth is a disease.

Only the infant will admire
The vulgar opulence of fire
 To tyrannize the dumb
 Patient continuum.

And, while the buds burst, hug and hold
A cancer that must be controlled
 And moulded till it fit
 These forms not made for it.

FROM 'THE CIRCULAR PAVANE'

They thought they'd see it as parenthesis –
 Only the naked statement to remember,
Cleaving no logic in their sentences,
 Putting no feelers out to the waking dreamer –

So they might reassume untaken seats,
     Finish their coffee and their arguments,
From the familiar hooks redeem their hats
     And leave, with the complacency of friends.

But strand is locked with strand, like the weave of bread,
     And this is part of them and part of time –

'AT THE END OF THE DARK HALL'

At the end of the dark hall he found his love
     Who, flushed and gay,
     Pounded with walking hand and flying fingers
     The grinning stained teeth for a wassail of singers
That drooped around, while on the lid above
     The dog unnoticed, waiting, lolling lay.

He noticed, cried, dragged her away from laughter.
     Lifts on the frantic road
     From loaded lorries helpful to seek safe south
     Slyly sidestreeted north. Each driver's mouth,
Answering her silly jokes, he gasped at after
     The cabin-door slammed shut: the dogteeth showed.

At last, weary, out of the hot noon's humming,
     Mounting his own stair
     It was no surprise to find a mother and daughter,
     The daughter she. Hospitable, she gave him water.
Windless, the shutters shook.

     A quiet voice said: 'I'm coming.'
     'Oh God God it's the dog', screamed the daughter,

But he, up the miles or leaden water,
Frantically beat for air.

INDEPENDENCE DAY

Anciently the man who showed
Hate to his father with the sword
Was bundled in a dark sack
With a screaming ape to claw his back
And the screaming talk of a parrot to mock
Time's terror of air's and light's lack
Black
And the slimy litheness of a snake.
Then he was swirled into the sea.
But that was all balls and talk
Nowadays we have changed all that
Into a cleaner light to walk
And wipe that mire off on the mat.
So when I knew his end was near
My breath was freer
Aerating a shedding then
Of all the accidents of birth,
And I had a better right to the earth
And knew myself more of a man,
Peeling the last squamour of the old skin.

But never underestimate
The comic cunning of the dead.
The snake that slithers in at night
To occupy most of the bed
Has learnt to wear my father's head.
And one day in the filthy shop

Of ancient rubbish I wound up
A 1914 gramophone
To a parrot voice intone
Some nonsense about sun and air,
The two things that were lacking there.
And, like a fetal marmoset,
Something is swinging when I fix
Eyes upon eyes in the bathroom glass
A load of stupid monkey tricks
Turns me to him as the months pass:
Hair, eyes, jowl, teeth.
I hear him mine the floor beneath
Muffled: You'll not be rid of me.
Each morning when you shave you'll see.

'THEY FEAR AND HATE'

They fear and hate
the Donne and Dante in him, this
cold
gift to turn heat to a flame, a kiss
to the gate
of a monster's
labyrinth. They hold
and anchor a thin thread
the tennis party, the parish dance:
stale pus out of dead
pores.

'SO WILL THE FLOW OF TIME AND FIRE'

So will the flux of time and fire,
The process and the pain, expire,
And history can bow
To one eternal now.

The greenstick snaps, the slender goldenrod
Here cannot probe or enter. Thin spring winds
Freeze blue lovers in unprotected hollows, but
Summer chimes heavy bells and flesh is fed
Where fruit bursts, the ground is crawling with berries.

SEPTEMBER, 1938

There arose those winning life between two wars,
Born out of one, doomed food for the other,
Floodroars ever in the ears.
Slothlovers hardly, hardly fighters:
Resentment spent against stone, long beaten out of
Minds resigned to the new:
Useless to queue for respirators.
Besides, what worse chaos to come back to.
Home, limbs heavy with mud and work, to sleep
To sweep out a house days deep in dirt.
Knowing finally man would limbs loin face
Efface utterly, leaving in his place
Engines rusting to world's end, heirs to warfare
Fonctionnant d'une manière automatique.

SUMMER, 1940

Summer swamps the land, the sun imprisons us,
The pen slithers in the examinee's fingers,
And colliding lips of lovers slide on sweat
When, blind, they inherit their tactile world.
Spectacles mist, handveins show blue, the urge to undress
Breeds passion in unexpected places. Barrage balloons
Soar silver in silver ether. Lying on grass,
We watch them, docile monsters, unwind to the zenith.

Drops of that flood out of France, with mud and work
Stained, loll in the trams, drinking their cigarettes,
Their presence defiling the flannels and summer frocks,
The hunters to hound out safely, spoil the summer.

SPRING IN CAMP, 1941

War becomes time, and long logic
On buried premises; spring supervenes
With the circle as badge which, pun and profundity,
Vast, appears line and logical,
But, small, shows travel returning.
Circle is circle, proves nothing, makes nothing,
Swallows up process and end in no argument,
Brings new picture of old time.
Here in barracks is intake of birds,
The sun holds early his ordered room,
The pale company clerk is uneasy
As spring brings odour of other springs.
The truckdriver sings, free of the war,
The load of winter and war becomes

Embarrassing as a younger self.
Words disintegrate; war is words.

THE EXCURSION

The blue of summer morning begs
The country journey to be made,
The sun that gilds the breakfast eggs
Illuminates the marmalade.
A check is smiling on the desk.
Remembered smells upon the lane
Breed hunger for the picaresque
To blood the buried springs again.
Here is the pub and here the church
And there our thirty miles of sun,
The river and the rod and the perch,
The noonday drinking just begun.
Let beer beneath the neighbour trees
Swill all that afternoon away,
And onions, crisp to sullen cheese,
Yield the sharp succulence of today.

Today remembers breaking out
The fire that burned the hayfield black.
An army that was grey with drought
Shows to my stick its fossil track.
Returning evening rose on rose
Of pomegranate rouge and ripe;
The lamp upon the pavement throws
The ectoplasm of my pipe.

EDEN

History was not just what you learned that scorching day
Of ink and wood and sweat in the classroom, when mention
Of the Duke of Burgundy lost you in voluptuous dream
Of thirst and Christmas, but that day was part of history.

There were other times, misunderstood by the family,
When you, at fifteen, on your summer evening bed
Believed there were ancient towns you might anciently visit.
There might be a neglected platform on some terminus

And a ticket bought when the clock was off its guard.
Oh, who can dismember the past? The boy on the friendly bed
Lay on the unpossessed mother, the bosom of history,
And is gathered to her at last. And tears I suppose

Still thirst for that reeking unwashed pillow,
That bed ingrained with all the dirt of the past,
The mess and lice and stupidity of the Golden Age,
But a mother and loving, ultimate Eden.

One looks for Eden in history, best left unvisited,
For the primal sin is always a present sin,
The thin hand held in the river which can never
Clean off the blood, and so remains bloodless.

And this very moment, this very word will be Eden,
As that boy was already, or is already, in Eden,
While the delicate filthy hand dabbles and dabbles
But leaves the river clean, heartbreakingly clean.

'AND AS THE MANHATTAN DAWN CAME UP'

And as the Manhattan dawn came up
Over the skyline we still lay
In each other's arms. Then you
Came awake and the Manhattan dawn
Was binocularly presented in your
Blue eyes and in your pink nipples
Monostomatic heaven…

'THEN AS THE MOON ENGILDS THE THALIAN FIELDS'

Then as the moon engilds the Thalian fields
The nymph her knotted maidenhead thus yields,
In joy the howlets owl it to the night,
In joy fair Cynthia augments her light,
The bubbling conies in their warrens move
And simulate the transports of their love.

'SO THE WORLD TICKS, AYE, LIKE A TICKING CLOCK'

So the world ticks, aye, like to a ticking clock
On th'wall of naked else infinitude,
Am I am hither come to lend an ear
To manners, modes and bawdries of this town
In hope to school myself in knavery.
Aye, 'tis a knavish world wherein the whore
And bawd and pickpurse, he of the quartertrey,
The coneycatcher, prigger, jack 'o the trumps

Do profit mightily while the studious lamp
Affords but little glimmer to the starved
And studious partisan of learning's lore.
There, I say, am I come hither, eye,
To be enrolled in knavish roguery.
But soft, who's this? Aye, marry, by my troth,
A subject apt for working on. Good den,
My master, prithee what o'clock has thou,
You I would say, and have not hast, forgive
Such rustical familiarity
From one unlearn'd in all the lore polite
Of streets, piazzas and the panoply
Of populous cities –

'YOU WENT THAT WAY AS YOU ALWAYS SAID YOU WOULD'

You went that way as you always said you would,
Contending over the cheerful cups that good
Was in the here-and-now, in, in fact, the cheerful
Cups and not in some remotish sphere full
Of twangling saints, the pie-in-the-sky-when-you-die
Of Engels as much as angels, whereupon I…

'THE WORK ENDS WHEN THE WORK ENDS'

The work ends when the work ends,
Not before, and rarely after.
And that explains, my foes and friends,
This spiteful burst of ribald laughter.

Let the stamps in the album,
Free of their mucilage,
Smile and mow in homage,
And the railway museum
Steam and clank and cry
At one who more than any
Palped the pulse of the age,
Finding the English mass
And the whole of the O. E. D.
Relevant to our need
Of a voice and ear that knew
The European mess
And fronted it with a creed
Shining as a machine.
China and Berlin,
Iceland and Brooklyn too
Danced with a lexis which
Johnson would have approved.
And above all the craft
Coaxed to a new cuisine
The language that he loved.
Is he a climate too?
The winds and the squalls are gone,
And the patches of metal sun,
Along with Wystan Hugh,
But Auden remains, remains,
A name as rounded as
A decent artifact
One can hold in the hand,
The joy of the maker's act
Immanent in its round
And smooth irregular

Ultimate uselessness,
All art, said Wilde, being useless.
Wherever, Sir Wystan, you are,
Frown on our careless craft,
And pray for us, pray for us.

A CHRISTMAS RECIPE

Of shining silver crystal be your bowl,
Big as a priest's paunch or a drunkard's soul.
Take spongecakes then to fill it, very dry.
Divide them lengthwise, lengthwise let them lie,
Inner face upwards. Smear these faces then
With raspberry jam, then jam them shut again –
Dispose them in the bowl. Take Jerez wine
Or Mavrodaphne; liberally incline
The bottle till, like rain on earth sun-baked,
The liquor has not drenched but merely slaked
That spongy thirst. With milk and eggs well-beaten
Seethe up a custard, thick; with honey sweeten –
Then on your drunken spongecakes swiftly pour
Till they are sunk beneath a golden floor.
Cool until set. Whip cream and spread it deep.
Strew dragées in a silver swoop or sweep.
Cool, and keep cool. A two-hour wait must stifle
Your lust to eat this nothing, this mere TRIFLE.

LIMERICK: THE ANGLER OF KINSALE

An angler who lived at Kinsale

Encountered a bilingual whale;
He swore that it sounded
A Yank as it grounded,
But was, when caught, blowing a Gael.

'I HAD NOT THOUGHT TO HEAR'

I had not thought to hear
A thrush in the heart of Ealing
Like a heart throbbing, unsealing
My waxed London ear.

'THUS KNEELING AT THE ALTAR RAIL'

Thus kneeling at the altar rail
We ate the Word's white papery wafer.
Here, so I thought, desire must fail,
My chastity be never safer.
But then I saw your tongue protrude
To catch the wisp of angel's food.
Dear God! I reeled beneath the shock:
My Eton suit, your party frock,
Christmas, the dark, and postman's knock!

'DO YE THE SAVAGE OLD LAW DENY'

Do ye the savage old law deny.
Let me repay, in age or youth –

An infinitude of eyes for an eye,
An infinitude of teeth for a tooth.

'THE KIND OF LAUGH THAT WODEHOUSE IMPARTS IS'

The kind of laugh that Wodehouse imparts is
Extremely popular with the Nazis.
On his covers let's stamp (am I being too caustic?) a
Crumpet, an egg, a bean and a swastika.

'A GLANCE OR GANDER OF THIS GANDY DANCER'

A glance or gander of this gandy dancer,
    Ganef gannet of mind I mean,
        Takes in seasky's immensities,
Black wingtips hid, see crass beak pincer
    Thoughtfish, gulp, in a wavewhite preen
        On rock rests nor questions what rock is.

'THE YOUNG THINGS WHO FREQUENT MOVIE PALACES'

The young things who frequent movie palaces
Know nothing of psychoanalysis.
    But Herr Doktor Freud

Is not really annoyed.
Let them cling to their long-standing fallacies.

THE WIGGLE POOF

Sometimes, in winter, just for fun,
    It flies round and disturbs
Poor youngsters who are trying hard
    To swot up Latin verbs

The colour of the Wiggle Poof
Is green with purple spots.
It's harmless as a chimpanzee:
    I'm sure you'd love it lots.

'A PRISM IS A USEFUL THING'

A prism is a useful thing:
    Besides refracting light,
When tied on to a piece of string,
    It's useful in a fight.

Warmed in a sauce or chilled with ice,
    It makes a splendid meal,
With prunes, asparagus or rice,
    Or even candied peel.

'I WROTE ON THE BEACH, WITH A STICK OF SALTY WOOD'

I wrote on the beach, with a stick of salty wood,
    'Our deeds are but as writings on the shore',
    Believing it: I never thought them more
Than prey for growling time: all ill, all good
Were friable a sand. There where I stood,
    The wild wind whistled, driving all before,
    And the inexorable waves, with a damped roar,
Strode on, like beasts that smell their living food.

So I forgot. But, ages older grown,
    Revisiting, I caught that distant day.
The sands will stretched, without life and alone,
    But one spot the waves had sheered away,
Fearful to touch it. There, as if on stone
    Stark and clear-chiselled, that inscription lay.

'CALM LIES OUR HARBOUR, WHILE THE MAIDEN DAY'

Calm lies our harbour, while the maiden day
    Leans forth her arms to night and bids it go,
    Smiling, and waits to wake with gentlest glow
Quayside and sea, and tall gaunt ships that sway.
I wait no longer now: wide lies the way,
    Unsure, uncharted. Only this I know:
    That sea has dubious currents, tides that flow
Frustrating all the havened ancients say…

'FATHER OF FIRE, WITH BOLD SIMONY'

Father of fire who, with bold simony,
    Didst steal the seed, catched high on Olympus
Now in my mind relive that felony
    And lean down to my praying, piteous.
    Be thou again as brave bounteous
As when thou first didn't bring that art of heat
    To nations bestial still and barbarous,
And fetch a match to light my cigarette.

'J.B.W.'

J.B.W.,
Girls won't trouble you
He's the fella for Llewela
French without tears.
Or, All's Llwell that Ends Llwell.

'THE SEA, GREEN AND DEEP'

The sea, green and deep,
Seems like a beast asleep.
The beach and seaweed gleam,
And the sea breathes, heaves, sleepily,
In its deep green dream.

'WINTER WINS'

Winter wins
Freeze the trees.
Winter winds
Chill the knees.
Bitter, shrill,
They whistle, shriek,
Nip and whip
Chin and cheek.
Shiver, shiver, bird on tree,
Shiver, shiver, fish in sea.
Stream and river, frozen be.
Soon will spring
Bring the sun,
Linnets sing,
Winter done.

'OUT OF THE STATION PUFFS THE TRAIN'

Out of the station puffs the train
Under the bridge, then up the hill,
Down the hill, across the plain,
Beside a river, till once again
It comes to a station and stands still.

SONNET FROM 'THE END OF THINGS: THREE DIALOGUES FOR OLD MEN'

Crippled, the antarctic fire with chiselled skill
And fraught with allomorphs deforms the climb

To netherness and, opportune, clangs time
Out of the waldorf-coloured chlorophyll.
Undoubt, unbuild the wharf-encrusted thrill
That doubts redouts of most discordant slime
Where, weathered to a clink of the sublime,
The sheaths of allergy must work their will.
Enough – or else too much, which means too little.
Unbreach, consider neither jot nor tittle,
The swarthy Nordics out of Dusseldorf.
You find it mollient? I found it brittle,
And hence exploded with a beery skittle
Each brooding titan and resplendent dwarf.

'IMAGINATION IS YOUR TRUE APOLLO'

Imagination is your true Apollo.
    In our translunar skills the moon's small beer.
Fact's fancy's cripple. Acts are dim to follow
    Words (small cheese, I meant – small *green* cheese).
We're too long beyond the moon. The moon's too near.

Bored with the merely visible, SF
    Spends trillions on each fresh galactic race
Yet shells out not one cent to make us deaf
    To the shrill signals from that silver face,
    Attuning us to tunes from deeper space.

Still, it was all romance, drawn up from wells;
    Or myth – an uncertain lantern in the air,
Or Prester John's balloon, the Christian hell's
    Chill annexe, or the huntress in her chair.
    Now Armstrong (Neil) and Aldrin (Ed) are there,

And Collins in his clucking mothercraft.
    Old Glory on the consecrated crust
Is all th' old glory that, alas, is left.
    Glory in, in your progressive lust,
    These heroes who sift silver for its dust.

Where the black gods deliciously prevail,
    You find cool tribes. Our hot entropic plan
Submits to seeing human order fail,
Erects inhuman order where it can
    And smiles and sighs at lunonautic man.

'OUR NORMAN BETTERS'

Our Norman betters
Taught English letters
To bathe in the fresh
Warm springs of the south.
So turn your backs on
Anglo-Saxon,
The þ in the flesh
And the æ in the mouth.

NOSTALGIA IN HEAD PLUNGING

----------different topic

a rose is a rose is a rose   yes, but try:
a street is a street is a street
a bridge is a bridge is a bridge

rosa no buscaba rosa buscaba otra cosa
gli archi fanno più belli i ponti

is everything art,
is everything structuralism?

'DREAMING WHEN DAWN'S LEFT HAND…'

Dreaming when dawn's left hand…
Break break break…
Grrr there go my heart's abhorrence
Out of the cradle endlessly rocking
Simon Danz has come home again
Earth hath not anything…
A thing of beauty…
O wild west wind…
Loveliest of trees…
Before the Romans came to Rye…

AN ELEGY FOR X

X is unnecessary, like his brother
That 'whoreson zed' (King Lear) or like the other
That stands between thoses two – the Grecian i,
As Latins call it. You may ponder why
We need an X in taxi when you queue
(There's Norman tyranny. C double U
Will do, and did do for the Saxons when
A queen had not dethroned a native *cwen*),
Lugging your luggage from a train or bus,

For tacsis at a Cymric terminus.
In Russia, if you have the time to wait,
A takcu is delivered by the state.
St Cyril gave the barbarous Russians X
For a good Grecian purpose. Even sex,
A western import, has a K and C.
The Welsh, though far from sexless, like to be
X-less. And yet that letter was a brand
Of Celticness when Claudius stormed the land,
Raping and pillaging, firing farmer's ricks,
Subduing what he thought were knavish tricks –
Asterix, Obelix, Vercingetorix.
X stands for sh in Malta; Taxxbiex.
Venetians, scornful of the Roman leash,
Mock X in rex and lex bidding it dance
In place of voiced and unvoiced sibilants.
Only in Xmas do we pay our dues
To the harsh velar Greeks and Russians use,
For Christ is Xristos, and who spoke or wrote
The sacred name paid homage in his throat.
Now phoneticians sensibly denote
That fishbone-clearing phoneme with the letter
Which marks the sounds that K and S do better.
Was XXXXXX the ghastly agonizing rasp
St Andrew uttered in his final gasp
Spreadeagled on his special, chi-shaped cross?
It's a sad letter. We won't mourn its loss,
Let it be buried, vapourised or drowned
At least when it essays a double sound.
X is a cypher, X the unknown,
The sign of the analphabete, alone,
Along with brewing strengths, the pseudonyms
Of spies and co-respondents. Sing no hymns
Save frog-croaks. Only note where it is not
With this sole epitaph: 'X marks the spot'.

WORDS FOR MUSIC

FROM MUSIC FOR MOSES THE LAWGIVER

PRINCESS'S LULLABY/QUEEN'S LULLABY

Out of the desert the wind blows strong, but cool from out of the
    sea.
The desert burns and the day is long, but night sends my loved one
    back to me.

CHANT

Lord of the river and of that quickening mud
Whence all manner of lowly things are brought to birth,
Bring to thy servant the gift of fecundity,
That she be not despised among the lowlier daughters of the earth,
And the worth of her birth be matched by the worth of thy gift.
Lift her, O river god, to the ranks of the mothers, the mothers,
    the mothers.

SOLDIER'S SONG

Here's the way we earn our pay.
Who's the enemy we slay?
Baby slaves so long as they have
Balls between their legs.

That's no way to earn your pay.
We would rather any day
Take their mothers and then lay our
Balls between their legs.

legs legs legs legs legs legs legs legs (repeat ad lib)

PRAYER

You who nourish the palm and tamarind,
The date-palm and the pepper-tree,
From whose mud the crocodile breeds,
Many-toothed, strong as a chariot.

LULLABY

Out of the desert the wind blows strong, but cool, but cool from
    out of the sea
The desert burns and the day is long
But night sends my loved one back to me

PASTORALE

What will my love bring when he comes?
A silver ring.
Earth will ring with his tread,
I when he comes.
On his head a kingly crown

When he comes down the hill.
What will he bring?
A silver ring,
When he comes,
When he comes…

WATER SONG

So sang the water, so sang the water:
I was here before man began
And though I will cleanse him and slake his thirst…
I will make him know that I was first,
And when man's brief day is past,
I will be last.
So sings the water,
So sings the water:
I will obey in the little things, but
I'm not his cattle, his cattle or sheep.
He may bid me go, ocean or rain, or the snow but
I remain

DESERT SONG FOR MOSES

Burning day
Brims into the burning skies
Where only the vulture flies,
Alert for his prey.
Only faith imparts
Hope to hopeless hearts
And bids us brave the dust of our desolate way.

Airless air,
A kingdom of stone and sand
That stretches on hand and hand
Unbounded and bare.
Still we dare the sun
Till our goal is won
And brave the hell that leads to a heavenly land.

TRAVELLING SONG

Sing praise to our God,
Praise to Israel's Lord.
He strikes down our foes:
Praise the might of his sword.
He will lead us to land
Where our flocks may graze
And temples will stand
To hymn his praise.
His mercy is great as the
Power of his sword –
Hear ye, Israel –
Praise your Lord!

MIRIAM'S SONG OF TRIUMPH

Sing ye to the Lord for he has
Triumphed gloriously
The horse and his rider hath he thrown into the sea
Halleluluiah

Sing ye to the Lord for he has
Triumphed gloriously
The horse and his rider hath he thrown into the
Sea hath he thrown into the sea
Praised be his name for ever and ever.
Halleluiah! Halleluiah! Halleluiah! Halleluiah!
(repeat and ad lib.)

MIRIAM'S SONG OF TRIUMPH

The Lord is our captain,
his helmet the sun,
the moon his shield,
the night sky is full of his arrow holes.
Halleluiah
The hands of the Lord were with us.
They pushed the water aside and aside
Like the hands of a farmer dividing grain

The Lord is just, quick to smite the tyrant
Quick to heal the oppressed,
Comfort the comfortless.
He dips his sword in honey, his spear in balm.
Halleluiah
We have seen the wonders of the Lord, in fire and hail,
in plague and famine, in the parting of the waters.
He leads us to a green abode bursting with richness.
Praised be his name for ever and ever.
Halleluiah
Halleluiah
Halleluiah

MARRIAGE ROUND

Where will our wedding wedding be?
Up in the fronds of a dikla tree.
What will we drink and what will we eat?
The moon for wine and the sun for meat.

MOSES'S SONG

Give ear O ye heavens and I will speak
And hear O earth the words of my mouth.
My doctrine shall drop as the rain,
My speech shall distil as the dew,
As the small rain upon the tender herb
And as the showers upon the grass
The Lord is the rock, his work is perfect.
Rejoice O ye nations with his people
For he will arrange the blood of his servants
And will be merciful merciful merciful
Unto his land
And to his people.

TRAVEL SONG

We go, we go to the unknown land
Where the hand of the Lord showers blessings
And the sun fails not nor the soil,
And the man's toil is a prayer of thankfulness
To the Lord.
There it lies beyond our eyes

And yet within reach of our hand
We go to the unknown land, to the unknown land

BULL SONG

His strength is the strength of the bull that charges in thunder
Again and again
Above in the skies and under the skies
In the golden noon and the moon's gold
His power and wonder are told.
Halleluiah

GOLDEN CALF SONG

His head is the sun, he bears the moon on his brow.
His legs are the North and the West and the East and South
From his mouth blow the words thereof.
His coat is speckled with the stars.
He strides in power over all the world.
Halleluiah.

BARD'S SONG

And we turned and went up by the way of Bashan.
And Og the king of Bashan went out against us.
He and all his people, to the battle at Edrei.
And the Lord said unto Moses: fear him not,
And thou shalt do to him as thou didst

Unto Sihon king of the Amorites.
So we smote him, and his son, and all his people.
Until there was none left alive.
And we possessed his land.

JUBILEE ANTHEM
FOR MALAYAN BOYS' VOICES

I

What have we seen in fifty years?
     Worlds rise, worlds decay.
Blasts of war have shattered our eyes, our ears,
     And threats of war, as terrible as they,
Fed us with fears, blinded with useless tears.

And even this green land
     Land of mountain, jungle, birdsong-haunted,
Of sun- and rain-washed earth, sea-beaten sand,
     Has seen the conqueror's garish banner flaunted
And felt the conqueror's hand.

Nor has the conflict ceased,
     The blindfold war to liberate the free.
The untamed jungle hides another beast
     Clenching its teeth in evil glee
To see blood rise in the unhappy east.

But we must celebrate
     Something achieve, something with labour won
From the devouring jungle crouched in hate
     To trample time and swallow up the sun,

A work as nobly great
    As any in this noble land begun
Whether to conquer death, impose the rule
    Of law on chaos, re-create
The merging of the many into one –
    This growth and slow maturing of our school.

II

Young Boys

Beside the silver river
    In the silver land
Changing ever-never,
    With bright devotion planned,
In green and glory stand
    The halls of our endeavour.

Older Boys

Where the only strife
    Is to seek and learn –
Here the key of life,
    There the hand to turn.

Young Boys

The river swiftly flowing
    Tells us that the time
For acting and for knowing
    For learning how to climb,
Time that never waits

Begs us to begin
Open up the gates,
    Let the truth come in.
We pledge ourselves to borrow
    The strength they had of old
Who learned through pain and sorrow
    The only wealth to hold
Is that unminted gold
    Which hides in each to-morrow

Prelude

Trumpets sound
    For Jubilee,
Drums pound
    For Jubilee,
Flutes shrill,
Bells beat their fill
    For Jubilee!

Older Boys

Let us use the past
    As a road to reach
    That enormous beach
Rich with sail and mast
    Seas for us to chart
    Call the eager heart:
Let the voyage start!

Young Boys

Remembering the ruins.

III

Let us praise those men whose vision
Scorned a sneering world's derision,
Dreamed a dream and then fulfilled it,
Dreamed a school and went to build it.

Let us praise the boys before us
Whom we echo in our chorus
Who became the men who freed us
Who became the men who lead us.

'THE THREE DIMENSIONS'

Watch me trace
The three of space:
Up, down, and then across
The three dimensions, as they say.
But there's another,
An elusive sort of brother –
Time!
I'm
Giving all my attention
To treating that fourth dimension
As if it were a spatial one.
I can walk up and down it or run,
Even fly. My
Time journey's almost begun.

The past is hidden,
The future's forbidden.
We don't care why or how.
We're happy enough with now.
No discomfort, no disease,
Gentlemen living at their ease,
Everything designed to please
In good Victoria's reign.
Darwin, Marx, electric light,
The Church of England taking fright
As new ideas put old to flight

Were they right, I wonder –
Stay as you are, refuse to move,
Stick in your comfortable groove,
Sheltered from storm and thunder.
But destiny beckons me yonder
To dare the unknown, unseen.
Back to my time machine.

WORDS GETTING IN THE WAY

The man without words
    Wants to be in love
Without words getting in the way.
    What words could match
Her fairness of face?
What words could catch
Her grace?
The language of birds
    In the blue above –
Even that's unequipped to say

In the magic sand
What magic she brings
    To all surround-
Ing things.

Why should I waste
    Time and brain and breath
On what bores me to dusty death?
Let me taste
Her lips, not your words on mine –
Entwine her within my strong embrace

To a wordless man like this
    A sigh can say no more
Than all of your bor-
Ing intellectual play.
How can I kiss
    With words getting in the way?

I'm sick of each day
    With each tiresome tome
That you drag from a special shelf.
I know a tree
    Where poetry may
Proceed to hang itself

I'm sick of each night
    That I spend at home
    With a polysyllabic theme.
    Insipid alien
    Sesquipedalian writings
    Make me scream

Don't answer me when
    I ask once again:
By all that's sacred, how may
I hold her tight
    With words getting in the way?

No matter how powerful or subtle or fine
I'm weary of working with words that you write
    An actor enacting another man's lines
But now that I'm seeing her, now it's tonight
    The things I must say are the things I must say.

It's she and it's I,
It's her and it's me –
No one but we
Tonight.

No poet need try
To fly in the way
Singing's the right
Sonnets to say.

It's she and it's me,
And I and it's her –
And I prefer
It so.

As soon as I see
The flame on her cheek,
Then I will know
Just how to speak

I'm sick of each day
With each tiresome tome

That you keep on a special shelf.
I know a tree
Where poetry
May proceed to hang itself.

'SLAVERY'

Slavery slavery
Which he's dressed up in his bravery
Up to some unsavoury escapades
I'm made
To moan in my slavery.
Slavery slavery
Which he's returned from his knavery
Full of what he gave her and she gave him
I grimly groan in my slavery.
Slavery
Oh the anguish
No language
Cut off from my culture,
Served from my sect
The viper and the vulture
The tribal dialect
with a loincloth round my middle
And a priest upon the griddle
I would gambol to a fiddle
Made of human gut
But I'm cut
Off

'NONE BUT THE COWARD'

None but the coward
    Deserves the fair, for
    Brave men die
But the coward's always there.

What should a woman
    Supremely care for –
    Two live arms
Or a statue in the square?

I admit that bull or rogue ram
Will need an eventual butcher's knife
But it's not in my programme –
A medium sensual sort of life.
I don't like to eat
Meat raw in my paw,
I prefer it dressed by my wife

Hardly empowered
To get in there,
I'd rather survive
And thrive
And if you're agreeable, wive.
And, like every coward,
Stay alive.

I am, let one imagine
Lord Hamlet – one imagin-
-ation that can take in every side,
But wide to take a murder in its stride.
But not wide enough.

'HE BOUGHT ME FROM A SARACEN'

He bought me from a Saracen
Who bought from some Turks
Who used me in the garrison
To build the public works.
Though he keeps me in food
And no longer in the nude

...

He bought me from a Grecian
    Minister of works
Who'd bought me from a Venetian
    Who bought me from the Turks
    Who'd bought me from the Arabs

'SEVILLA, SEVIYA – OR SEVIJA'

Sevilla, Seviya, Sevija – or Seville.
Call it what you will
It's the same town,
Not a tame town – no shame at all
Nothing much happens in the morning:
They're recovering from the evening.
Nothing much happens in the afternoon:
They're waiting for the moonlight to fall
On Sevilla, Seviya, Sevija – or Seville.
Come here when you will.
Crane your necks at
All the sex at your beck and call.

'I LOVE HATE'

I love hate.
The teeth that growl and grate
And bate me.
So hate me.
Hate is the wind
That sweeps the winter clean,
Scoured and unskinned
By the gold and green.
As for love,
And the dove-cooing lies
And the eyes that glow –
Love can get up and go.
So hate me, hate me,
Make me tough.
I hate love,
I love hate.
I'd love the world more
If it would hate me enough.

Hate is the state
That turns men tough
I'd adore
The world more
If it would only hate me enough.
Hate me.
Hate.

A TIME FOR MUSIC

You've got to liv wiv zest Liz luv
If you farm port of a *roman fleueve*
On the riverain on the sane side
Where I'll fake you for a ride,
An Avon of a joke
Inn Eden where you've been rest to soak
Down the wurling Winderpool
Of a swashbuckling machine,
Bint shrunk into a minikin.
It's a long ford that has no crossing
And its lakes a tot of frank pakenhamming
With hots of katzenjamming
Chopping up the best back notes
To fate you with flewts and notes
And a host of hobos.
I hope I've taught your dido heart
Numbling your private parts
In an anthem of praise I've raised
A cannibal in a hamilcart;
I shope itsall bean great greene fun
Liz luv and you've slept your cool
Sunlike a river hooligan
Assort of Rogue Riderhood cum again
In a bally Volga boat-school
My dearest moncybun

'WHAT I'D LIKE TO DO'

What I'd like to do
To you

Is too painful to be true.
I'd like to
Thrust here
Grind there
Behind there.
Ooooo –
What I'd like to do to you!

Eight and twenty years
The Scythians scourged Asia
With insolence and oppression
But King Cyaxares smote them,
Smote them, smote them,
Brought them low.

King Cyaxares – praise him –
Toppled Nineveh's towers.
King Cyaxares – praise him –
Had the Assyrian by the beard.

Lo, the empire of the Medes
Stretches almost to Babylon.

Praise the son of Cyaxares,
Our noble Astyages,
Who keeps the peace
And maintains our empires.

'TO BE A KING, TO BE A KING'

To be a king, to be a king
Is a high and mighty thing.
The one who's wise and not the fool
Shall wear the crown and rule.
And rule.

To be a king, to be a king
Is a high and mighty thing.
The one who's strong and also clever
Shall wear the crown for ever.
For ever.

To be a king, a king
Is a mighty thing.
He who's wise and not the fool
Shall rule and rule.

To be a king, a king
Is a mighty thing.
He who's strong and clever
Shall rule for ever.

'A DRINK. WHAT IS A DRINK?'

A drink. What is a drink?
A machine for cooling the throat,
Injecting speedy sugar into the pancreas,
Getting high.
Eating's not a feast.
It's an existential function.

Administering extreme unction,
The waiter's not a priest.

A drink. What do they think a drink is? What is a drink?
A machine to wet the dry.
For sugaring the pancreas.
For getting high.
Highballs.
I don't like it
What? I like it.
I don't like it.
What? Liking it.
Liking these folks
Who like to be slaves
Liking their cokes
And Gillette shaves
Liking their bosses
And buses and bikes
Like the likes and dislikes.
The people don't talk
They bully or whine,
They snort or they squeak
I don't like it.
What? Your liking it.
I don't like it.
What? Your not
Liking me liking it.
How do you stomach
The stuff that they scoff?
Even its look
Puts me off.

BED

'Rest', says my bed.
'When all is said,
Rest, rest is best.
The day is fled,
All red,
Into the west.
Forget, forget
The men you met,
The book you read,
The bread you ate.
Sleep lies ahead.
Rest your head,
Heavier than
A chest of lead.
I am ready
To hold your heavy head
Steady,
Steady,
Steady.'

'Heady.'
Ho hez hy hed.

BEAR

'See – there, there.'
Where?
'There –
A hairless bear,
Walking about the square.'

But you shouldn't stare
At a hairless bear.
You wouldn't care
For folk to stare
If you didn't have
Your share of hair,
Like that poor bear there,
That hairless bear,
That bare bear,
Bare bear –
'Black sheep?'
No, that hairless bear
Glaring around
The square.

'I'M WEARY OF WORKING WITH WORDS THAT YOU WRITE'

I'm weary of working with words that you write
An actor enacting another man's lines.
But now that I'm seeing her, now it's tonight,
The things I must say are the things I must say.

It's she and it's I,
It's her and it's me –
No one but we
Tonight.

No poet need try
To fly in my way
Justify the night
Say sonnets to say.

It's she and it's me,
It's I and it's her –
And I prefer
It so.

As soon as I see
The flame on her cheek,
Then I will know
Just how to speak

'HOW DARE I DARE TO DREAM'

How dare I dare to dream
That all I dream is in vain?
And dare I dare believe
That sweet joy
Springs from pain?

How dare I dare to hope
That such a lowly thing as I
Could steal himself a pair silver wings
And fly,

To dare the heavens
Where she in beauty
Dares me –
Unworthy me,

How dare I head the call
That bids me claim the final prize?
I'd stumble and I'd fall – before her eyes.

How dare I dare to dream
That all I dream is not in vain?
And dare I dare believe
That sweetness
Springs from you

How dare I dare to hope
That such a lowly thing as I
Could steal himself a pair of silver wings
And fly.

To dare the heavens
Where she in *beauty*
Dares men
Unworthy me

How dare I hear the call
That bids me claim the final prize?
I'd stumble and I'd fall – before her eyes

'HIS BOWELS ARE OF GOLD, HIS VEINS
OF SILVER'

His bowels are of gold, his veins of silver.
The blood of his veins is rubies fine-powdered.
His head is a city, strong of wall and turret,
His member is the straightest tree of the forest…

'I'M SICK OF A KINGDOM WHICH IS A JEWELLED PRISON'

I am sick of a kingdom which is a jewelled prison,
Of the wine of bondage and the roasted meats of
       servitude.
Give me the free wind of the morning and the sun
       that burns not from malice,
And the brook for wine and the berries and nuts
       of the wild wood.
I am sick of kinds and princes, for their words
       are an emptiness,
Their favour is water in a furnace, their smiles
       are shadows.
A voice within says: the king is but a king,
But you Gyzat, are a man and a free man.
Your nobility outreaches the king's hand and
       outtops his crown.

'LEX FOR LAW AND ORDER'

Lex for law and order,
Peace within our border,
Factory wheels are turning,
Here's an end of yearning.
Loyal hearts are burning
With patriotic joy.
Lex is our boy.

'I WOULDN'T FRIRK URANUS'

I wouldn't frirk Uranus,
He gives me a pain in the anus.
I wouldn't frirk with Neptune,
Neptune's tune is not a hep tune.

So pounce on me, Puma.
You're no idle rumor, right?
I'm in the humor,
So pounce on me, Puma, tonight.

I don't want to frirk with Mars.
Mars is covered with stars and scars.
I don't want to frirk with Venus,
That blind kid Cupid would get between us.

So pounce on me, Puma, etc.

'HERE ON THE FINAL PYRE'

Here on the final pyre
See that page with its curled ends
Rolling into the fire.
Here's what the poet sang:
This is the way the world ends:
Not with a whimper. BANG.

'A BIRD SAT HIGH ON A BANYAN TREE'

A bird sat high on a banyan tree,
Carolling night and carolling day,
And on the heads of the passers-by

And each bemerded passer-by
Cried loud in anger on that bird
Carolling night and carolling day,
Wiping from his eye.

And still that bird upon the tree,
Carolling night and carolling day,
Ignored the plaints of the passers-by.

Let us like birds upon the tree,
Carolling night and carolling day,
Ignore each hairless passer-by,
And say...

'BEASTS AND MEN ARE MADE THE SAME'

Beasts and men are made the same –
  Here a one and there a two,
And with these three they play the game
  Of doing what they have to do.

'OH, LOVE, LOVE, LOVE'

Oh, love, love, love –
Love on a hilltop high,
Love against a cloudless sky,
Love where the scene is
Painted by a million stars,
Love with martinis
In the cabarets and bars.
Oh, love, love, love...

'WE WILL BUILD A BRIDGE TO HEAVEN'

We will build a bridge to heaven,
Build in earnest, not in play;
Night and morning, noon and even,
We will watch and we will pray.

'WE'LL BE COMING HOME'

We'll be coming home,
Coming, coming home.
Some day soon,
January or June,
Evening, morning or afternoon –
– So just you stand and wait
By the garden gate
Till my ship comes bouncing o'er the foam.
We'll be together
For ever and ever,

Never more to roam –
– He'll be coming,
We'll be coming,
I'll be coming home.
We'll be together
For ever and ever,
Never more to roam –
We'll be coming home,
Coming, coming home.
Some day soon,
January or June,
Evening, morning or afternoon –

'MY ADORABLE FRED'

My adorable Fred:
He's so, so sweet,
From the crown of his head
To the soles of his feet.
He's my meat.

'MY DEAD TREE. GIVE ME BACK MY DEAD DEAD TREE'

My dead tree. Give me back my dead dead tree.
Rain, rain, go away. Let the earth be still
Dry. Kick the gods back into the cakey earth,
Making a hole, for that purpose, with a drill.
The northern winds send icy peace,
The southern gales blow balmy.

Pelagius is fond of police;
Augustine loves an army.

'THIS LOVELY QUEEN, IF I SHOULD WIN HER'

This lovely queen, if I should win her,
Shall have my heart for a medallion.
She'll never lack a hearty dinner,
This lovely queen, if I should win her.
My fire shall rouse the fire that's in her,
She'll ride my sea, a golden galleon,
This lovely queen. If I should win her,
She'll have my heart for a medallion.

'HOW COME THAT SUCH A SCHOLAR'

How come that such a scholar
Can put up with such a squalor?
Just gimme hafe a dollar
And I'll make it spick and span, man.

'ICH NEM' EIN' ZIGARETT'

Ich nem' ein' Zigarett'
Un ich fuhl du liebst much nicht mehr
Und ich weiss es ist aus
Un da macht mein Herz so schwer.
Yet

With my cigarette
Thought I give no more than I get
There's no sigh of regret
At the end of my cigarette.

'YOU WHOM THE FISHERFOLK OF MYRA BELIEVE'

You whom the fisherfolk of Myra believe
To have power over the sea
Acknowledge a power as old as Eve –
The sea's goddess, Venus, me!

O tue che a Mira ogni pescatore
Venera pel potere che hai sul mare
Conoscer devi la potenza arcana
Di Vener, dea del mar, me, sovrunmana.

'WAKING AND SLEEPING'

Waking and sleeping
It's always the same,
Sleeping and waking
I call on your name.
Sleeping I cry,
Waking I sigh,
Knowing there's no reply.

We're versing and voicing
Our heartfelt rejoicing,

Your troubles belong to the past
So nuzzle and nestle,
For you've said it, Cecil,
At last.

'MONEY ISN'T EVERYTHING'

Money isn't everything –
It's only board and bed,
The only thing distinguishing
Being living, being dead
(So I've heard it said).

'I'LL CRASH THE MOON'

I'll crash the moon
To fetch a spoon
Of precious lunar dust.
I'll fly as high
As heaven's eye.
I'll even die
If I must.

Anything at all
I'll gladly do
To prove a lasting
Love for you.
Each and every task
Beneath the sun:

You only have to ask –
It's done.

UNE P'TITE SPÉCIALITÉ CALLED L'AMOUR

Meet her at a *table*
Out side some small café,
Say she's *adorable*
In such a Gallic way.
Let your lady fair know
That she is all you see,
Prime her with a Pernod
Or three.
Make the chestnuts blossom
And keep away the rain,
Under the gossamer
Soon you'll start to eat like an epicure –
Une p'tite spécialité called l'amour.

Take another *table*
Inside a *restaurant*,
Somewhere *formidable*
Where you'll be *très contents.*
Comfort her with oysters
In quite the classic style –
Succulent and moist as
Her smile.
See her crack a lobster
And strip it to the buff,
Rough as when a mobster
Gets tough.
Keep the wine cascading and you'll ensure

*Une p'tite sp*écialité called *l'amour.*

When you had dined,
You find some boîte
Whereat they're inclined
To l'érotique.
Keep her close entwined
Till your minds
Grow weak.

When you have danced,
Chance takes you where
The air is entranced
With Paris spring.
There you'll hear her whisper
The thing
You'll want to hear till

All the city sparrows
Are chirping to the sun,
Market stalls and barrows
Say morning has begun.

Light as gold as taffy
Is sugaring the day
While you drink your café
Au lait.
Bite into a *croissant*
And smile upon your love;
Hear the larks *en passant*
Above.

They make it ev'ry day in
Their own Parisian way:

Paris may be sinful, but one thing's pure –
It's *une p'tite spécialité* called l'amour.

CABBAGE FACE

CABBAGE
F A C E: Cabbage Face.
If you were in Paris, you
Might be called *mon petit choux*,
But you're in a different place,
So I call you Cabbage Face.

NATHAN'S SONG

David's people we,
Seeking David's town.
A simple shepherd he
Who acquired a crown.
David, kind of Israel,
Wish well.

'THY MOUTH, A FIG, THY TEETH'

Thy mouth, a fig, thy teeth
Troops in ivory array.
Of the treasures ranged beneath
I may yet nothing say.
Must I wait till the nuptial day?

'MY LOVE LAY ACROSS THE WATERS'

My love lay across the waters,
Twenty leagues away,
Fairest of fifteen daughters
So they used to say.
I'll go back to her some day.

'FISH GREY, FISH BROWN'

Fish grey, fish brown,
Will you come up, or must we go down?
Fish silver, fish white,
Will you permit us to eat you tonight?

Fish green, fish red,
How on earth can the people be fed?
Fish dull, fish bright,
Will you permit us to catch you tonight?

THE PRODIGAL SON

There was a man who had two sons,
And he loved them both in equal measure.
He put aside, so the story runs,
Gold for both from his ample treasure.
Oh, the prodigal son.

'Father, father, the time is come',
So said the younger son one day,

'To give to me my promised sum.
Thank you, father'. And he went away.
Oh, the prodigal son.

He wasted his gold on whores and wine,
And very soon the gold was gone.
A famine came to Palestine
And it did not spare this spendthrift one.
Oh, the prodigal son.

So he became, against his will,
A swineherd, far from Galilee.
He would have eaten of the porkers' swill,
Had he not been something of a Pharisee.
Oh, the prodigal son.

'My father's men have bellies full
With bread and wine and roasts to carve.
They are snug and warm in leather and wool,
While I must shiver and I must starve.'
Oh, the prodigal son.

He has left the swine, he has left the trough,
He has left the foul hut wherein he slept.
His father saw him a good way off
And ran to him, kissed him, laughed and wept.
Oh, the prodigal son.

'Father, I'm but a worthless thing,
I am not fit to be your son.'
But his father gave him a costly ring
And the finest robe that was ever spun.
Oh, the prodigal son.

'Bring out the fatted calf', he cried.
'Let us eat and drink and stamp the ground,
For he is alive that I deemed had died.
Rejoice, for he that was lost is found.'
Oh, the prodigal son.

The elder was an angry one,
He would have no part in feast or song.
'All these years I have been a good son,
Asking no favour, doing no wrong,
Never a prodigal son.'

THE GOOD SAMARITAN

There was a man of Israel,
    A brother of our faith and blood.
He bought and sold and his work went well.
    Like us, he was neither bad nor good.

He travelled one day from Jerusalem
    To do some business in Jericho.
He fell among thieves and was stripped by them
    And beaten with many a savage blow.

He lay at the side of the road near dead.
    A priest of the temple came riding by.
A dying man, to himself he said.
    What can I do but let him die?

A man of the Levites rode on his way,
    Yea, one of Moses' and Aaron's race.

His horse said nothing but he said nay,
    And they cantered on at a merry pace.

Now who should come next but a foreign man,
    A son of a race that the Jews despise,
Yes, as you guess, a Samaritan,
    But he halted and pity flooded his eyes.

He cared for this wretch all blood and rage,
    He washed his wounds in wine and oil,
He tore white linen from his saddlebags,
    He did not scorn the surgeon's toil.

He set him tenderly on his steed,
    Rode to a nearby inn, and then
His only care was to tend and feed
    And bring that wretch to life again.

'Landlord, landlord, I must go away.
    Care for this sick man, I pray.
Whatever the cost I will gladly pay.
    I will be back in a week and a day.'

Now who was the kindly neighbour here
    In the eyes of that robbed and wretched man –
The Levite, to the Lord most dear,
The priest he had been taught to revere,
    Or the despised Samaritan?

PASSOVER HYMN

He showed the power of that mighty hand
And out of its bondage Israel came,
From bondage to the promised land.
Blessed be his holy name.
Alleluia alleluia.
Blessed be his holy name.

1. *An Essay On Censorship.* Previously unpublished. Poem dated 10 April 1989.
2. *The Creation of the World.* Previously unpublished variant text. Same title as in *ABBA ABBA*, Based on a second draft that does not have the title, but is otherwise the same. This draft version uses the word 'his' instead of 'us', presumably erroneously. See also *ABBA ABBA* (London: Faber, 1977), p. 92.
3. *The Earthly Paradise of the Beasts.* Previously unpublished variant. Titled 'The Beastly Paradise' in *ABBA ABBA*, p. 92. Some differences in line indentation. The *ABBA ABBA* version uses the phrase 'roughish fun was rife'. The last three lines have no space before them in the *ABBA ABBA* version.
4. *Back to the Roots.* Previously unpublished variant. Titled 'Origins' in *ABBA ABBA*, p. 93. Some variations in indentation.
5. *Man.* Previously unpublished variant. Titled 'Adam' in *ABBA ABBA*, p. 93. Variations in indentation. The spaces between 'om nip o tence' are not present in the published version. 'Say' was originally typed, but corrected to 'prove' in line 4.
6. *His Own Image and Likeness.* Previously unpublished variant. Titled 'Image and Likeness' in *ABBA ABBA*, p. 93. Variations in the indentation. 'Old Nick' appears in the published version, and 'Satan' is used in line 8. This is a hand correction on the typed MS, which was originally 'The devil'. Line 14 has 'fucking' in the published volume, changed from 'bloody' in the MSS.
7. *All About Eve.* Previously unpublished variant. Titled 'About Eve' in *ABBA ABBA*, p. 95. Some variations in indentation. Word substitutions in this MS version include: 'divil' (which became 'divvle'); 'handkerchief' (which became 'snotrag'); 'She' in the last stanza (which

became 'who'). The MS shows that Burgess put 'Mother' in as an after-thought.

8. *A Reply*. Previously unpublished variant. Titled 'Another Point of View' in *ABBA ABBA*, p. 95. Some variations in indentation. The first line in the published version was 'But some say: Scorn her not. Remember, she'.

9. *The First Mouthful*. Previously unpublished variant. Titled 'Greed' in *ABBA ABBA*, p. 96. Some variations in indentation.

10. *Adam's Sin*. Previously unpublished variant. Titled 'Original Sin' in *ABBA ABBA*, p. 96. Variations present in the indentation, and also in use of italics (for 'why').

11. *The First Clothes*. Previously unpublished variant. Titled 'Knowledge' in *ABBA ABBA*, p. 97. Some variations in indentation.

12. *The State of Innocence (1)*. Previously unpublished variant. Titled 'What Might Have Been' in *ABBA ABBA*, p. 97. Some variations in indentation.

13. *The State of Innocence (2)*. Previously unpublished variant. Titled 'A Problem' in *ABBA ABBA*, p. 98. Some variations in indentation. A cancelled version of line three begins: 'And spuds –' The first line of stanza two uses commas instead of the brackets used in the final version. Likewise, collective pronouns are used in lines 13 and 14, in place of what would become the personal 'I' in the published version.

14. *Holy Starvation*. Previously unpublished variant. Has the same title as in *ABBA ABBA*. Some variations in indentation. 'Yes' and 'O ye' are heavily overwritten on the MS in ink (the previous words are illegible). An em dash in the penultimate line is used in the typescript, whereas a semi-colon appears in the published version. See *ABBA ABBA*, p. 98.

15. *Cain and the Lord*. Previously unpublished variant. Titled 'Cain 1' in *ABBA ABBA*. Some variations in indentation. The MS version uses 'hell' instead of the 'fuck' of the published version. See *ABBA ABBA*, p. 99.

16. *Cain's Crime*. Previously unpublished variant. Titled 'Cain 2' in *ABBA ABBA*. Some variations in indentation. See *ABBA ABBA*, p. 99.

17. *The Second Sin*. Previously unpublished variant. Titled 'Cain 3' in *ABBA ABBA*. Some variations in indentation. See *ABBA ABBA*, p. 100.

18. *The Universal Deluge*. Previously unpublished variant. Is called 'The Ark 1' in *ABBA ABBA*. Some variations in indentation. See *ABBA ABBA*, p. 100.

19. *Noah's Ark*. Previously unpublished variant. Titled 'The Ark 2' in *ABBA ABBA*, p. 101. Some variations in indentation. *Honey for the Bears* is the title of Burgess's 1963 novel, written around nine years before this sequence. 'Parmiggiano' becomes 'gorgonzola' in the published version.

20. *The New Wine*. Variant text. Titled 'Noah on Land' in *ABBA ABBA*, p. 101. Some variations in indentation.

21. *The Age of Man*. Variant text. Titled 'Age' in *ABBA ABBA*, p. 102. Some variations in indentation.

22. *The Tower*. Variant text. Same title in *ABBA ABBA*, p. 102. Some variations in indentation.

23. *Abraham's Sacrifice (1)*. Unpublished variant. Titled 'Abraham 1' in *ABBA ABBA*, p. 104. Some variations in indentation. This is sonnet 25 in the published version. Burgess re-wrote the sestet twice. The first (deleted) version reads:

> And called to Isaac: 'Pack the bags and
> > This donkey, get the boy to bring a nice
> > > Sharp axe, kiss mum goodbye, no you won't need your
> Best shirt. Fetch my hat, let's take the road.
> > The blessed Lord requires a sacrifice.
> > > The time has come to teach you the technique.

This variant may have been abandoned due to its complex indentations. The second previously unpublished MS version is hand-corrected in ink, substituting 'then kiss' for 'and kiss', and 'Bring coats and hats we're' for 'At sunrise we are'. The final line was originally 'The time has come to teach you the technique.'

24. *Abraham's Sacrifice (2)*. Variant text. Titled 'Abraham 2' in *ABBA ABBA*, p. 105. Some variations in indentation. This is sonnet 26 in the published version.

25. *Abraham's Sacrifice (3)*. Variant text. Titled 'Abraham 3' in *ABBA ABBA*,

p. 105. Some variations in indentation. This is sonnet 28 in the published version.

26. *Joseph the Jew (1)*. Variant text. Is called 'Joseph 1' in *ABBA ABBA*. Some variations in indentation. This is sonnet 30 in the published version. Corrections in AB's hand include adding 'and' to the end of the first line, and removing the same word from the second line. In the original MS, the phrase 'get a wetnurse' is hand-corrected to 'gave him fodder'. Transcribed from MS draft. See *ABBA ABBA*, p. 106.

27. *Joseph the Jew (2)*. Unpublished variant. Is called 'Joseph 2' in *ABBA ABBA*. Some variations in indentation. This is sonnet 29 in the published version. Published in *ABBA ABBA*, p. 106.

28. *Lot at Home*. Unpublished variant. Titled 'Lot 1' in *ABBA ABBA*. Some variations in indentation. This is sonnet 23 in the published version. The word 'arrived' in line three eventually became 'came'. 'His window lamp' was eventually changed to 'his lamp'. On the MS, 'buggers' is written in AB's hand to replace 'asses'. Published in *ABBA ABBA*, p. 103.

29. *Lot's Wife*. Unpublished variant. Titled 'Lot 2' in *ABBA ABBA*. Some variations in indentation. This appears as sonnet 24 in *ABBA ABBA*, p. 103.

30. *Lot in Repose*. Unpublished variant. Is called 'Lot 3' in *ABBA ABBA*. This is sonnet 25 in the published version. From this poem on, Burgess used the same indentation as featured in the final published version. The word 'so' is hand-deleted on the MS from the very start of line one, and 'then' is added later on the same line. 'The daughters' was eventually changed to 'Lot's daughters' in the final published version. On the MS, Burgess has hand-corrected 'Morality' to 'Propriety.' Published in *ABBA ABBA*, p. 104.

31. *Exodus*. Previously unpublished variant. Same title as the version published in *ABBA ABBA*, p. 107. Burgess originally typed line three as 'Making them toil under sadistic knaves'. On the MS, the word 'wander' is substituted for 'frig'. From here, the sequence follows the same order as in *ABBA ABBA*.

32. *Balaam's Ass*. Previously unpublished variant. Same title and order as the version published in *ABBA ABBA*. On the MS, Burgess substitutes

the word 'number'[?] for 'donkeys'. The 'Asperges me' is a rite sung during feasts and mass in the Catholic Church. The phrase describes ritual cleansing through sprinkling. See Jon R. Stone, *The Routledge Dictionary of Latin Quotations* (London: Routledge, 2013). See *ABBA ABBA*, p. 107.

33. *The Battle of Gideon*. Previously unpublished variant. Same title and order as the version published in *ABBA ABBA*. On the MS, 'Boos with[?]' is re-typed as 'Boos in'. Possibly 'Rudely –' has been deleted on the MS just before 'Ta-rah'. Line 12 originally read: 'Look at us now. We have our martial brawls.' See *ABBA ABBA*, p. 108.

34. *The Foxes*. Unpublished variant. Same order as the version published in *ABBA ABBA*. Was published as 'Foxes'. The MS has some substantial corrections in AB's hand. The published lines 'Where are the foxes now? It seems they're shunning/Our hounds as we shun syphilitic doxies' were originally 'Though vermin then, where are they now? They're shunning/Our hounds, like bishops shunning heterodoxies'. However, it seems as though Burgess was keeping his options open, as Burgess has also typed 'Our hounds as we shun syphilitic doxies,' suggesting this variant was adopted during typesetting. In addition to this, 'With scores of foxes sniffing round his skirt, you' was originally intended to be 'Laden with fucking foxes, I assert you'. Hand-written on the typescript is an abandoned last line, 'But back to foxes –'. See *ABBA ABBA*, p. 108.

35. *God Helps Those Who Help Themselves(1)*. Previously unpublished variant. Same order as the version published in *ABBA ABBA*. Was published as 'Revenge 1'. Line 9 originally read: 'God frowned and made a memo.' Originally numbered with a Roman numeral and no brackets. See *ABBA ABBA*, p. 109.

36. *God Helps Those Who Help Themselves(2)*. Unpublished variant. Same order as the version published in *ABBA ABBA*. Was published as 'Revenge 2'. The final version uses a space in 'agag agag'. See *ABBA ABBA*, p. 109.

37. *David's Duel*. Unpublished variant. Same order as the version published in *ABBA ABBA*, p. 110. Was published as 'David 1'. 'Powerful' was

originally intended as 'strong'; 'He sent' was originally typed as 'Once he', and 'tough and scary' was a hand-correction of 'strong and scary'; likewise, 'very easy' is hand-corrected on the MS to 'rather easy'.

38. *Holy King David*. Previously unpublished variant. Same order as the version published in *ABBA ABBA*. Was published as 'David 2'. 'He spoke with God, he much preferred the bar-p-/Arlour' was originally intended as 'And that, off duty, he much preferred the bar-p-/ (Hic) Arlour'. See *ABBA ABBA*, p. 110.

39. *The Judgment of Solomon*. Unpublished variant. Published as 'Wisdom' in *ABBA ABBA*, p. 111.

40. *The Fair Judith*. Unpublished variant. Same order as the version published as 'Judith' in *ABBA ABBA*, p. 111, with variant indentation.

41. *Guessing Game*. Unpublished variant. Same order as the version published in *ABBA ABBA*. Was published as 'Susannah' with slight differences in punctuation in the last six lines, and the 'Ach' substituted for 'Aaaargh'. See *ABBA ABBA*, p. 112.

42. *Belshazzar's Feast*. Previously unpublished variant. Same title and order as the version published in *ABBA ABBA*, p. 112.

43. *The Eighth of December*. Unpublished variant. Same title (as 'Dec. 8') and order as the version published in *ABBA ABBA*. Burgess substituted the original 'Absquatulate' for 'Evacuate'. The MS here has a short a sequence of 13 sonnets that were originally selected for inclusion into Playboy, which then carry on in the correct sequence from 44 onwards. Each page in the 'Playboy' selection is simply marked 'Playboy' at the bottom of each presumed photocopy MS. Burgess evidently intended the following sonnets for publication in Playboy, and presumably in this order: '27. Joseph the Jew (II)'; '7. All About Eve'; '8. A Reply'; '11. The First Clothes'; '12. The State of Innocence'; '13. The State of Innocence', and; '24. Joseph the Jew (I)'. See *ABBA ABBA*, p. 113.

44. *The Annunciation*. Unpublished variant. Same title (as 'Annunciation') and order as the version published in *ABBA ABBA*. In the first line, 'day' was inserted by hands, the 'even the year' was originally written as 'you even know the year'. Line five (deleted and corrected by hand) originally read: 'He crashed a window like a well-aimed spear'. The last

two lines were subject to substantial redrafts, and were originally written as:

> 'A hen?' she blushed, 'for I know nothing of –'
> Gabriel nodded, knowing that she meant cocks.

Line thirteen has a corresponding handwritten note, which reads 'A hen, they say, if she knew nothing of (so leer the blasphemous facetious) cocks.' See *ABBA ABBA*, p. 113.

45. *The Madonna's Marriage*. Previously unpublished variant. Same order as the version published in *ABBA ABBA*. Was published as 'Enter Joseph'. In line 12, the word 'dribbler' was substituted for the original 'fellow.' See *ABBA ABBA*, p. 114.

46. *The Visit*. Previously unpublished variant. Same title, order, and wording as the version published in *ABBA ABBA*. See *ABBA ABBA*, p. 115.

47. *Epiphany*. Previously unpublished variant. Eventually published in *ABBA ABBA* as 'The Magi'. Minor handwritten corrections were added by Burgess: 'painted' was originally 'rainbow'; 'with their caravan' was originally 'in their caravan', and 'it seems' was originally 'alas'. See *ABBA ABBA*, p. 115.

48. *The Circumcision*. Previously unpublished variant. Same title (as 'Circumcision'), order, and wording as the version published in *ABBA ABBA*. Line six was eventually published as 'The Jewish law, so look the Lord of Earth', but no pen corrections were made to this effect on the original MS. See *ABBA ABBA*, p. 115.

49. *Christ's Foreskin*. Previously unpublished variant. Same order and wording as the version published in *ABBA ABBA*. Eventually published as 'The Living Prepuce'. The MS was originally typed with following order in the second stanza:

> You look incredulous, my friend. But know
> That faith, though buffeted, must never fail.
> In eighty other Christian lands they show
> This self-same prize for reverent eyes to hail.

Arrows are drawn on by Burgess that indicate the final change in order. Another heavily hand-corrected variant in included elsewhere in the MS, as follows:

> The sacred relic that had long been hid,
> Preserved in camphor, pickled or else iced
> So previous that its worth could not be priced,
> At last we saw. His Holiness undid
> The holy lock, then raised the holy lid –
> Behold, the foreskin of our saviour Christ,
> Shrimplike in shape, most elegantly sliced,
> To profane eyes, exhibited.
>
> You look incredulous. I know, I know –
> But faith, though fiercely tried, should never fail.
> In eighty other Christian lands they show
> This self-same prize for reverent eyes to hail.
> His heavenly father must have made it grow,
> When was stripped out just like a fingernail.

See *ABBA ABBA*, p. 116.

50. *The Flight of the Holy Family*. Previously unpublished variant. Same order and wording as the version published in *ABBA ABBA*. Later published as 'The Slaughter of the Innocents 1'. See *ABBA ABBA*, p. 116.

51. *The Slaughter of the Innocents*. Previously unpublished variant. Same order and wording as the version published in ABBA ABBA. Later published as 'The Slaughter of the Inncents II'. Lines nine and ten were originally intended as: 'Christ, as I said, was halfway to the delta / So did not smell the filthy bloody water.' See *ABBA ABBA*, p. 117.

52. *Original Sin*. Previously unpublished variant. Same order and wording as the version published in *ABBA ABBA*. Later published as 'Baptism'. Line ten was originally intended as: 'As staunch a Jew as any on the earth.' See *ABBA ABBA*, p. 117.

53. *The Wedding at Cana (1)*. Previously unpublished variant. Same order and wording as the version published in *ABBA ABBA*. Originally titled using Roman numerals with no brackets. Has been altered for the purposes of consistency. See *ABBA ABBA*, p. 118.

54. *The Wedding at Cana (2)*. Previously unpublished variant. Same order and wording as the version published in *ABBA ABBA*. 'Teeth' was originally intended as 'pegs'. Originally titled using Roman numerals with no brackets. Has been altered for the purposes of consistency. See *ABBA ABBA*, p. 118.

55. *The Wedding at Cana (3)*. Previously unpublished variant text. Same order and wording as the version published in *ABBA ABBA*. 'Rhapsody' was originally intended as 'symphony'. Originally titled using Roman numerals with no brackets. Has been altered for the purposes of consistency. See *ABBA ABBA*, p. 119.

56. *The House of God*. Previously unpublished variant. Same order and wording as the version published in *ABBA ABBA*, as 'Anger'. 'Moneychangers preying' was originally intended as 'moneymen who battoned'. Transcribed from MS draft. Published in *ABBA ABBA*, p. 119.

57. *Martha and Mary*. Previously unpublished variant. Same order and wording as the version published in *ABBA ABBA*. Compared with the *ABBA ABBA* version, there is a very minor variant in line eight, in the italicized phrase and the lower-case 'w'. Transcribed from MS draft. See *ABBA ABBA*, p. 120.

58. *First Communion*. Previously unpublished variant. Same order and wording as the version published in *ABBA ABBA*, as 'Communion'. 'To eat' was originally intended as 'Gobble'. At this point in the MS, Burgess clearly makes a mistake the numbering of the sequence. Hence, each sonnet from here on was originally assigned the number before it. For example, this – sonnet number 58 – is mistakenly hand-corrected to number 57. Correct numbers have been reassigned for the present edition. See *ABBA ABBA*, p. 120.

59. *Christ's Cross-Examination*. Previously unpublished variant. Same order and wording as the version published in *ABBA ABBA*, as 'Christ & Pilate'. See *ABBA ABBA*, p. 121.

60. *Christ at the Pillar*. Previously unpublished variant. Same order as the version published in *ABBA ABBA*, as 'At the Pillar 1'. The first line was eventually re-written as 'Bare as a Briton auctioned into slavery', but this phrase does not appear (typed or hand-written) on the MS. See *ABBA ABBA*, p. 121.

61. *Courage*. Previously unpublished variant text. Same order and wording as the version published in *ABBA ABBA*, as 'At the Pillar 2'. Burgess's numbering is once again correct from this sonnet onwards. See *ABBA ABBA*, p. 122.

62. *Ill-Starred*. Previously unpublished variant. Same order as the version published in *ABBA ABBA*, as 'Pity'. Minor hand-corrections on MS made the following substitutions: 'on' for 'in' (line 2); 'Forced as' for 'And then' (line 3); 'To slave' for 'Slaving' (line 4); 'old saying' for 'saying' (line 13); 'spavined' for worn-out' (line 14). Burgess evidently abandoned a hand-written correction which intended to substitute 'All vermin' for 'flies'. See *ABBA ABBA*, p. 122.

63. *The Two Breeds*. Previously unpublished variant. Same order as the version published in *ABBA ABBA*, as 'The Two Kinds of Men'. Burgess later inserted the word 'Scarred'. Croesus, king of Lydia, apparently ruled for over a decade prior to being defeated by Cyrus the Great. Burgess wrote about Cyrus in a 1976 screenplay, poems from which appear above on p. 433. See: Herodotus. *Complete Works of Herodotus* (Delphi Classics, 2013). See *ABBA ABBA*, p. 123.

64. *Guilt in the Ghetto*. Previously unpublished variant. Same order as the version published in *ABBA ABBA*, as 'Guilt'. 'When Christ left home' was eventually changed to 'When Christ went' in the *ABBA ABBA* version. The last three lines have corrected by hand in the typescript, and were originally:

> Doomed-to-die (put it another way)
> Has to be matched, alas, by doomed-to-slay.
> Somebody had to take this business on.

These corrections are so heavy on the MS, that Burgess retyped the stanza in the form shown in the present edition. Transcribed from MS draft. See *ABBA ABBA*, p. 123.

65. *Limbo*. Previously unpublished variant. Same title and order as the version published in *ABBA ABBA*. This, and subsequent sonnets, are not given a number by Burgess, but the sequence of the MSS follows that seen in the eventual published form in *ABBA ABBA*. The numbers are added by the editor from here onwards. 'Saintly' was eventually substituted for 'holy' in the *ABBA ABBA* version. Transcribed from MS draft. See *ABBA ABBA*, p. 124.

66. *Christ in Hell*. Previously unpublished variant. Same title and order as the version published in *ABBA ABBA*. In the MS, 'can' is hand-corrected to 'could'. Transcribed from MS draft. See *ABBA ABBA*, p. 124.

67. *Doubting Thomas*. Previously unpublished variant text. Same order as the version published in *ABBA ABBA*, as 'Doubt'. The first three lines (undeleted in the MS, but then reworked) were originally began as:

> When Christ rose up, those somewhat timid gentry
> His friends screamed just like magpies. One apostle
> Though, St Thomas,

On the MS, 'Shove' is hand-corrected to 'Poke' on line nine. Published in *ABBA ABBA*, p. 125.

68. *Whitsun*. Previously unpublished variant text. Same order as the version published in *ABBA ABBA*. Burgess provides no title in the MS. For convenience and continuity, the title from *ABBA ABBA* is used here. See *ABBA ABBA*, p. 125.

69. *Spread the Word*. Previously unpublished variant. Same order as the version published in *ABBA ABBA*. Burgess provides no title in the MS. For convenience and continuity, the title from *ABBA ABBA* is used here. On the MS, 'Jesus' and 'Cassia' typewritten corrections of illegible deleted words. 'Took' in line three was originally intended as 'sought', and then hand-corrected. Line four – again, later hand-corrected – originally read as 'Some, tiring, went to feed the need/Of'. Transcribed from MS draft. See *ABBA ABBA*, p. 126.

70. *The Last Days.* Previously unpublished variant. Same order as the version published in *ABBA ABBA.* Burgess provides no title in the MS. For convenience and continuity, the title from *ABBA ABBA* is used here. Line nine was published in a variant form in *ABBA ABBA*, as: 'The prophet Enoch will lambast the liar.' Originally, line ten (subsequently corrected by hand) was intended as: 'Who will arise out of a big black hatch'. In the final line on the MS, 'The' is hand-corrected to 'And'. Transcribed from MS draft. See *ABBA ABBA*, p. 126.

71. *The Last Judgement.* Previously unpublished variant. Same order as the version published in *ABBA ABBA*. Burgess provides no title in the MS. For convenience and continuity, the title from *ABBA ABBA* is used here. Line nine (subsequently hand-corrected on the MS) was originally intended as: 'And there the Lord, cool, careful, systematic'. 'Er-phwoo' on the last line was originally written as 'Phwoo', and then corrected by hand. The last three sentences in this line appear, in *ABBA ABBA*, on separate stepped lines of their own. The current version follows the indentations selected by Burgess in the original MS. This is the last of the sonnets in the *ABBA ABBA* version, but other sonnets can be found either in the HRC and IABF collections. See *ABBA ABBA*, p. 126.

72. *The Father of the Saints.* Previously unpublished variant. Inserted in the sequence of sonnets in the MS in its current position. It is very different to the version that eventually appeared in the novel; it is not included in the appendix, but is embedded within the prose of the main story. In the novel, the poem is given by Belli to John Keats, who hides it amongst his papers. Two full variants of this sonnet are known to exist. The version selected for inclusion in the main body of the present edition is thought to be the first draft. What is presumed to be the second draft is much closer to the version read by Keats in the novel:

> These are some names, my son, we call the prick:
> The chair, the yard, the nail, the kit
> The holofernes, rod, the cock, in rock,
> The dickery, the dick, the liquorice stick,
> The lust, Richard or the listless dick,

The old blind bob, the just on twelve o'clock,
Mercurial finger, or the lead-filled sock,
The monkey, or the mule with – kick.

The squib, the rocket, or the Roman candle,
The dumpendebat or the shagging shad
The lovelump or the pump or the pump handle
The tap of venus, the leering lad,
The hand-dandy, stiff proud as a-dandle
But most of all our sad glad bad mad dad.

In the presumed second draft MS, these lines are appended to this poem, which cannot be seen on the presumed first draft:

And I might add
That learned patents by their midnight tapers
After endless low standing high
Fat phallus done – papers

These unfinished lines are similar to those included in the novel. Note that the version used in the present sequence is much longer than a sonnet. It is presumed that the last six lines were included as a possible variant, but both are included. This also follows the pattern of lines that are embedded in the novel, which also includes extra material.

73. *Local Industry.* Previously unpublished. The typescript from here includes versions of 'The Bet', 'Two Uses for Ashes', and 'The Fair Judith' (see item 40, above). After these, the 'Three Apocryphal Sonnets of Belli' also includes 'The Bet', 'Two Uses for Ashes', 'The orchidaceous catalogue begins', and the sonnet that was eventually published in *ABBA ABBA* as 'Privy Matters'. To avoid duplication, the present edition tackles the Apocryphal sonnets only once, and this is explained below. Choosing to do so allowed for the inclusion of previously unpublished sonnets 'Local Industry', 'Spaniards', and 'Work' at a point that seems most logical.

74. *'Spaniards'*. Previously unpublished. MS on diary paper pre-printed Sabato/Gennaio 3. Title added by editor.

75. *'Work'*. Previously unpublished. Title not given by Burgess, but adopted by editor.

76. *The Bet.* Previously unpublished variant. Same title as the version published in *ABBA ABBA*, but with different indentation. Marked, on the MS, as one of 'Three Apocryphal Sonnets of Belli'. Note that this sub-title has not been adopted in the present edition, as there are four such sonnets. Minor variants between this and the *ABBA ABBA* version include: use of 'Ah' on line five (later removed), 'Albert', which became 'one man', 'Right', which became 'Reet', and 'pound', which became 'quid'. Another variant MS exists that shows these substitutions being made in Burgess's hand. On this variant, the following lines were considered and then redrafted by Burgess: 'Some chaps was arguing, as chaps often will' (first line); '"Coming up" was the first thing that he spoke' and '"Get ready" was the first thing that he spoke' (line 12). See *ABBA ABBA*, p. 88.

77. *Two Uses for Ashes.* Previously unpublished variant poem. Geoffrey Grigson's full name is present in the MS version, but not in the *ABBA ABBA* version. In the novel, this sonnet is ascribed to J. J. Wilson, who apparently writes it having been present at a University Literary Society lecture by the Oxford poet G—y G—n. The 'swinging censors' is comparable with the phrase 'swinging like twin censers', which Burgess re-uses in his long poem about Augustine and Pelagius. Geoffrey Grigson wrote two negative reviews of Burgess's work in 1960 and then in 1970. See Biswell, *The Real Life of Anthony Burgess*, pp. 217, 315. See *ABBA ABBA*, p. 88.

78. 'The orchidaceous catalogue begins.' Previously unpublished variant poem. Geoffrey Grigson's full name is present in the MS version, but not in the *ABBA ABBA* version. In the novel, this sonnet is ascribed to J. J. Wilson, who apparently writes it having been present at a University Literary Society lecture by the Oxford poet G—y G—n. The 'swinging censors' is comparable with the phrase 'swinging like twin censers', which Burgess re-uses in his long poem about Augustine and Pelagius.

Geoffrey Grigson wrote two negative reviews of Burgess's work in 1968 and 1970. See *ABBA ABBA*, p. 89.

79. *Privy Matters*. Previously unpublished variant poem. In *ABBA ABBA*, this sonnet by Burgess is ascribed to the character J.J. Wilson, a literary historian. The indentations are not present in the *ABBA ABBA* version. Other variations include: 'neighbour box', which became 'next nook', 'be damned', which was eventually removed, 'scatographic theses' which became 'a scatographic thesis', and the last line, which was published in *ABBA ABBA* as 'Lucky? I haven't got me kecks down yet.' Another version of the sonnet in this MS uses capital letters for the speech in line eight and line fourteen, and uses the word 'cabinet' for 'box'. Following this variant sonnet in the archive MS is another copy of the poems intended for *Playboy* magazine, plus a number of intermediate prose transliterations that were used as part of the translation process, plus some very early drafts of sonnets included in the present sequence. See *ABBA ABBA*, p. 88.

80. *Foreword 1974* (from *Moses*). Previously unpublished. IABF, AB/ ARCH/A/MOS/28.

81. *Foreword 1976* (from *Moses*). Previously unpublished in this form. The original English spelling (from the MS) has been restored. IABF. AB/ ARCH/A/MOS/29.

82. *Moses – The Bondage*. IABF. AB/ARCH/A/MOS/28.

83. *Moses – The Young Moses*. IABF. AB/ARCH/A/MOS/29.

84. *Moses – The Burning Bush*. IABF. AB/ARCH/A/MOS/3.

85. *Moses – Return Into Egypt*. IABF. AB/ARCH/A/MOS/3.

86. *Moses – The Plagues*. IABF. AB/ARCH/A/MOS/3.

87. *Moses – The Passover*. IABF. AB/ARCH/A/MOS/3.

88. *Moses – The Exodus*. IABF. AB/ARCH/A/MOS/3.

89. *Moses – Miracles Of The Desert*. IABF. AB/ARCH/A/MOS/3.

90. *Moses – The Mountain*. IABF. AB/ARCH/A/MOS/3.

91. *Moses – A Restive People*. IABF. AB/ARCH/A/MOS/3.

92. *Moses – The Golden Calf*. IABF. AB/ARCH/A/MOS/3.

93. *Moses – Death And The Law*. IABF. AB/ARCH/A/MOS/3.

94. *Moses – Unrest*. IABF. AB/ARCH/A/MOS/3.

95. *Moses – The Death Of Dathan*. IABF. AB/ARCH/A/MOS/3.

96. *Moses – Balaam*. IABF. AB/ARCH/A/MOS/3.

97. *Moses – Zimri*. IABF. AB/ARCH/A/MOS/3.

98. *Moses – Abominations Before The Lord*. IABF. AB/ARCH/A/MOS/3.

99. *Moses – Jordan*. IABF. AB/ARCH/A/MOS/3.

100.   'And if there be no beauty, if god has passed some by.' Previously unpublished. *St Winefred's Well* [by Gerard Manley Hopkins and Anthony Burgess], broadcast on BBC Radio 3, 23 December 1989. BBC Written Archives Centre, ref. SBS950/89DA6366. Transcribed from the audio recording.

101.   'Talk is easy. Easiest for one who.' From *St Winefred's Well*.

102.   'Thank you. Enough, brother Teryth.' From *St Winefred's Well*.

103.   'I choose no tail or toy! Truth – a light that outdoes this sun.' From *St Winefred's Well*.

104.   'Say nothing, Priest, father, mother.' From *St Winefred's Well*.

105.   *The Pet Beast*. This text published posthumously in Paul Phillips, *A Clockwork Counterpoint*, pp. 405-6. Typescript at Angers University Library.

106.   *Signs (Dogs Of Peace)*. Previously unpublished. IABF, AB/ARCH/A/POE/18.

107.   'Augustine and Pelagius.' *A Clockwork Testament, or Enderby's End*. (London: Hart-Davis, MacGibbon, 1974), pp. 22–67. Transcribed from IABF, AB/ARCH/A/TCT, IABF. Title added by editor.

108.   *The Princely Progress*. A review of Clive James's *Charles Charming's Challenges on the Pathway to the Throne* (London: Jonathan Cape, 1981). *Times Literary Supplement*, 12 June 1981, p. 656.

109.   'Sick of the sycophantic singing, sick.' 'Five Revolutionary Sonnets', *Transatlantic Review*, 21 (1966), pp. 30–32.

110.   'Bells broke in the long Sunday, a dressing-gown day.' 'Five Revolutionary Sonnets', *Transatlantic Review*, 21 (1966), pp. 30–32.

111.   'A dream, yes, but for everyone the same.' 'Five Revolutionary Sonnets', *Transatlantic Review*, 21 (1966), pp. 30–32.

112.   'They lit the sun, and then their day began.' This sonnet appears, with the first line missing, in *Enderby Outside* (London:

Heinemann, 1968), pp. 88–9. 'Five Revolutionary Sonnets', *Transatlantic Review*, 21 (1966), pp. 30–32.

113. 'Augustus on a guinea sat up straight.' 'Five Revolutionary Sonnets', *Transatlantic Review,* 21 (1966), pp. 30–32.

114. *To Vladimir Nabokov On His 70th Birthday.* IABF, AB/ARCH/A/POE/23.

115. *The Sword.* The swordstick, and the New York subway setting also appear in *A Clockwork Testament*, when Enderby defends himself and others against thugs on a train. *The Transatlantic Review,* No. 23 (Winter 1966-7), pp. 41–43.

116. *O Lord, O Ford, God Help Us, Also You.* 'Hinc illae lacrimae' means 'hence these tears'; see: Terence. Andria (ed. by George Pelham Shipp). (London: Bristol Classical Press, 1960:2002). Burgess describes organised cannibalism, and it leading to canned food called, amongst other things, 'Mench'. Here, Burgess partially reuses material from his dystopian novel *The Wanting Seed* (London: Heinemann, 1962). *New York Times,* 29 December 1974.

117. *A Sonnet for the Emery Collegiate Institute.* Previously unpublished. Addressed to: Warner Winter, Esq. and dated St. Bridget's Day, 1976. Typescript at IABF.

118. 'Advice to would-be writers? Simple. *Don't.*' Previously unpublished. Dated July 24, 1974, and sent to a Mrs Fischer. Burgess wrote the following note to accompany the sonnet: 'Dear Mrs Fischer – Many thanks for your kind letter of May 4. The delay in getting it and hence replying (it came a couple of days ago) must be blamed on the Italian postal services, which are now sunk in ultimate chaos. Here is a sonnet.' Typescript at IABF.

119. 'I send these lines to you in Agincourt.' Previously unpublished. Transcribed from an image of a Burgess manuscript posted online in 2007. Graphical analysis of the image showed that on the back of the sonnet is a letter from 16 February 1974 in which Burgess thanks someone for an (unknown) act of kindness. In the fragment, he tantalisingly mentions a birthday, 'electronic equipment', and a photograph. From a scanned image of an original MS. Location unknown.

120.   'End of the world – cosy, something thrilling.' Previously unpublished. Sent to the editors, *Yale News*. Typescript at IABF.

121.   'Late as I am, but blame the mails, not me.' Previously unpublished. Sent to Mr Selwyn C. Gamble. Typescript at IABF.

122.   'Forgive the lateness, please, of this reply.' Previously unpublished. Sent to Mr Alan Fox. Typescript at IABF.

123.   'Some consider love is great.' Previously unpublished. From the screenplay for *Eternal Life* (1991). The character Stauff notes of this: 'There used to be a poem. I forget who composed it. I remember these lines, however... You have read no history [he tells Golisha]. You have been forbidden books. The epics of the human past are unknown to you.' Transcribed from MS draft.

124.   *To Chas*. Previously unpublished. Attributed to Burgess. 'To Chas'. Emailed to IABF on 21 May 2012. The correspondent described the work as 'a poem that Anthony Burgess wrote for a member of my family [who was] suffering from terminal lymphoma when he shared a room with Mr Burgess in Columbia Presbyterian Hospital in New York in 1991 or 1992.' Typescript at IABF.

125.   'What can I say? I'd better try a sonnet.' Previously unpublished. Addressed to Mr Peter Brule and dated 31 March 1974. Typescript at IABF.

126.   'Forgive my writing verse: I get so bored.' Previously unpublished. Untitled sonnet to Mr S.G. Byam. Typescript at IABF.

127.   'Dear Chris, the trouble is, as you must know.' Previously unpublished. Untitled sonnet to Mr Chris Mahon, dated 14 September 1974. Typescript at IABF.

128.   *Happy Birthday Tae Andrew*. Previously unpublished. Anthony Burgess. 'Happy Birthday tae Andrew'. Hand-written and illustrated booklet of loose paper. Dated August 9 1979. Typescript at IABF.

129.   'So will the flow of time and fire.' Previously unpublished. This is deleted in the published novel. Burgess gives no indication as to why this is to be deleted, but there is a confident scrawl and deletion mark next to it. In terms of the context of the story, the second half is more believable as it is less finished:

And something something something can
Take partners for a plonk pavane,
The blinded giant's staff
Tracing a seismograph.

This is a poem that comes to Enderby upon waking. The use of 'something' and 'plonk' is not reflective of Burgess's general drafting technique, which – generally – involves leaving an obvious space in the line, rather than using a temporary word. Transcribed from MS draft.

130. *Whisky*. Previously unpublished. This is the longest of two drafts. The other draft includes these slightly varied stanzas:

Double you aitch eye ess kay ee wye spells
Irish an, without an ee, spells Scotch.
Saxon stupidity ha made a botch
Out of the autocratic pose,
Celtic uisgebaugh, which tells
The paternal strictness he distrusted, still
    Clung to his utterance and features,
    It was a protective imitation

For one who lived among enemies so long;
If only he was wrong and at times absurd,
To us he is no more a person
    Now – but a whole climate of opinion.

IABF, AB/ARCH/A/POE/26.

131. *A Ballade for Christmas*. Previously unpublished. Photocopy typescript, signed Liana, Anthony, Andrew, and Bettie [i.e. Bettina Culham, Liana's secretary]. Pencilled on the top of this MS is a note, indicating that it was 'Sent to Gabriele and Leslie for Christmas 1984'. Gabriele Pantucci was Burgess's agent, who married the agent Leslie Gardner.

132.   *January 1.* Previously unpublished.

133.   *A l'Hôtel Le Clos Voltaire.* Previously unpublished. Hand-written MS on paper headed *Hôtel Le Clos Voltaire.* In a typewritten essay draft, dated 15 May 1978, and written for *Saturday Review,* Burgess provides some comtext for this poem: 'In May I was able to get as far as Geneva, where they were getting ready to celebrate the feast of the Ascension [...] The only writing I did in this week and more was an acrostical sonnet on the name *Le Clos Voltaire,* the cheap hotel in Geneva where we stayed. For this, of course, I received no payment.' Clos Voltaire is now a community centre, located at 49 Rue de Lyon, Geneva. Thomas Stearns are the first two names of T. S. Eliot. The theologian Michael Servetus also features in *Byrne* (1995). Typescript at IABF.

134.   'The verses of E. Lucie-Smith.' Previously unpublished. Typescript at IABF.

135.   You were there, and nothing said.' Previously unpublished variant text. Appears, with variants, in *Enderby* (p. 44). Dated 1937 on the MS, although this is probably a much later recalling of the poem. On the back of the MS is an extract from the 'Pet Beast'.

136.   *Catullus 1.* Previously unpublished. Burgess's translation is found in his copy of Tibullus Catullus, *Pervigilium Veneris* (trans. F. W. Cornish *et al.*) (Cambridge, Mass.: Harvard University Press, 1913:1976). Typescript at IABF.

137.   *Catullus 2.* Previously unpublished. Burgess's translation is in his copy of *Pervigilium Veneris* at IABF.

138.   'Heroes are dead to us.' Previously unpublished variant text. Also in the novelised version of *The Eve of St Venus* but with collective, rather than personal, pronouns used. Banbury diary, c.1954[?]. MS in notebook at IABF.

139.   From typescript.

140.   *That The Earth Rose Out Of A Vast Basin Of Electric Sea.* Written as J. B. Wilson, Burgess's real name. *Manchester Xaverian,* Easter Term, 1936. Copy at IABF.

141.   *Sonnet In Alexandrines.* John Burgess Wilson (JBW). *The Manchester Xaverian* (Easter Term, 1936). Copy at IABF.

142.　*A Rondel For Spring.* Described as 'After Charles D'Orléans'. Appears on same MS as 'My father, his wife', with minor variants (title, and no comma after 'rain'). The manuscript version appears to be typed quite late in Burgess's life. John Burgess Wilson (JBW), 'A Rondel for Spring' in *Manchester Xaverian.* Easter Term, 1936.

143.　*When It Is All Over. The Serpent,* vol. 24 (1939–1940), p. 15.

144.　*Wir Danken Unsrem Führer. The Serpent,* vol. 24 (1939–1940), p. 4.

145.　*Girl.* This poem has been attributed to two fictional poets in Burgess's career: to Lavinia Grantham, and to Enderby. Kevin Jackson notes that the pronouns are changed in the re-attribution from J.B. Wilson to F.X. Enderby. Jackson does not mention the re-attribution that occurred in *A Vision of Battlements,* which pre-dates Enderby, even if it was published later. Jackson notes that this poem was originally published in *The Serpent.* Later on in *A Vision of Battlements,* the content of the poem bleeds into Burgess's description of Ennis's thoughts on Lavinia: 'Her yellow hair, sheaves shed by summer, was irradiated by the last of the sun…' (p. 155). The last part of this sentence, although not appearing in the poem, maintains the rhythm of the line. *A Vision of Battlements* (London: Sidgwick and Jackson, 1965), p. 153; *The Serpent,* vol. 24, p. 26 (see Biswell, p. 73).

146.　*To Amaryllis After The Dance. The Serpent,* vol. 24, p. 89 (see Biswell, p. 73).

147.　*Orpheus And Eurydice. The Serpent,* vol. 24, p. 96 (see Biswell, p. 73).

148.　'All the ore.' *The Serpent,* vol. 24, p. 63.

149.　*A History. The Serpent,* vol. 24, p. 56.

150.　*The Lowdown On Art Or Æsthetics For The Science Student. The Serpent,* vol. 244, p. 9.

151.　*Dead Leaves. The Serpent,* vol. 24, p. 33.

152.　*Sonnet on Examinations. The Serpent,* vol. 24.

153.　*Sixth-form Triolets.* Line three of part II originally read 'It ages children to adults, –'. The em dash has been removed to regulate the punctuation. *The Serpent,* vol. 24.

154.　*Jack's Story.* A fragment of an unfinished autobiographical poem.

155.　'Prudence! Prudence!' the pigeons call.' *Inside Mr. Enderby,* pp. 32–35.

156. *Fish And Heroes. Inside Mr. Enderby*, p. 73.

157. 'Nymphs and satyrs, come away.' *Inside Mr. Enderby*, p. 105.

158. 'And in that last delirium of lust.' Written by Enderby, as part of the *Arry and Thelma* cycle that he composes for a kitchen chef. *Inside Mr. Enderby*, p. 110.

159. *Epithalamion*. Prior to writing this, Enderby invokes Shelley. For Shelley's own Epithalamion, see P.B. Shelley, *The Works of P.B. Shelley* (Ware: Wordsworth Poetry Library, 1994), p. 412. *Inside Mr. Enderby*, p. 138.

160. *To Tirzah*. Described as a 'gnomic telegraphic message'. In *Little Wilson and Big God* (p. 185), Burgess says this was printed in the University of Manchester student magazine, *The Serpent*. He also says 'I never quite understood this poem'. On the same page, he provides the title of the poem. See: Damon, S. Foster (2013) *A Blake Dictionary: The Ideas and Symbols of William Blake*. (Lebanon, NH: University Press of New England, 2013, p. 407): 'TIRZAH was the fifth, last, and most important of the daughters of Zelphehad. As the fifth, she represents sex... Tirzah is the creator of the physical body... and thus the mother of death.' *Inside Mr. Enderby*, p. 230.

161. 'Your presence shines about the fumes of fat.' Written by Enderby, as part of the *Arry and Thelma* cycle that he composes for a kitchen chef. *Inside Mr. Enderby*, p. 45.

162. 'The Dragon's mouth will consummate our search.' Written while Burgess lived in Adderbury, 1950-1954. Jackson calls this poem 'Adderbury', but Burgess does not provide a title. The poem appears in two separate parts in *The Worm and The Ring*. The first stanza given here appears on p. 99. On pp.150-1, the final two stanzas appear in exactly the same format as they do in Burgess's autobiography, *Little Wilson and Big God*. The first stanza is thus missed by Jackson. In *The Worm and the Ring*, the character-poet is described as 'a shrunken journalist who was writing a long comic epic in heroic couplets on the town and its denizens.' (p. 99) *The Worm and the Ring* (London: Heinemann, 1961), pp. 99 and 150-151.

163. 'Where sweat starts, nothing starts...' This Empsonian poem is

written by Fenella Crabbe, dealing with the idea that '[c]ivilisation is only possible in a temperate zone'. See *Time for a Tiger* (London: Heinemann, 1956), p. 59.

164. 'Land where the birds have no song, the flowers.' This poem is written by Fenella Crabbe on a manuscript 'much scarred with fastidious alterations'. Victor Crabbe decides: 'It was not a very good poem – confused, the rhythms crude.' *The Enemy in the Blanket* (London: Heinemann, 1958), pp. 103–4.

165. 'Cracks open the leaden corncrake sky with crass, angelic.' Recited by Talbot 'harshly and without nuance from a heavily corrected manuscript'. *The Enemy in the Blanket*, pp. 245, 365, 393.

166. 'The afternoon hour has struck for you to.' Crabbe finds it 'impossible' that his wife's poem should have 'a proleptic Eliotian image of an aged eagle with tired wings demanding to be released from the dressing-mirror'. *Beds in the East* (London: Heinemann, 1959), pp. 127–8.

167. 'Rice-paper land, O lotus-footed.' The lead character Denham tell us: 'to my surprise, [Everett] began to quote one of his own, or Harold's, or John's, or Alfred's poems.' Who these people are is not explained. *The Right to an Answer* (London: Heinemann, 1960), p. 206.

168. 'You take my heart with such unformed grace.' Denham tells us that his friend Everett had written the verses about Imogen 'when she was seven, though I only read them myself for the first time long after [our] first meeting.' *The Right to An Answer*, p. 52.

169. 'Beryl is the daughterly daughter.' Lead character J. W. Denham attributes the poem to 'some modern poetaster', from which he has substituted the name 'Ethel' for 'Beryl.' *The Right to An Answer*, p. 4.

170. *Epigraph On A Printer*. Denham remarks to Everett that, even though he wrote it for Denham's father, it could well be the poet's own epitaph. *The Right to An Answer*, p. 211.

171. *The Music Of The Spheres*. Versions of this poem also appear in *Byrne* (1995) and *The Worm and the Ring* (1961). This, the longest version, from *Inside Mr Enderby*, p. 95.

172. 'Not, of course, that either of us thought.' The mention of steak and kidney pie with potatoes appears at the end of the poem. Janet Shirley, to whom it is read, 'must have sort of nodded off while [her husband] Howard was reading this poem. It seemed to me to be a very boring poem, with no rhymes or rhythm in it either and I must have just dropped off.' This poem acts a precursor to the attempted assisted suicide of Janet, which would have been followed by Howard's suicide. *One Hand Clapping* (London: Peter Davies, 1961), pp. 102–103.

173. 'In this spinning room, reduced to a common noun.' Ascribed to F. X. Enderby, who composes the poem in a lavatory. *Inside Mr. Enderby*, pp. 54–8. See also *Byrne* (London: Hutchinson, 1995), p. 139.

174. "Perhaps I am not wanted then,' he said. Enderby finds this in a number of anthologies, including '*Poetry Now, A Tiny Garner of Modern Verse, Best Poets of Today, They Sing for You, Soldier's Solace… Voices Within*, and other volumes…' *Inside Mr. Enderby*, p. 78.

175. 'Tomorrow will be love for the loveless, and for the lover love.' The first stanza also appears in *The End of the World News* (p. 118) when Courtland Willett sings the song to mark an early transit of Venus. The only difference in the 1982 version is that Willett's verse has an exclamation mark at the end. See *The Eve of St Venus* (London: Hesperus, 2006), pp. 76–8.

176. 'The moon awaits your sleeping: fear to be kissed'. This is the first of Lavinia Grantham's poems that Richard Ennis reads 'in a small tea shop.' *A Vision of Battlements* (London: Sidgwick & Jackson 1965), p. 152.

177. 'The stoat's cry tears long slivers of the night.' Lavinia is singularly impressed when Ennis mentions the personal meaning of the poem: 'Don't you think you ought to eat your mixed grill?' *A Vision of Battlements*, p. 155.

178. 'And his hooves hammer me back into the ground.' *A Vision of Battlements*, p. 180.

179. 'Pigs snort from the yard.' Lavinia plays down this poem: 'That's

nothing to be proud of … that bit of nonsense. I wrote it as a joke.'
A Vision of Battlements, p. 182.

180.   'Gasping in the dunny in the dead of dark.' *Enderby Outside* (London: Heinemann, 1968), pp. 122–3.

181.   'Dragged from his doings in the roar of youth.' *Enderby Outside*, pp. 190–1.

182.   'Archangels blasting from inner space.' This is one of two cut-up style poems that are read by radical/psychedelic poets in this scene. *Enderby Outside*.

183.   'Bells broke in the long Sunday, a dressing-gown day.' 'Five Revolutionary Sonnets', *Transatlantic Review*, no. 21 (1966), pp. 30–32. Also in *Enderby Outside*, p. 8.

184.   'Useless to hope to hold off.' Enderby, interrupted at the end of the poem, doesn't have the opportunity to complete the penultimate line which, in the Jackson, version appears as follows: 'The final kiss and final/Tight pressure of hands.' *Enderby Outside*, pp. 30–31.

185.   *Curtal Sonnet*. The Curtal Sonnet is most closely associated with Gerard Manley Hopkins. For example, 'Peace', written in 1879 is an eleven-line sonnet: 'A Curtal Sonnet in "standard" Alexandrines'. See Hopkins, *Poems and Prose*, ed. W.H. Gardner (Harmondsworth: Penguin, 1953), pp. 42, 232. *Enderby Outside*, p. 45.

186.   'Shrewsbury, Shrewsbury, rounded by river.' *Enderby Outside*, pp. 80–1.

187.   'I sought scent, and found it in your hair.' *Enderby Outside*, p. 102.

188.   'The urgent temper of the laws.' In response to this, 'Out of a trance somebody farted.' *Enderby Outside*, pp. 141-2

189.   From *The Circular Pavane*. *Enderby Outside*, pp. 181–2.

190.   'At the end of the dark hall he found his love.' *Enderby Outside*, p. 209.

191.   '*Independence Day*.' This is labelled c. 1993. 'And, like a fetal marmaset [sic]' is a restored, previously struck-through line from the MS. The last five lines follow the version used by Paul Phillips in *A Clockwork Counterpoint*. A shorter version appears with a variant line ('My brain was freer/And scrawled a cancellation then') in

Little Wilson and Big God, p. 194. See Phillips, *A Clockwork Counterpoint*, p. 407.

192.   'They fear and hate.' *Enderby Outside*, pp. 219–21.

193.   'So will the flux of time and fire.' Described as lines towards a Horatian ode for the king of Denmark. *Enderby Outside*, p. 227.

194.   *September, 1938. Enderby Outside*, pp. 239–240.

195.   *Summer, 1940. Enderby Outside*, p. 240.

196.   *Spring In Camp, 1941. Enderby Outside*, p. 240.

197.   *The Excursion. Enderby Outside*, p. 241.

198.   *Eden. Enderby Outside*, p. 242.

199.   'And as the Manhattan dawn came up.' This poem is read out by another of Enderby's composition students, a Nordic man called Sig Hamsun. This verse is described by Enderby as 'rather sloppy and fungoid', like 'its execrator'. *The Clockwork Testament, or Enderby's End* (London: Hart-Davis, MacGibbon, 1974), p. 60. 'Then as the moon engilds the Thalian fields.' Specimen lines from a play called *The Love of Hostus for Primula* by a Gervase Whitelady. Both the play and the playwright are fictions, created by Enderby. *The Clockwork Testament*, p. 49.

200.   'So the world ticks, aye, like to a ticking clock.' Soliloquoy by a minor character named Retchpork. Enderby produces this work of fiction, under pressure to sustain the lie he has told about the existence of an Elizabethan poet named Gervase Whitelady. He tells his students that this comes from a play called 'Give you good den good my masters'. See *The Clockwork Testament*, p. 51.

201.   'You went that way as you always said you would.' Enderby encounters these lines in a volume of his own work that is brought to him by a psychopathic woman. Although he cannot remember writing them, he decides that he possessed genius at the time. *The Clockwork Testament*, p. 112.

202.   'The work ends when the work ends.' This is an improvised verse recited by a time traveller child called Edmund in order to mark the death of Enderby. His teacher decides that the verse is inappropriate, and accordingly rebukes him. *The Clockwork Testament*, p. 122.

203. *In Memoriam Wystan Hugh Auden KMT. Mark Twain Journal*, vol. 17, no. 4 (Summer, 1975). Copy at IABF.

204. *A Christmas Recipe*. Hand stitched and bound booklet. Limited edition of 100 copies. Labelled 'Seasons Greetings from Anthony & Liana Burgess. Buon Natale 1977.' *A Christmas Recipe* (Verona: Plain Wrapper Press, 1977).

205. *Limerick: The Angler Of Kinsale*. Burgess provides this limerick as an example of Irish place name limericks, which he says Patrick Stevenson was engaging in. Patric(k) Stevenson (1909-1983) was a poet and prolific painter, who lived in County Down, Ireland. 'Something lyrical, something terrible.' *Times Literary Supplement*, 26 April 1978, p. 576.

206. 'I had not thought to hear.' The verse is recited by Toomey after remembering how he met the character Valentine Wrigley: 'He had read an article I had contributed to the English Review on the poetry of Edward Thomas and had written me a letter saying that he had thought himself to be the only admirer of Thomas's work.' The poem is enclosed in this letter. *Earthly Powers*, p. 61.

207. 'Thus kneeling at the altar rail.' Dawson Wignall is the fictional poet laureate who Toomey meets via the British Council in Malta. Toomey owns a 'revised *Oxford Book of English Verse*, bloody Val Wrigley as editor... I did not care for what I found – insular, ingrown, formally traditional, products of a stunted mind. Wignall's themes derived from Anglican church services, the Christmas parties of his childhood, his public school pubescence, suburban shopping streets; they occasionally exhibited perverse valleities of fetischistic order' (*Earthly Powers*, p. 23).

208. 'Do ye the savage old law deny.' Of this, the lead character Toomey notes, after performing it to his friend Val: 'It needs tidying up a little, of course.' He smiled, not at me, but in pleasure at his performance' (*Earthly Powers*, p. 62).

209. 'The kind of laugh that Wodehouse imparts is.' The fictional poet Wrigley writes this in response to P.G. Wodehouse being 'captured by the Germans in his French villa and persuaded to talk very

freely and indiscreetly, though also humorously, on Berlin radio'. See *Earthly Powers*, p. 438.

210. 'A glance or gander of this gandy dancer.' Toomey notes that this verse is 'A long way from the thrush in the heart of Ealing.' The verse is one of Wrigley's published works: 'From a big side pocket, he pulled a thin book. Valentine Wrigley. Faber and, highly reputable. The title: A Feast of Cinders.' The style of this verse is reminiscent primarily of Hopkins ('wavewhite preen', 'gandy dancer') but there may be elements of Whitman, too. See *Earthly Powers*, p. 214.

211. 'The young things who frequent movie palaces.' Carl Jung, who hears this limerick in the novel, is 'prudishly embarrassed' by it. *End of the World News: An Entertainment* (London: Hutchinson, 1982).

212. *The Wiggle Poof*. This is purportedly juvenilia, but bears the same neat-rhymed style of the children's verse Burgess write in the late 1970s, especially in *Long Trip to Teatime*. Published in *Little Wilson and Big God*, p. 101.

213. 'A prism is a useful thing.' Claimed as another piece of juvenilia in *Little Wilson and Big God*, p. 101.

214. 'I wrote on the beach, with a stick of salty wood.' The colliding 's' sounds are comparable with the linguistic experimentation of G. M. Hopkins. *Little Wilson and Big God*, p. 101.

215. 'Calm lies our harbour, while the maiden day.' Burgess says he sent this sonnet 'to the *Sunday Times*, which sent it back'. No copy of this correspondence is listed in either the IABF or HRC archives. *Little Wilson and Big God*, p. 150.

216. 'Father of fire who, with bold simony.' 'There was my father [in the poem] proffering a flaring Swan Vesta. He had become both myth and comedy.' *Little Wilson and Big God*, p.195.

217. 'J.B.W.' *Little Wilson and Big God*, p. 210.

218. 'The sea, green and deep.' Burgess describes this verse as a mnemonic rhyme for the phoneme /I:/. *A Mouthful of Air*, p. 330.

219. 'Winter wins.' This, according to Burgess, is a mnemonic rhyme for the phoneme /I/. *A Mouthful of Air*, p. 330.

220. 'Out of the station puffs the train.' This also appears in Burgess,

Language Made Plain (London: Fontana, 1975), p. 147. Following this verse, Burgess notes: 'Meanwhile, read. The Bantam dual language books and the Penguin anthologies of foreign verse are cheap and useful. They have literal translations next to the text. Whatever the view of poetry held by the average Englishman, most other peoples are fond of it. Read a French poem in a French café and people will applaud. Read a Russian poem to Russians, and they will kiss you and buy you drinks. Learn short poems by heart. That is a sure way into the heart of the language and the hearts of the people' (p. 147). See also *A Mouthful of Air*, p. 129.

221.   'Crippled, the antarctic fire with chiselled skill.' This poem appears in the typescript of an unpublished play, 'The End of Things: Three Dialogues for Old Men' (1991). After the poem has been recited, one of the three characters in the dialogue, Aubrey, comments: 'That sonnet is about something, and that something is the impossibility of making sense of the world. Its meaning is the necessary cancelling out of meaning. It is art, hence it is beauty.'

222.   'Imagination is your true Apollo.' IABF, AB/ARCH/A/POE/5.

223.   'Our Norman betters.' IABF, AB/ARCH/A/POE/8.

224.   *Nostalgia In Head Plunging*. IABF, AB/ARCH/A/POE/4.

225.   'Dreaming when dawn's left hand.' IABF, AB/ARCH/A/POE/4.

226.   'An Elegy for X' in Stephen Spender (ed). *Hockney's Alphabet*. (London: Faber, 1991).

227.   *Princess's Lullaby/Queen's Lullaby*. Previously unpublished. From 'Music for Moses the Lawgiver' (IABF, AB/ARCH/A/MOS).

228.   *Chant*. Previously unpublished. From 'Music for Moses the Lawgiver'.

229.   *Soldier's Song*. Previously unpublished complete version. Variant published in *Revolutionary Sonnets* without final line. From 'Music for Moses the Lawgiver'.

230.   *Prayer*. Previously unpublished, from 'Music for Moses the Lawgiver.

231.   *Lullaby*. Previously unpublished, from 'Music for Moses the Lawgiver'.

232.   *Pastorale*. Previously unpublished, from 'Music for Moses the Lawgiver'.

233. *Water Song.* Previously unpublished, from 'Music for Moses the Lawgiver.

234. *Desert Song For Moses* . Previously unpublished, from 'Music for Moses the Lawgiver'.

235. *Travelling Song.* Previously unpublished. From 'Music for Moses the Lawgiver'.

236. *Miriam's Song of Triumph.* Previously unpublished, from 'Music for Moses the Lawgiver'.

237. *Miriam's Song of Triumph.* Previously unpublished. From 'Music for Moses the Lawgiver'.

238. *Marriage Round.* Previously unpublished, from 'Music for Moses the Lawgiver'.

239. *Moses's Song.* Previously unpublished, from 'Music for Moses the Lawgiver'.

240. *Travel Song.* Previously unpublished, from 'Music for Moses the Lawgiver'.

241. *Bull Song.* Previously unpublished, from 'Music for Moses the Lawgiver'.

242. *Golden Calf Song.* Previously unpublished, from 'Music for Moses the Lawgiver'.

243. *Bard's Song.* Previously unpublished, from 'Music for Moses the Lawgiver'.

244. *Jubilee Anthem. For Malayan Boys' Voices.* Previously unpublished, from handwritten MS, c.1955. Written to be sung by boys of Malay College Kuala Kangsar, whose golden jubilee was celebrated in 1955 (IABF, AB/ARCH/A/POE/15). For more detail, see Sholto Byrnes, 'Unveiled: Work by Anthony Burgess Suppressed for Years', *Independent*, 5 December 2010.

245. *The Three Dimensions.* This poem appears on pp. 51–3 of the prose draft of *Byrne* (published 1995). The full verse does not appear in the final version, although it is alluded to.

246. *Words Getting In The Way.* Previously unpublished. Transcribed from undated MS. It is not clear as to whether the poem was intended for a novel, play, or translation. The section beginning

'No matter how powerful or subtle or fine' is from another draft (IABF, AB/ARCH/A/CYR/20).

247. 'Slavery slavery.' Previously unpublished. From red notebook of the brand 'Block Notes Mediolanum ICCI Produzione 5'.

248. 'None but the coward.' Previously unpublished.

249. 'He bought me from a Saracen.' Previously unpublished. MS draft.

250. 'Sevilla, Seviya, Sevija – or Seville.' Previously unpublished. MS draft.

251. 'Take him, you don't have to pay for him.' Previously unpublished.

252. 'I love hate.' Previously unpublished. IABF, AB/ARCH/A/POE/3.

253. 'What I'd like to do.' Previously unpublished. From 'The Doctor is Sick: Motion Picture Typescript', p. 52. Stage direction on p. 51: 'A teenage group [called The Kneetremblers] is at work, almost inaudible for adulation. There are TV cameras trained on them, along with a fullfledged TV team.'

254. 'Eight and twenty years.' Previously unpublished. From the script for *Cyrus the Great*. Sung by a bard with a harp. The stage directions indicate that the character Astyages 'sits with Harpagus at supper […] There is a feast of venison'.

255. 'To be a king, to be a king.' Previously unpublished. From the script for *Cyrus the Great*. Sung by a number of boys. Verses one and two are from one draft, and three and four are from another draft.

256. 'A drink. What is a drink?' Previously unpublished. MS on a diary page, preprinted with date 'Samedi 12 Novembre'. 12 November fell on a Saturday in 1966, 1977, 1983 and 1988. The correct date is probably 1977.

257. *Bed.* Previously unpublished. IABF, AB/ARCH/A/POE/12.

258. *Bear.* Previously unpublished. IABF, AB/ARCH/A/POE/12.

259. 'I'm weary of working with words that you write.' Previously unpublished. IABF.

260. 'How dare I dare to dream.' Previously unpublished. IABF.

261. 'His bowels are of gold, his veins of silver.' Previously unpublished. From the script for *Cyrus the Great* (1977). Gyzat's song, sung by a Eunuch. Belshazzar notes that this is 'nothing new' and consists of

the 'same weary old images … must get me a new court poet, must I not? There is already one ready there, smirking, young, handsome, catamitic.'Typescript draft.

262. 'I am sick of a kingdom which is a jewelled prison.' Previously unpublished. From the script for *Cyrus the Great* (1977).Having sung this song, Gyzat asks 'Is that enough, your majesty?'. Belshazzar replies 'I think so, Gyzat … will you scream in metre, groan in numbers? I am, you see, something of a poet myself…'. He then sends for whips, 'Gyzat,' we are told, 'awaits the worst.'

263. 'Lex for law and order.' Previously unpublished. *Dawn Chorus* is a film script about a specialist in ornithological sounds, and a producer of avant-garde music based on birdsong and electronic music. The lead character becomes an unwitting part in a political scandal that involves hyper-conservative leader Lex Penninck. The film is set 'in a tropical zone undefined'. Some revolutionary thugs sing this with 'fervour'. Lex is a right-wing politician, who appears on TV earlier in the film script in front of a sign that reads 'Lex means Law'. Typescript draft.

264. 'I wouldn't frirk Uranus.' From a draft of the novel *Puma*, dated 31 January 1976.

265. 'Here on the final pyre.' Previously unpublished. From draft of *Puma*, dated 31 January 1976.

266. 'A bird sat high on a banyan tree.' Song sung by the character Kartar Singh. In Burgess's original text, this song appears in various pages, embedded in prose text; in the novel, verse breaks are delineated by ellipses, which have here been replaced by line breaks. The final ellipsis has been retained. *The Enemy in the Blanket*, pp. 88–91.

267. 'Beasts and men are made the same.' This song is sung by Kartar Singh, who 'raised his tuneless voice in a doubtful ballad'. *The Enemy in the Blanket*, p. 130.

268. 'Oh, love, love, love.' Sung, 'relaxed without effort, against the pre-Raphaelitish chords of early Debussy' in *Beds in the East*, pp. 146-7.

269. 'We will build a bridge to heaven.' This appears to be a Burgess

original, although 'Night and morning, noon and even' is taken directly from 'Sound Sleep' by Christina G. Rossetti. *Devil of a State* (London: Heinemann, 1961), p. 43.

270. 'We'll be coming home.' Song sung to a mouth organ tune by soldiers. *The Wanting Seed* (London: Heinemann, 1962), pp. 240-6.

271. 'My adorable Fred.' Described as 'a song that had recently become popular'. This song is said to be 'much burbled on the television by epicene willowy youths.' *The Wanting Seed*, p. 3.

272. 'My dead tree. Give me back my dead dead tree.' A song recited by 'one of the bearded homos'. 'Bloody nonsense,' said the man' who was listening next to Tristram. *The Wanting Seed*, p. 38.

273. 'This lovely queen, if I should win her.' This poem is recited by 'Melvin Johnson (illustrious surname) who, balanced on his head, feet high in the air, recited loudly a triolet of his own composition. It was strange to see the upside-down mouth, hear the right-way-up words...' *The Wanting Seed*, p. 182.

274. 'How come that such a scholar.' Described as a song 'from a silly college musical of the thirties'. *The Clockwork Testament*, p. 146. Transcribed from AB/ARCH/A/TCT (IABF).

275. 'Ich nem' ein' Zigarett'. Receited by a character called Dorothy in 'Dietrich style'. *Earthly Powers*, p. 473.

276. 'You whom the fisherfolk of Myra believe.' Song ascribed to Kenneth Toomey, and sung by Dominico Campinati. *Earthly Powers*, p. 508.

277. 'Waking and sleeping.' These are verses from a musical comedy which, according to Toomey, 'you could hardly call this sort of thing literature ... A young man named Cecil loves a girl called Cecilia but cannot bring himself to utter the ultimate endearment. In August 1914 he said I love you to a girl and immediately war broke out.' *Earthly Powers*, pp. 90-91.

278. 'Money isn't everything.' A chorus from an opera by Domenico Campinati and Kenneth Toomey, which they sing as they reach the casino in Monaco. IABF, AB/ARCH/A/EAR.

279. 'I'll crash the moon.' A popular song sung through a microphone.

Toomey recalls: 'Popular songs were, at that time, going through a brief phase of literacy.' *Earthly Powers*, pp. 347-8.

280.   *Une P'tite Spécialité Called L'Amour.* Toomey is called upon by a ship's steward to sing this in a ship's lounge bar. Toomey is clearly ashamed of the words: 'I could not well deny knowing this song, since I had written the word. It came in that wartime horror Say It, Cecil.' A version with a different line order and only very slight wording differences is held at the IABF. The *Earthly Powers* version used here is more complete. *Earthly Powers*, p. 225.

281.   *Cabbage Face.* This, according to Burgess, 'was for use in a mock music lesson in a pantomime. The refrain-title was a spelling out of the notes that made up the melody'. *Little Wilson and Big God*, p. 161.

282.   *Nathan's Song.* Nathan's song. 'The words said something to the effect that the singers were the descendants of David, a shepherd who had become kind, and that they wished the spirit of David to watch over them.' *Man of Nazareth* (London: Magnum/Methuen, 1980), p. 49.

283.   'Thy mouth, a fig, thy teeth.' Jesus' flattering language. Burgess notes that, in his adolescence, Jesus 'found time in the cool of the evening to engage in… speaking flattering language to the dark-eyed girls, even singing songs to a two-string fiddle accompaniment'. *Man of Nazareth*, p. 93.

284.   'My love lay across the waters.' This song is sung by Philip while he is fishing with Jesus. James and John's following verses (see below) are taken as a 'more practical song.' *Man of Nazareth*, p. 150.

285.   'Fish grey, fish brown.' James and John's song to the fish. *Man of Nazareth*, pp. 150–1.

286.   *The Prodigal Son.* Sung by Philip in *Man of Nazareth*, pp. 158-9.

287.   *The Good Samaritan.* Sung by Philip in *Man of Nazareth*, pp. 196-7.

288.   *Passover Hymn.* This is the song that the disciplines sing on their way to their lodgings, following the Last Supper with Jesus. Judas, we are told, 'did not join in'. *Man of Nazareth*, p. 284.

SOURCES AND FURTHER READING

Books and Articles about Burgess

Aggeler, Geoffrey, *Anthony Burgess: The Artist as Novelist* (University of Alabama Press, 1979)

Biswell, Andrew, 'Introduction' in Anthony Burgess, *A Clockwork Orange. The Restored Edition*, ed. by Andrew Biswell (London: Heinemann, 2012), pp. xv–xxxi

Biswell, Andrew, *The Real Life of Anthony Burgess* (London: Picador, 2005)

Bloom, Harold, ed., *Anthony Burgess* Modern Critical (New York and Philadelphia: Chelsea House Publishers, 1987), pp. 13–28

Boyntinck, Paul, *Anthony Burgess: An Annotated Bibliography and Reference Guide* (New York: Garland, 1985)

Bradbury, Malcolm, 'Anthony Burgess: A Passion for Words', *Independent on Sunday*, 28 November 1993, p. 3

Brewer, Jeutonne, *Anthony Burgess A Bibliography*, Scarecrow Bibliographies, no. 47 (Metuchen NJ, and London: Scarecrow Press, 1980)

Cabau, Jacques, 'Anthony Burgess *par lui-même, un entretien inédit avec l'auteur*' in *TREMA*, no. 5 (1980), 93–110

Clarke, Jim, *The Aesthetics of Anthony Burgess: Fire of Words*. (Basingstoke: Palgrave Macmillan, 2017)

Coale, Samuel, *Anthony Burgess* (New York: Frederick Ungar, 1981)

Daiches, David, 'Ambulant Prophet', *Times Literary Supplement*, 21 January 1977, p. 50

Dix, Carol M, *Anthony Burgess*, Writers and Their Work, no. 222 (Harlow: Longman for the British Council, 1971)

Farkas, A.Í, *Will's Son and Jake's Peer* (Budapest: Akadémiai Kiadó, 2002)

Jeannin, Marc, ed., *Anthony Burgess: Music in Literature, Literature in Music* (Newcastle: Cambridge Scholars, 2009)

Monod, Sylvère, 'Enderby le minable magnifique' in *TREMA*, no. 5 (1980), 19-29

Monod, Sylvère, 'Poets and Poetry in the Enderby Cycle', *Anthony Burgess Newsletter*, no. 6 (December 2003)

Morrison, Blake , 'Introduction' in Anthony Burgess, *A Clockwork Orange* (London: Penguin, 1996)

Phillips, Paul, *A Clockwork Counterpoint: The Music and Literature of Anthony Burgess* (Manchester: Manchester University Press, 2010)

Roughley, Alan, ed., *Anthony Burgess and Modernity* (Manchester: Manchester University Press, 2008)

Sophocles, *Oedipus the King*, trans. by Anthony Burgess (Minneapolis: University of Minnesota Press, 1972)

Véza, Laurette, 'Anthony Burgess: de la poésie à la parodie' in *TREMA*, no. 5 (1980), 31–8

Woodroffe, Graham, ed., *Marlowe, Shakespeare, Burgess: Anthony Burgess and his Elizabethan Affiliations* (Presses l'Université d'Angers, 2012)

Works Containing Poetry by Burgess, or Burgess's Commentaries on Poetry

'A Babble of Voices' in *Index on Censorship*, 9.2 (1980), 38-41

'A mingled chime', *Times Literary Supplement*, 16 January 1975, p. 50

'Authors on Translators' in *Translation*, 11.74 (Winter 1974), 5–8

'Bless Thee Burgess, Thou Art Translated', *Independent*, 27 November 1993, p. 2

'Burgess... on Film, Television and Radio', http://www.anthonyburgess. org/about- anthony-burgess/burgess-on-filmtelevision-and-radio

'Chatsky, or The Importance of Being Stupid' in *Chatsky*, Almeida Theatre programme (London: Almeida Theatre, 1993), pp. 6–7

'European Lecture', *Guardian*, 27 November 1993, G2 section, p. 2. Originally given at Cheltenham Festival of Literature, 9 October 1992

'Five Revolutionary Sonnets', *Transatlantic Review*, 21 (1966), 30-32

'Five sonnets by G.G. Belli translated by Anthony Burgess', *Times Literary Supplement*, 23 January 1976, p. 76

'Introduction' in Edmond Rostand, *Cyrano de Bergerac*, trans. by Anthony Burgess (London: Nick Hern Books, 1985: 1991), pp. i-xii

'Is Translation Possible?' in *Translation: The Journal of Literary Translation*, 12 (1974), 3–7

'Making Them Sing' (review of W.H. Auden and Chester Kallmann, *Libretti and other Dramatic Writings*) in *Observer*, 29 October 1993, p. 18

'Poèmes Inédits', ed. by Sylvère Monod, in *TREMA*, no. 5 (1980), pp. 5-17

'The Bond of Words', *Times Literary Supplement*, 5 April 1984, p. 487

'The Ecstasy of Gerard Manley Hopkins', *New York Times*, 27 August 1989, p. 15

'The Magus of Mallorca', *Times Literary Supplement*, 21 May 1982, p. 547

'The Princely Progress', *Times Literary Supplement*, 12 June 1981, p. 656

'Viewpoint', *Times Literary Supplement*, 11 March 1973, p. 2

ABBA ABBA (London, Faber, 1977)

Beds in the East (London: Heinemann, 1959)

Blooms of Dublin: A Musical Play Based on James Joyce's Ulysses (London: Hutchinson, 1986)

Carmen: An Opera in Four Acts. By H. Meilhac and L. Halevy, trans. by Anthony Burgess (London: Hutchinson, 1986)

A Christmas Recipe (Verona: Plain Wrapper Press, 1977)

A Clockwork Orange: A Play With Music (London: Hutchinson, 1987)

The Clockwork Testament, or Enderby's End (London: Hart-Davis, MacGibbon, 1974)

Cyrano de Bergerac. By Edmond Rostand, trans. by Anthony Burgess (London: Nick Hern Books, 1991)

Earthy Powers (London: Hutchinson, 1980)

End of the World News: An Entertainment (London: Hutchinson, 1982)

Enderby Outside (London: Heinemann, 1968)

The Enemy in the Blanket (London: Heinemann, 1958)

The Eve of Saint Venus (London: Sidgwick & Jackson, 1964)

Inside Mr Enderby (as Joseph Kell) (London: Heinemann, 1963)

*Little Wilson and Big God: Being the First Part of the Confessions of Anthony
    Burgess* (London: Heinemann, 1987)

A Long Trip to Teatime (London: Dempsey & Squires, 1976)

Man of Nazareth (London: Magnum/Methuen, 1980)

MF (London: Cape, 1971)

A Mouthful of Air (London: Hutchinson, 1992)

Napoleon Symphony (New York: Alfred A. Knopf, 1974)

Oberon Old and New (London: Hutchinson, 1985)

One Hand Clapping (as Joseph Kell) (London: Peter Davies, 1961)

One Man's Chorus, ed. by Ben Forkner (New York: Carroll and Graf, 1998)

Revolutionary Sonnets, ed. by Kevin Jackson (Manchester: Carcanet, 2002)

The Right to an Answer (London, Heinemann, 1960)

They Wrote in English: A Survey of British and American Literature, 2 vols
    (Milan: Tramontana, 1979)

Time for a Tiger (London: Heinemann, 1956)

A Vision of Battlements (London: Sidgwick & Jackson, 1965)

The Wanting Seed (London: Heinemann, 1962)

The Worm and the Ring (London: Heinemann, 1961)

You've Had Your Time (London: Heinemann, 1990)

ALPHABETICAL LIST OF TITLES
OR FIRST LINES

Poems with titles are given in *italics*. Those not given titles by Burgess
appear without italics.